Glass Elephants

Early, Depression, & Beyond

Myra Coe-Hixson

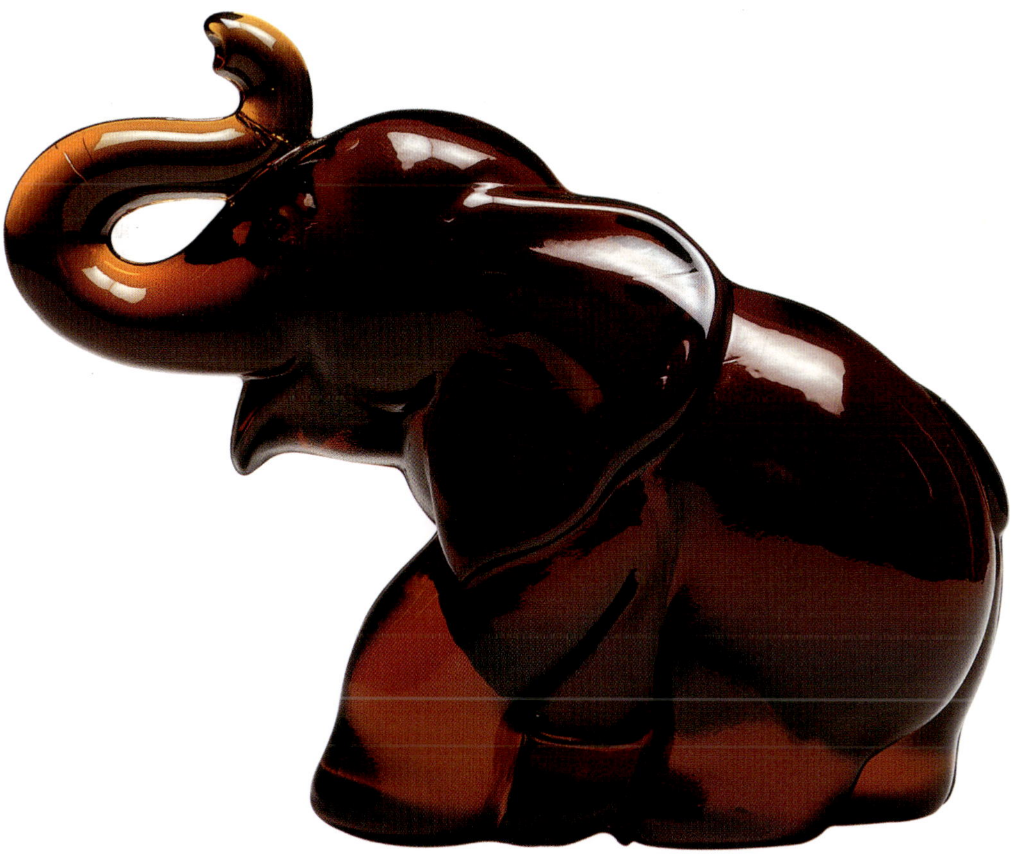

Schiffer Publishing Ltd®
4880 Lower Valley Road, Atglen, PA 19310 USA

Dedication

To Stephen Hixson, for all the love and support he has provided along the way. He is my number one fan and believes in me for everything I do.

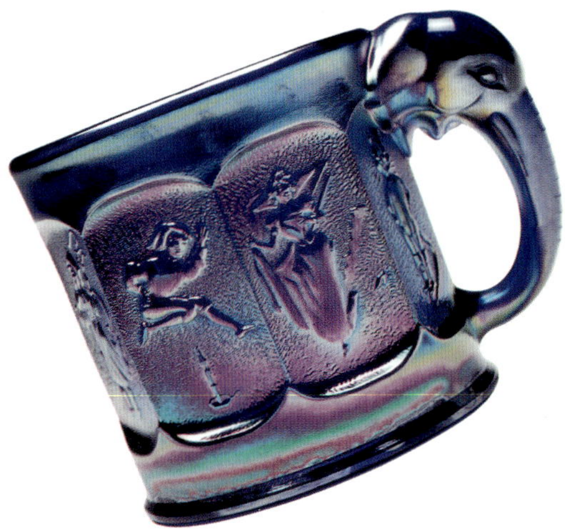

Library of Congress Control Number: 2003108465

Designed by Ellen J. (Sue) Taltoan
Type set in Seagull Hv BT/Souvenir Lt BT

ISBN: 0-7643-1935-3
Printed in China
1 2 3 4

Published by Schiffer Publishing Ltd.
4880 Lower Valley Road
Atglen, PA 19310
Phone: (610) 593-1777; Fax: (610) 593-2002
E-mail: Schifferbk@aol.com
Please visit our web site catalog at
www.schifferbooks.com
We are always looking for people to write books on new and related subjects. If you have an idea for a book, please contact us at the above address.

This book may be purchased from the publisher. Include $3.95 for shipping. Please try your bookstore first.
You may write for a free catalog.

In Europe, Schiffer books are distributed by
Bushwood Books
6 Marksbury Ave. Kew Gardens
Surrey TW9 4JF England
Phone: 44 (0)20 8392-8585; Fax: 44 (0)20 8392-9876
E-mail: Bushwd@aol.com
Free postage in the UK. Europe: air mail at cost.
Please try your bookstore first.

Contents

Acknowledgements

It would not have been possible to compile this book without the help from many people who provided me with information, let me study their glass, and assisted me in my work.

I greatly thank my parents, Debbie and Randy Coe, who have been my role models. They are true glass collectors and highly knowledgeable, and have passed their passion on to me. I truly could not have completed this book without their immense support. Their photography equipment enabled me to take the majority of the photographs presented here. Their priceless knowledge came forth during the research and they spent countless hours assisting me during the final stages.

I also thank Tara Jennings for assisting me with much of the final production work. Finalizing a book takes a lot of hours, and she was there to assist in every way possible

The following people provided me with glass to photograph and/or sent me photographs of a large variety of glass elephants that I could not have found alone. Thank you Alexander Ash, John and Inez Fallihee, Alta Miller, Donna and Ron Miller, Cecil Taylor, John Walk, and Juanita and Jonathan Williams. Walter Font was a great assistant at the Fort Wayne Historical Museum. A special thank you goes to Darlene and Gordon Cochran for all of their help, time, effort, and thoughtful consideration. Their generosity demonstrated the highest meaning to glass collecting and sharing.

Everyone associated with the Fenton Art Glass Company was of tremendous help. They are absolutely a great group to count on for information. Frank M. Fenton was of invaluable assistance answering questions and guiding me in the right directions. He also located some elephants that I needed to study and photograph. I especially thank Jon Saffell, a designer at the Fenton Art Glass Company, for his time, patience, and specific information. Howard Seufer, who has retired from Fenton, was an absolute wonder in obtaining needed photographs and providing assistance.

I would also like to give special thanks to the Boyd family, for their insightful knowledge. They were instrumental in obtaining much of the specific information about the Boyd Glass Company and details about the two glass elephants they created.

The staff at Suburban Photo in Beaverton, Oregon, assisted in technical ways and processed most of the photography.

My editor, Nancy Schiffer, has been helpful. Without her confidence in me, it would not have been possible to produce this valuable reference.

I sincerely value highly each person's expertise and assistance.

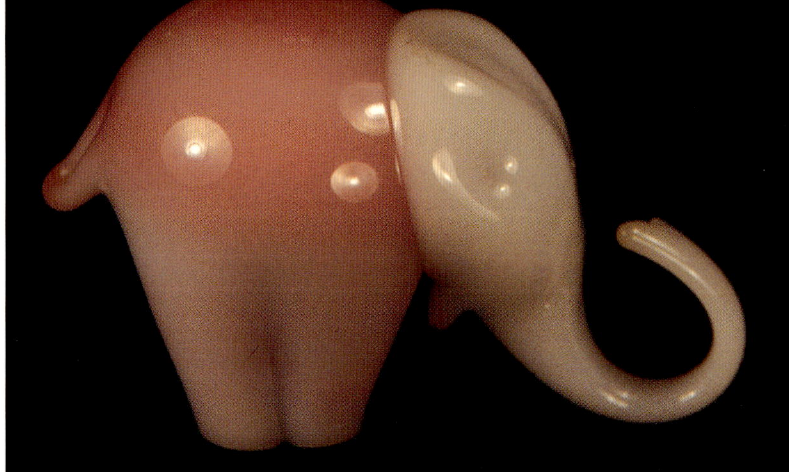

Preface

It is my understanding that a book like this has not been produced before. When seeking glass elephants and information about them, readers formerly had to consult many company-specific books, some readily available and some long out-of-print. I had the dream of bringing relevant information on glass elephants together in one book, where collectors could see and enjoy them and learn more.

This book focuses on American companies that made glass elephants. I wanted to focus on what has been created within our own country and pay tribute to that. There are many companies that made a multitude of elephant figures with varying colors. An attempt was made to gather as many as possible, but still this will serve only as a sampling. There also are companies that made only a few colors, yet I have tried to gather numerous ones to demonstrate their glass.

No one person can know everything, but we can rely on one another for continuing knowledge. I hope and request that readers provide me with further information and opinions that will add to what is known. I am sure many of you have your own collections and knowledge; if you would be willing, I would greatly enjoy hearing about them.

I aspire to gain more knowledge about glass elephants. Many important details can be found in old glass catalogs, reprints, original advertising, and such and I will appreciate anyone's willingness to provide or sell me any new resources. Thank you.

Introduction

Many great American glass companies created glass elephants. The Fenton Art Glass Company has produced the most elephants with seven different styles in a variety of colors. All the other major glass companies, such as Fostoria, Heisey, Imperial, and New Martinsville, are also included. Several of the contemporary companies, like Boyd and Mosser, also made elephants.

What is Included in American Glass Elephants?

While this is a book focused primarily on glass figural elephants, there are a few variations. Some of the elephants are containers, are part of a larger item, or have plastic additions. Every item is primarily glass.

Measurements

Actual measurements are used. For the majority of pieces, the height precedes the length or width. There may be slight discrepancies when you are measuring because each piece is subject to slight variables.

Value Guide

Values provided are for pieces in **MINT CONDITION ONLY**. Mint condition means that it is flawless. Flaws can include, but are not limited to, scratches, chips, and cracks. When flaws occur, the value is less. Values for damaged products cannot be offered, because it is impossible to determine the extreme variance that occurs with damage. It is possible for once-damaged pieces to be repaired, and when this happens the value should still be lower than those listed, because the piece would still not be in Mint condition. However, the collector/purchaser must be the final judge.

Further, values can vary according to different regions of the marketplace. This happens because there may be a limited supply in one place and a larger supply in another. Or it may be that demand may be higher in certain areas. Consider the market in which you are selling and/or buying.

In order to determine values, a variety of sources were consulted, including the sales of glass dealers, prices paid by customers, prices exhibited in different markets, and national publications. Information from several collectors and dealers were analized to find accurate prices.

This book is intended to be only a suggestive guide when people are trying to determine the possible worth of an item. Further, the final decision will be what the individual collector is willing to pay.

Neither the author nor the publisher assumes any responsibility for any transactions that may occur because of this book.

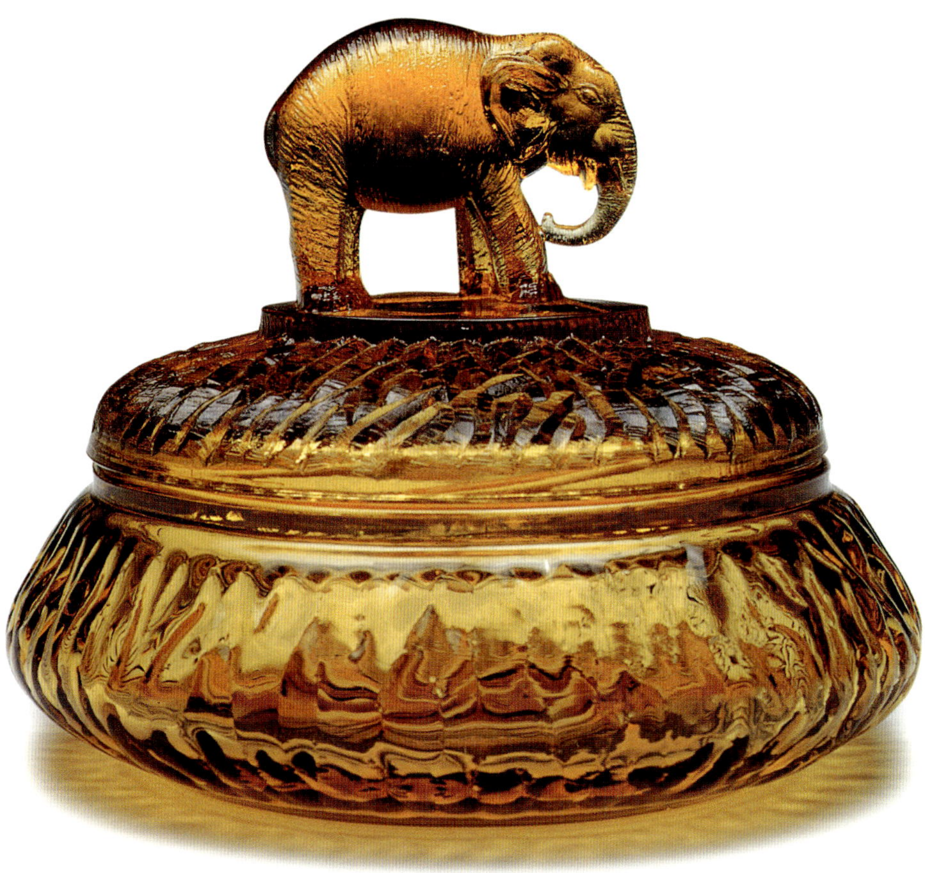

Aetna Glass & Manufacturing Company 1880-1889

Bellaire, Ohio was the home of Aetna Glass & Manufacturing Company. The company operated during the years of 1880-1889. It was R.T. Devries of the Baltimore and Ohio Railroad who founded the company. Henry Leasure was the manager and he had formerly been with Central Glass. The company primarily produced pattern glass tableware and stemware. Yet, they also made other items and one of them was an elephant.

The elephant they made was patterned after the famous "Jumbo," who was a circus elephant who performed with P.T. Barnum Circus. There was an advertisement in the 1884 *Crockery and Glass Journal* which described this piece as a perfect imitation of Barnum's elephant. In considering the very short period of production time, which was 1883-1884, it can be assessed that there were possibly problems during the production process, which often happens with large molds. This piece was not only large, but it was very heavy as well, weighing in at seven pounds. There have been guesses made that cracks or breakage could have occurred during the annealing process. If there were such problems then it is understandable that they would not want to keep it in line. Further, the ones that have survived today just might have some chips or slight damage because of the immense size of this piece. Taking this all into account, a person might consider accepting some minor problems because this is a piece rarely found.

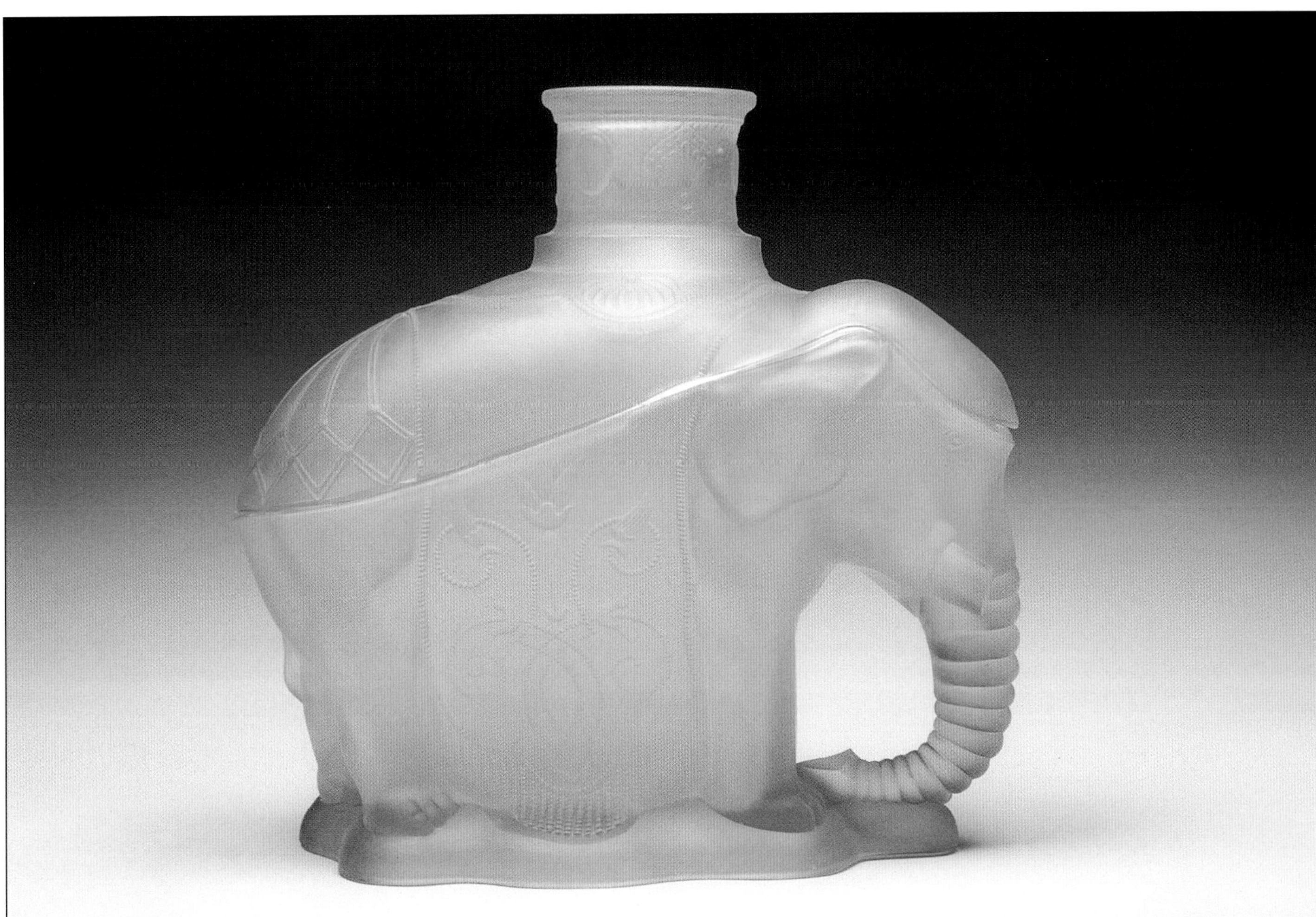

Jumbo covered dish, Crystal with satin finish, 10.3" tall 10" long, Circa 1883-84, **$450.00**

Avon Products Inc. 1886- present

David McConnell, son of a farmer, left home and became initially a book salesman. While selling books door to door, he listened to his customers' requests about other products. One of the most popular was quality perfume. Soon he and his wife were experimenting with a variety of fragrances. His female customers loved the idea of having perfume delivered to their door and soon these sales outnumbered books. The decision was made to end book sales and to develop a new company devoted to home products. The new company was called California Perfume Company, in honor of some friends that had just moved to California.

As sales increased, so did the need to increase production. A new laboratory was purchased in Avon, England. In honor of this new area, a line was developed and called Avon. In 1939, the company name was changed to Avon Products. Through the years, Avon has become versatile and added many different products to their home line. In the 1960s, Avon went to Wheaton Glass Company to have them design decorative bottles to hold their perfume, bubble bath, and after-shave lotions. In 1972, Avon moved into a much larger headquarters in New York City. Sales still remain strong across the country through home sales and on their web site.

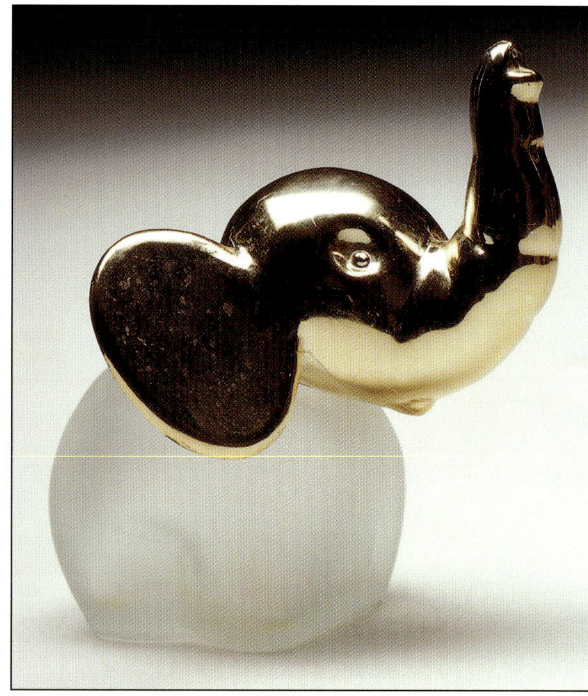

Elephant cologne bottle (called the Good Luck Elephant), Crystal with satin finish and gold plastic top, Made by Wheaton Glass for Avon and came filled with Patchwork cologne, 3.75" tall, 3" wide, Circa 1975-76, **$6.00**

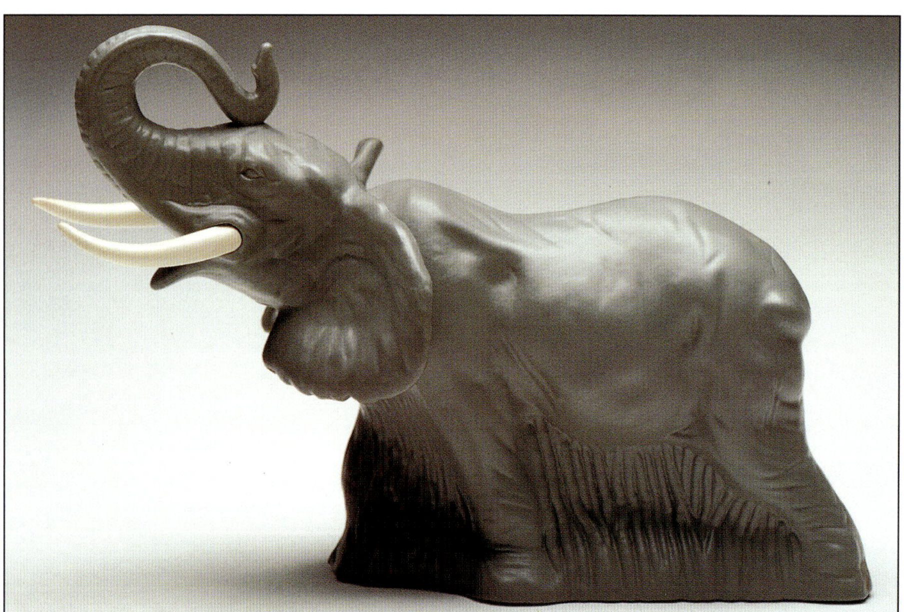

Elephant cologne bottle (called the Majestic Elephant), Crystal with gray paint, gray plastic head, Made by Wheaton for Avon and held 5.5 ounces of men's after shave, 5.25" tall, 7.5" long, Circa 1977, **$12.00**

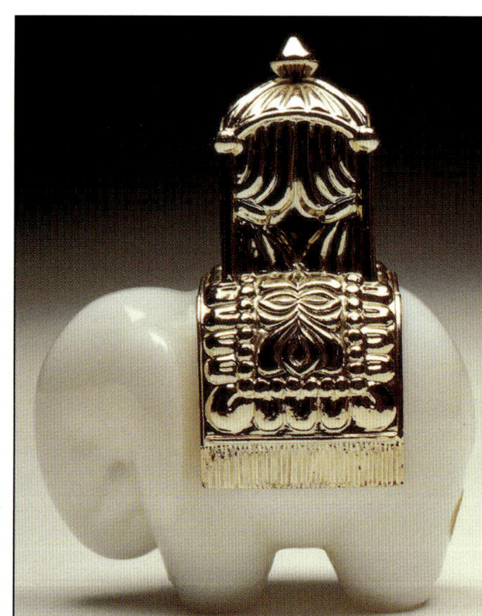

Elephant cologne bottle (called the Royal Elephant), Milk Glass with a gold plastic top, Made by Wheaton for Avon and held 0.5 fluid ounces of "Charisma" or "Topaze" perfume, 3.6" tall, 3" long, Circa 1977-79, **$5.00**

Blenko Glass Company 1921-Present

It was 1893 and William J. Blenko created his first glass factory. William later relocated to Milton, West Virginia, and established his fourth glass company. It became quite a family affair when his son, William Henry Blenko, joined him in 1923. The third generation, William Henry Jr., joined in 1946. Finally, the fourth generation, Richard Blenko, teamed up with his father in 1976.

Blenko Glass Company has prided itself with creating distinct, hand-blown glass. In fact, it was Blenko that created sixty table settings of glassware for President Ronald Reagan's inaugural dinner. The awards for the 1983 Country Music winners also were created by Blenko.

The current management seems to be aptly involved in all of the company's happenings, so that the continuation of Blenko looks very positive. A Blenko Glass Museum opened Seattle, Washington, in 2001, and hopefully it will bring in new collectors.

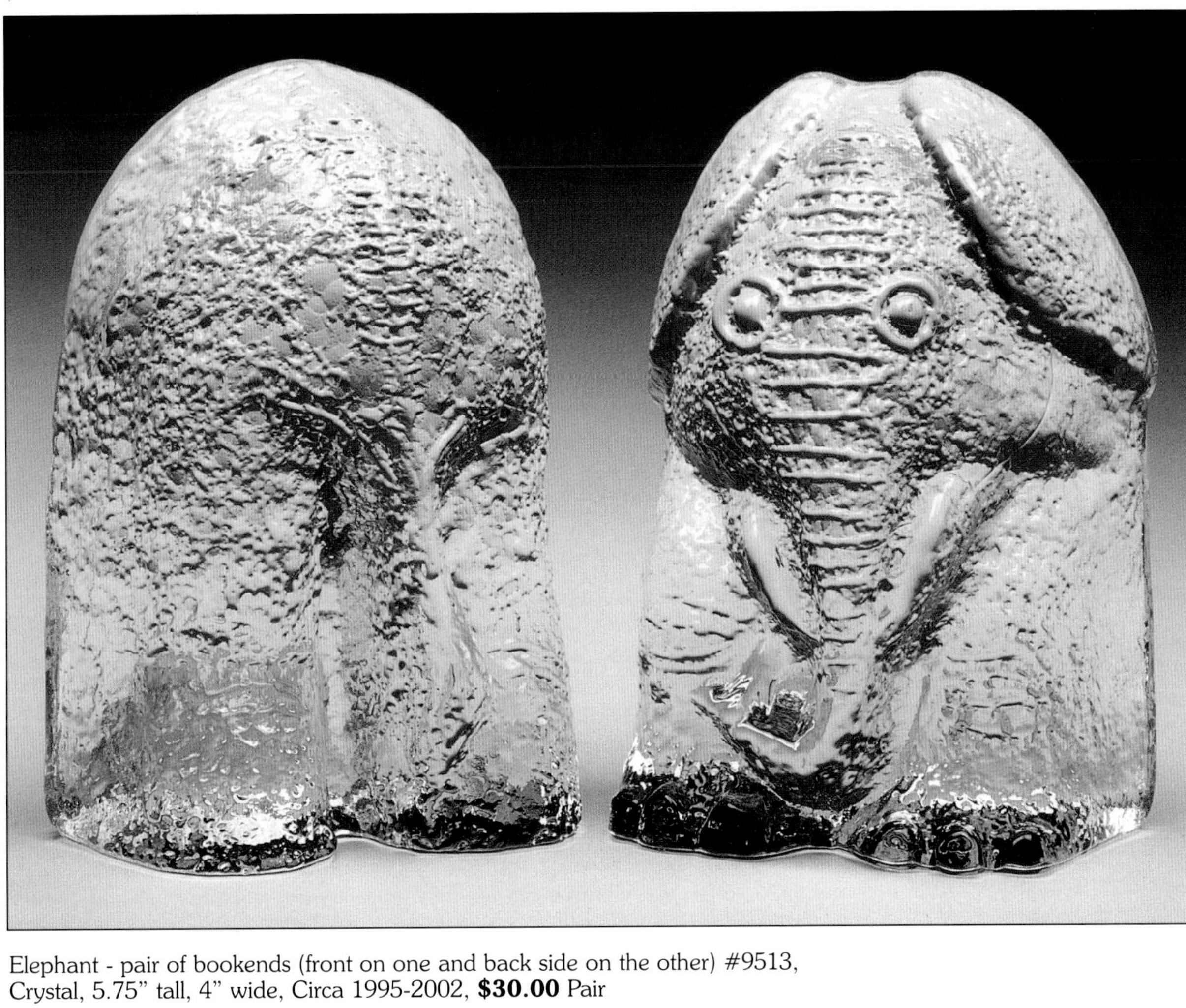

Elephant - pair of bookends (front on one and back side on the other) #9513, Crystal, 5.75" tall, 4" wide, Circa 1995-2002, **$30.00** Pair

Boyd Crystal Art Glass Company 1978-Present

Bernard C. Boyd was offered the first chance to buy the Degenhart glass factory after the death of Mrs. Degenhart in 1978, since she had put him in her will to do so. It was just a short six months later and the factory was open again. Most of the old Degenhart employees stayed, which was comforting. Since there was a transfer in companies, there was a need for a new logo, one that would be placed on every piece of glass.

The Boyd family has produced animals from the beginning and continues today. On average, new colors are made about every six weeks. Collectors enjoy the fact that each mould has a limited number for every color that is produced. The names of the moulds come from the names of family members or friends. This is a unique and personal touch. The colors are named as well.

Currently at Boyd three generations of the family are at work. They work at the factory in the daily activities and provide tours to educate people. To further assist their collectors, they publish a monthly newsletter that lists the current moulds and colors that they are producing, along with relevant information and updates.

Boyd ensures that their logo is on every piece of glass they make. Further, they change their logo every five years. This will be of assistance to collectors when they are dating pieces. The following are the Boyd logos that have been used:

1978-1983- a B in a diamond

1983-1988- a B in a diamond with a line underneath

1988-1993- a B in a diamond with lines above as well as underneath

1993-1998- a B in a diamond with lines to the right, above, and underneath

1998-2003- a B in a diamond inside a box

It is important to know the specifics of their two elephant moulds. Zack Boyd worked at the New Martinsville factory, in West Virginia, where they made a large elephant. Zack Boyd was highly talented and he could produce more elephants faster than any other worker who was there with him. This was all occurring in the 1930's, when many people were being laid off or out of work, so it was his talent that kept him in work. From this background the "Boyd Zack" was made, as a tribute to Zack Boyd. A smaller version of the New Martinsville elephant was made, and it was called "Zack to honor Zack Boyd." You can find the Zacks as solids or hollow. It is noted by Boyd that they tried to make it solid, but there was just too much breakage, so to increase productivity they changed the mould to be hollow. Island Mould Company, in Wheeling, West Virginia, made the Zack mould.

The very first Zack was made in the red color of Flame, on January 20, 1981. This Zack was made on the U. S. presidential inauguration day, and the Boyd family thought it would be appropriate to send it to President Ronald Reagan as a gift, since the elephant is the symbol of the Republican party. Red, as it turns out, was also Nancy Reagan's favorite color. The Boyd family was thrilled to receive an official presidential thank-you note from President and Mrs. Reagan.

Along with Zack elephant, there is also an elephant-head toothpick holder. This mould is a former Degenhart mould acquired when Boyd purchased the Degenhart estate and factory in 1978. There were many moulds, and one of them was this elephant head toothpick holder. Once purchased, Boyd took the mould and created many new elephant-head toothpick holders.

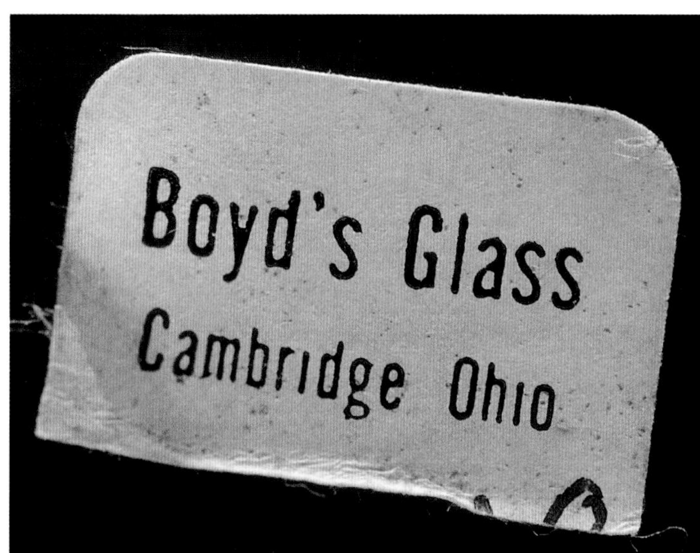

Original white and black label

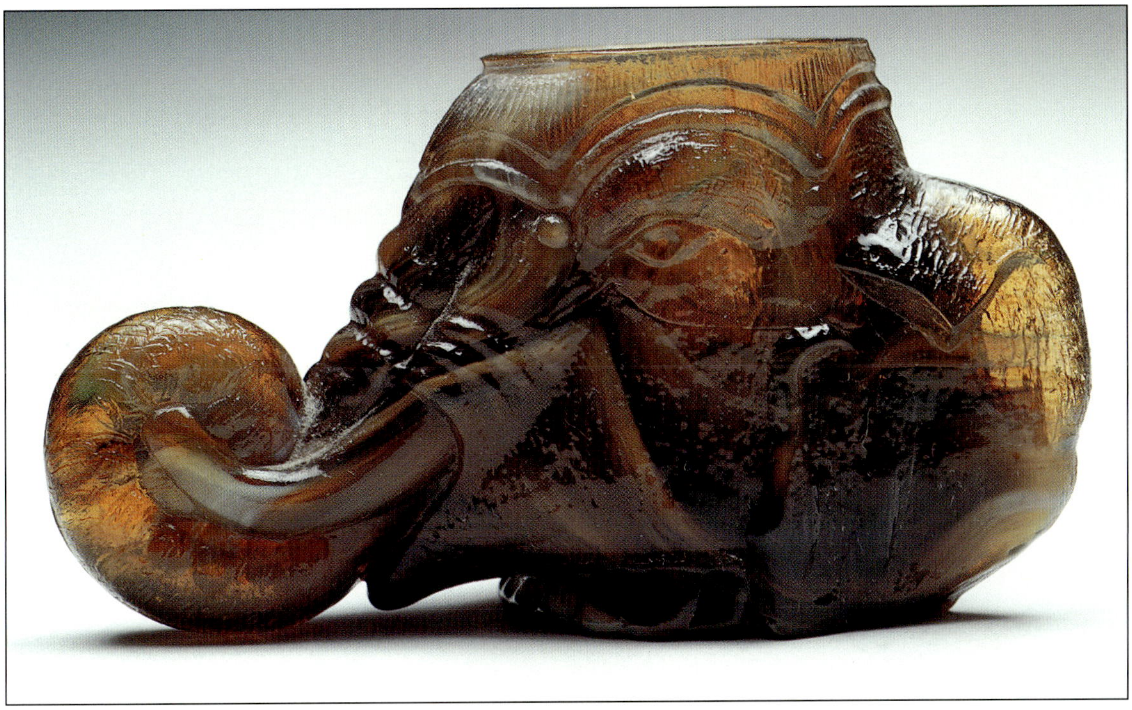

Elephant Head Toothpick, Walnut Slag, transparent brown and white slag, first Boyd mark, 2.5" tall, 4.4" long, March 1979, **$32.00**

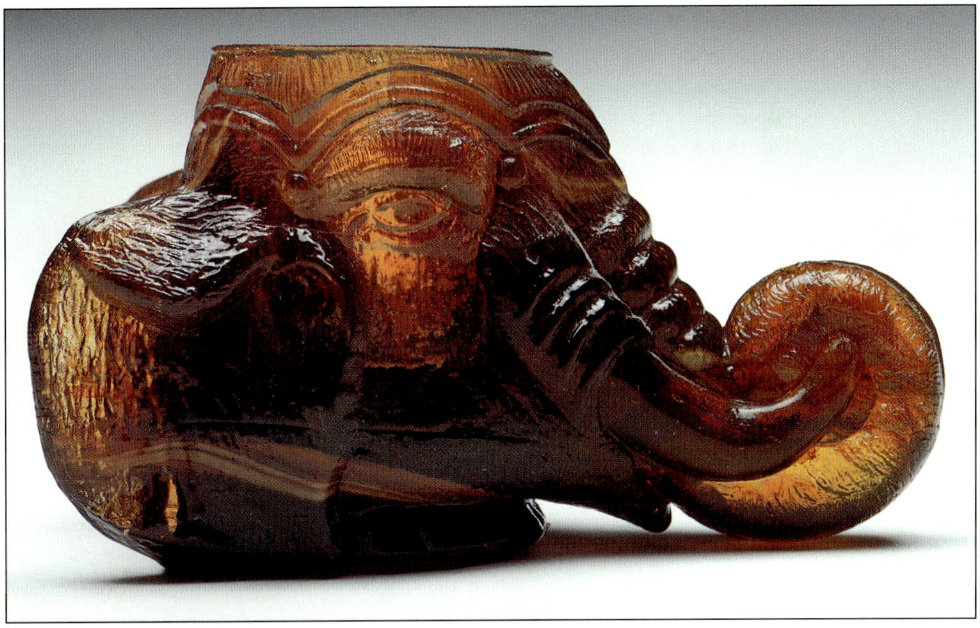

Elephant Head Toothpick, Root Beer Slag, transparent brown slag, first Boyd mark, 2.5" tall, 4.4" long, December 1980, **$30.00**

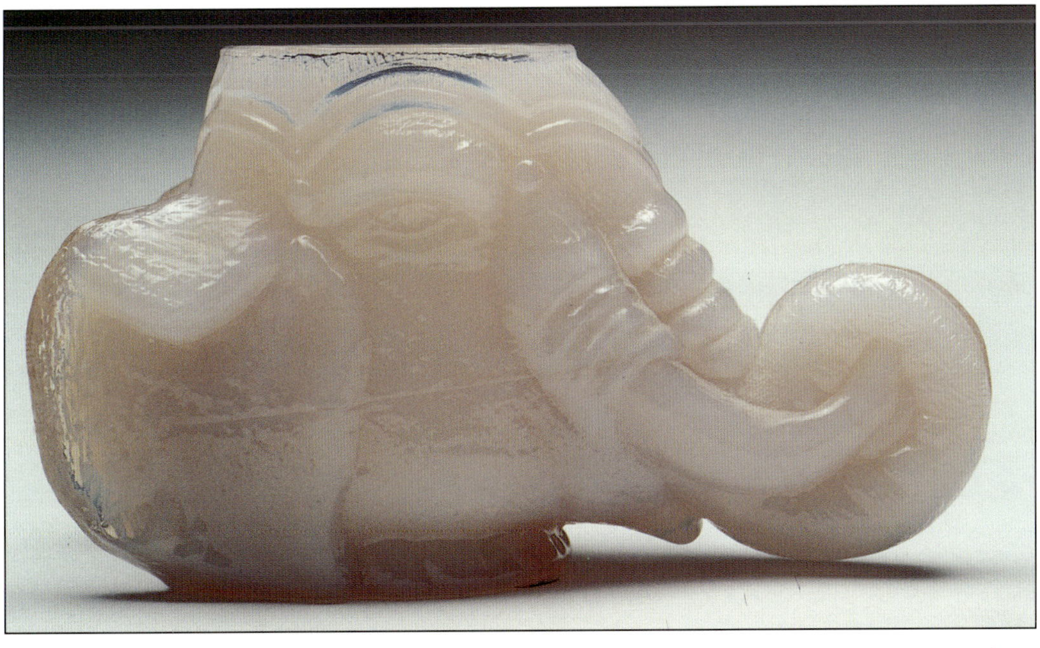

Elephant Head Toothpick, Crown Tuscan, opaque pink, first Boyd mark, 2.5" tall, 4.4" long, September 1982, **$18.00**

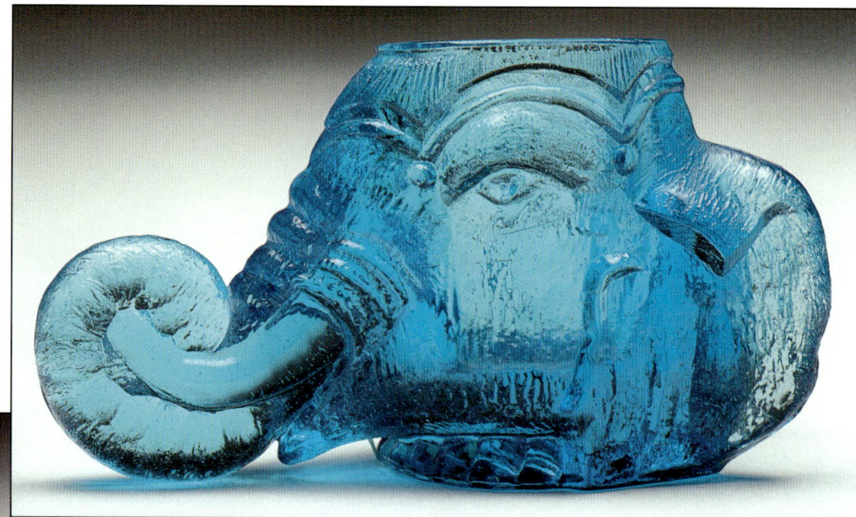

Elephant Head Toothpick, Alice Blue, transparent blue, first Boyd mark, 2.5" tall, 4.4" long, March 1983, **$28.00**

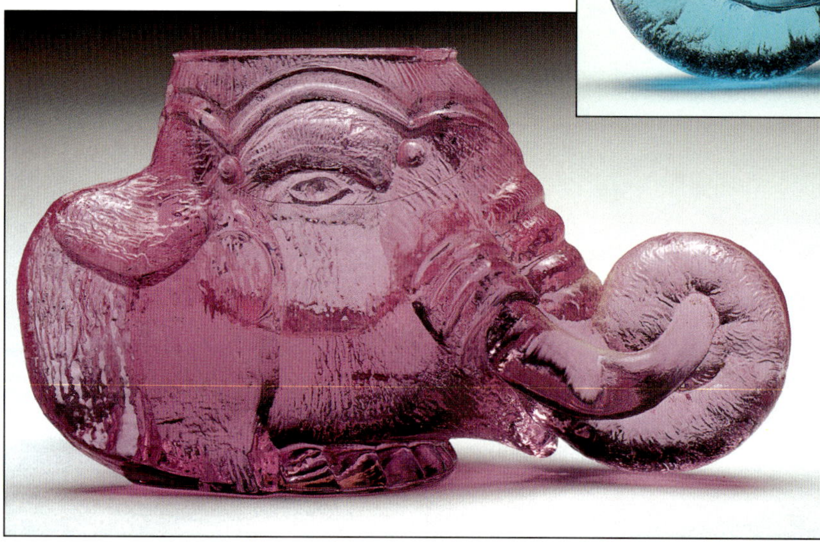

Elephant Head Toothpick, Alexandrite, third mark, 2.5" tall, 4.4" long, June 1989, **$26.00**

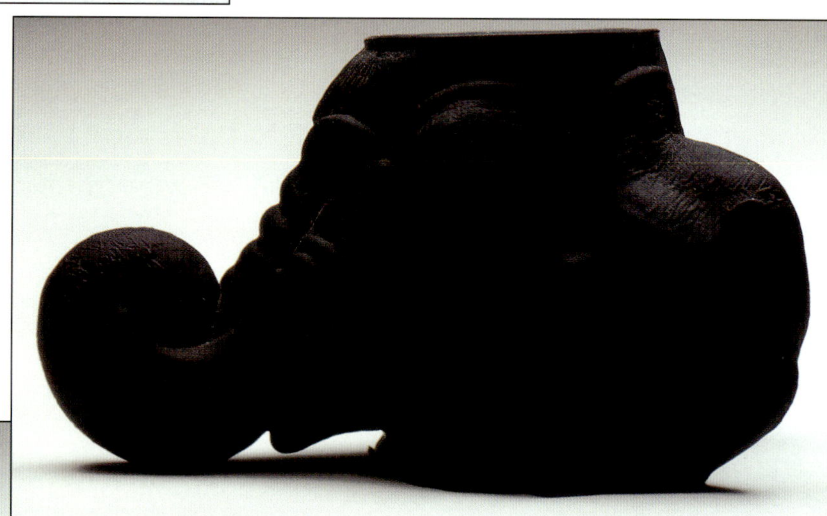

Elephant Head Toothpick, Classic Black with satin finish, second Boyd mark, 2.5" tall, 4.4" long, October 1991, **$22.00**

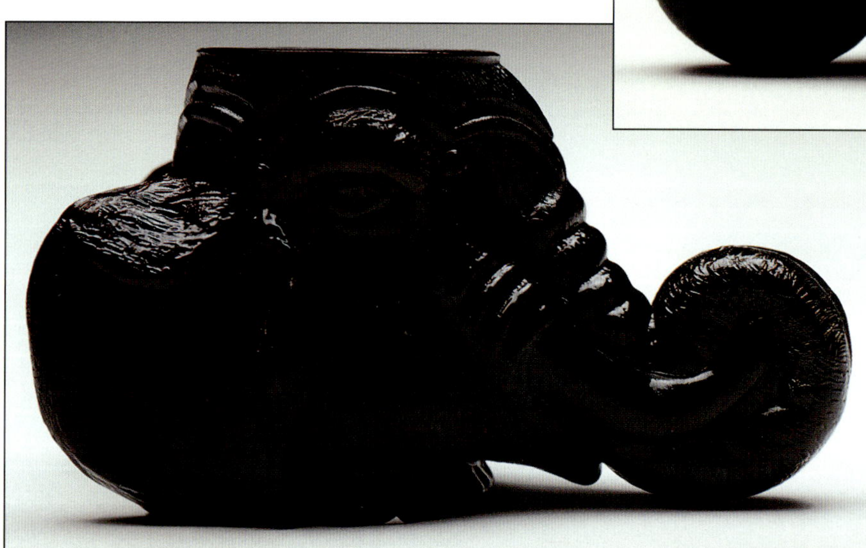

Elephant Head Toothpick, Classic Black, third Boyd mark 2.5" tall, 4.4" long, October 1991, **$18.00**

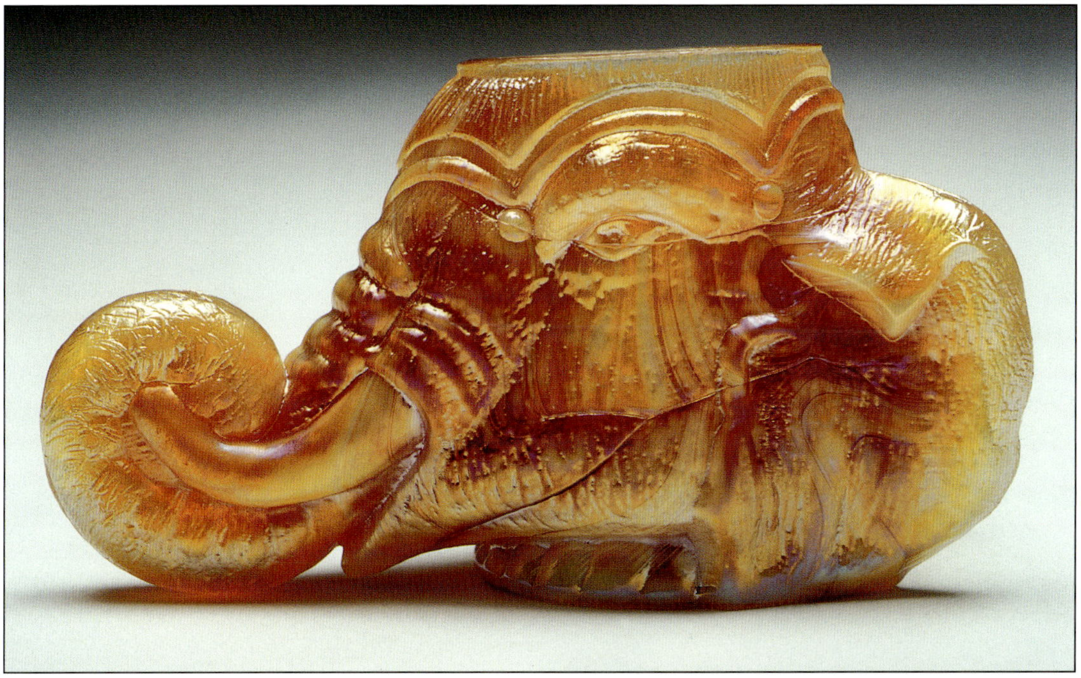

Elephant Head Toothpick, Sunkist Carnival, orange slag iridescent, fourth mark, 2.5" tall, 4.4" long, Circa February 1995, **$18.00**

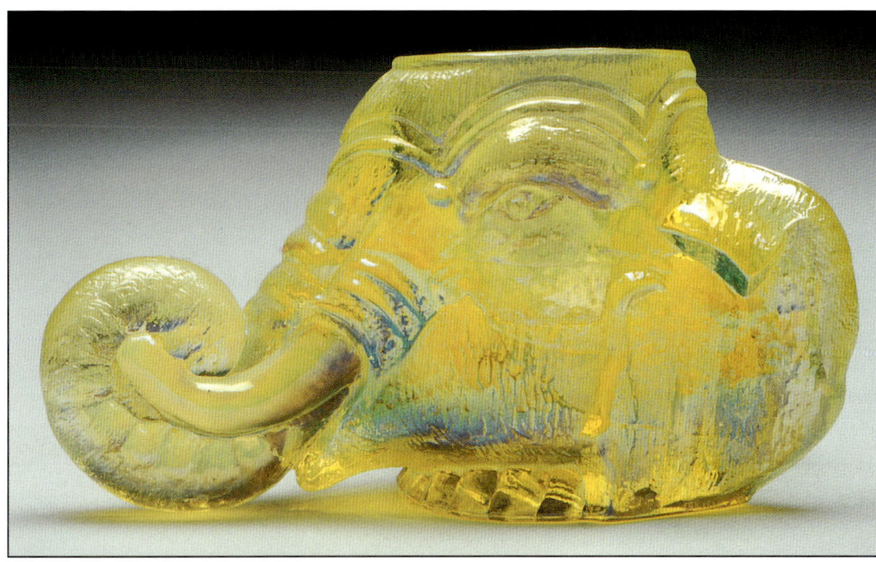

Elephant Head Toothpick, Vaseline Carnival, fourth mark, 2.5" tall, 4.4" long, August 1995, **$18.00**

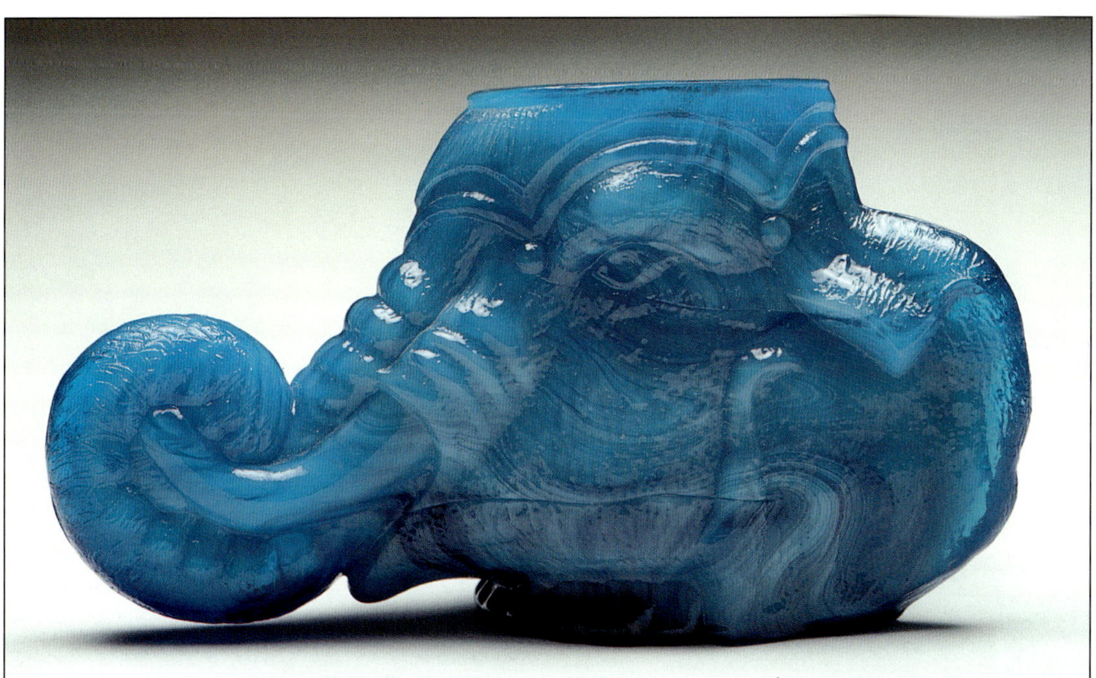

Elephant Head Toothpick, Capri Blue, opaque bright blue, fourth mark, 2.5" tall, 4.4" long, June 1996, **$16.00**

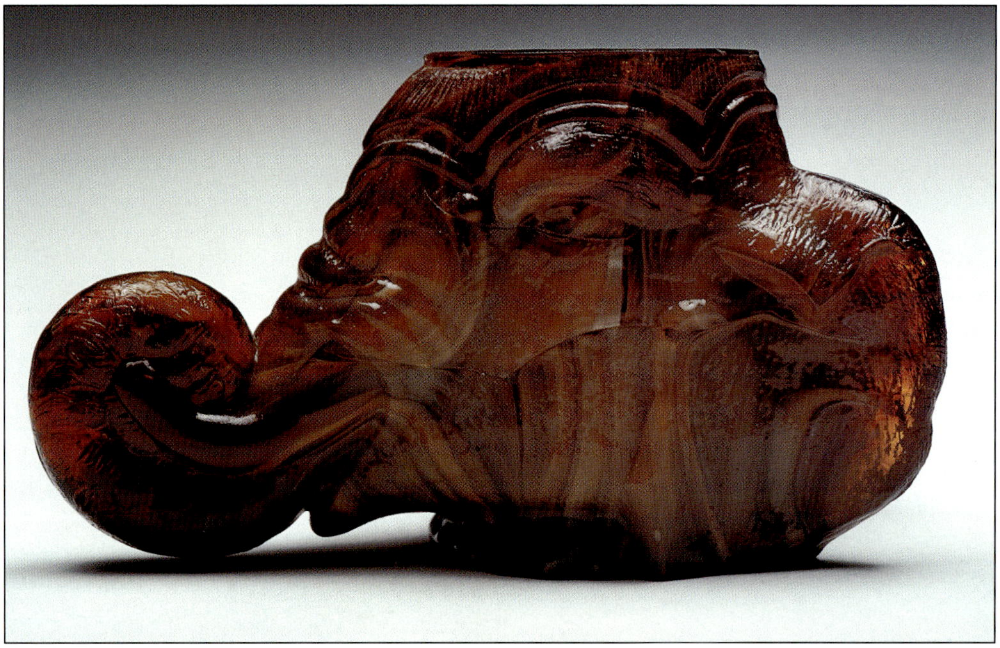

Elephant Head Toothpick, Milk Chocolate, brown opaque slag, fourth Boyd mark, 2.5" tall, 4.4" long, April 1996, **$18.00**

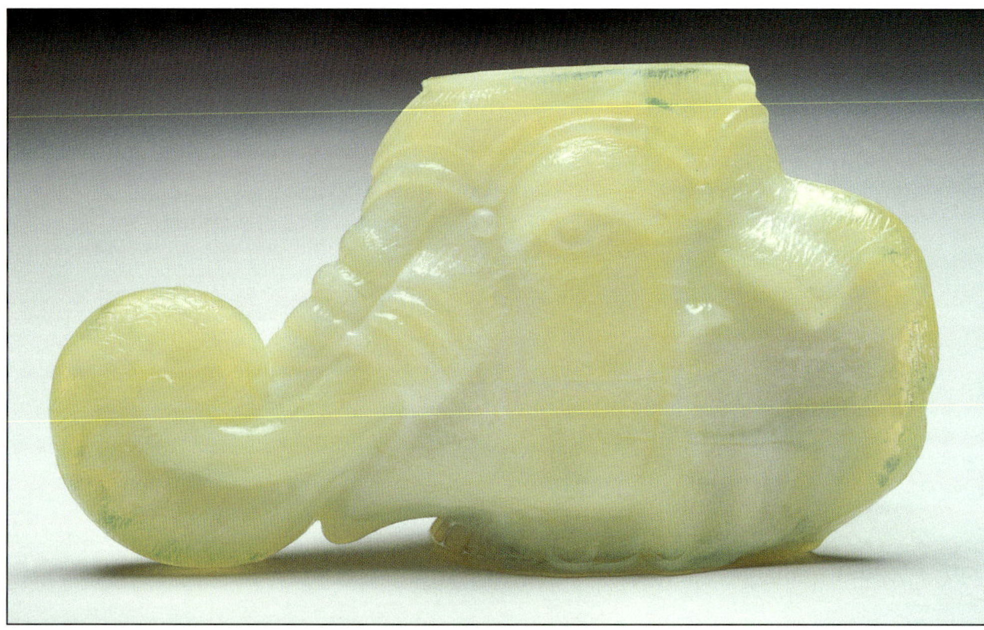

Elephant Head Toothpick, Lemon Custard, opaque yellow and milk slag, fourth Boyd mark, 2.5" tall, 4.4" long, December 1997, **$13.00**

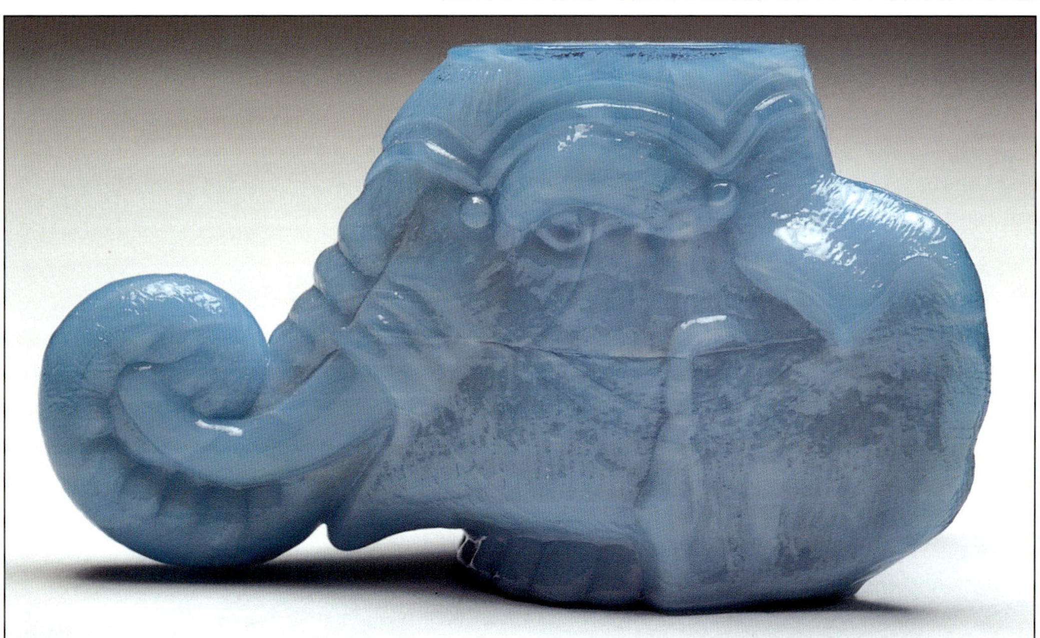

Elephant head toothpick, Alpine Blue, opaque blue and milk slag, fourth Boyd mark, 2.5" tall, 4.4" long, April 1998, **$16.00**

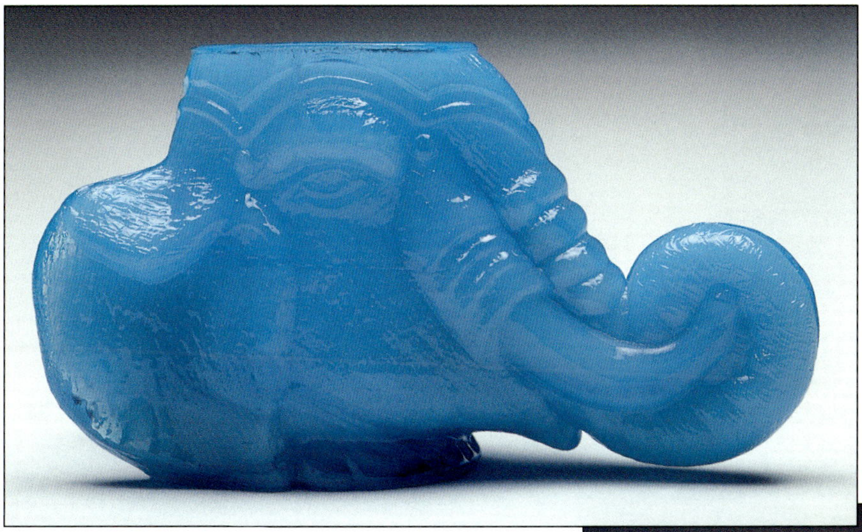

Elephant head toothpick, Alpine Blue, opaque blue and milk slag, fourth Boyd mark, 2.5" tall, 4.4" long, April 1998, **$16.00**

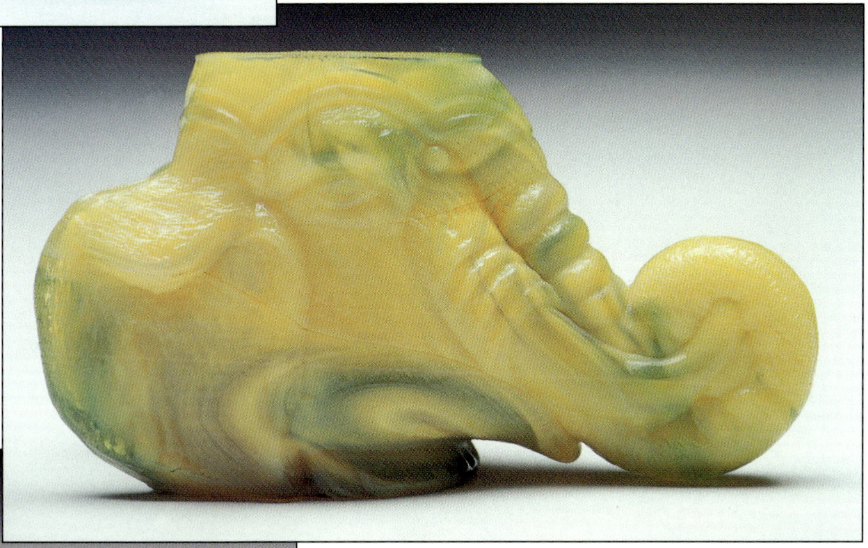

Elephant Head Toothpick, Harvest Gold, yellow and green opaque slag, fifth Boyd mark, 2.5" tall, 4.4" long, December 1999 **$14.00**

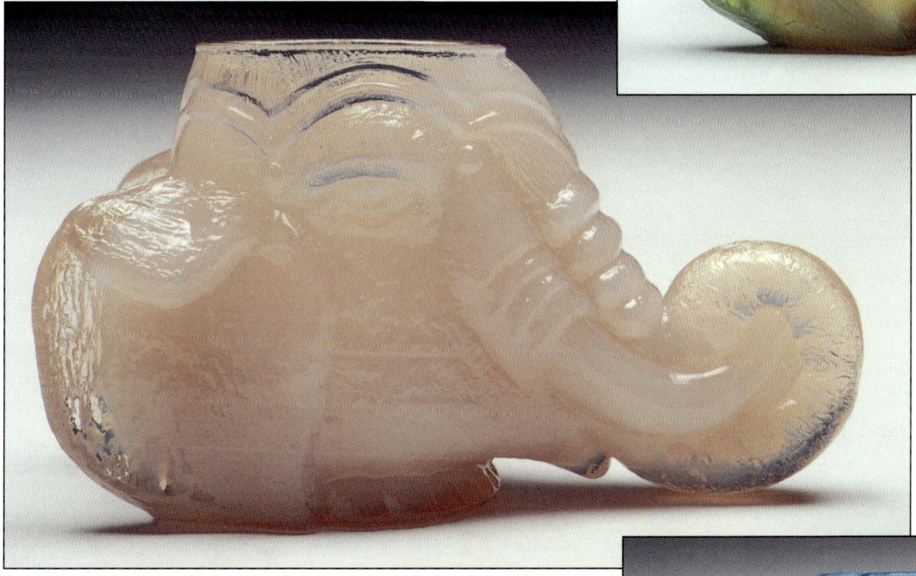

Elephant Head toothpick, Rosie Pink, fifth Boyd mark, 2.5" tall, 4.25" long, July 1999, **$10.00**

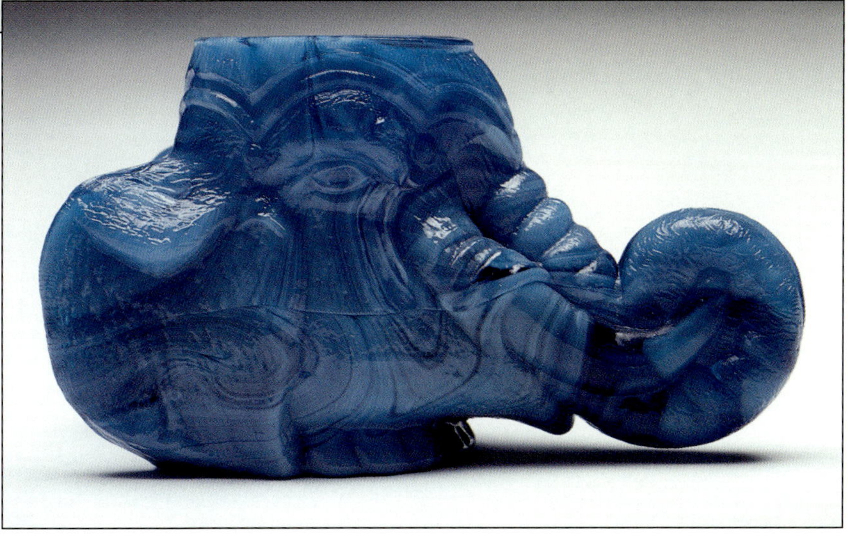

Elephant Head Toothpick, Millennium Surprise, opaque medium blue and dark blue slag, fifth Boyd mark, 2.5" tall, 4.4" long, April 2000, **$16.00**

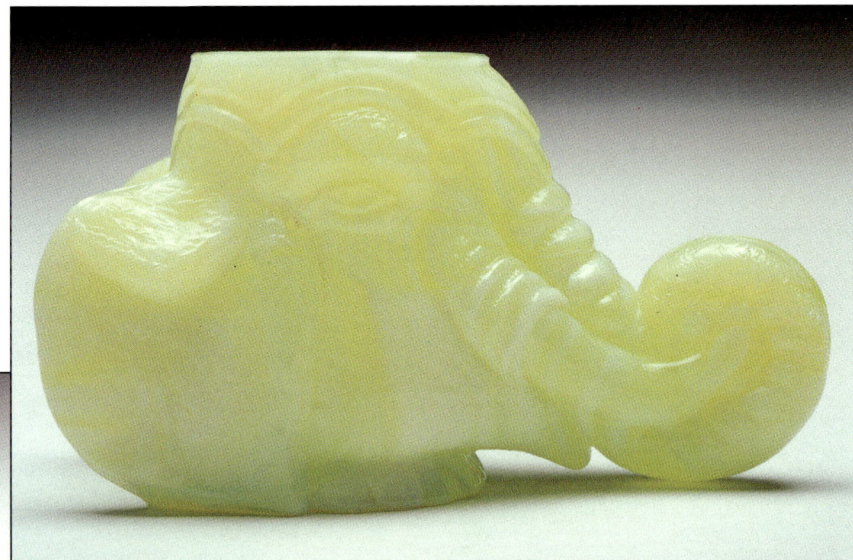

Elephant Head Toothpick, Lemon Splash, opaque milk, transparent Vaseline, fifth Boyd mark, 2.5" tall, 4.4" long, October 2000, **$13.00**

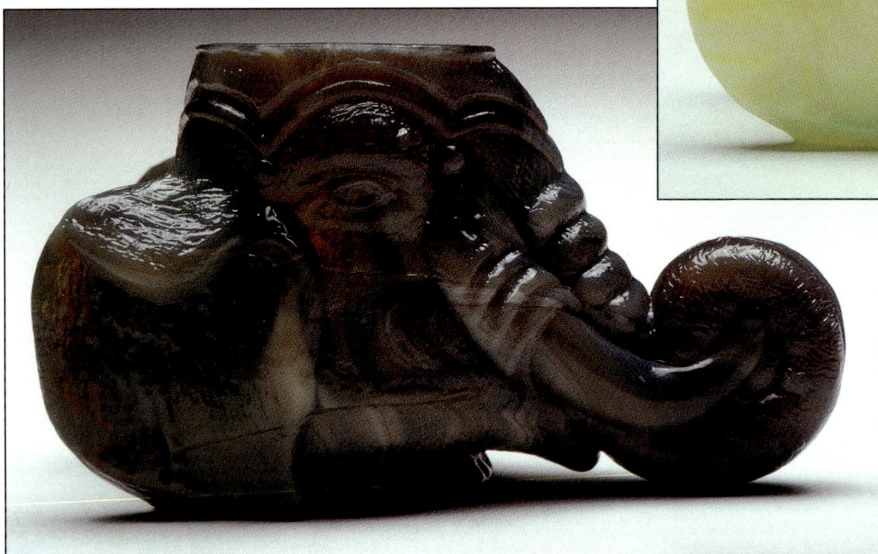

Elephant Head Toothpick, Toffee Slag, gray slag, fifth Boyd mark, 2.5" tall, 4.4" long, June 2000, **$16.00**

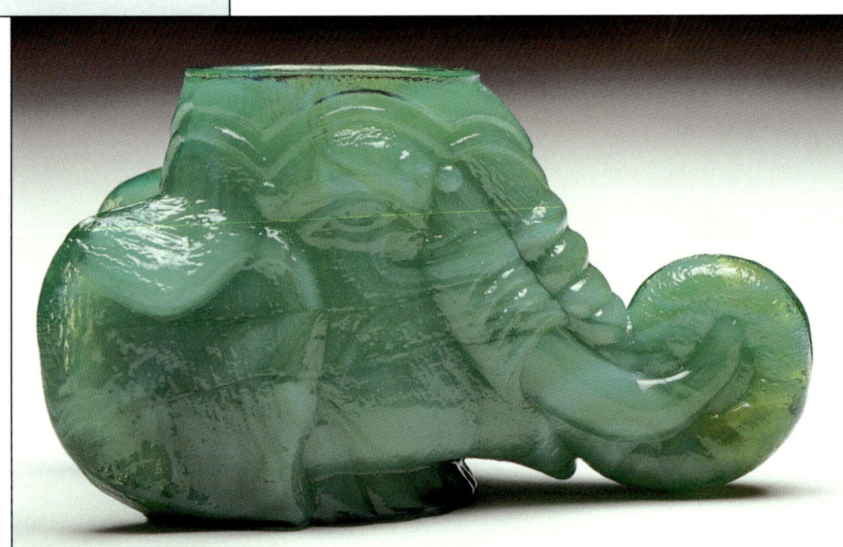

Elephant Head toothpick, Jade, fifth Boyd mark, 2.5" tall, 4.25" long, September 2000, **$14.00**

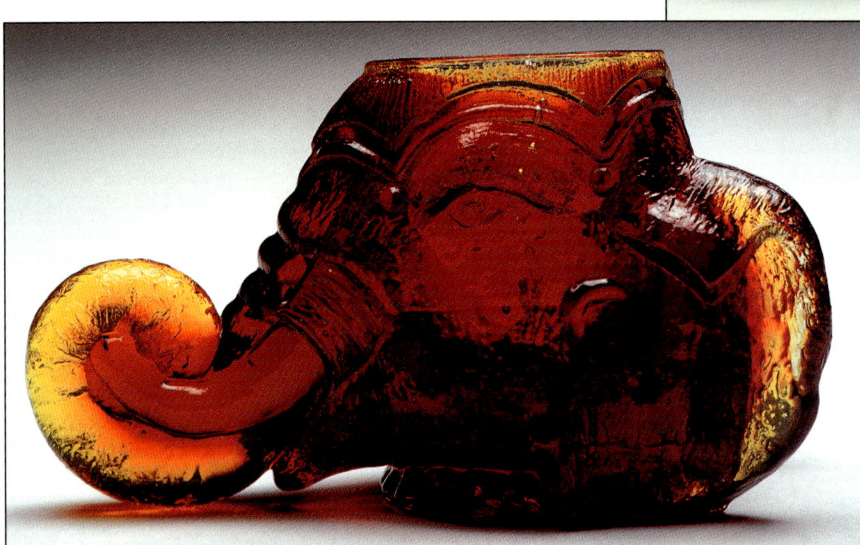

Elephant Head Toothpick, Cherry Red, transparent red, fifth Boyd mark, 2.5" tall, 4.4" long, October 2001, **$18.00**

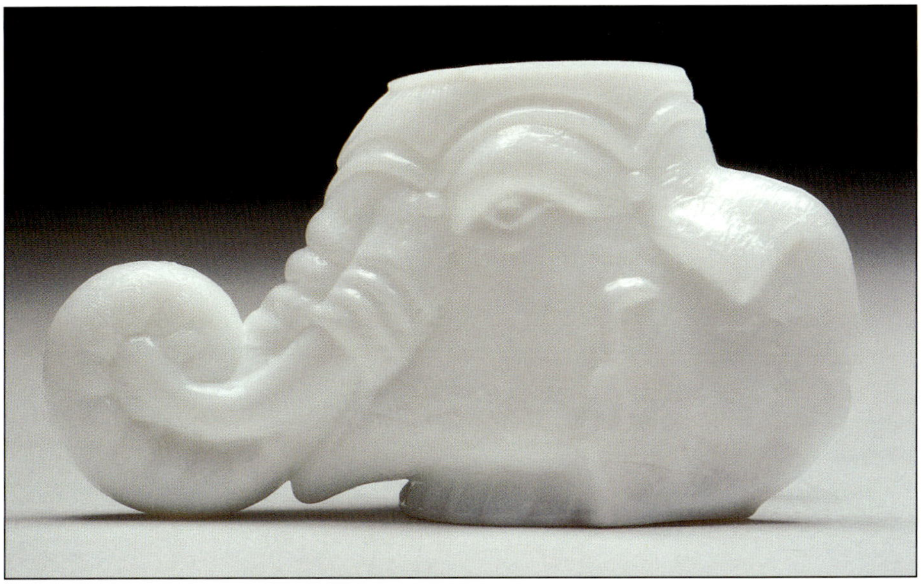

Elephant Head toothpick, Milk White, fifth Boyd mark, 2.5" tall, 4.5" long, April 2001, **$10.00**

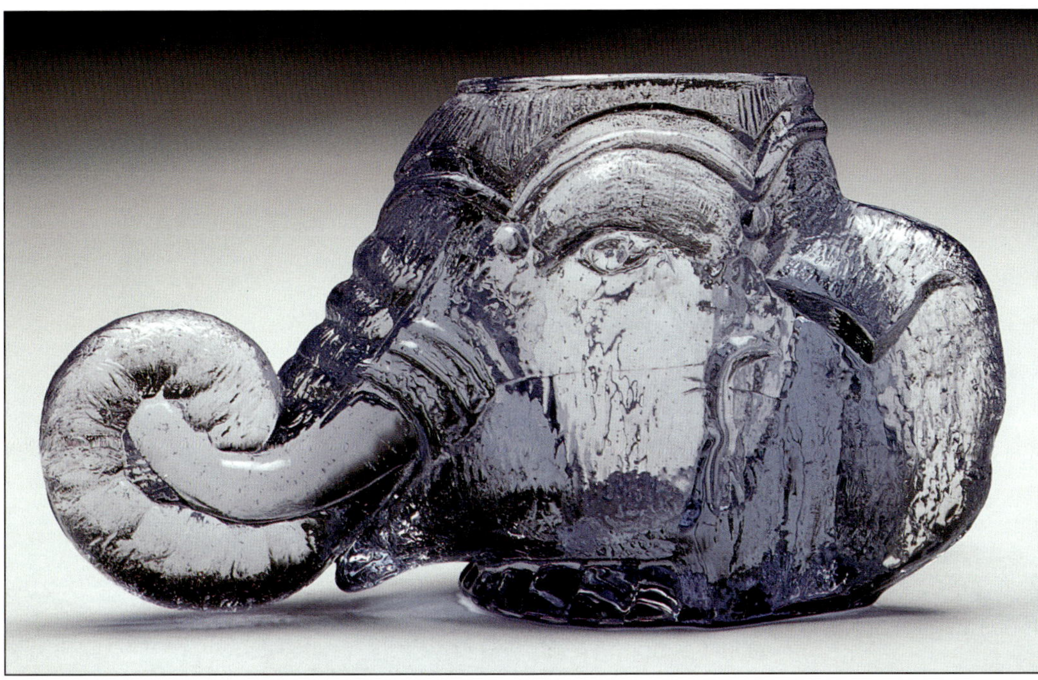

Elephant Head Toothpick, Purple Valor, transparent lilac, fifth Boyd mark, 2.5" tall, 4.4" long, January 2002, **$13.00**

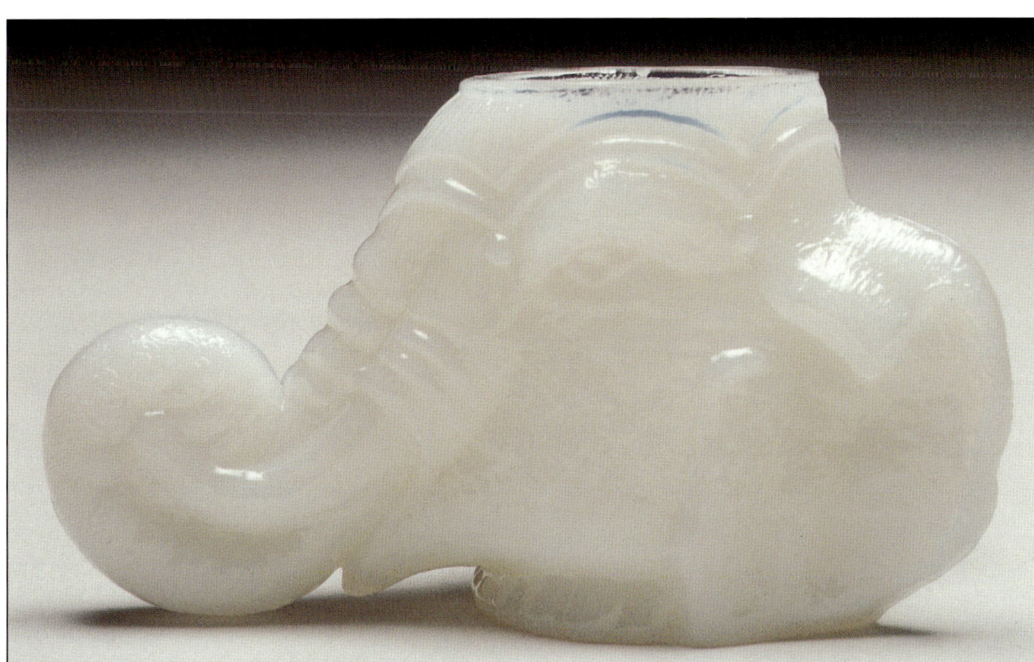

Elephant Head toothpick, White Salmon, fifth Boyd mark, 2.5" tall, 4.25" long, October 2002, **$10.00**

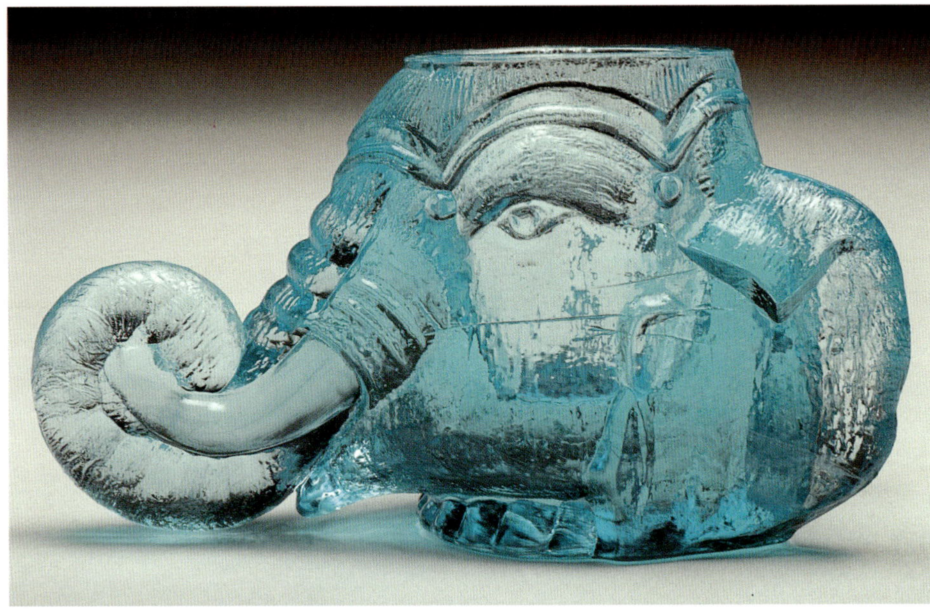

Elephant Head toothpick, Sky Blue, fifth Boyd mark, 2.5" tall, 4.25" long, November 2002, **$13.00**

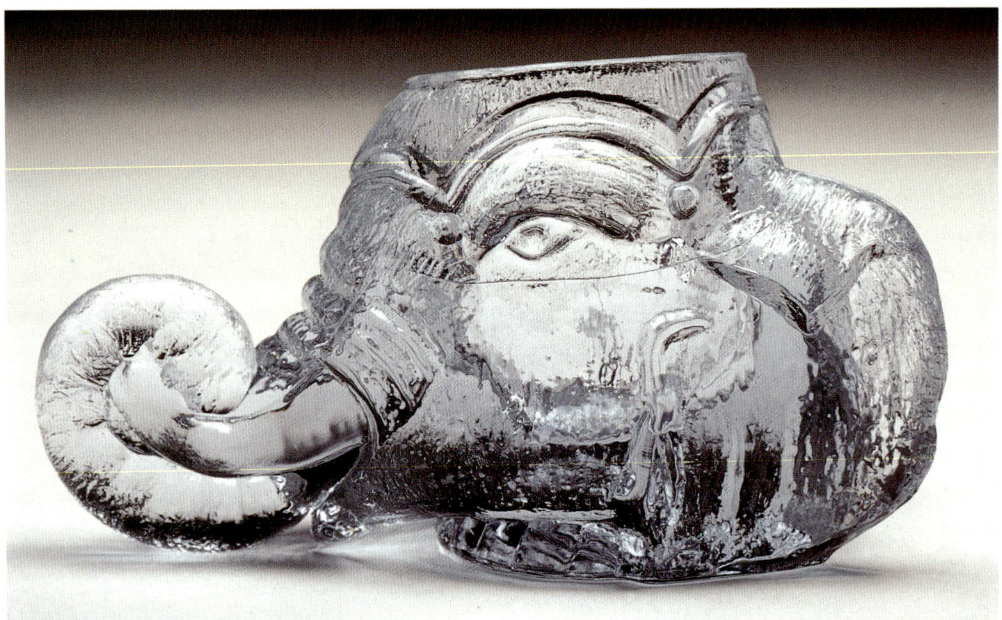

Elephant Head toothpick, Pearly Pink (diachromatic color changes under different types of lighting), fifth Boyd mark, 2.5" tall, 4.25" long, December 2002, **$10.00**

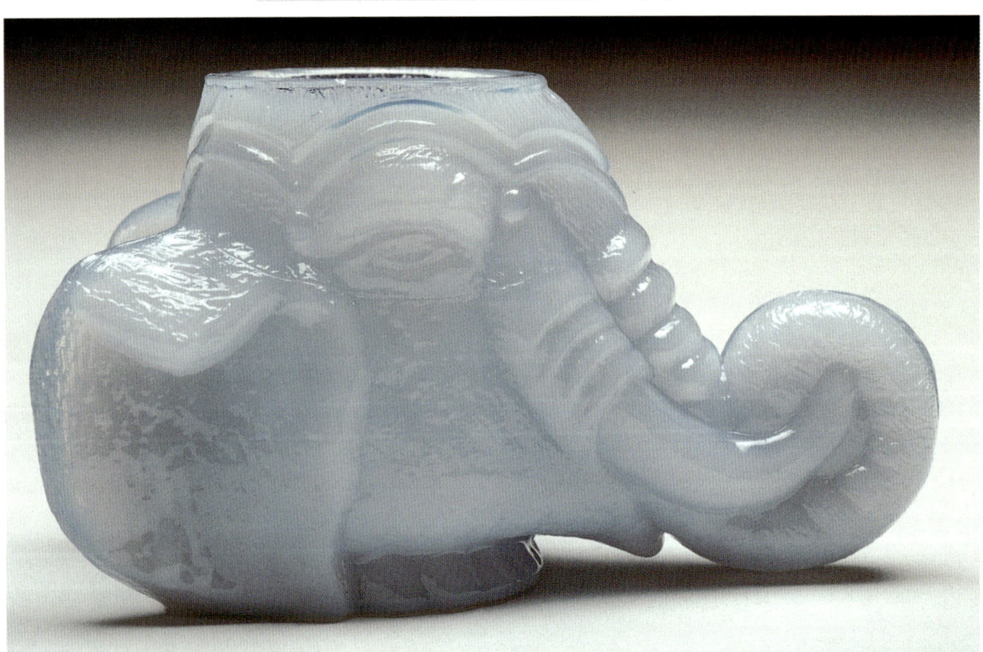

Elephant Head toothpick, Blue Orchid, fifth Boyd mark, 2.5" tall, 4.25" long, June 2002, **$12.00**

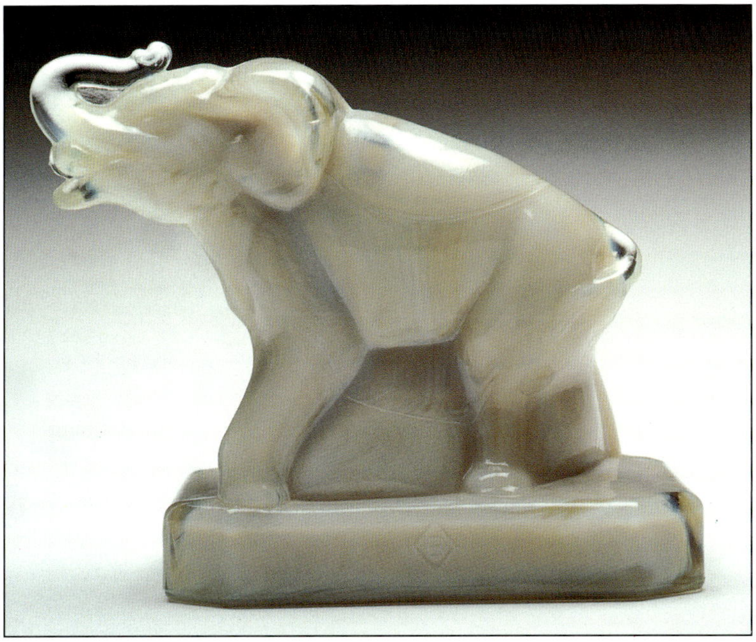

Zack the elephant, Sandpiper, opaque white and gray slag, solid base, first Boyd mark, 3.5" tall, 4.75" long, February 1981, **$35.00**

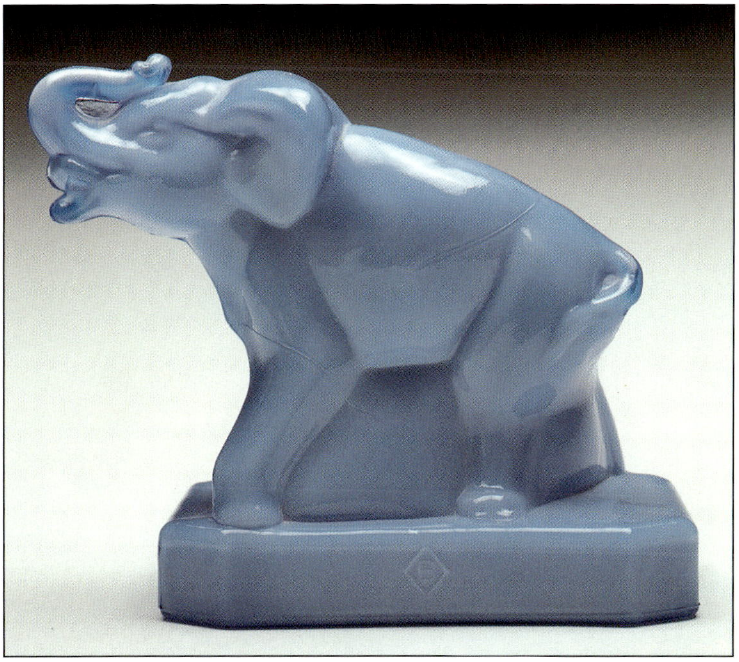

Zack the elephant, Delphinium, opaque medium blue, solid base, first Boyd mark, 3.5" tall, 4.75" long, March 1981, **$40.00**

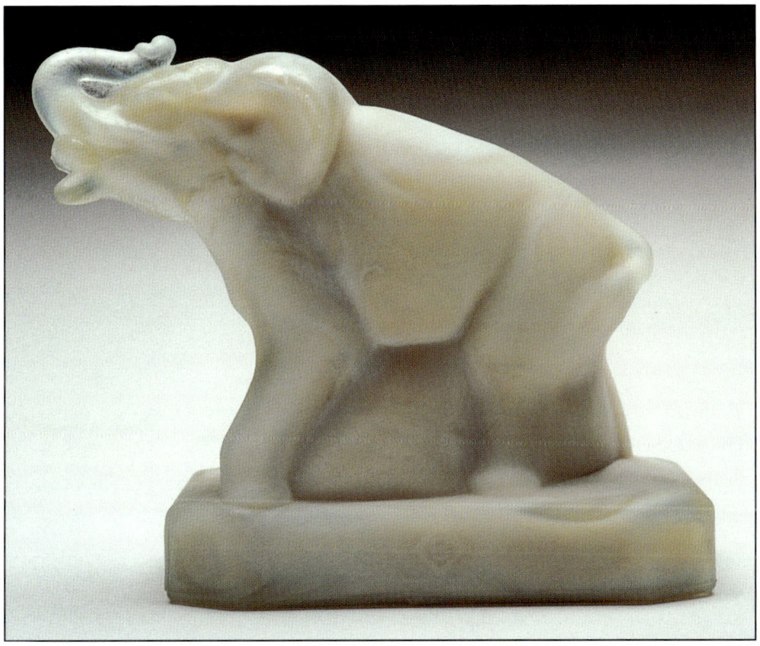

Zack the elephant, Sandpiper with satin finish, solid base, first Boyd mark, 3.5" tall, 4.75" long, February 1981, **$35.00**

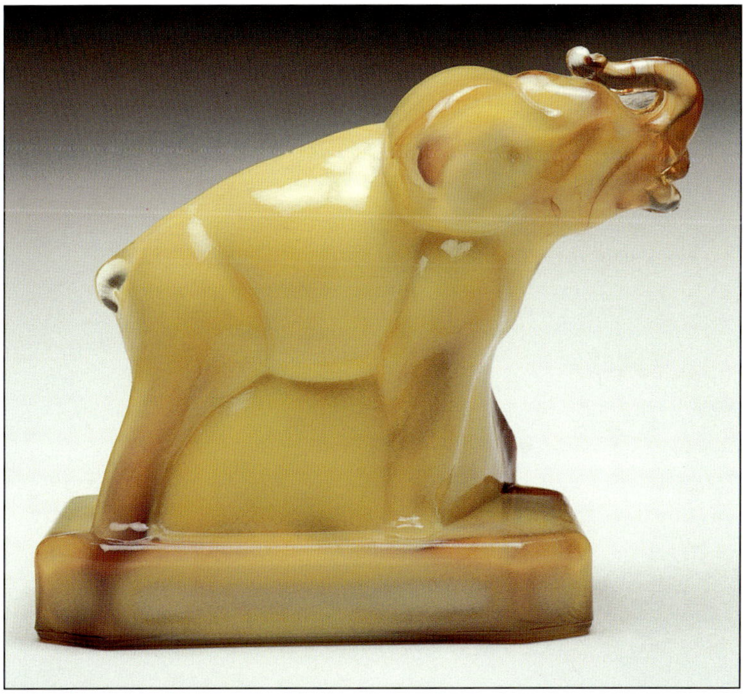

Zack the elephant, Olde Ivory Surprise, opaque yellow and brown slag, solid base, first Boyd mark, 3.5" tall, 4.75" long, May 1981, **$45.00**

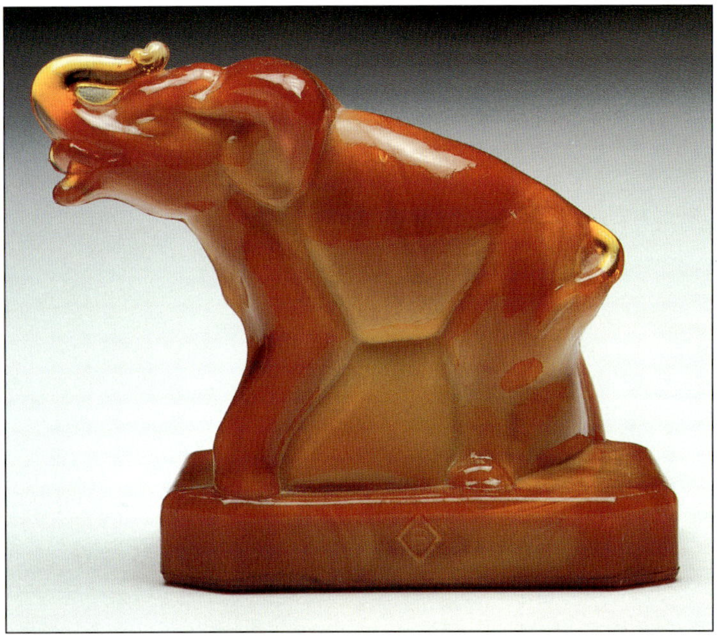

Zack the elephant, Mardi Gras, opaque orange, solid base, first Boyd mark, 3.5" tall, 4.75" long, June 1981, **$50.00**

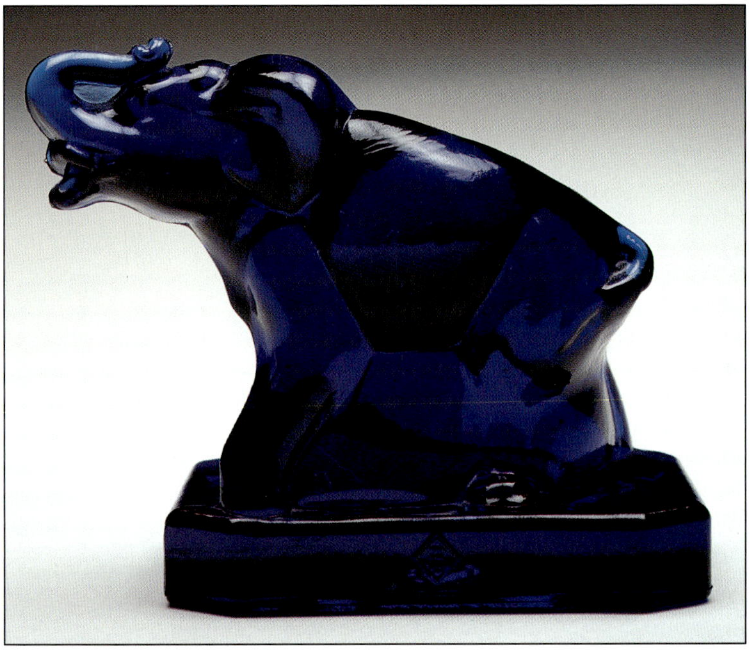

Zack the elephant, Cobalt, dark blue, solid base, first Boyd mark, 3.5" tall, 4.75" long, December 1981, **$45.00**

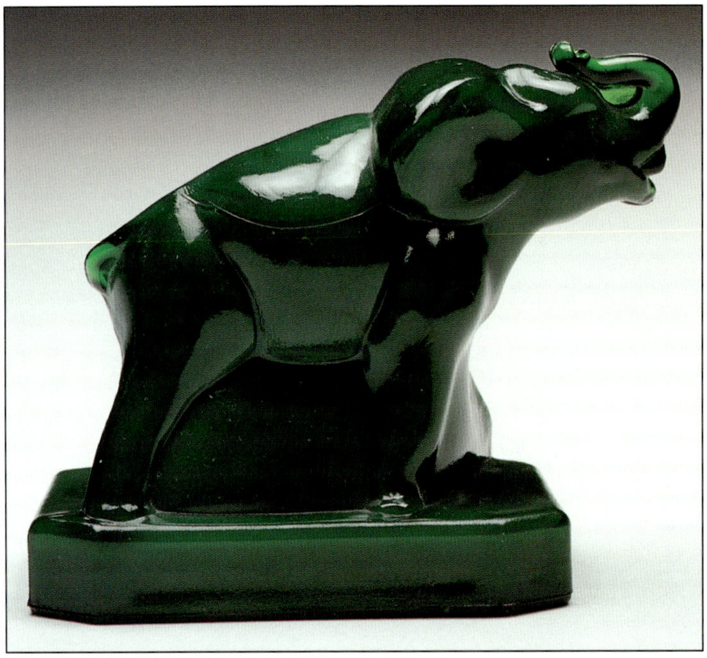

Zack the elephant, Furr Green, opaque green, solid base, first Boyd mark, 3.5" tall, 4.75" long, August 1981, **$40.00**

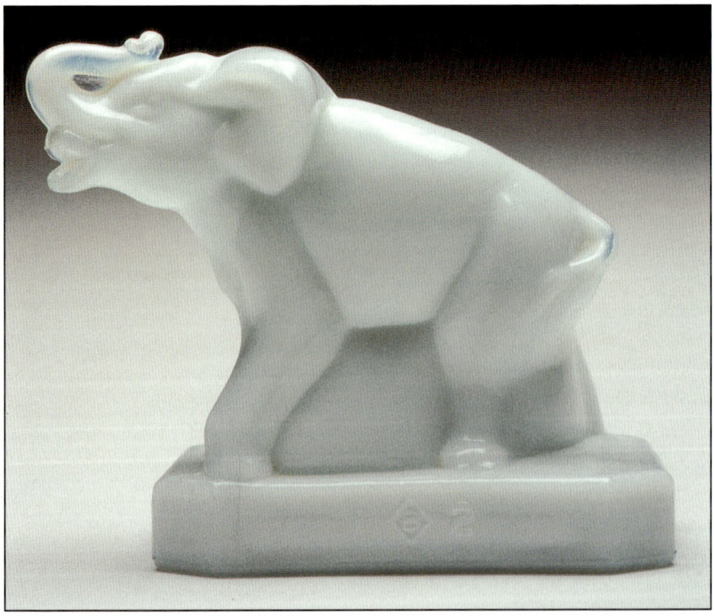

Zack the elephant, Snow, opaque milk glass, solid base, second Boyd mark, 3.5" tall, 4.75" long, February 1982, **$35.00**

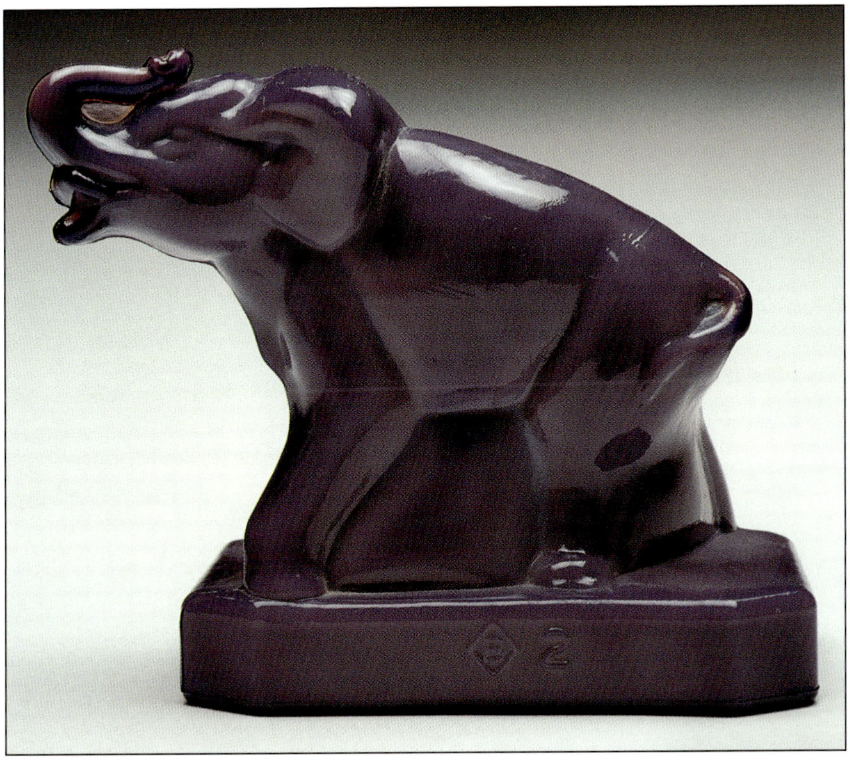

Zack the elephant, Lavender, opaque purple, solid base, second Boyd mark, 3.5" tall, 4.75" long, April 1982, **$45.00**

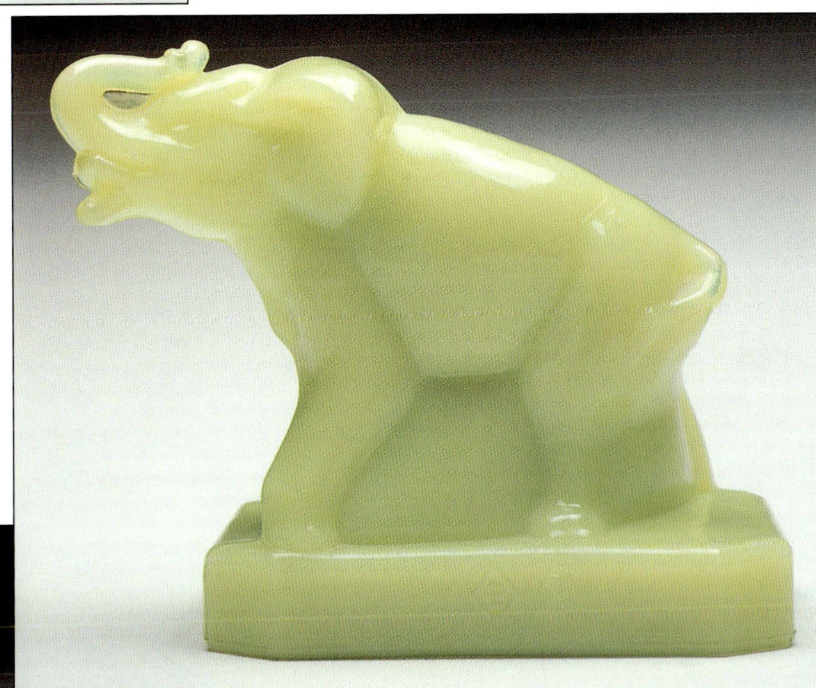

Zack the elephant, Pippin Green, opaque light yellow, solid base, second Boyd mark, 3.5" tall, 4.75" long, June 1982, **$40.00**

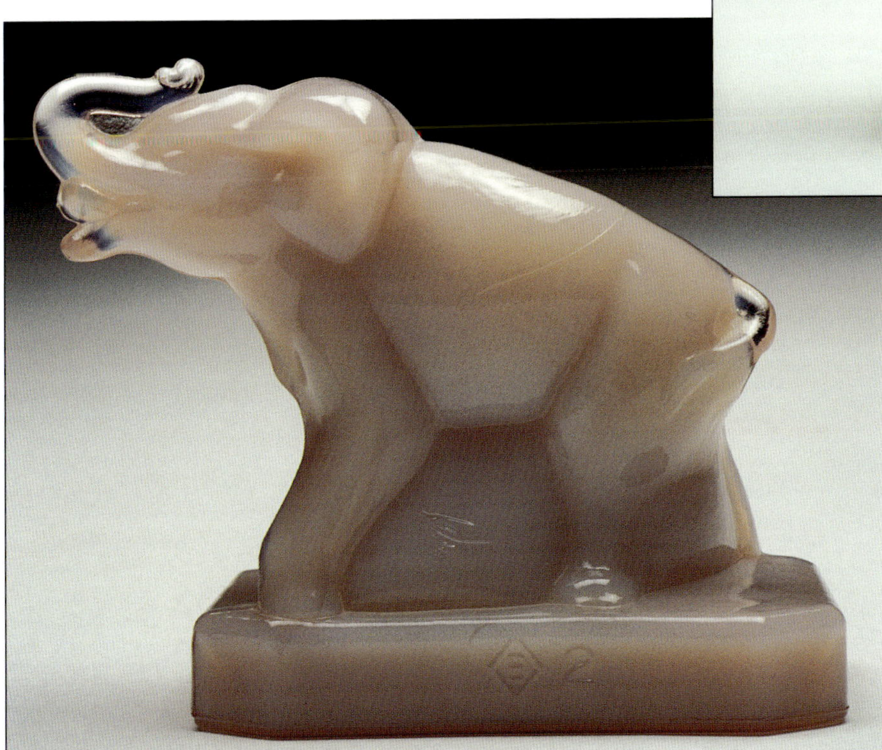

Zack the elephant, Crown Tuscan, opaque pink, solid base, second Boyd mark, 3.5" tall, 4.75" long, September 1982, **$35.00**

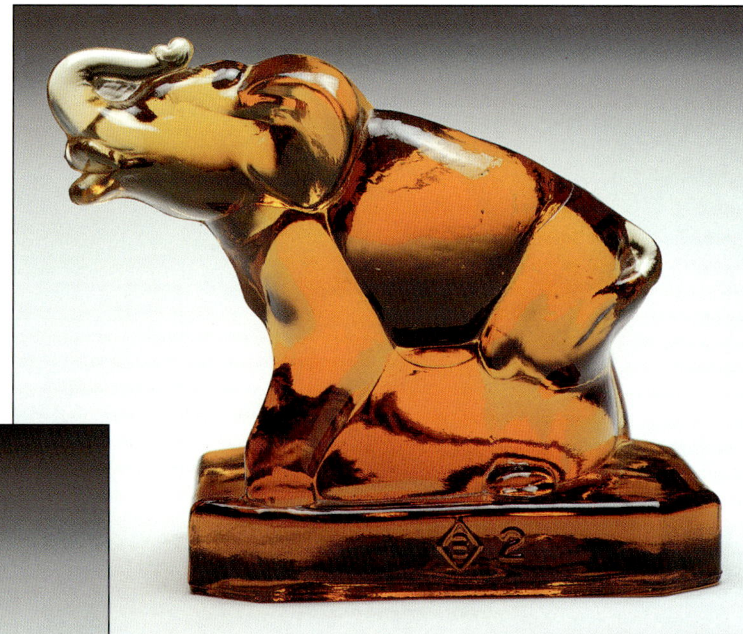

Zack the elephant, Golden Delight, amber, solid base, second Boyd mark, 3.5" tall, 4.75" long, November 1982, **$35.00**

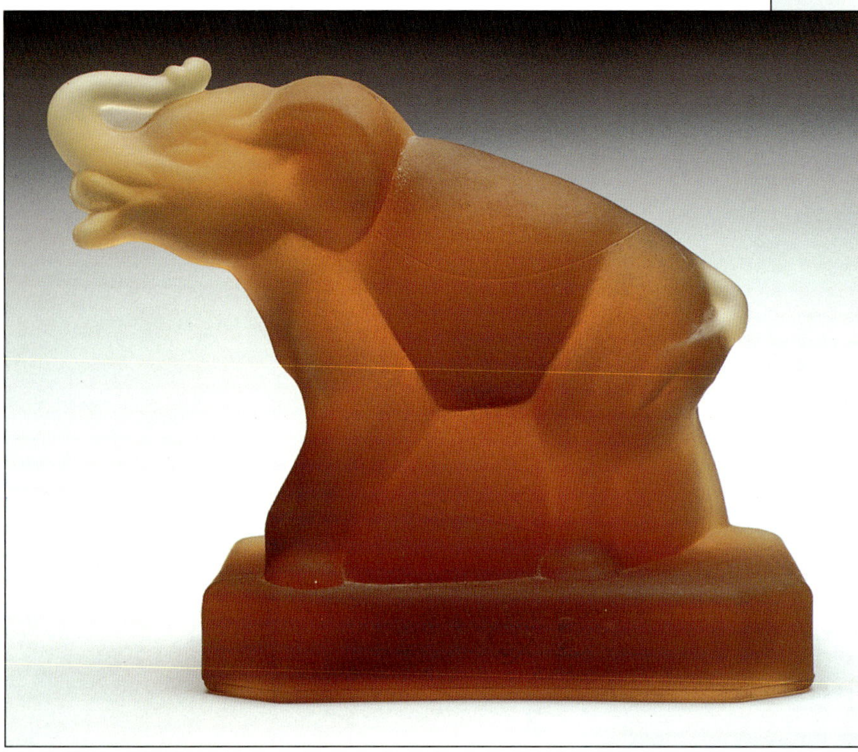

Zack the elephant, Golden Delight, amber with satin finish, solid base, second Boyd mark, 3.5" tall, 4.75" long, November 1982, **$38.00**

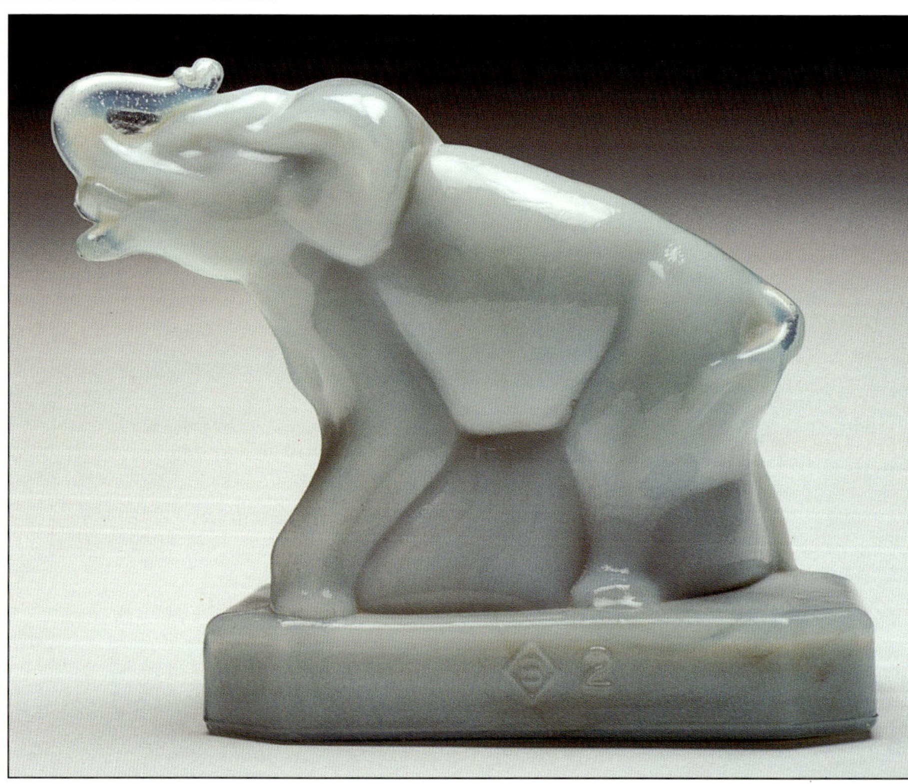

Zack the elephant, December Swirl, opaque, off white, solid base, second Boyd mark, 3.5" tall, 4.75" long, December 1982, **$35.00**

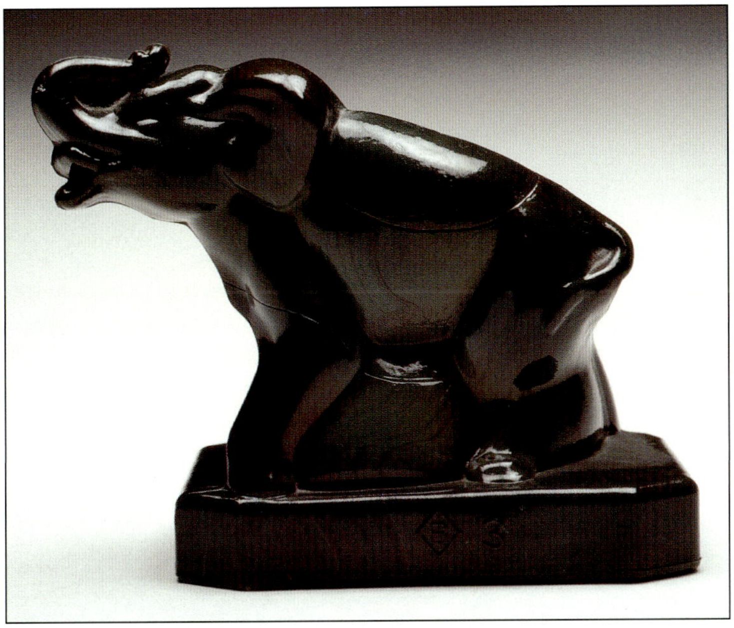

Zack the elephant, English Yew, opaque dark green with red streaks, solid base, third Boyd mark, 3.5" tall, 4.75" long, February 1983, **$38.00**

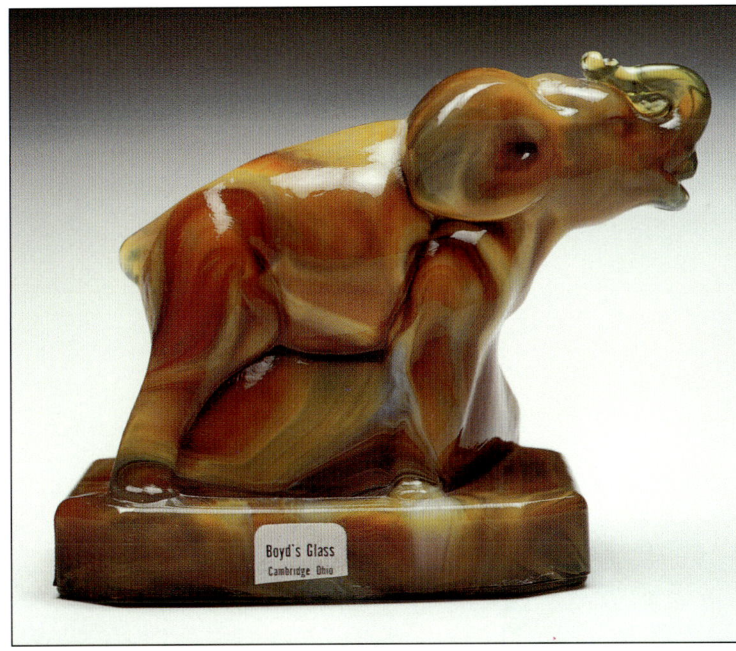

Zack the elephant, September Swirl, opaque mustard and orange slag, hollow base, third Boyd mark, original Boyd label, 3.5" tall, 4.75" long, September 1983, **$38.00**

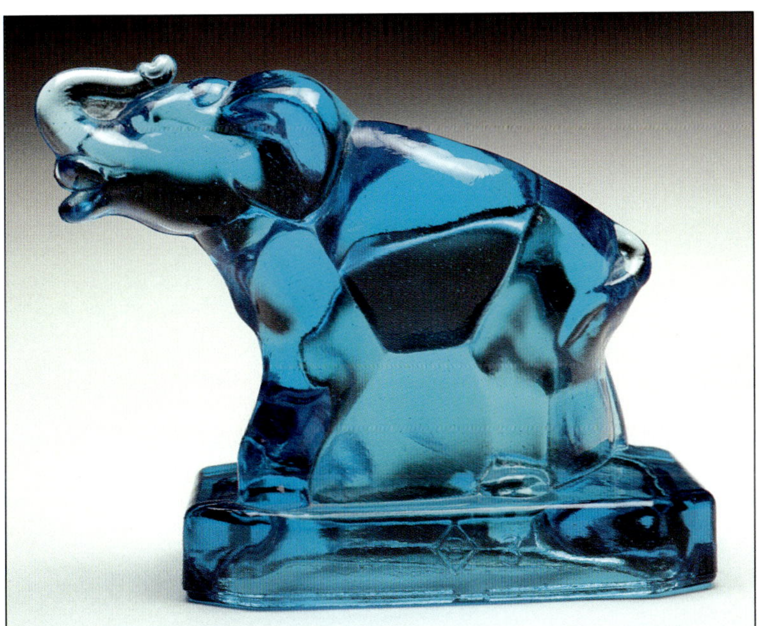

Zack the elephant, Alice Blue, transparent medium blue, hollow base, third Boyd mark, 3.5" tall, 4.75" long, April 1983, **$38.00**

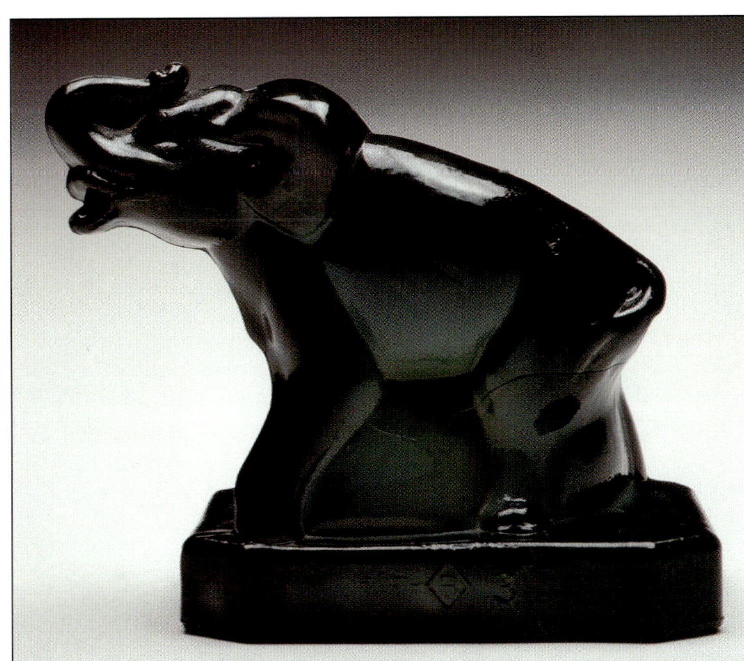

Zack the elephant, Mint Green, opaque medium olive green, solid base, third Boyd mark, 3.5" tall, 4.75" long, October 1983, **$30.00**

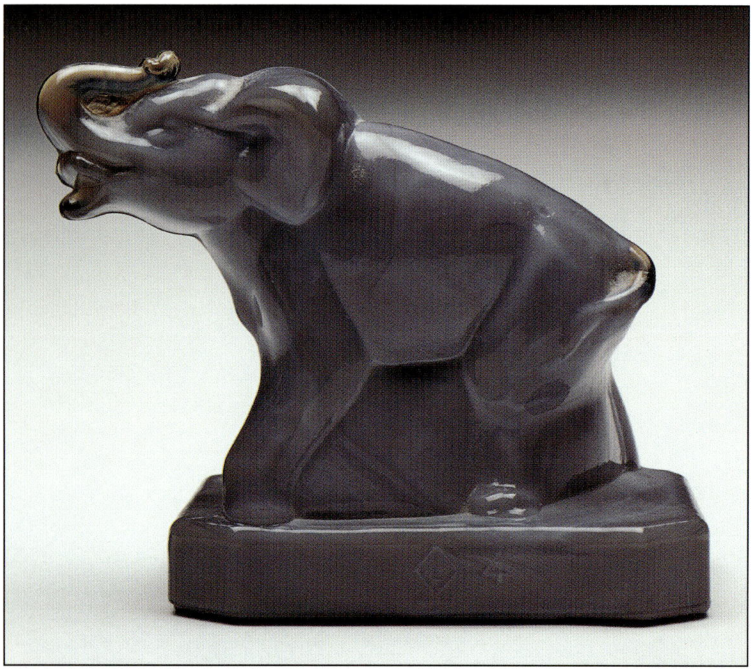

Zack the elephant, Violet Slate, opaque light gray, hollow base, fourth Boyd mark, 3.5" tall, 4.75" long, January 1984, **$25.00**

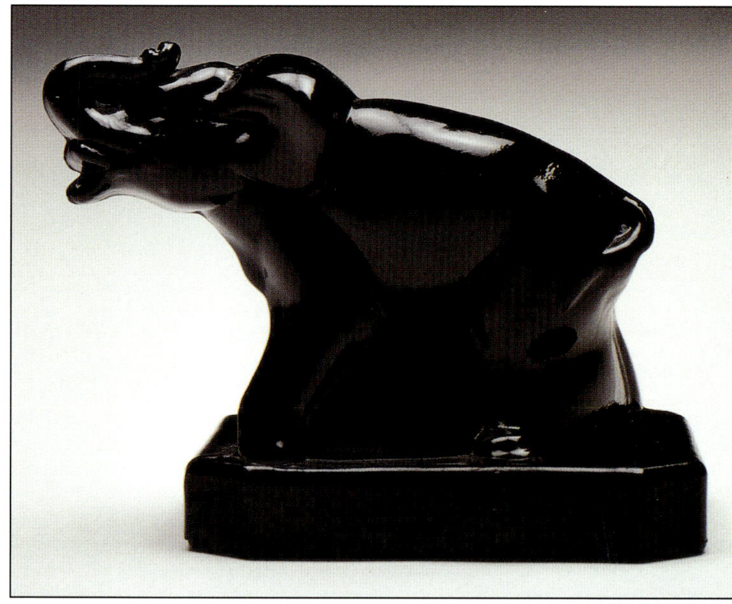

Zack the elephant, Ebony, opaque black, hollow base, fourth Boyd mark, 3.5" tall, 4.75" long, March 1984, **$32.00**

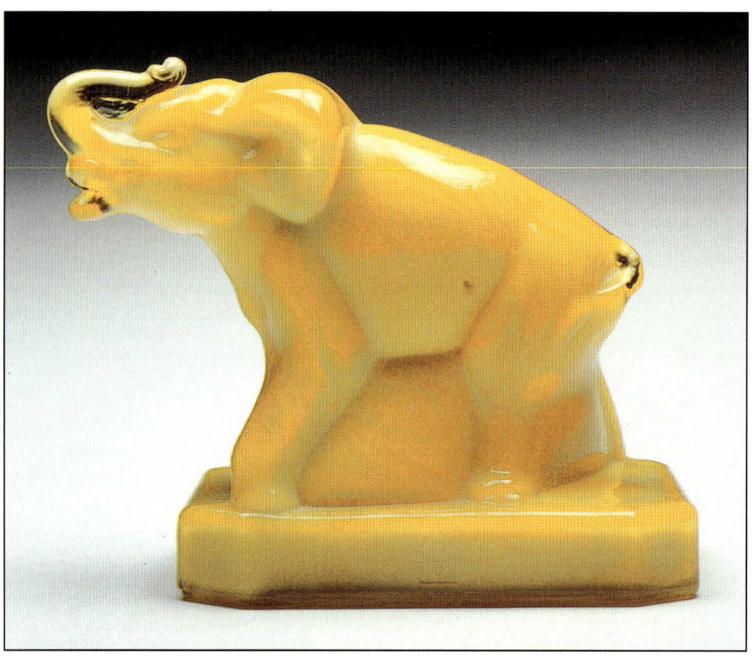

Zack the elephant, Daffodil, opaque yellow, hollow base, fourth Boyd mark, 3.5" tall, 4.75" long, January 1984, **$38.00**

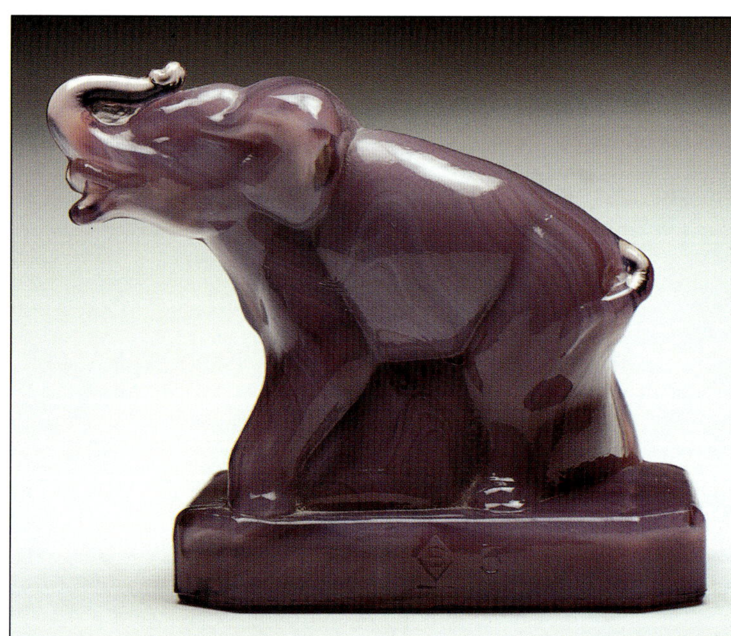

Zack the elephant, Lilac, opaque medium purple, hollow base, fifth Boyd mark, 3.5" tall, 4.75" long, June 1985, **$30.00**

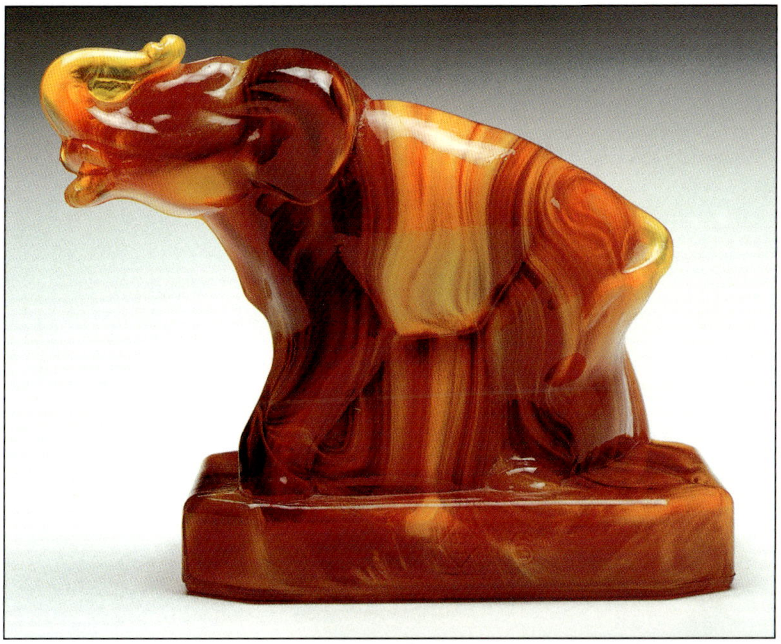

Zack the elephant, Kumquat, opaque orange and red slag, hollow base, sixth Boyd mark, 3.5" tall, 4.75" long, November 1986, **$38.00**

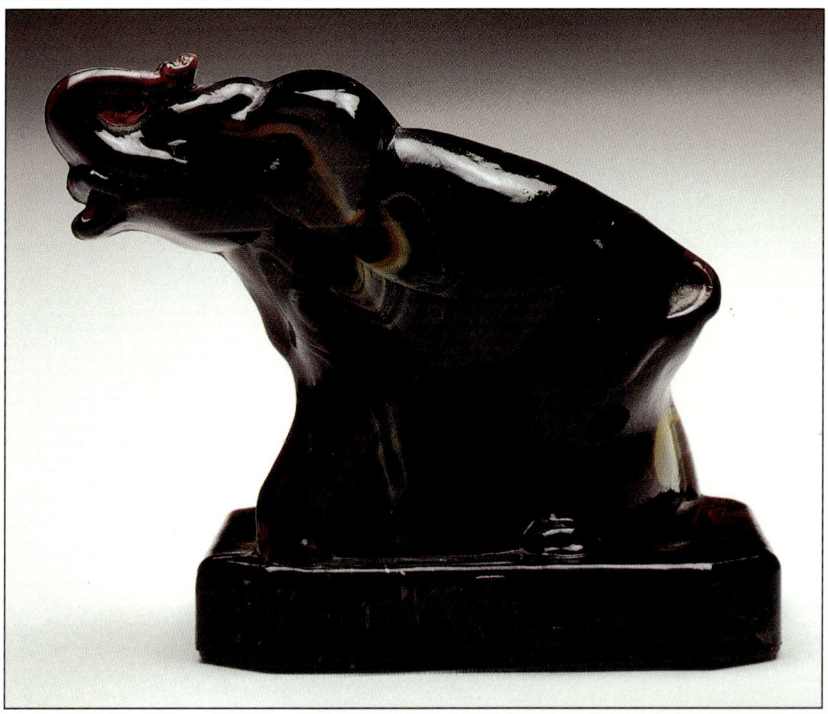

Zack the elephant, Plum Slag, black and yellow slag, hollow base, sixth Boyd mark, 3.5" tall, 4.75" long, November 1988, **$30.00**

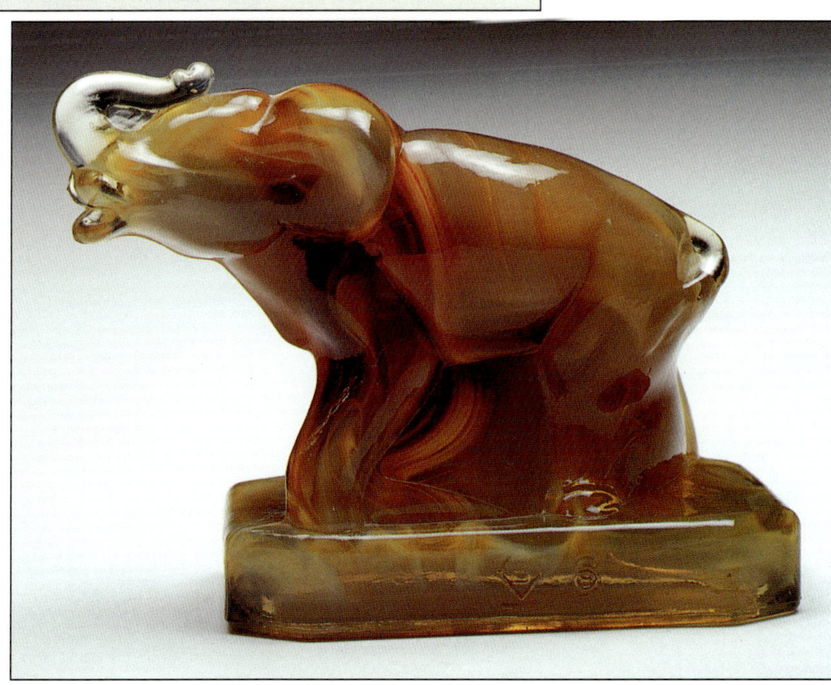

Zack the elephant, Autumn Splendor, opaque beige and orange slag, hollow base, sixth Boyd mark, 3.5" tall, 4.75" long, November 1989, **$32.00**

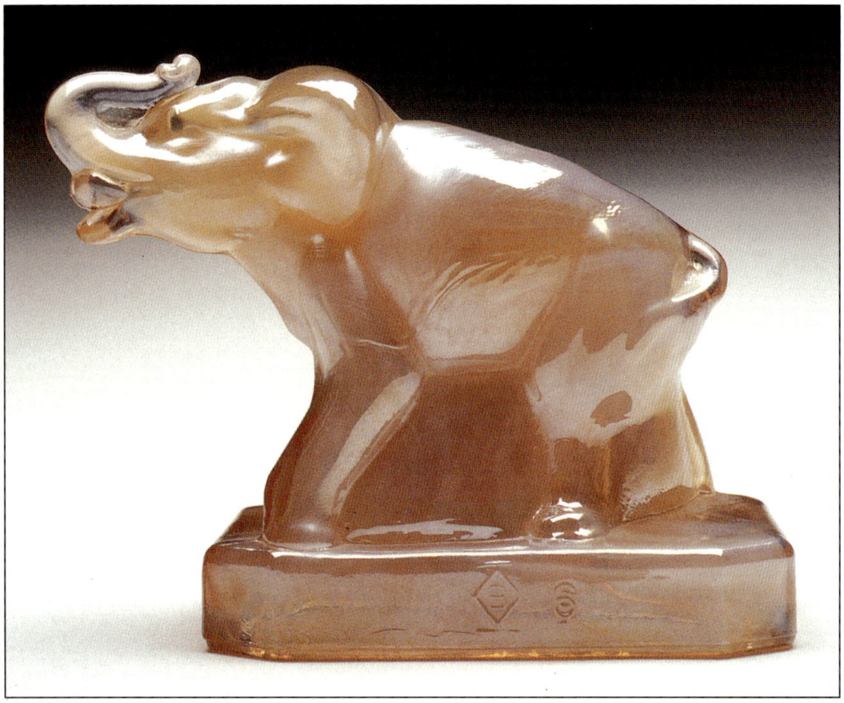

Zack the elephant, Crown Tuscan Carnival, opaque pink iridescent, hollow base, sixth Boyd mark, 3.5" tall, 4.75" long, September 1990, **$24.00**

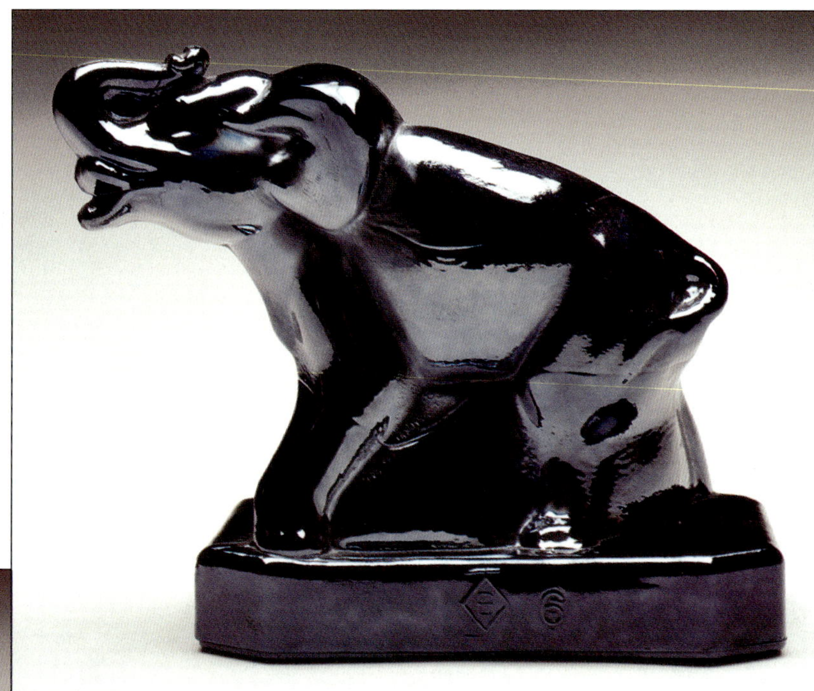

Zack the elephant, Classic Black Carnival, black iridescent, hollow base, sixth Boyd mark, 3.5" tall, 4.75" long, October 1991, **$26.00**

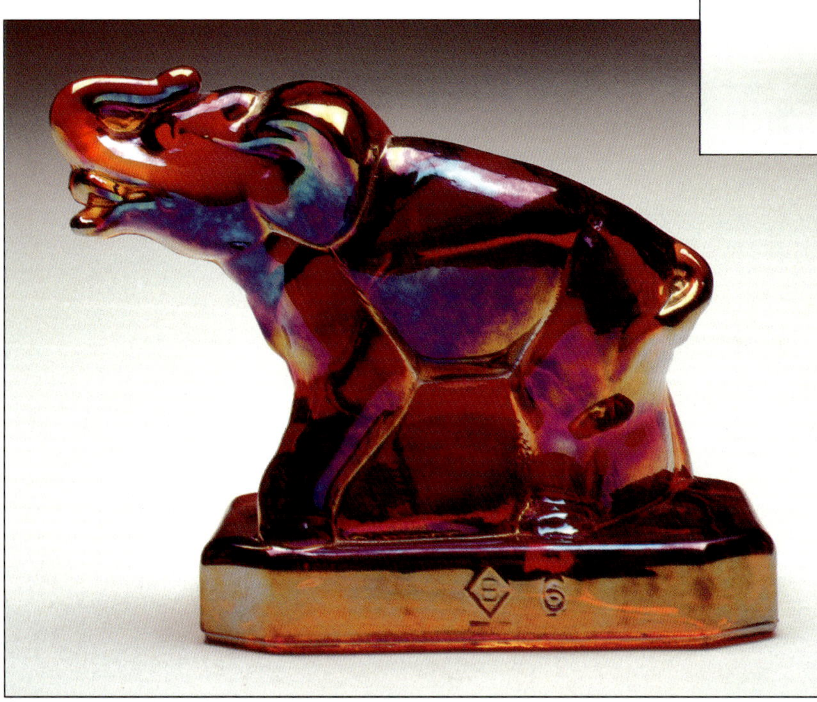

Zack the elephant, Cardinal Red Carnival, transparent red iridescent, hollow base, sixth Boyd mark, 3.5" tall, 4.75" long, May 1992, **$35.00**

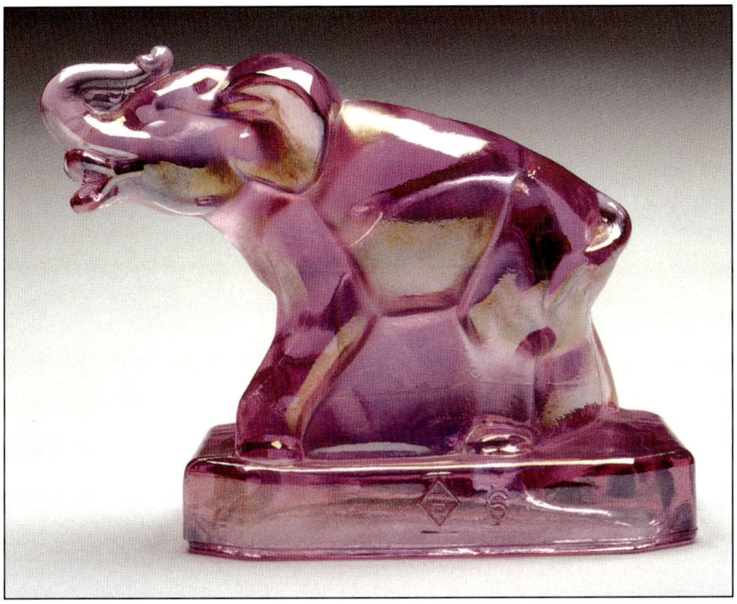

Zack the elephant, Alexandrite Carnival, transparent light purple, hollow base, sixth Boyd mark, 3.5" tall, 4.75" long, September 1993, **$35.00**

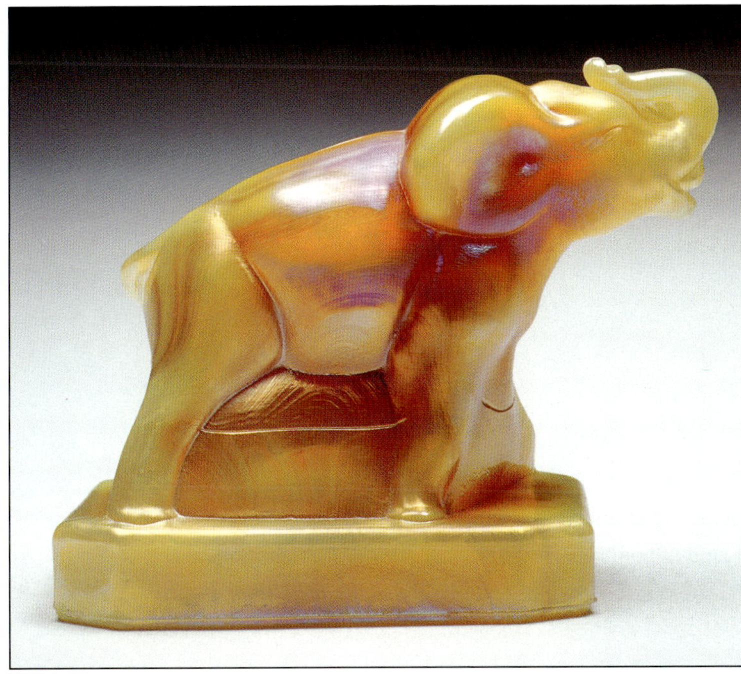

Zack the elephant, Sunkiste Carnival, opaque yellow and orange iridescent, hollow base, sixth Boyd mark, 3.5" tall, 4.75" long, February 1995, **$30.00**

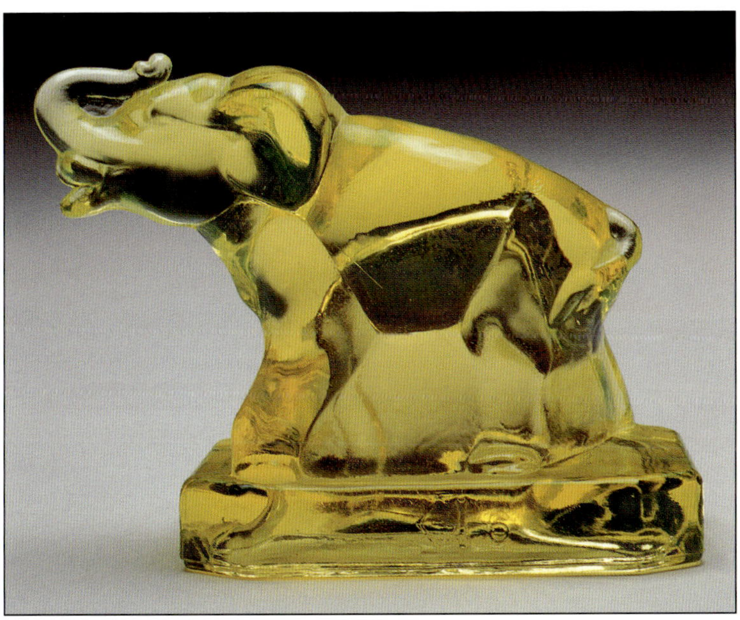

Zack the elephant, Vaseline, hollow base, sixth Boyd mark, 3.5" tall, 4.75" long, June 1994, **$28.00**

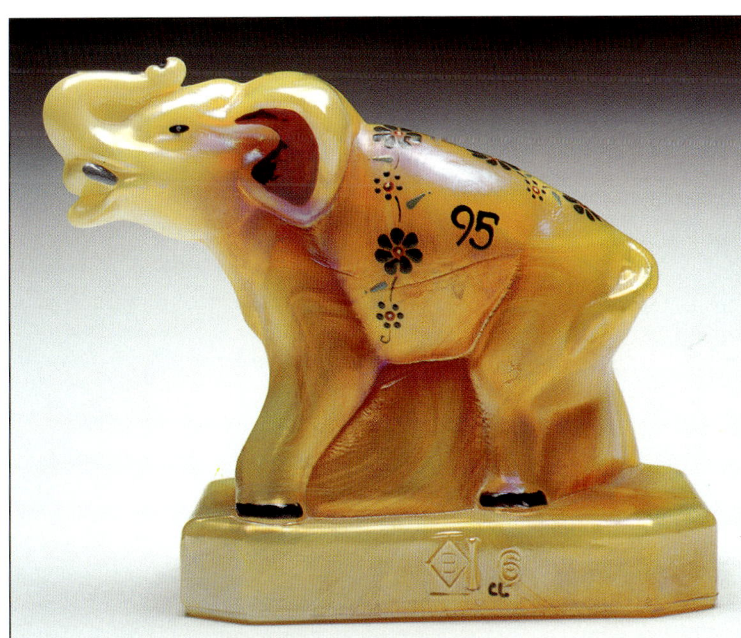

Zack the elephant, Sunkiste Carnival, opaque yellow and orange iridescent hand painted with flowers, hollow base, sixth Boyd mark, 3.5" tall, 4.75" long, February 1995, **$45.00**

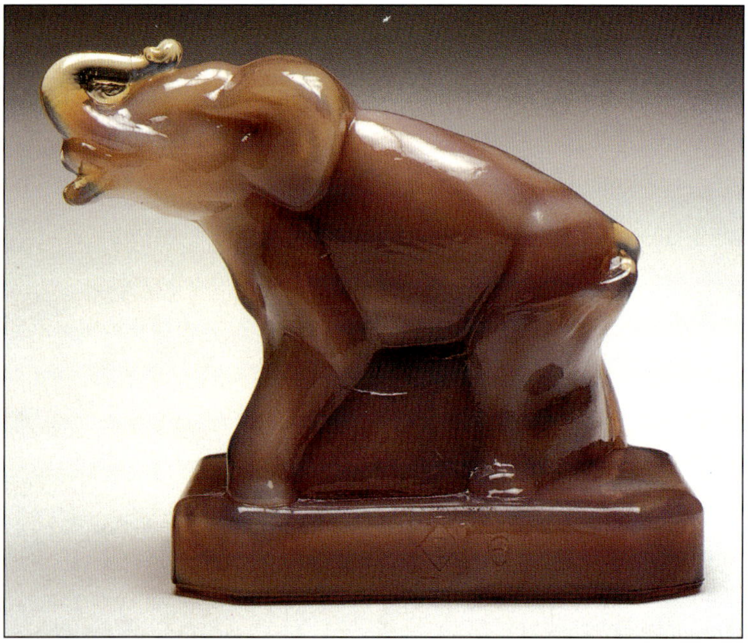

Zack the elephant, Mystique, hollow base, sixth Boyd mark, 3.6" tall, 4.5" long, October 1996, **$25.00**

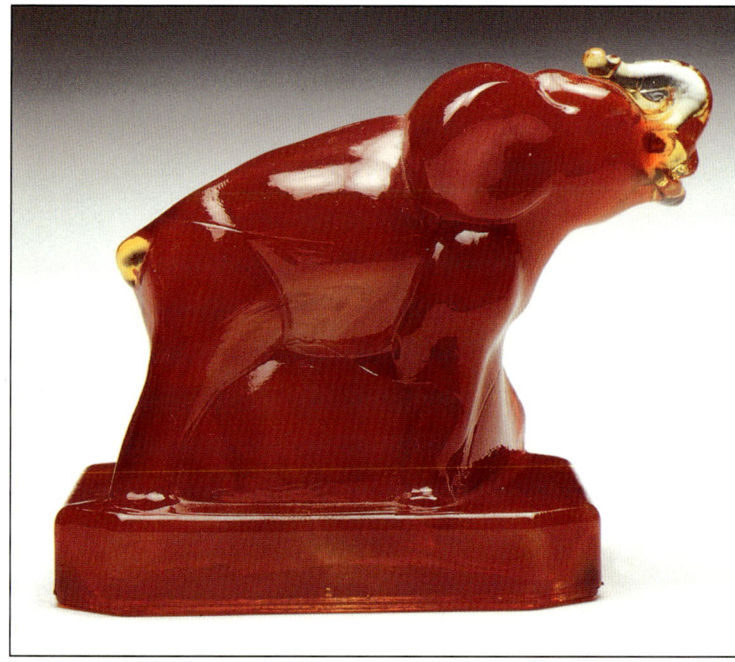

Zack the elephant, Spring Surprise, opaque red and orange, hollow base, sixth Boyd mark, 3.5" tall, 4.75" long, May 1997, **$30.00**

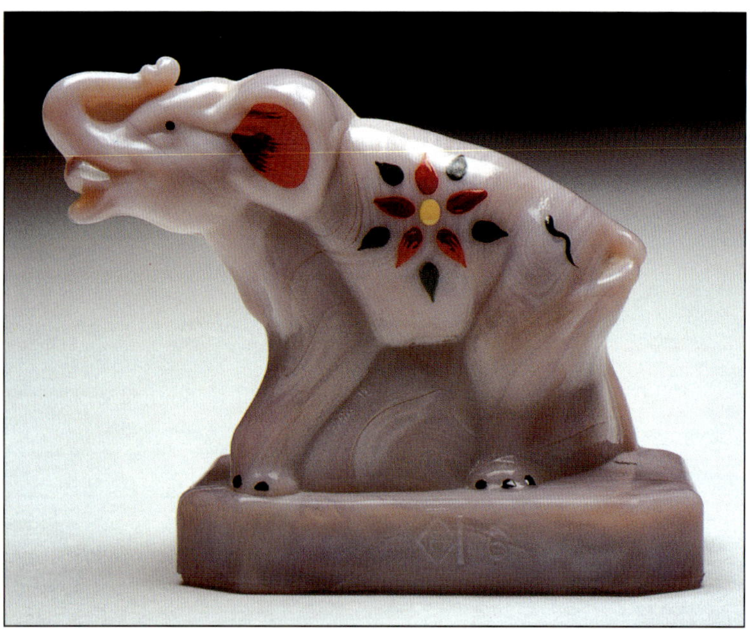

Zack the elephant, Mystique, opaque pink and purple hand painted with flowers, hollow base, sixth Boyd mark, 3.5" tall, 4.75" long, October 1996, **$38.00**

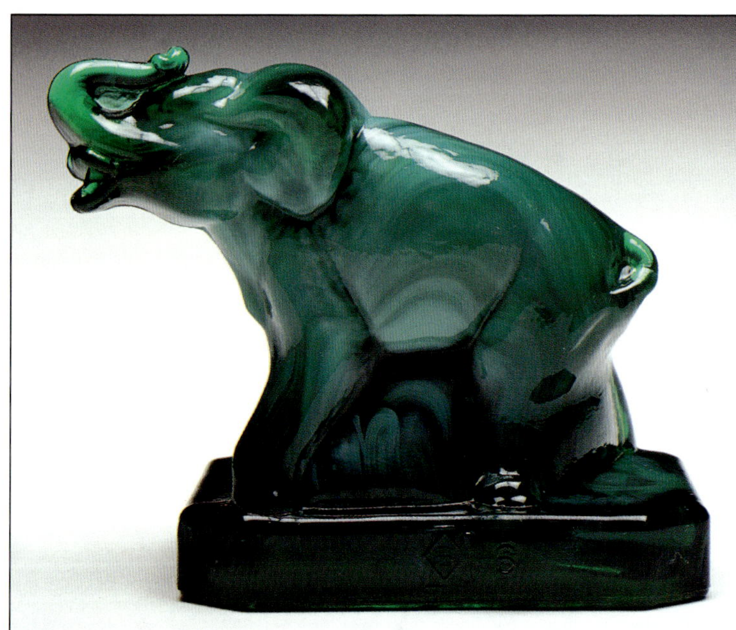

Zack the elephant, Moss Green, hollow base, sixth Boyd mark, 3.6" tall, 4.5" long, August 1998, **$25.00**

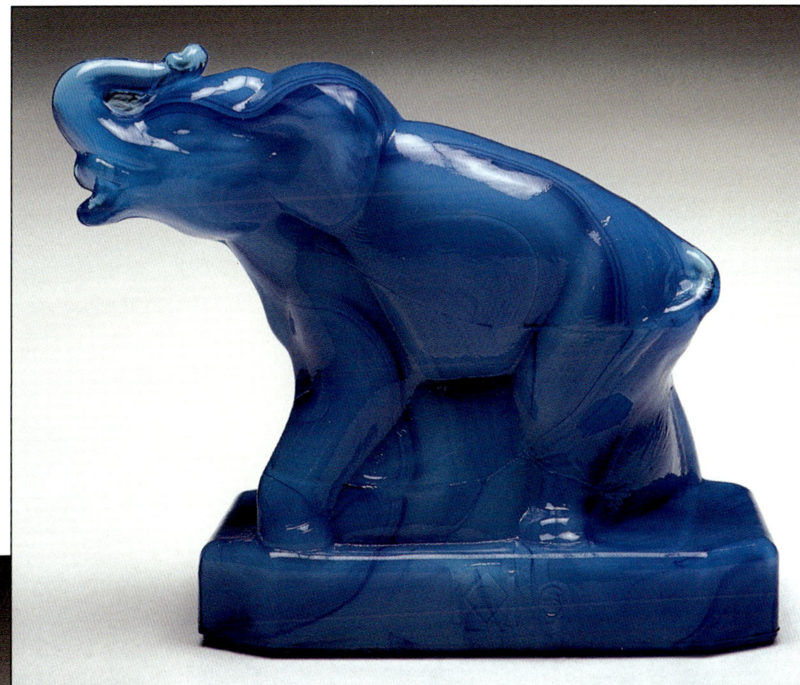

Zack the elephant, Peacock Blue Swirl, hollow base, sixth Boyd mark, 3.6" tall, 4.5" long, September 1999, **$28.00**

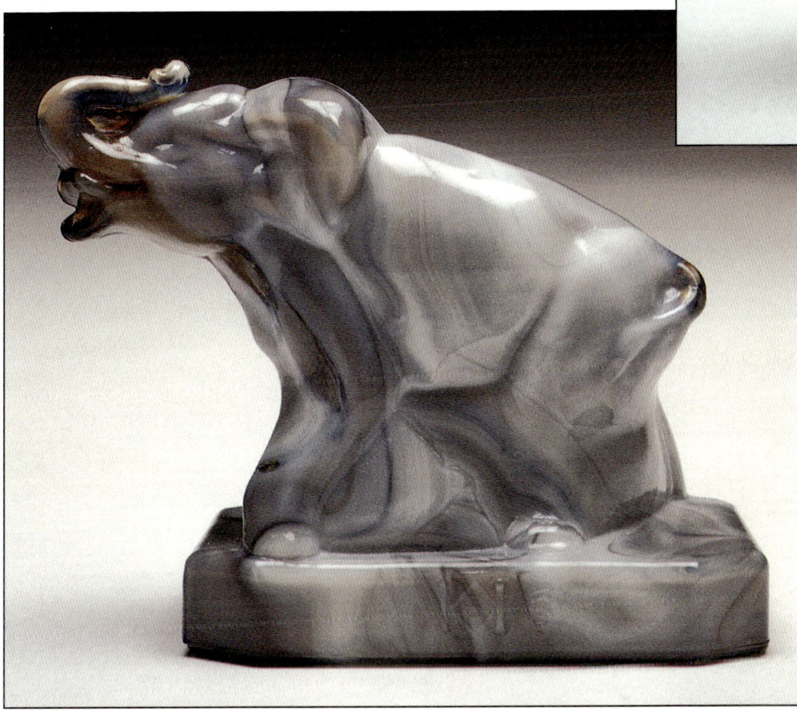

Zack the elephant, Toffee Slag, hollow base, sixth Boyd mark, 3.6" tall, 4.5" long, June 2000, **$25.00**

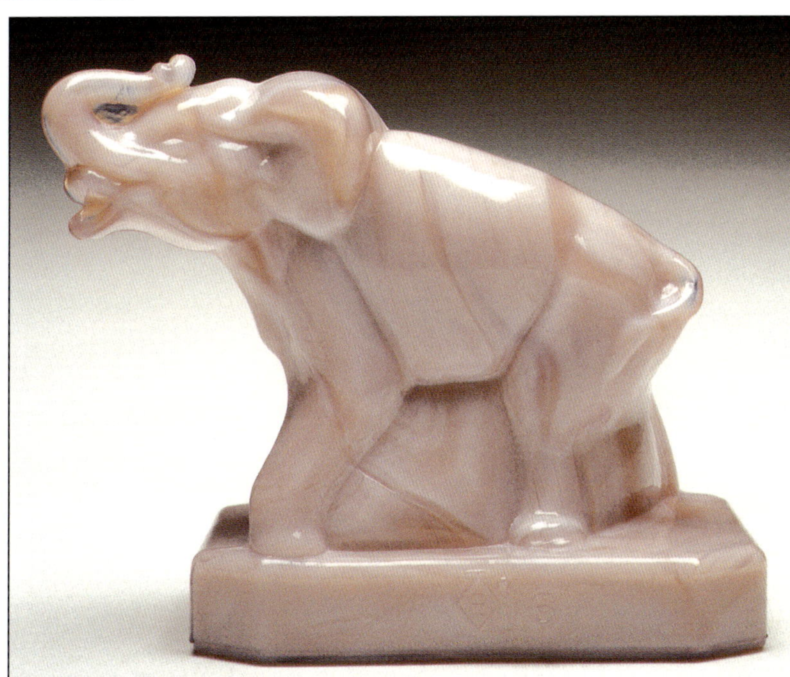

Zack the elephant, Ivory blush, 3 sided logo, hollow base, sixth Boyd mark, 3.6" tall, 4.5" long, August 2001, **$25.00**

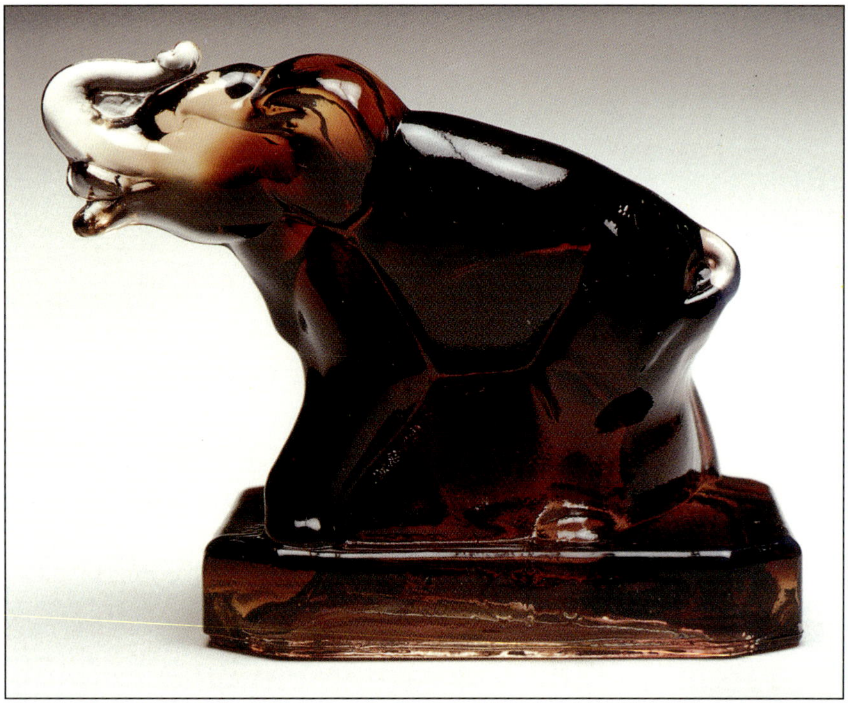

Zack the elephant, Cranberry, hollow base, sixth Boyd mark, 3.6" tall, 4.5" long, February 2002, **$30.00**

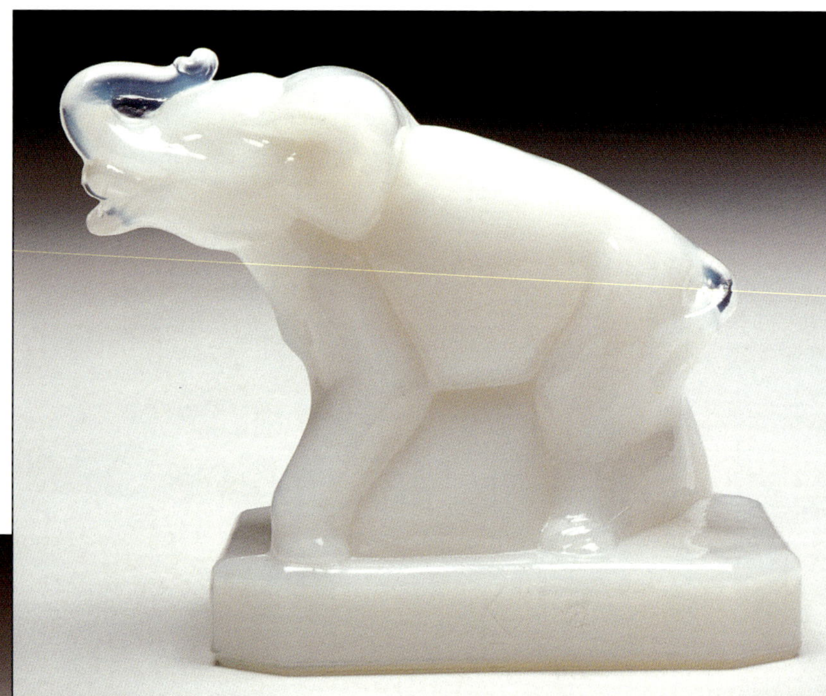

Zack the elephant, White Salmon, hollow base, sixth Boyd mark, 3.6" tall, 4.5" long, October 2002, **$20.00**

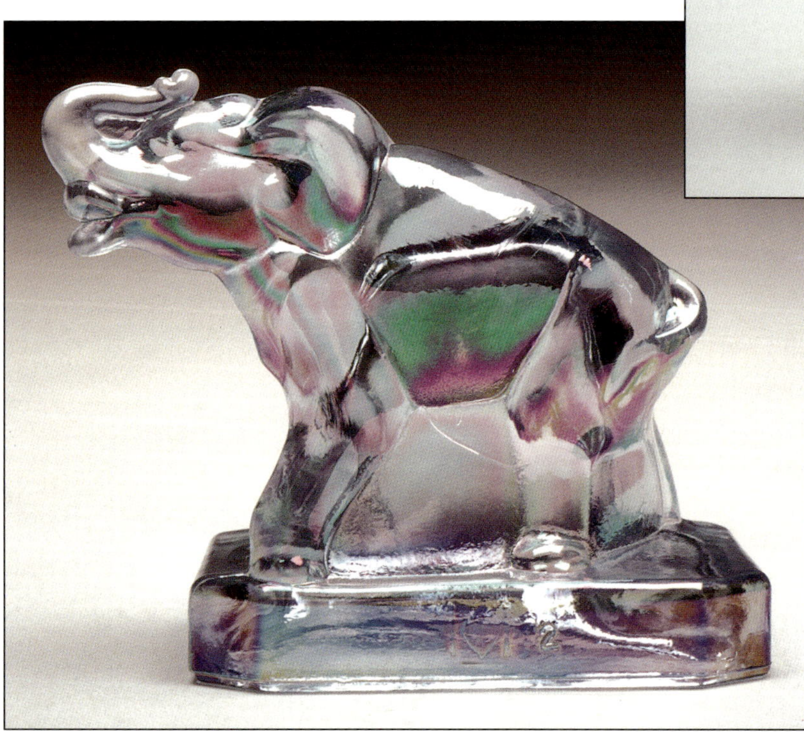

Zack the elephant, Pearly Pink Carnival (diachromatic color changes under different types of lighting), hollow base, sixth Boyd mark, 3.6" tall, 4.5" long, January 2002, **$20.00**

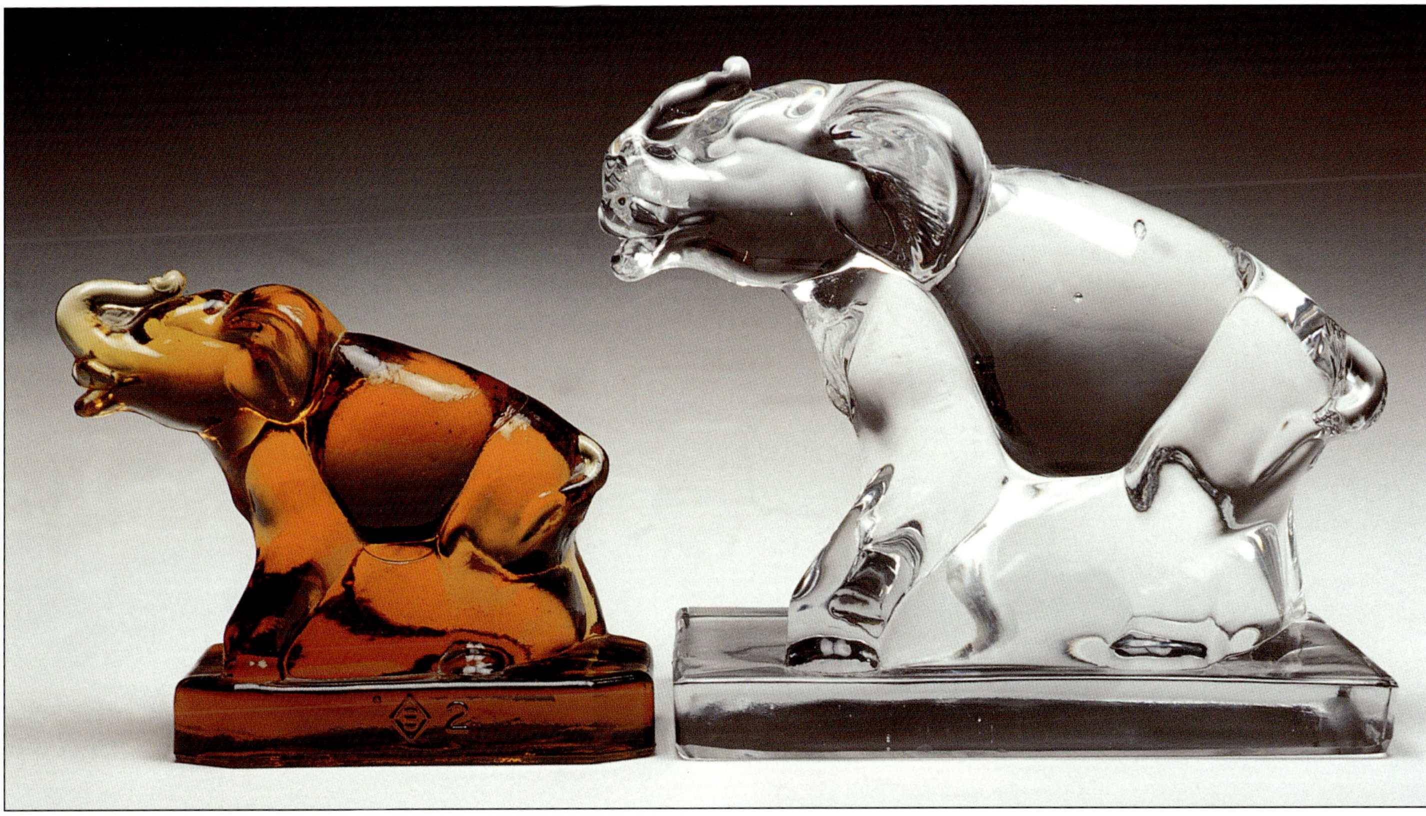

Comparison showing New Martinsville and Boyd elephant, **Left:** Boyd in Amber; **Right:** New Martinsville in Crystal

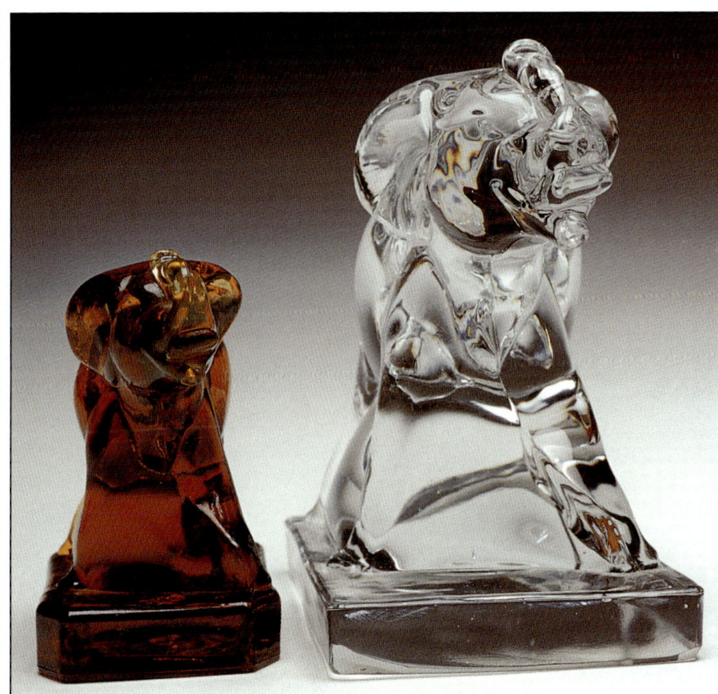

Comparison showing New Martinsville and Boyd elephant, **Left:** Boyd in Amber; **Right:** New Martinsville in Crystal

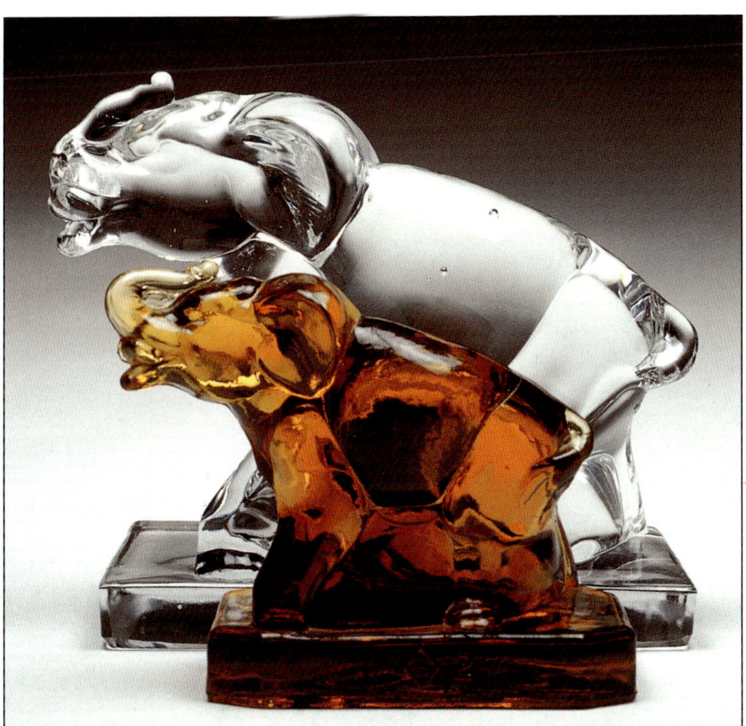

Comparison showing New Martinsville and Boyd elephant, **Back:** New Martinsville in Crystal; **Front:** Boyd in Amber

Cherokee Glass Unknown

Cherokee Glass is believed to be an American company, however further information has not been found about when, where, and how this company operated. Ironically, this elephant is well marked with the Cherokee name and the number 74. With "GOP" embossed on it, for the Republican Grand Old Party, this piece was obviously made for a political campaign. We have inquired of several knowledgeable glass people about this elephant, but nothing has yet been documented. If anyone has further information or knowledge about this company, contact the author.

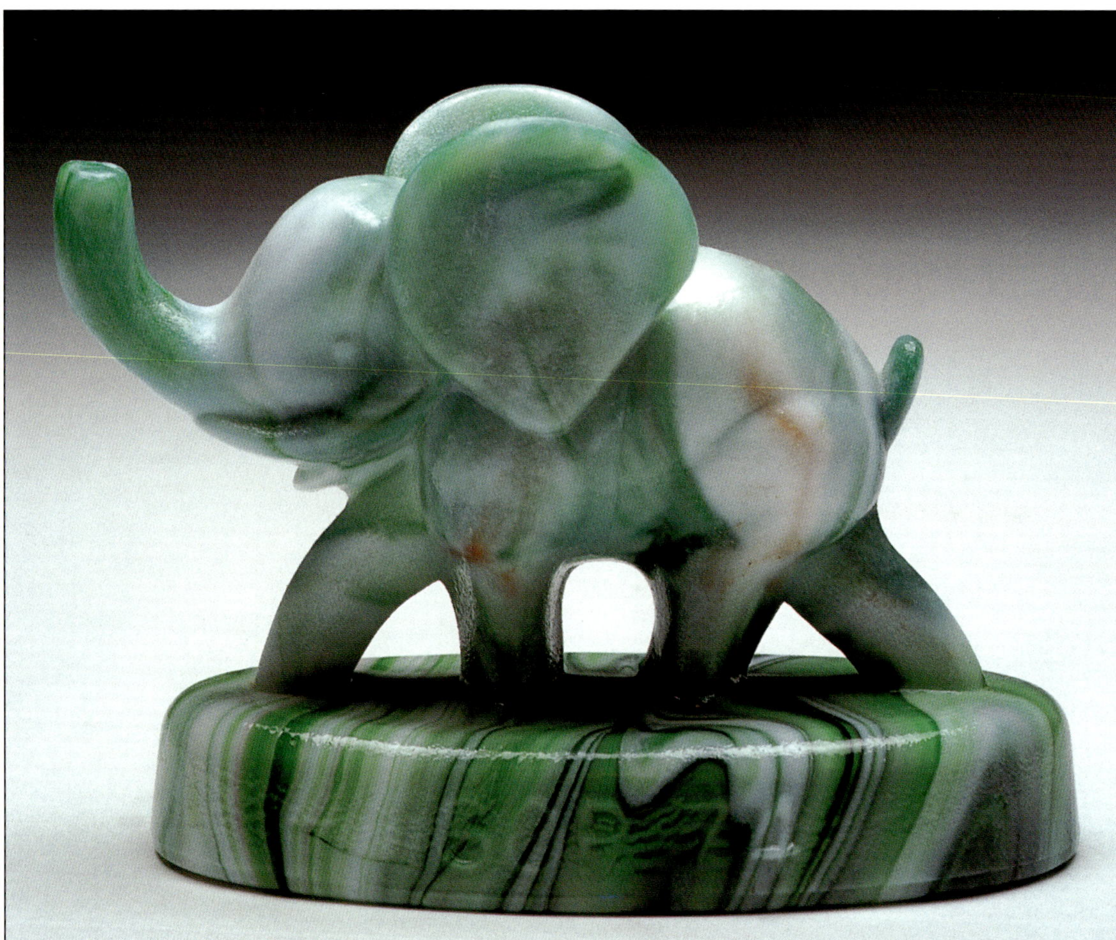

Elephant with raised trunk, Green and white slag, marked on base: GOP 74; marked on bottom: Cherokee Glass, 3.5" tall, 4.5" long, Circa 1974, **$28.00**

Co-Operative Flint Glass Company 1879-1934

It was 1879 in Beaver Falls, Pennsylvania, when Co-Operative Flint first began making glass. They began by producing glassware for restaurants and soda shops. Novelty and gift wares were made in the 1920s and 1930s, to give more variety.

An ad in the December, 1928, *Crockery and Glass Journal* described them as a top producer of glassware for hotels and restaurants with sales offices in the major cities of New York, Chicago, and Los Angeles.

However, tragically, during the economic strife of the Great Depression, this company was unable to survive and were forced to close their doors in 1934.

Some of the Co-operative colors had more than one name. For example, their Black and their Midnight Glass are, in fact, the same color.

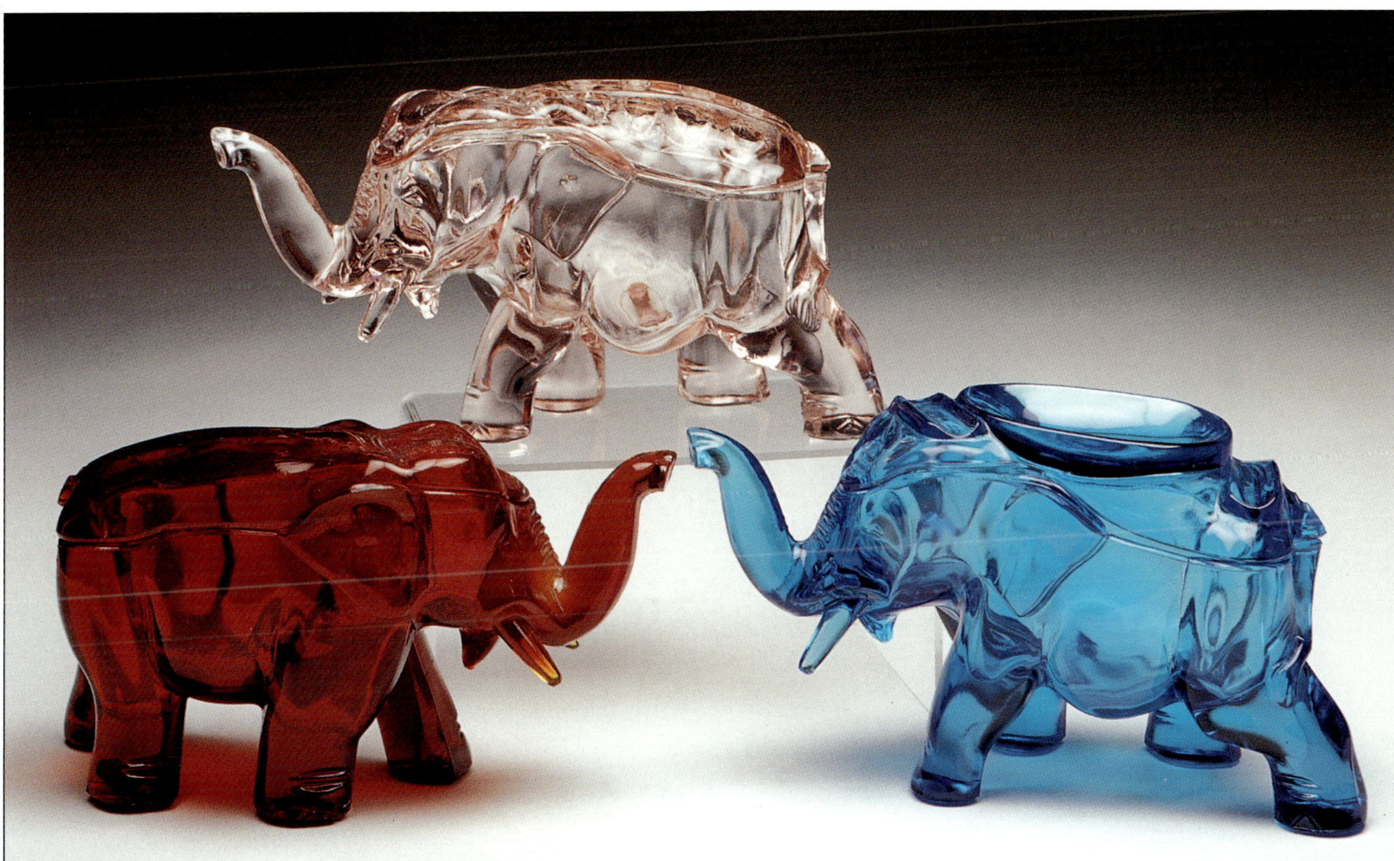

Group shot of covered Elephant dishes to show different types of backs
Back: Pink; **Front Left:** Red; **Front Right:** Dark Blue

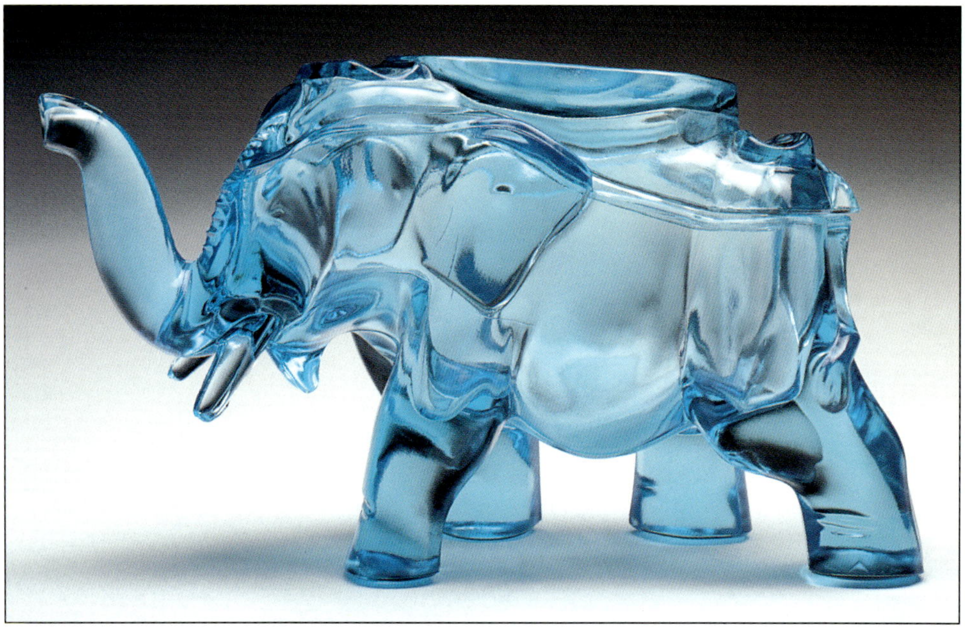

Elephant covered dish, Aqua Blue, ashtray and cigarette rest back, 4.5" tall, 7.5" long, Circa late 1920's to 1930's, **$275.00**

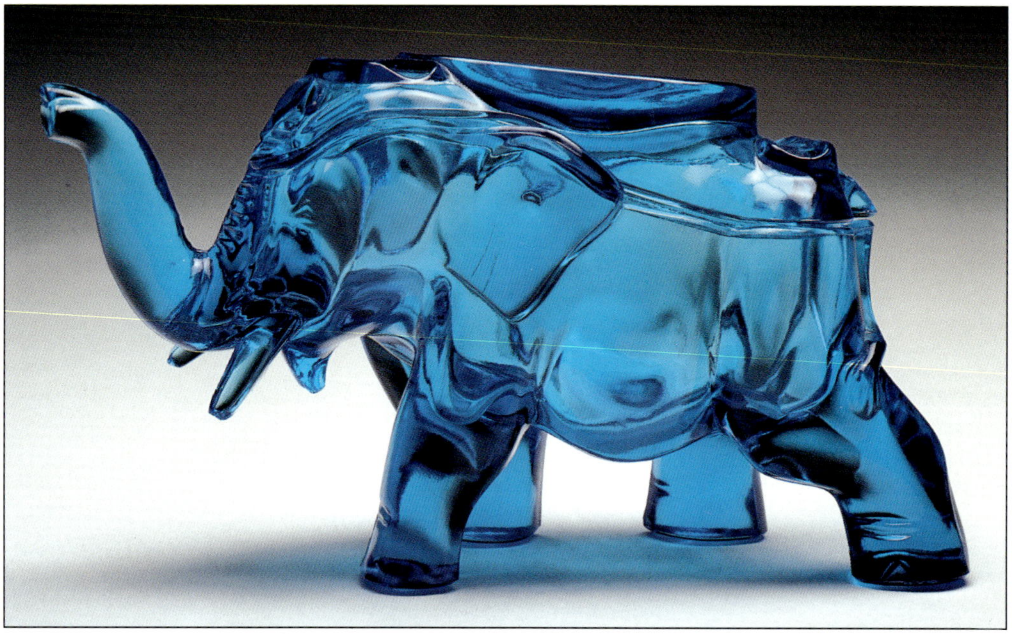

Elephant covered dish, Ritz Blue, ashtray and cigarette rest back, 4.5" tall, 7.5" long, Circa late 1920's to 1930's, **$350.00**

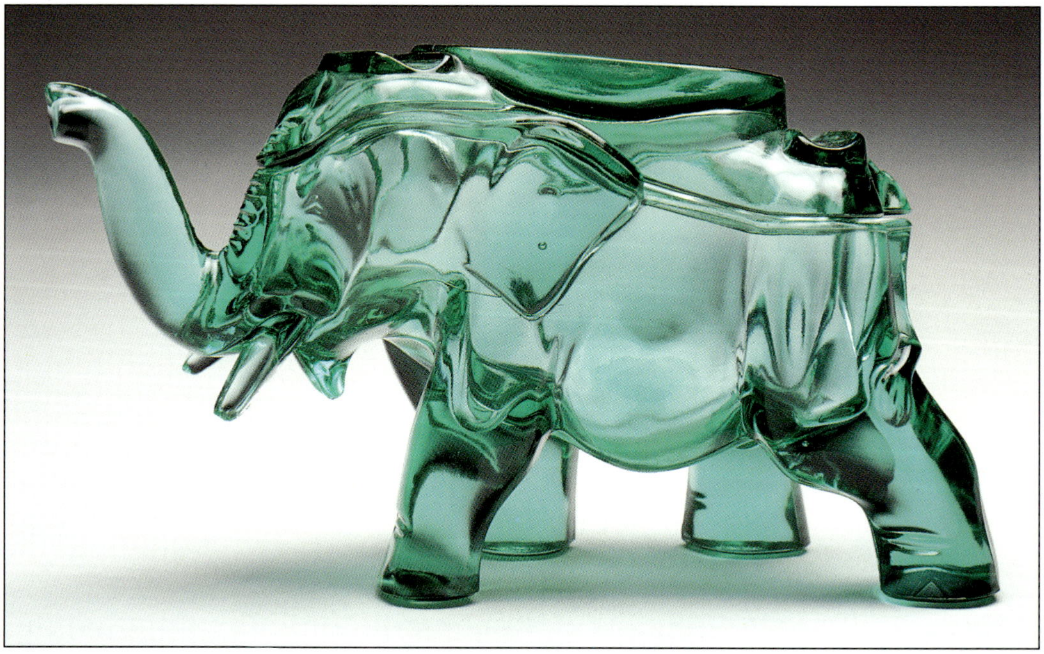

Elephant covered dish, Green, ashtray and cigarette rest back, 4.5" tall, 7.5" long, Circa late 1920's to 1930's, **$250.00**

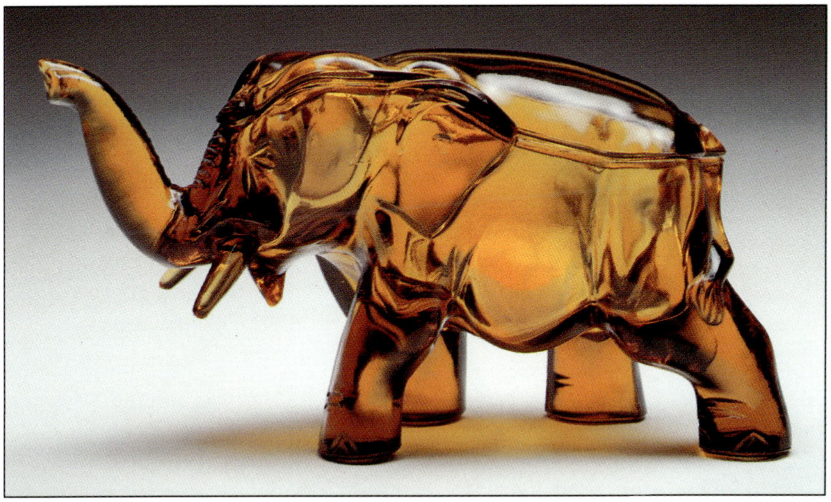

Elephant covered dish, Amber, domed back, 4.5" tall, 7.5" long, Circa late 1920's to 1930's, **$150.00**

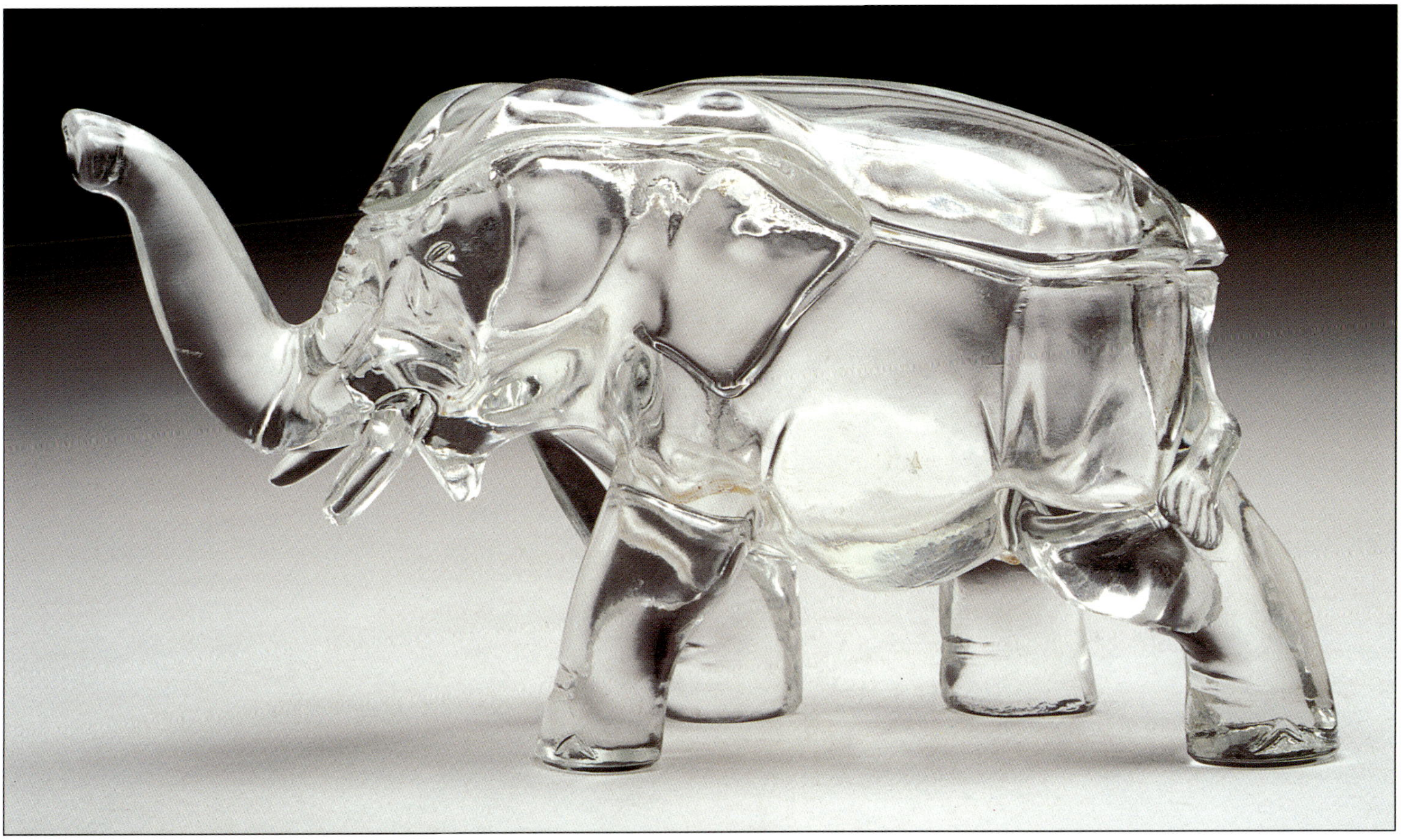

Elephant large size covered dish, Crystal, domed back, 7.25" tall, 14.5" long, Circa late 1920's to 1930's, **$300.00**

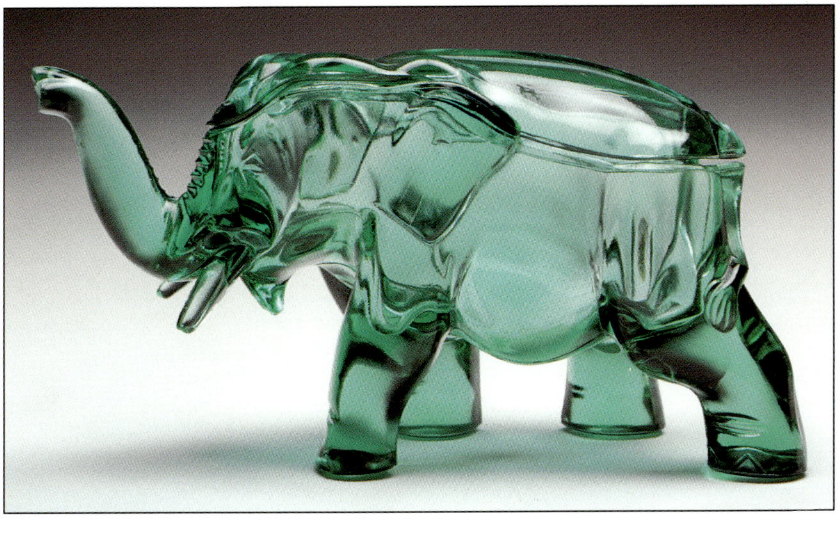

Elephant covered dish, Green, domed back, 4.5" tall, 7.5" long, Circa late 1920's to 1930's, **$200.00**

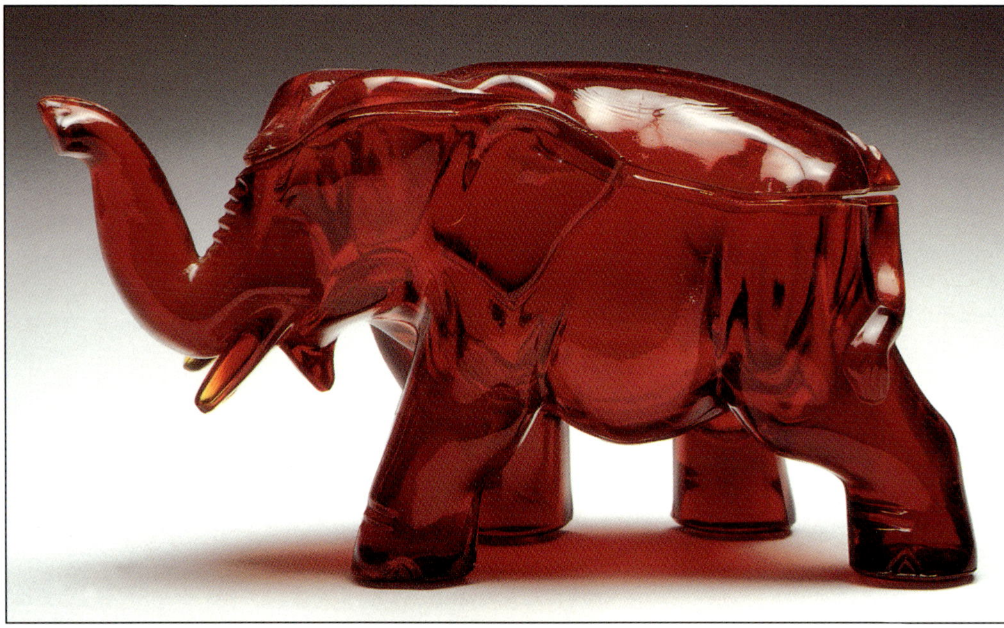

Elephant covered dish, Red, domed back, 4.5" tall, 7.5" long, Circa late 1920's to 1930's, **$250.00**

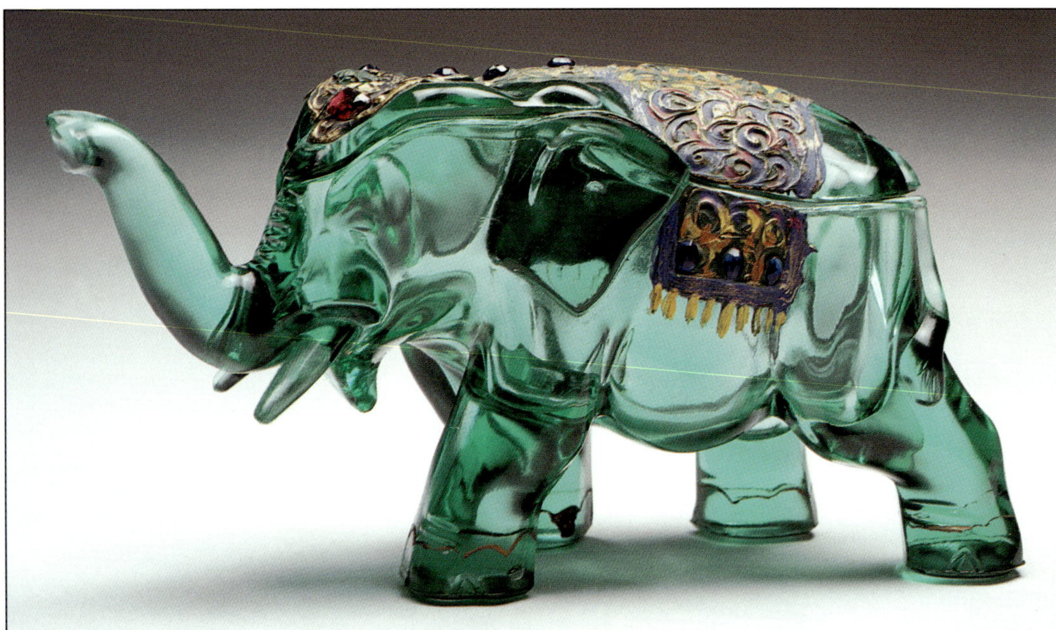

Elephant covered dish, Green, domed back, hand painted, 4.5" tall, 7.5" long, Circa late 1920's to 1930's, **$275.00**

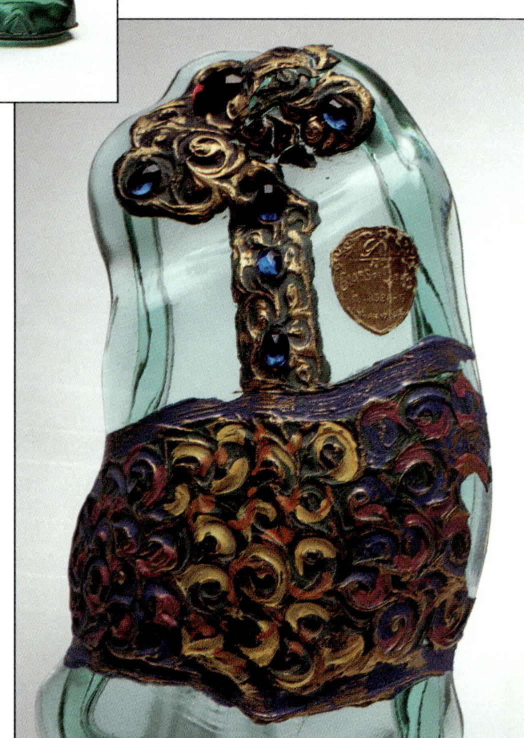

Detail of hand painted back and original label on Elephant covered dish

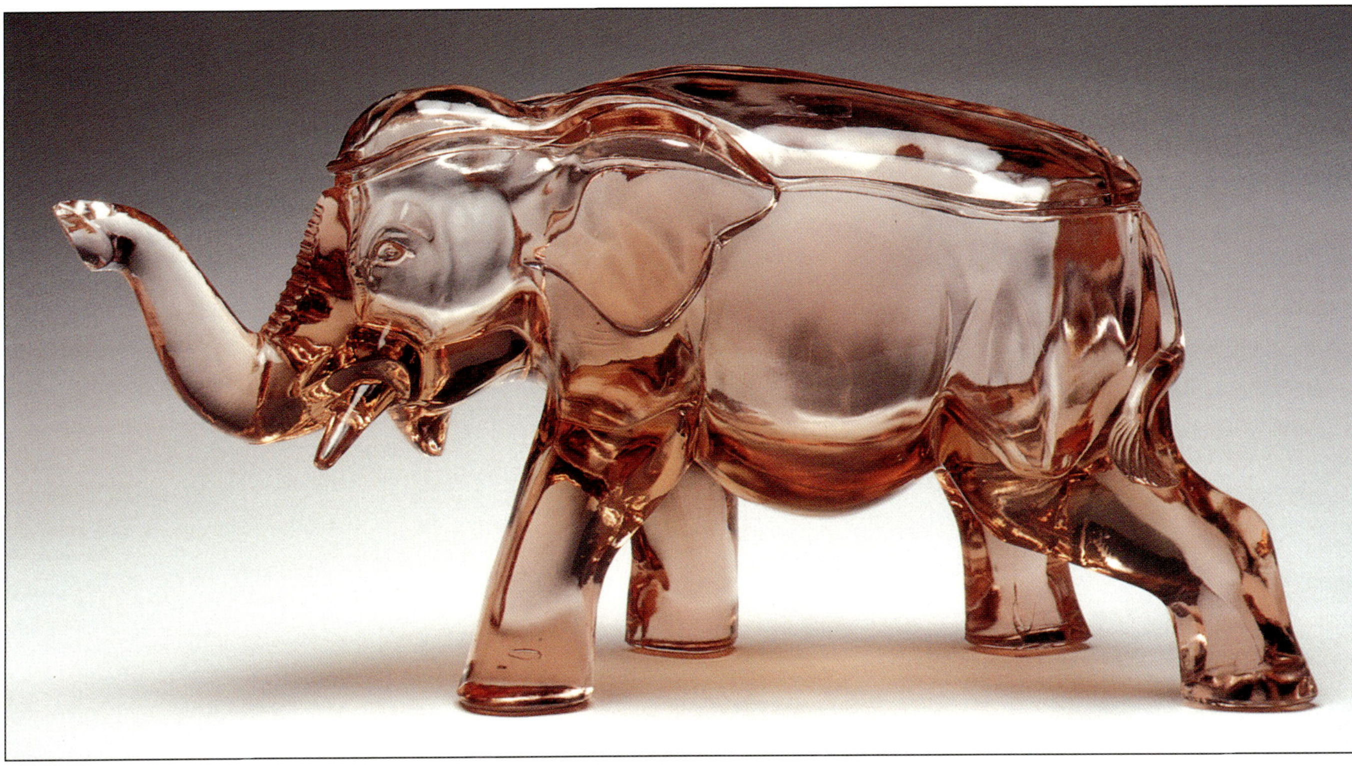

Elephant large size covered dish, Pink, domed back, 7.25" tall, 14.75" long, Circa late 1920's to 1930's, **$550.00**

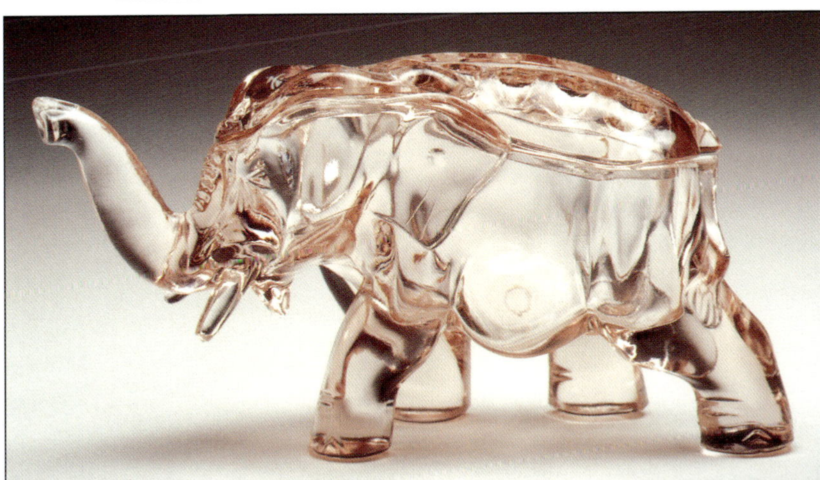

Elephant covered dish, Pink, domed flower frog back, 4.25" tall, 7.5" long, Circa late 1920's to 1930's, **$350.00**

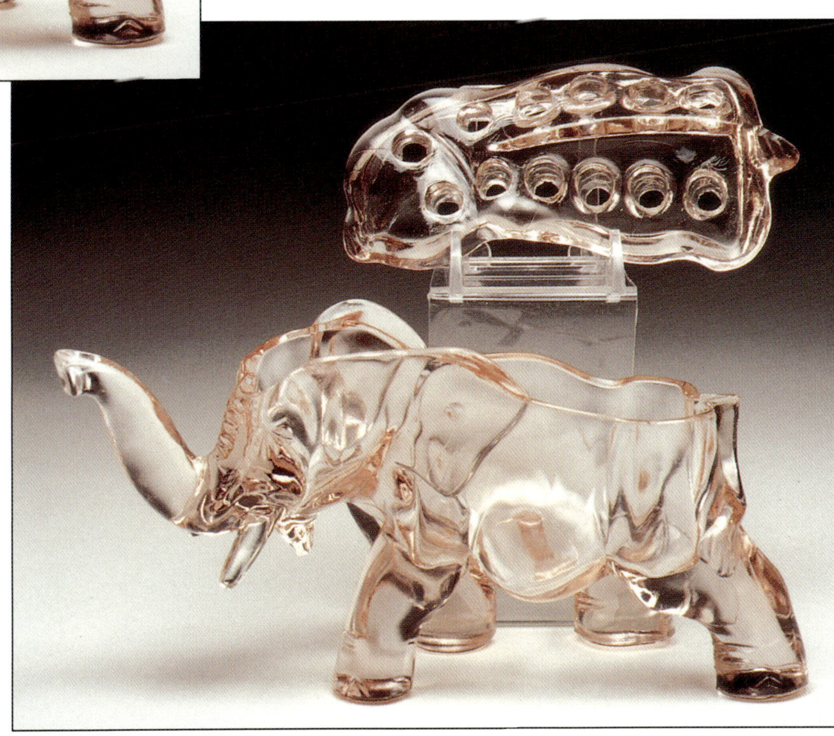

Elephant covered dish, Pink, domed flower frog back, shown with back off so you can see detail of cover

Craigs Glass Art Collectibles 1980s

Betty and Jerry Craig, of Ft. Wayne, Indiana, founded Craig's Glass Art Collectibles company in 1980. Their elephant, which they called Packy, was issued in a new color every month since it began in September, 1980. Fewer than 1,000 elephants were to be made in each of the colors, and there were only 652 made in the first color, which was Carnival Mardi Gras Slag.

Information is not readily available on this company, so it is not known how many Packys were made. During the 1980s, many ads could be found in the *Glass Review*, and then all advertising disappeared. It is assumed that they went out of business.

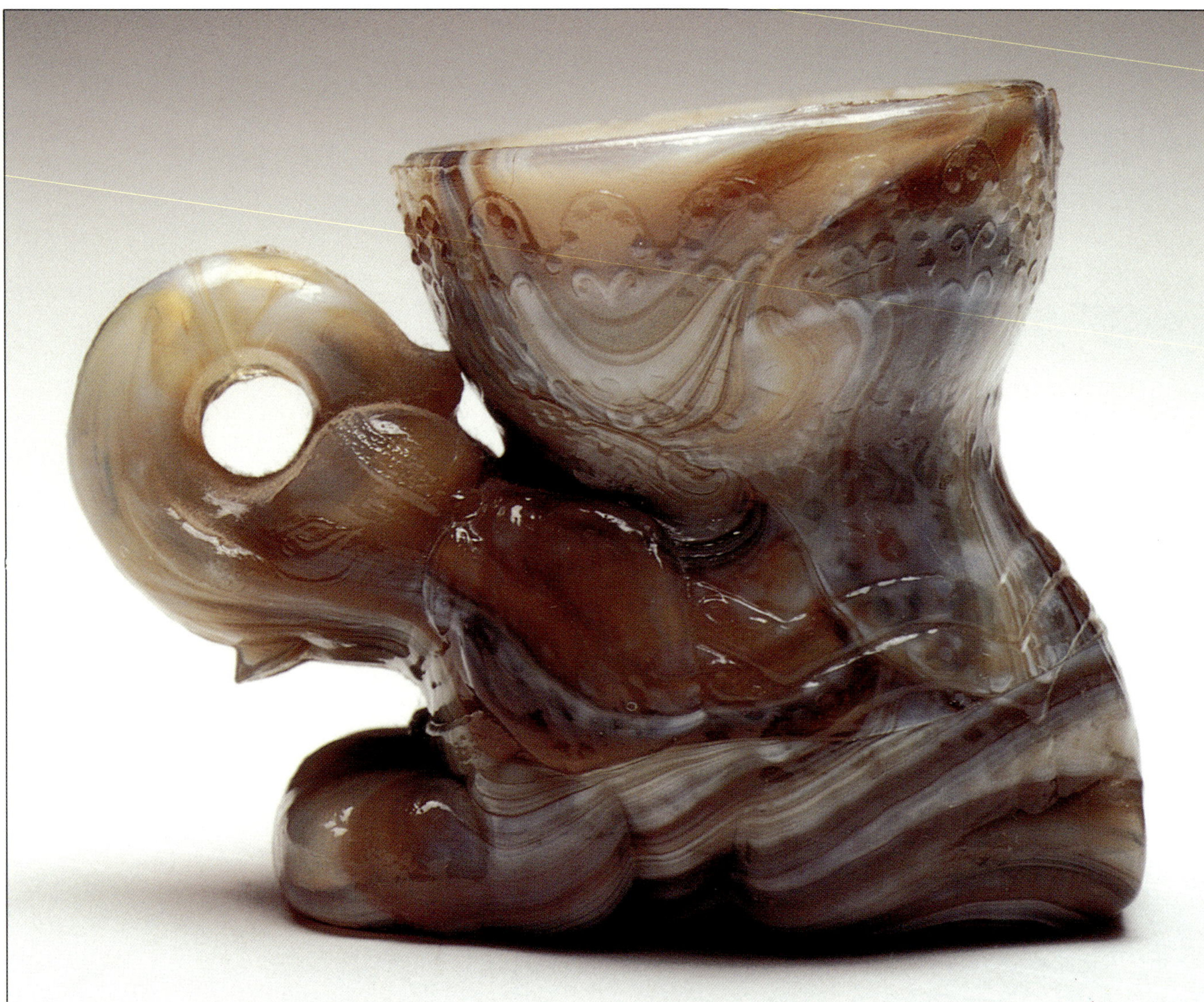

Elephant "Packy", Carmel Slag, 2.5" tall 3.25" long, Circa 1980's, **$18.50**

Dereume (Raymond) Glass Company 1921-Present

Founded in 1921 in Punxsutawney, Pennsylvania, Dereume Glass Company was originally a wholesaler of specialty glassware and a producer mainly of religious glassware for use in churches.

The Kanawha Glass Company closed in 1985 and was then sold to Raymond Dereume. This provided Dereume with the opportunity to expand into the giftware business. Currently, it is still in operation, even utilizing some of the Kanawha moulds.

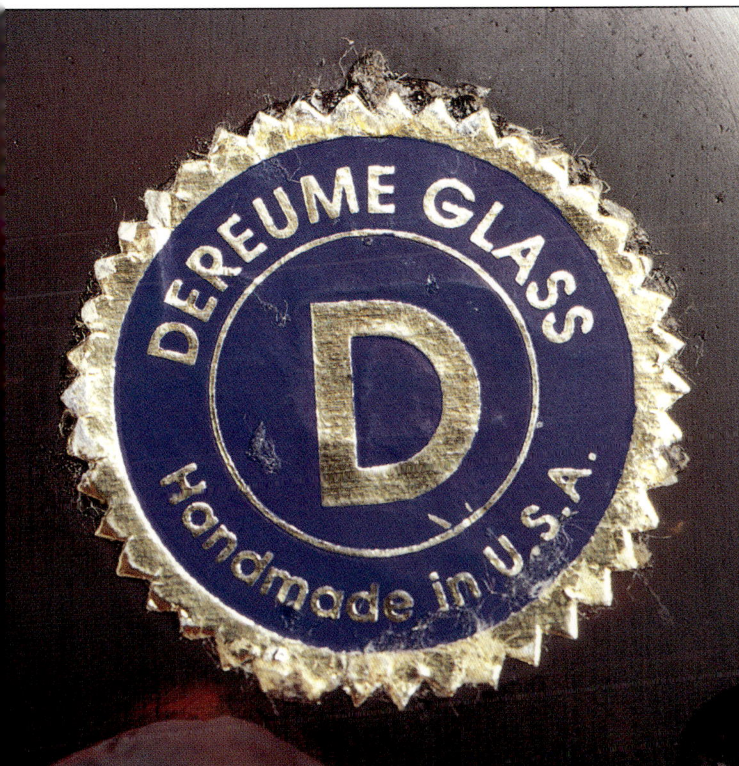

Original gold and dark blue label

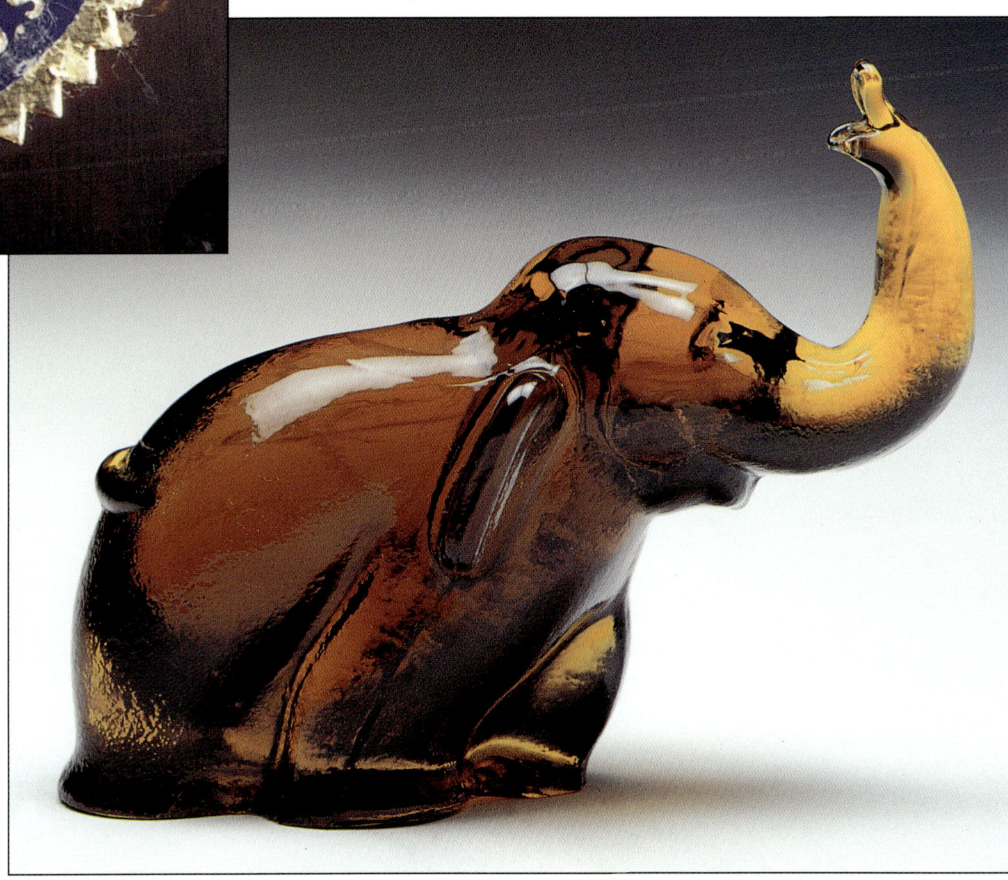

Small Elephant, Amber, 3.5" tall, 5" long, Circa 1990's, **$15.00**

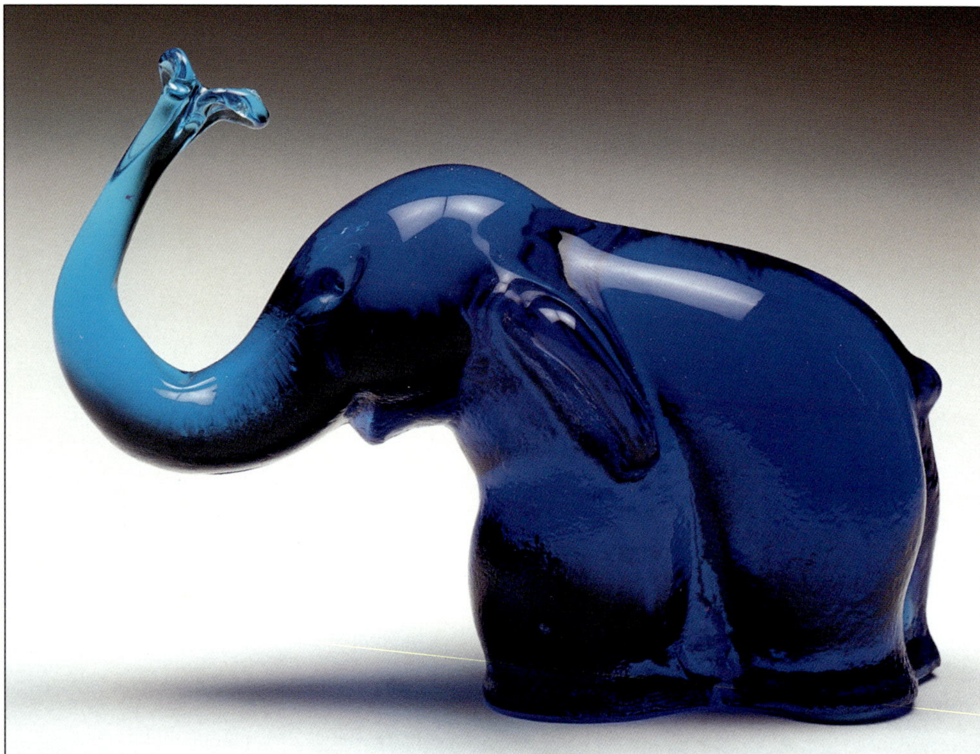

Small Elephant, Dark Blue, 3.5" tall, 5" long, Circa 1990's, **$20.00**

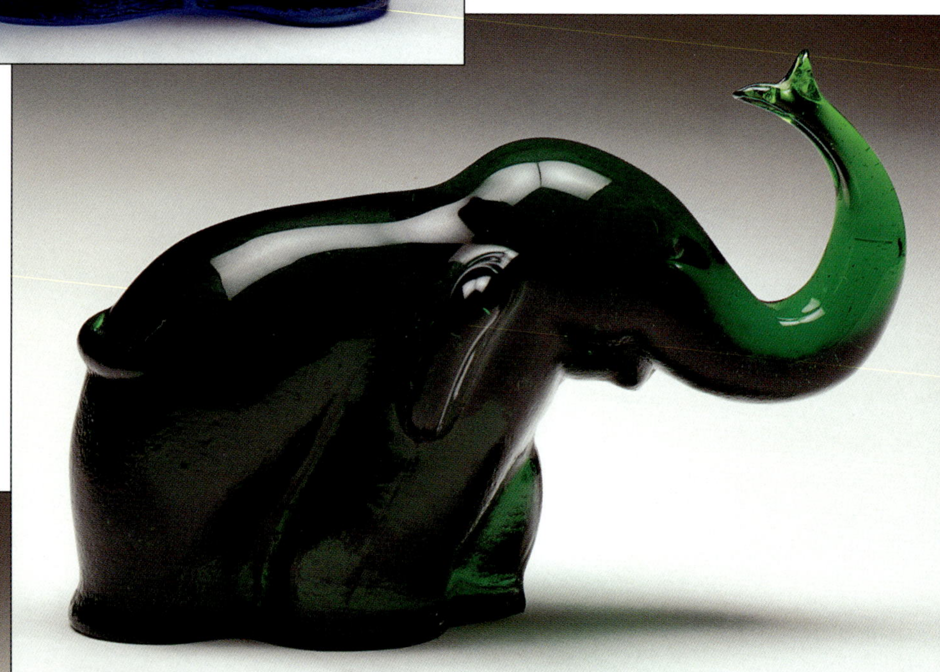

Small Elephant, Dark Green, 3.5" tall, 5" long, Circa 1990's, **$18.00**

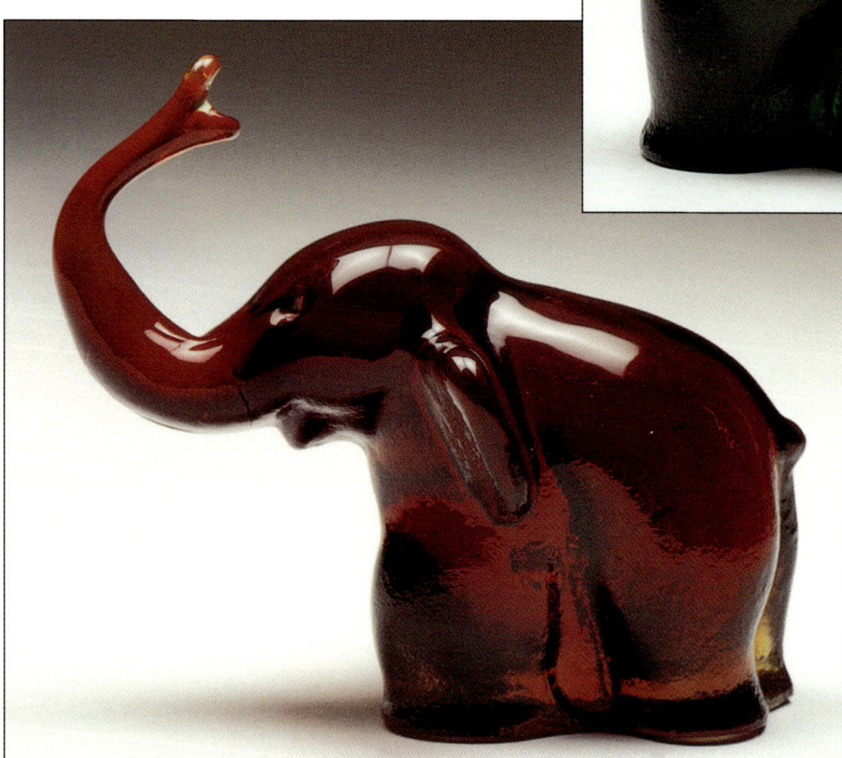

Small Elephant, Ruby, 4.1" tall, 5" long, Circa 1990's, **$20.00**

Walt Disney Productions 1925-Present

Walt Disney was interested in art at an early age and soon was enrolled in art classes starting at age 13. In 1920, he had his first animation job. His brother, Roy Disney, had moved to California in the 1920s and wanted Walt to join him there, since Hollywood was the center of the movie world. Walt made the move and soon had numerous jobs drawing many types of cartoons. It was Roy Disney, though, in 1929, who realized the importance of licensing merchandise to go with the cartoons. His initial relationship wasn't successful, but it did lead to other opportunities to capitalize on Walt's drawings. Every movie that was produced had companion toys and merchandise to go along with it. Many different types of companies are contracted with to produce various types of merchandise, such as glass, pottery, cloth, metal, plastic and paper.

With the establishment of Disneyland, and later Walt Disney World, many more items were developed to sell at the theme parks' gift shops. Now, with Disney Stores and their online catalog, merchandise of many types remains popular and fans can have their favorite characters at home to enjoy. Many companies compete each year to produce merchandise for Walt Disney Productions.

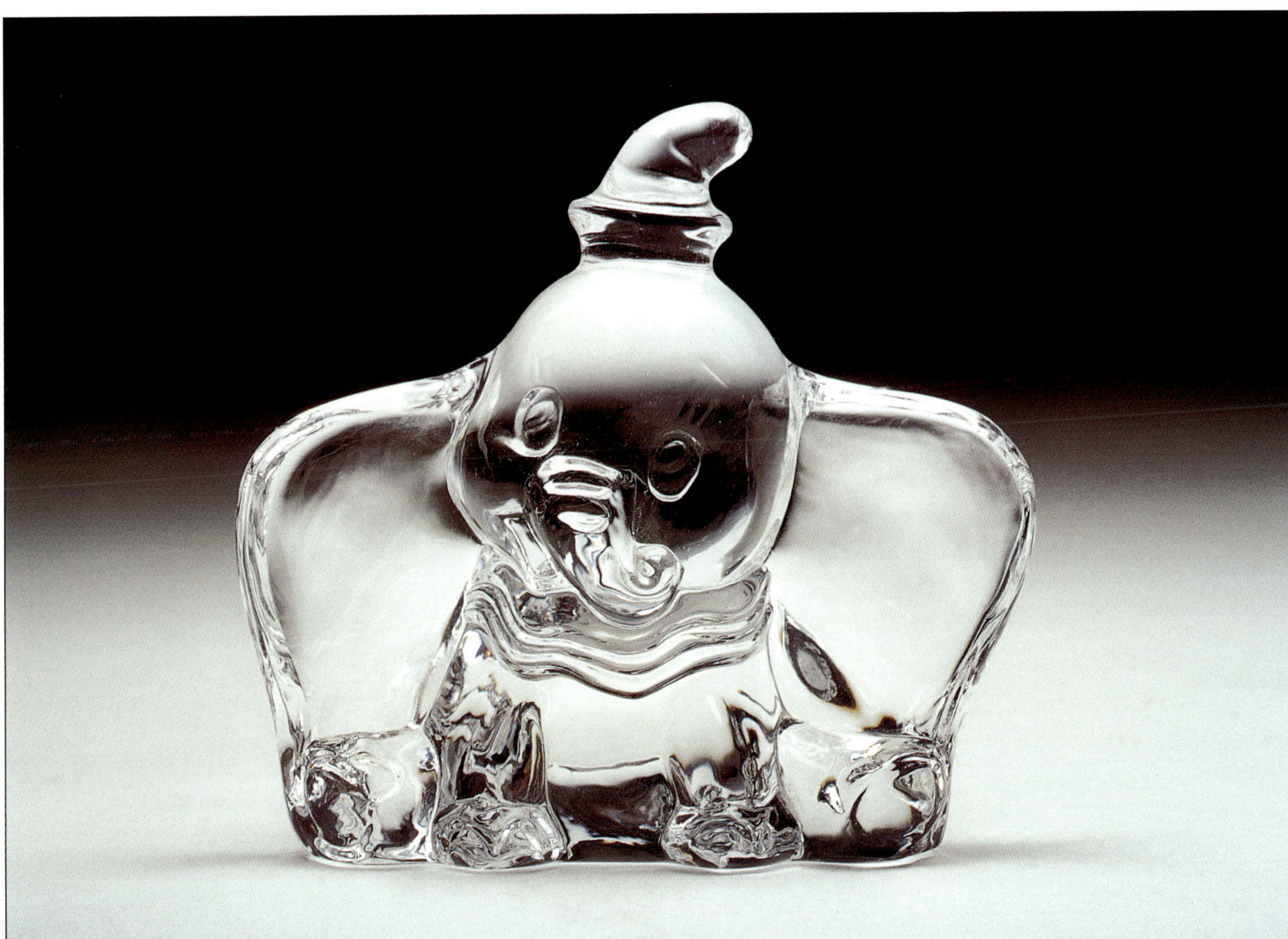

Dumbo, Limited edition #671 out of 1000, 5" tall, 4.75" wide, Circa 1980's, **$95.00**

Enterprise Manufacturing Company 1878-1883

Created in 1878, in Akron, Ohio, Enterprise Manufacturing Company was originally a maker of lamp chimneys, but they later expanded to produce novelty items.

Ad appeared in the 1883 *Glass and Crockery Journal* with an elephant pictured and labeled "Baby Jumbo." The ad suggested uses for it, such as a salt dish, a toothpick holder, or a mustard pot. The ad includes a guarantee for their product and if you are not happy/satisfied, you may return it at the expense of the company.

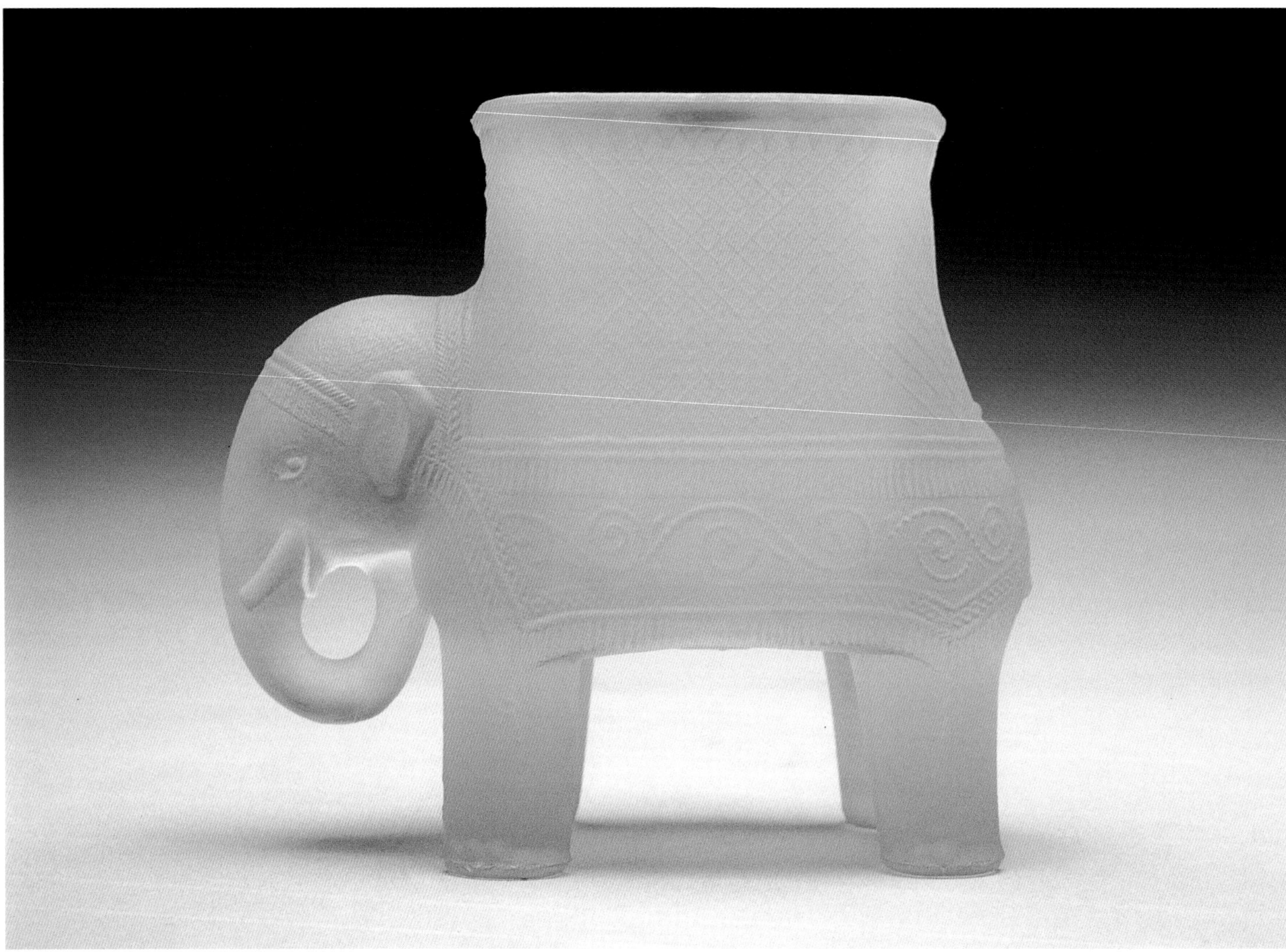

Elephant with basket on back, Crystal with satin finish, marked on bottom "Baby Mine", 3.5" tall 3.75" long, Circa 1883, **$45.00**

Fenton Art Glass Company 1905-Present

Frank L. Fenton founded the Fenton Art Glass Company in 1905 after he worked for Indiana Glass, Jefferson Glass, Bastow Glass, and eventually, Northwood Glass Company. He gained valuable experience and finally decided to start a company of his own with his brother, John. They combined their assets and created a company in Martins Ferry, Ohio. Their brother, Charles, quit his job at Northwood Glass and joined them. Together they decided to build a factory in Williamstown, West Virginia, in 1906, and the official opening of that factory was 1907. John Fenton left the group and ventured on his own in 1909, founding Millersburg Glass. Yet, the Fenton family structure continued with the addition of two more brothers, James and Robert.

Fenton Art Glass Company became a successful business. When the Great Depression came, Fenton was able to survive because they created binding retail accounts with Wrisley and Kresge department stores.

Fenton Art Glass was thriving when tragedy hit the company. The founder, Frank L. Fenton, died in May, 1948. It was time for others to step up and take over. Frank M. Fenton and his brother Bill Fenton were ready for the challenge, with the memories of their father, Frank L. Fenton, and uncles with them. They understood the importance of their company to the community and the market place and made a vow to ensure the success and continuation of Fenton Art Glass.

In the 1960s and 1970s, the third generation of Fentons aided the company: Frank M.'s sons, George, Mike, and Tom; along with Bill's children, Don, Randy, Shelly, and Christine. They all shared a passion for the business and became important role models within the company. George became the company president in 1986.

Fenton Art Glass understands that the market changes and that they must change with it to keep in the competitive business. One way they did this was by introducing items for sale on the QVC television shopping network that could attract brand new audiences for Fenton glass. Many Fenton glass pieces can be found through this program, including the Fenton elephants.

Currently, Fenton Art Glass is thriving through the staff's dedication and passion for glass. The fourth generation of family members, Lynn and Scott, help to ensure the successful future of the company as well. The history of Fenton Art Glass Company demonstrates the endurance of the company.

Fenton has hand-made blown-glass specialties that include animals, and within this category are their elephants. Fenton has made six different elephants and are in the process of creating a new one.

The first elephant was the elephant flower bowl, affectionately known to collectors as "Jumbo." It was designed by Frank L. Fenton and made in the 1920s. The real-life circus star, Jumbo, was the inspiration for this design. It was a very large piece of glass and was difficult to make.

In the 1930s, Fenton produced the elephant whiskey bottle, which was most likely made as contract work for a liquor company. There was a gap of many years before Fenton made another elephant.

In the 1970s, the work elephant was introduced. This elephant was designed by Harry Bridges, who was a work foreman. It was a small, realistic-looking elephant with the trunk down.

Next, the freehand elephants, mould number 5012, were created in 1980s. These were produced by glassworker Delmer Stowasser. Then, in 1984, the standing elephant, mould number 5158, came into the line. It was designed by Tony Rosena, who retired in 1990. This elephant came to be a regular mould used by Fenton for their different lines.

In 1995, a new elephant, mould number 5136, was designed to bring in variety and attract new customers. It was designed by Kathy See, who was a Fenton decorator for about three years. Collectors began calling this the circus elephant, since it reminded them of the performing elephants in the circus, with its trunk and front leg held up in the air. The work elephant was redesigned and was put back in production after an absence of about 30 years. Currently, a baby elephant is being planned and Jon Saffell is working on its creation. It would be a pleasant addition to the Fenton elephant family.

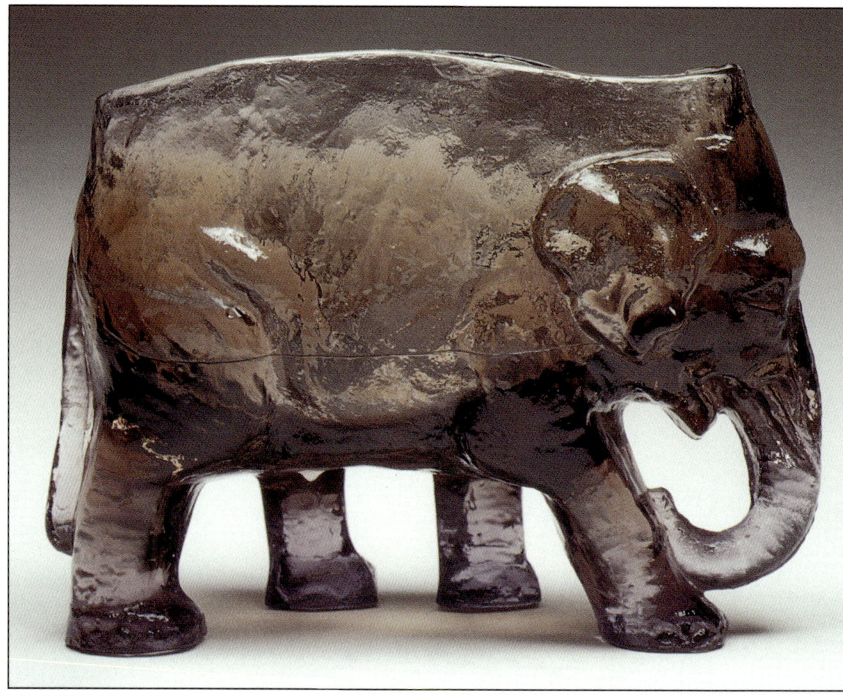

Jumbo flower bowl, Amethyst, 6.5" tall, 8.75" long, Circa late 1920's, **$500.00**

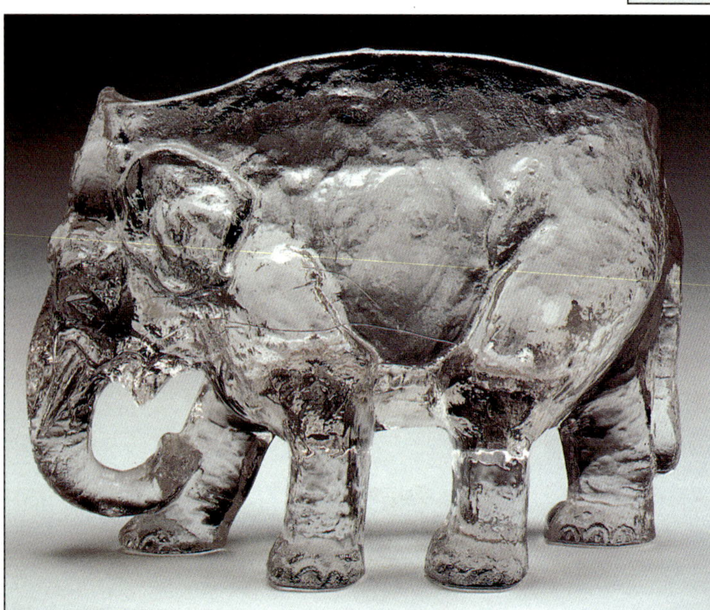

Jumbo flower bowl, Crystal, 6.5" tall, 8.75" long, Circa late 1920's, **$400.00**

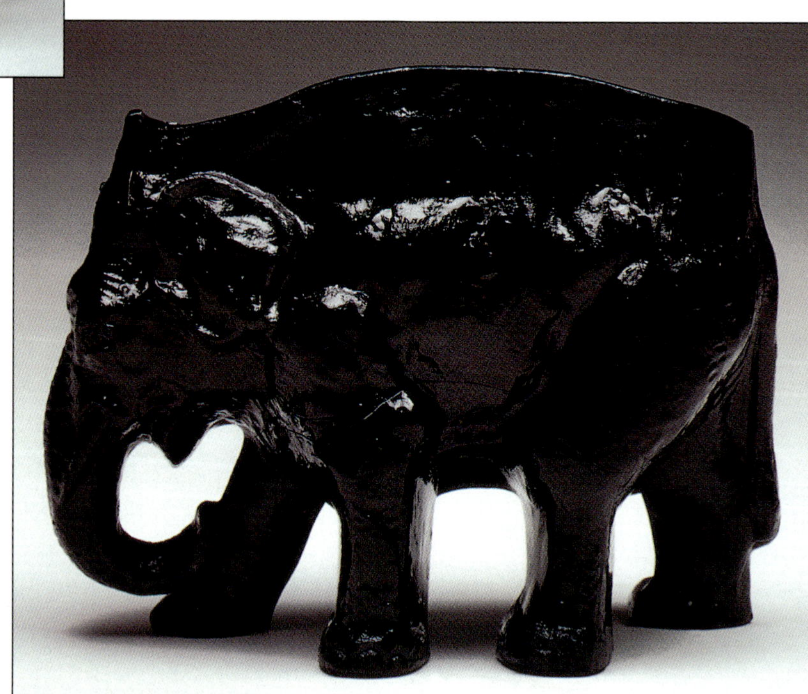

Jumbo flower bowl, Ebony, 6.5" tall, 8.75" long, Circa late 1920's, **$500.00**

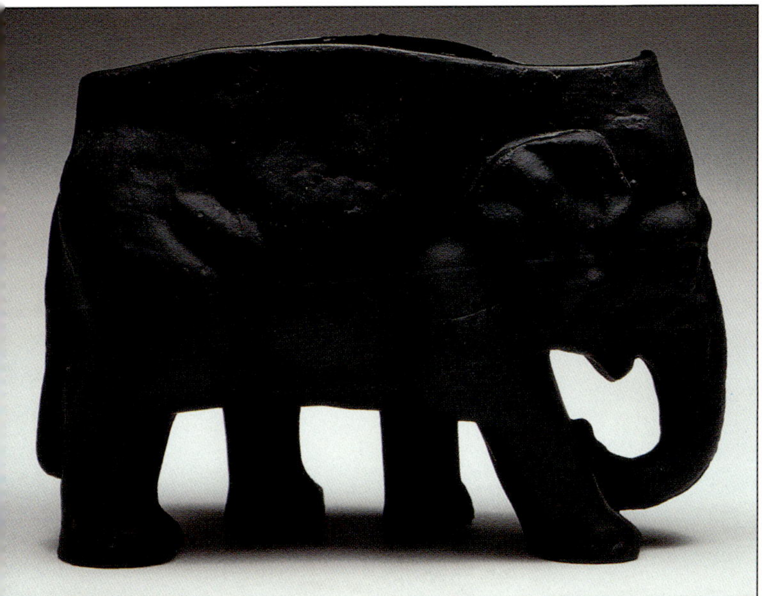

Jumbo flower bowl, Ebony with satin finish, 6.5" tall, 8.75" long, Circa late 1920's, **$650.00**

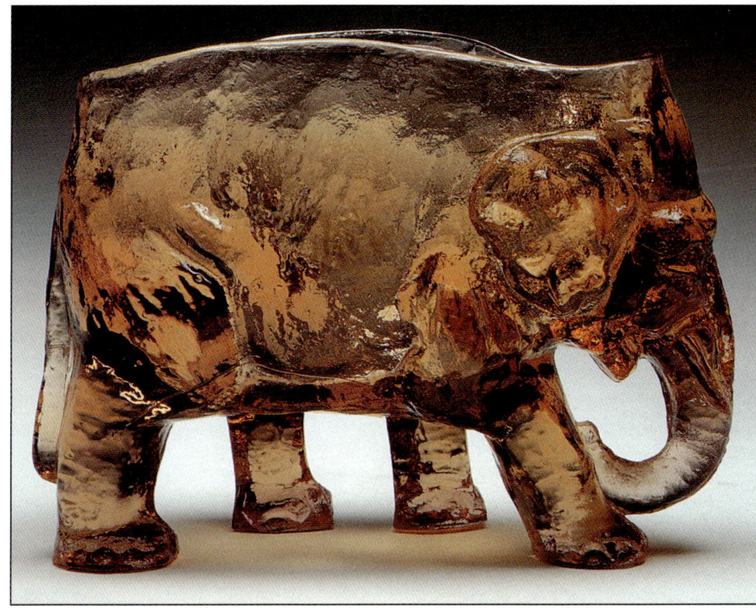

Jumbo flower bowl, Rose, 6.5" tall, 8.75" long, Circa late 1920's, **$500.00**

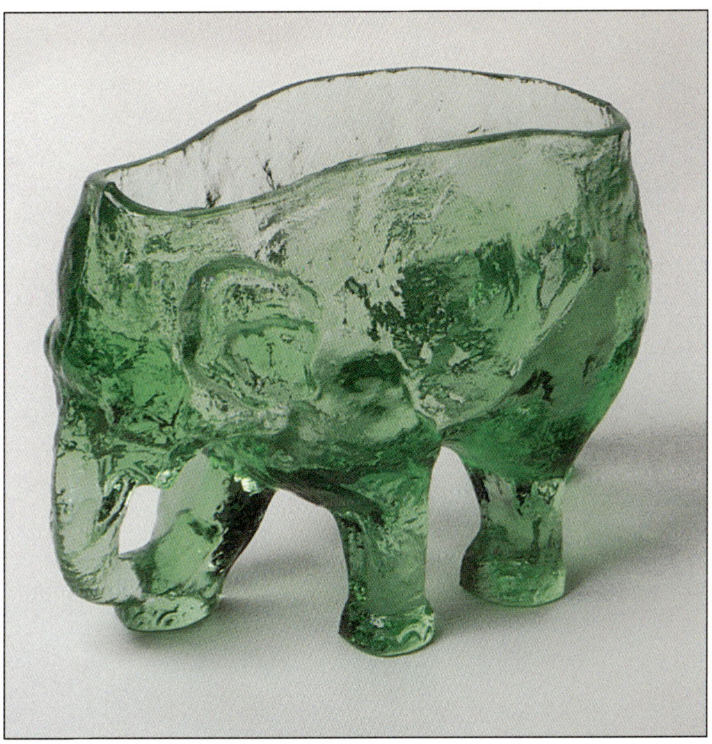

Jumbo flower bowl, Transparent Green, 6.5" tall, 8.75" long, Circa late 1920's, **$500.00**

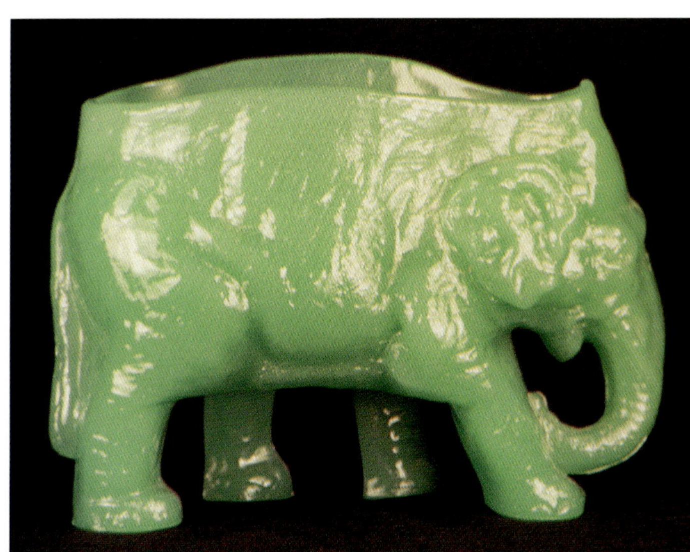

Jumbo flower bowl, Jade, 6.5" tall, 8.75" long, Circa late 1920's, **$750.00**

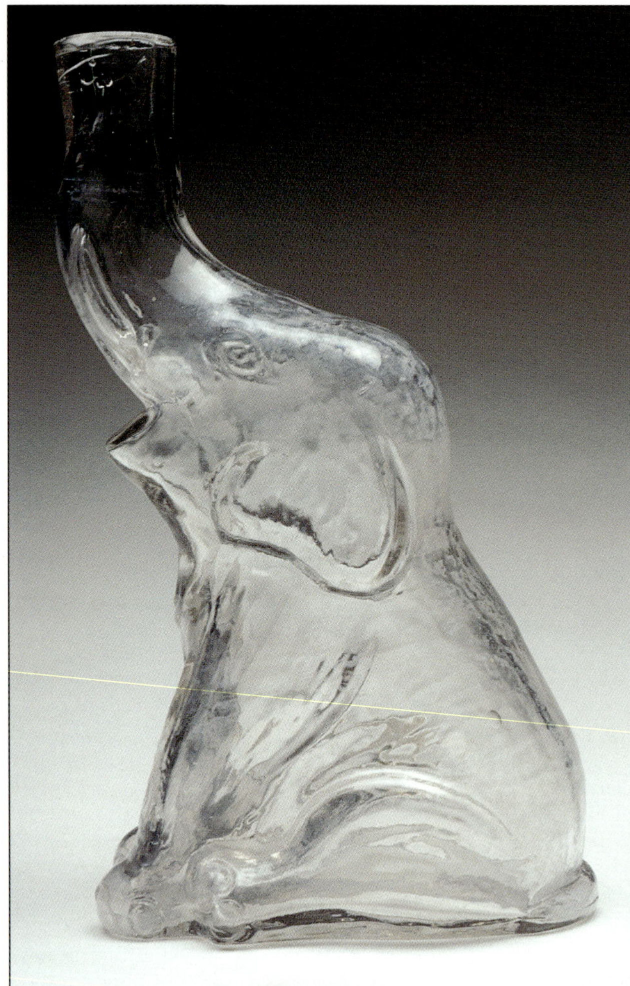

Elephant whiskey bottle (decanter), crystal, 8.5" tall, 5" long, Circa 1935, **$195.00**

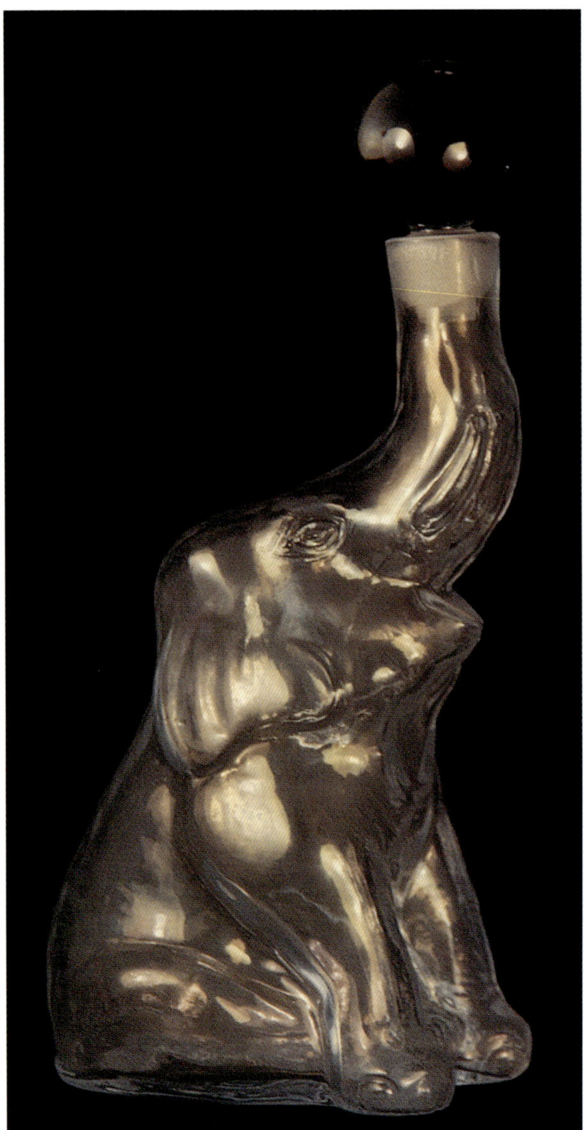

Elephant whiskey bottle (decanter), Mermaid Blue, 8.5" tall, 5" long, Circa 1935, **$650.00**

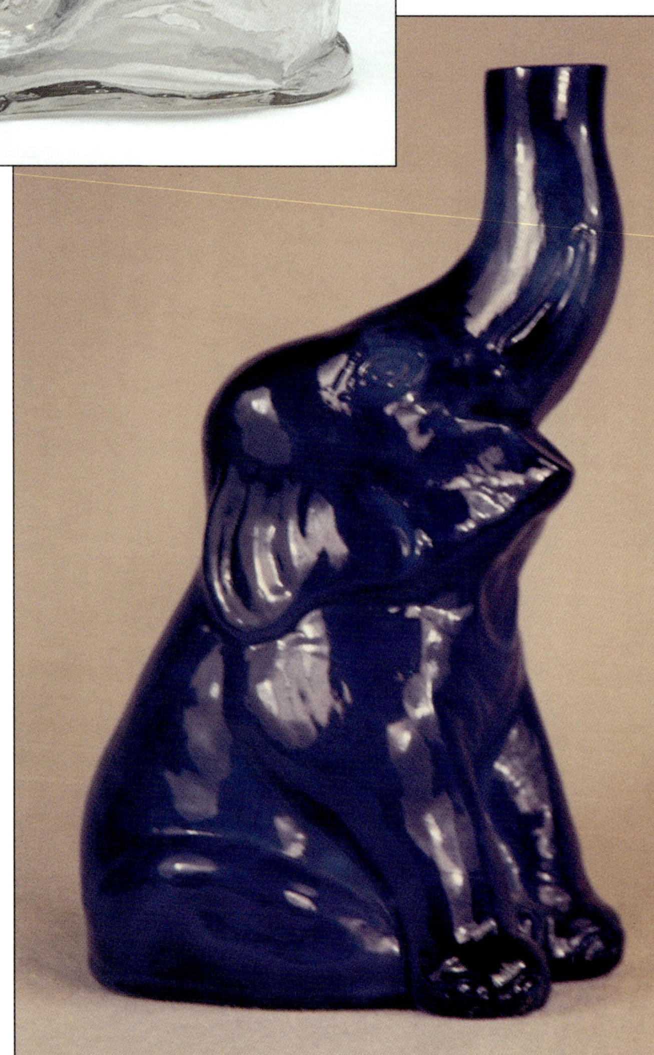

Right: Elephant whiskey bottle (decanter), Periwinkle blue, 8.5" tall, 5" long, Circa 1935, **$1,200.00**

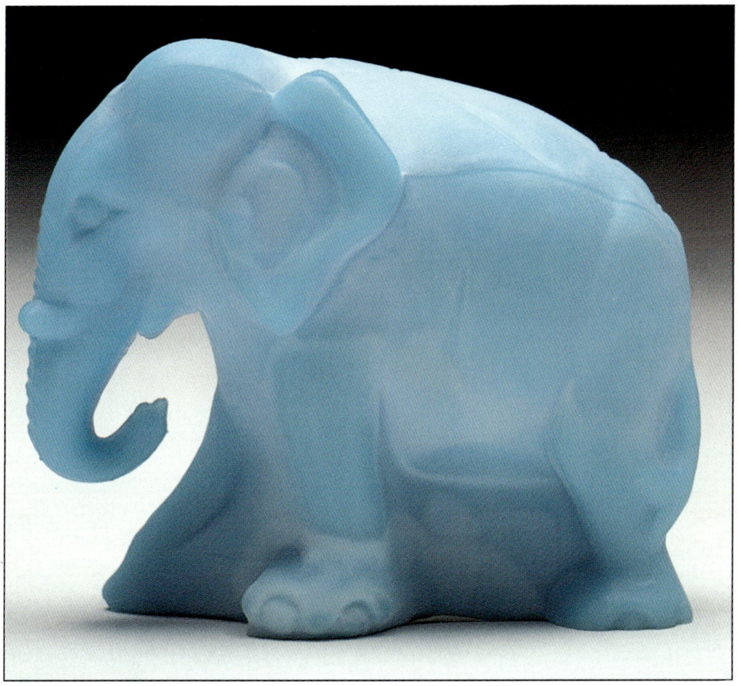

Work elephant, #5123BA, Blue with satin finish, 3" tall, 3.5" long, Circa 1970's, **$350.00**

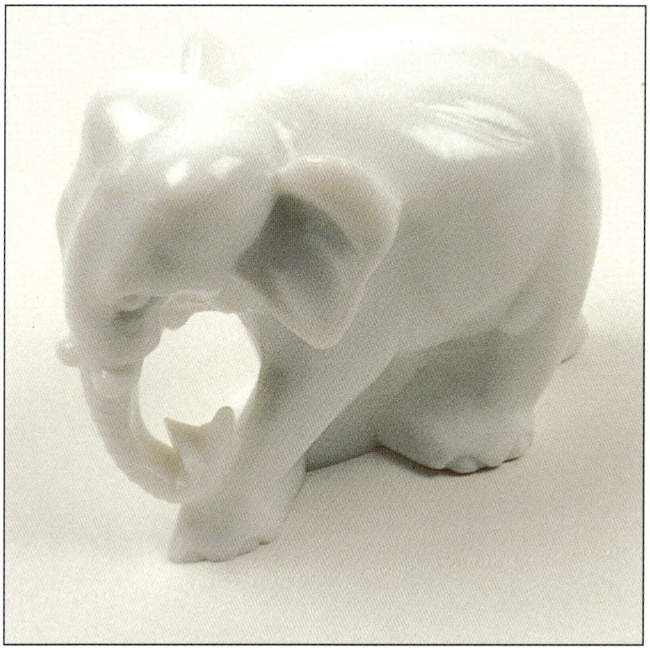

Work elephant, #5123MI, Milk Glass, 3" tall, 3.5" long, Circa 1970's, **$300.00**

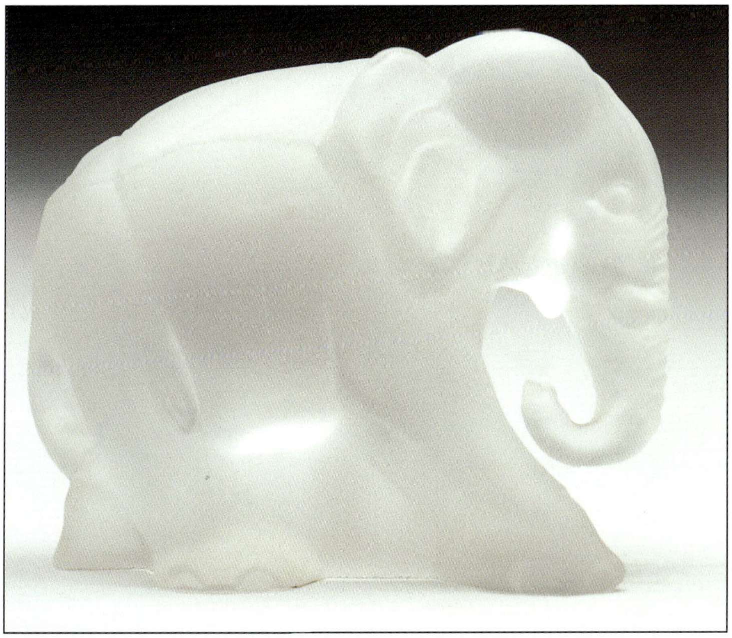

Work elephant, #5123CS,Crystal with satin finish, 3" tall, 3.5" long, Circa 1970's, **$250.00**

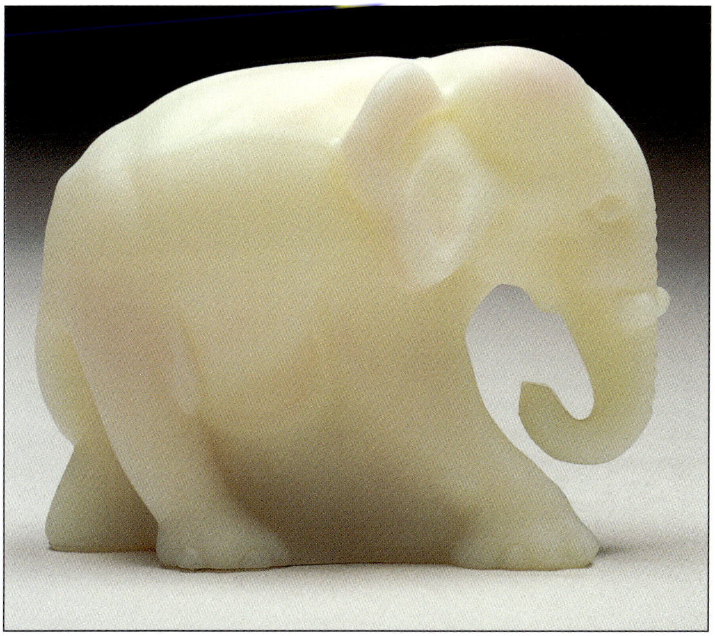

Work elephant, #5123BR, Burmese with satin finish, 3" tall, 3.5" long, Circa 2001, **$45.00**

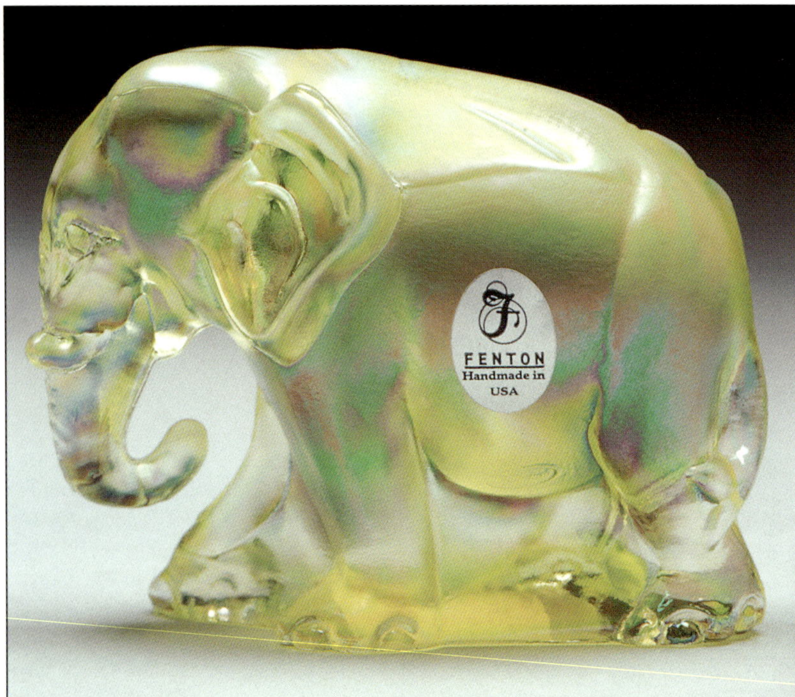

Work elephant, #5123TS, Topaz Iridescent with oval black and silver foil label, 3" tall, 3.5" long, Circa 2001, **$30.00**

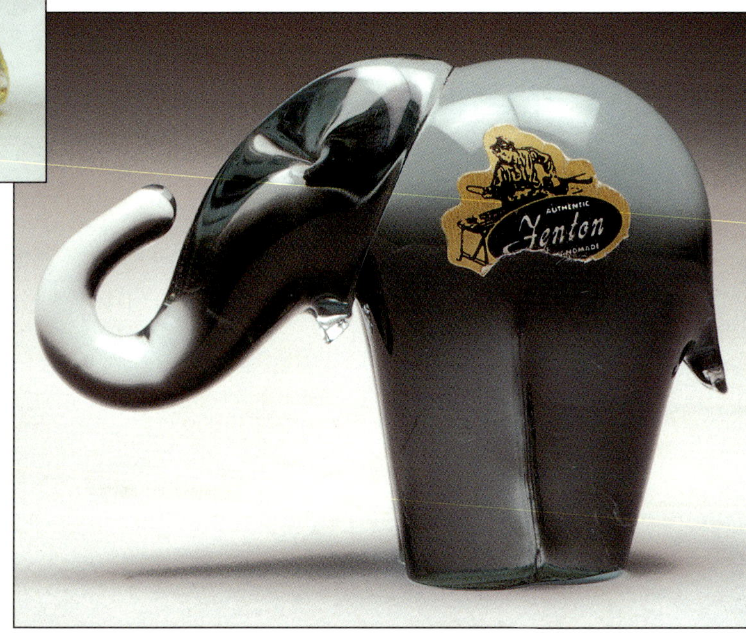

Free hand elephant #5012, Smoke, made for Fenton Gift Shop, with gold and black paper - glass blower label, sample color, 2.75" tall, 3.5" long, Circa 1980, **$150.00**

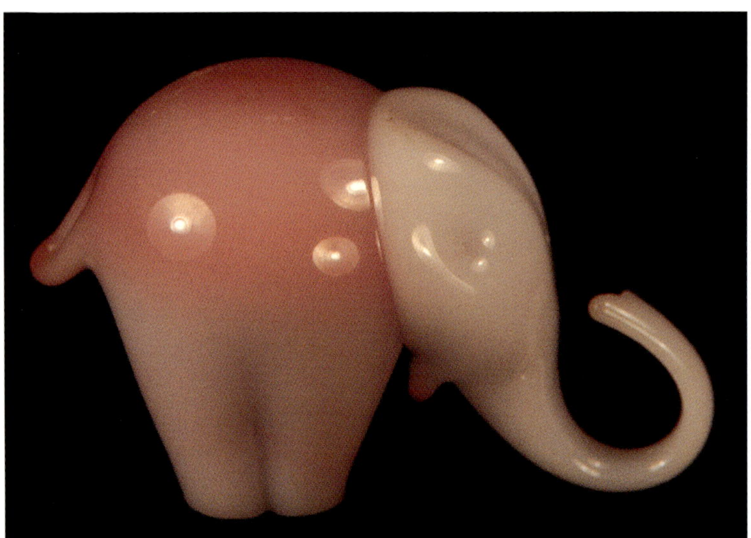

Free hand elephant #5012, Blue Burmese, made for Fenton Gift Shop, sample color, 2.75" tall, 3.5" long, Circa 1980, **$250.00**

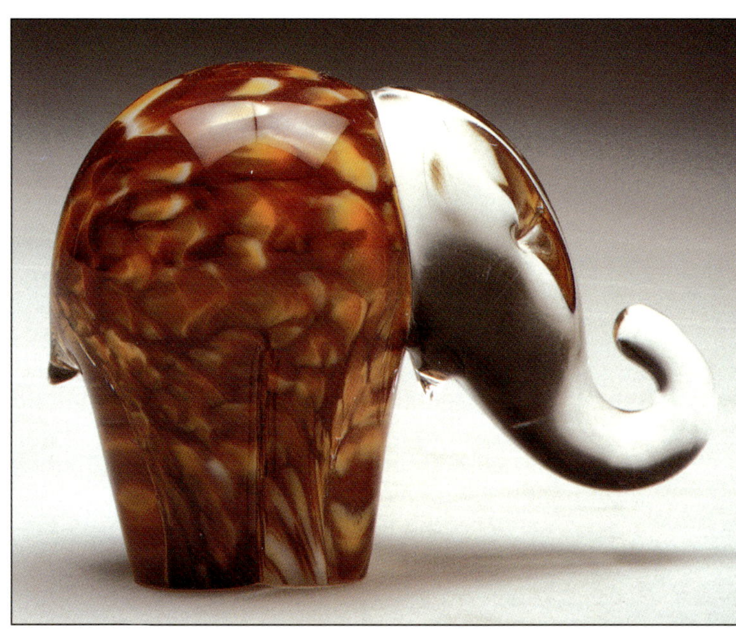

Free hand elephant #5012, Autumn Orange Vasa Murrhina, made for Fenton Gift Shop, 2.75" tall, 3.5" long, Circa 1984, **$125.00**

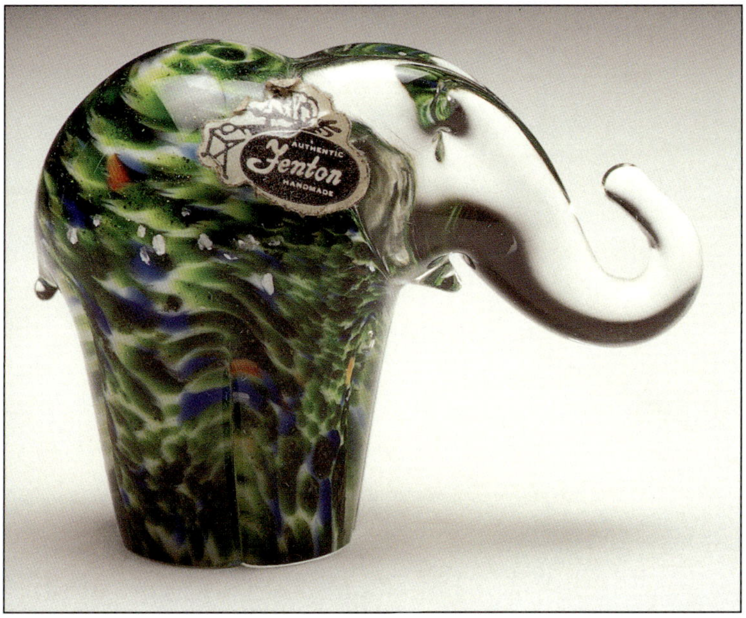

Free hand elephant #5012, Green Vasa Murrhina, made for Fenton Gift Shop, with gold and black paper - glass blower label, sample color, 2.75" tall, 3.5" long, Circa 1984, **$150.00**

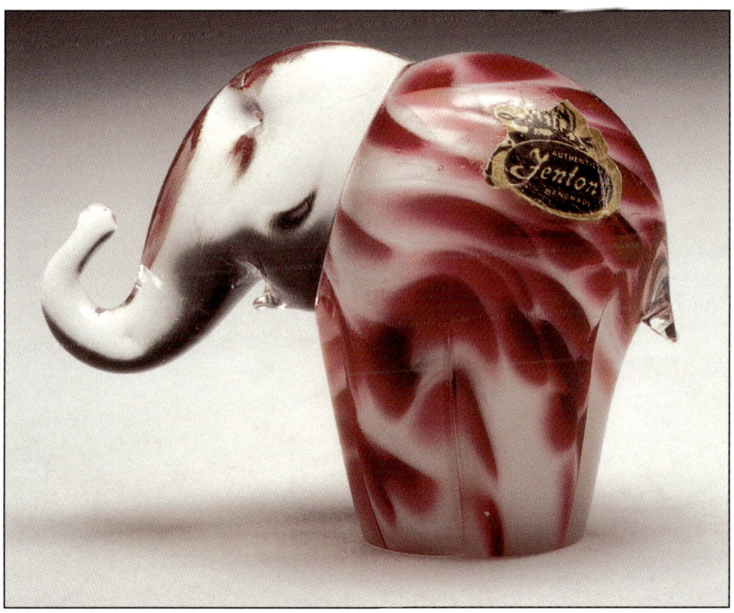

Free hand elephant #5012, Rose Vasa Murrhina, made for Fenton Gift Shop, with gold and black paper - glass blower label, 2.75" tall, 3.5" long, Circa 1984, **$175.00**

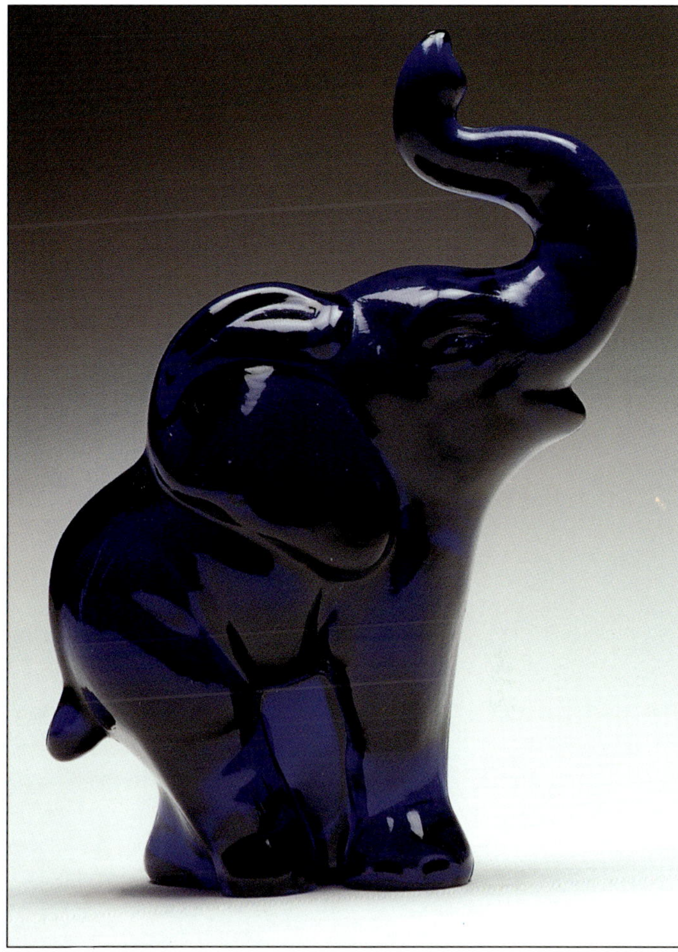

Standing elephant, #5158KK, not in Fenton's regular line, Cobalt, 4" tall, 3" long, Circa 1984, **$65.00**

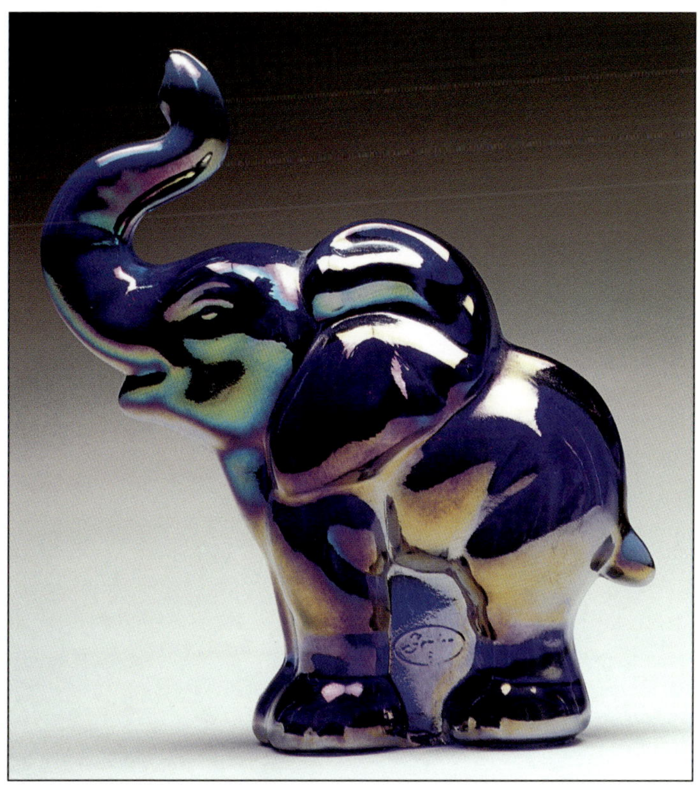

Standing elephant, #5158NK, Cobalt Marigold Carnival, 4" tall, 3" long, Circa 1984, **$48.00**

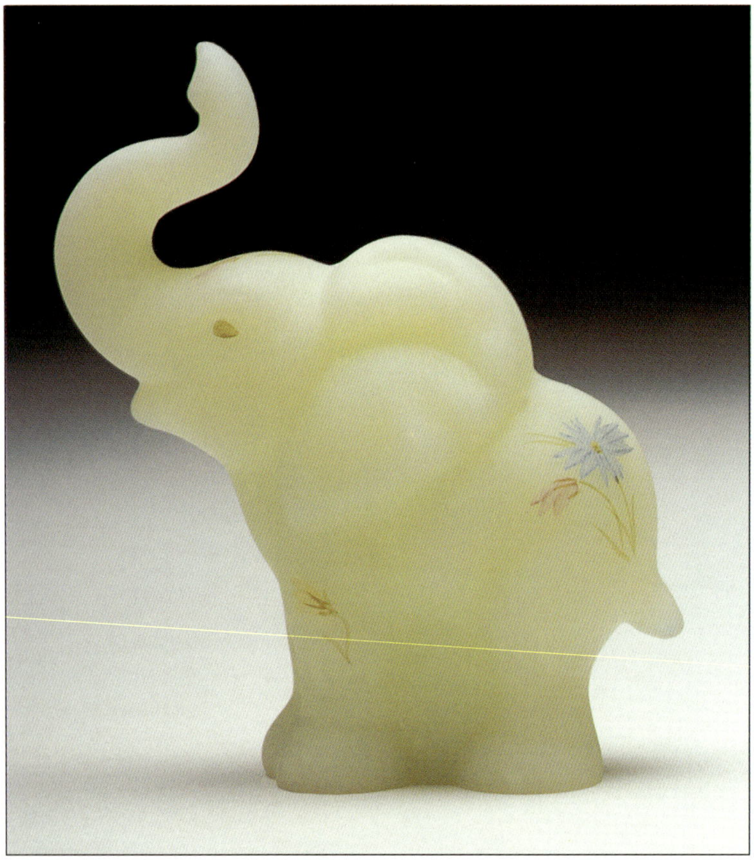

Standing Elephant #5158DN, Dianthus, hand painted on Custard, 3.75" tall, 3.5" long, Circa 1984, **$48.00**

Standing elephant, #5158FA, Frosted Asters, hand painted on blue satin, 4" tall, 3" long, Circa 1984-86, **$60.00**

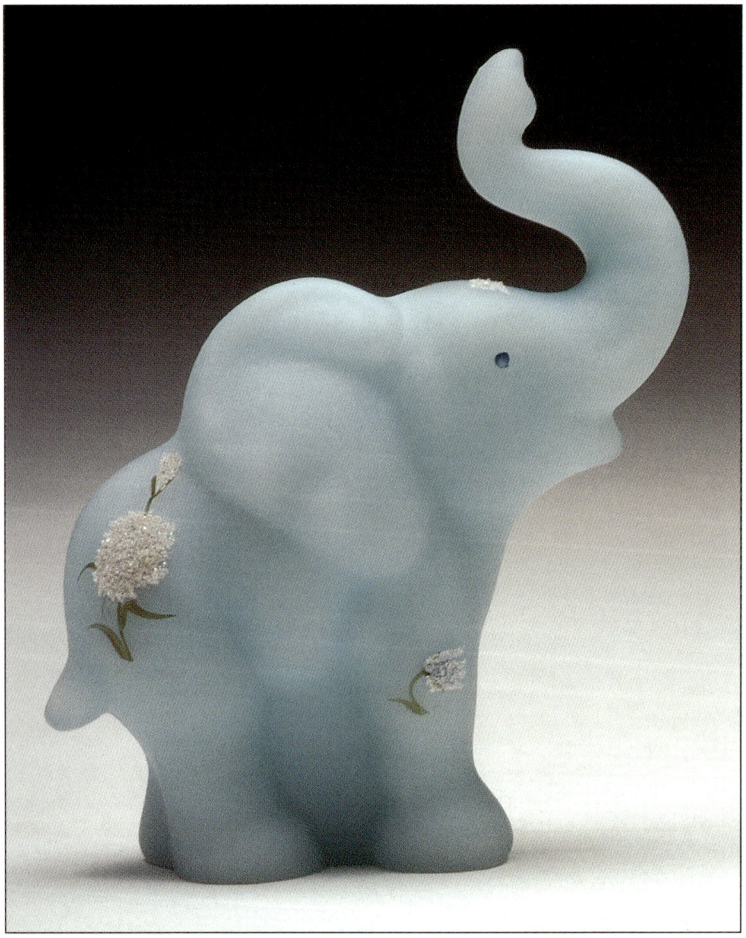

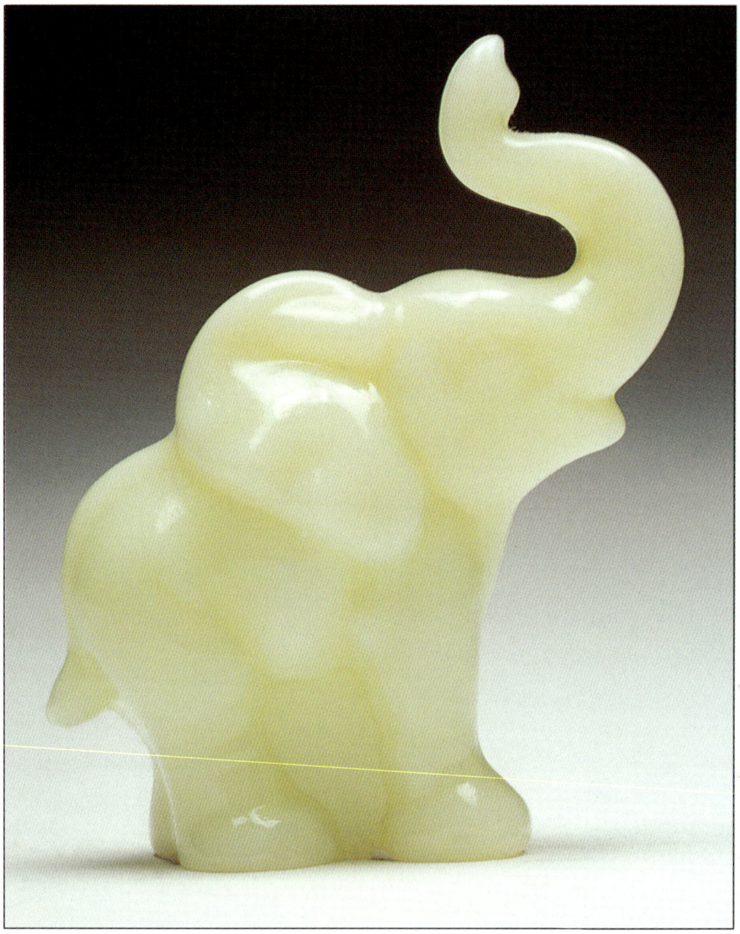

Standing elephant, #5158CU, not in Fenton's regular line, Custard with gloss finish, 4" tall, 3" long, Circa 1984-86, **$45.00**

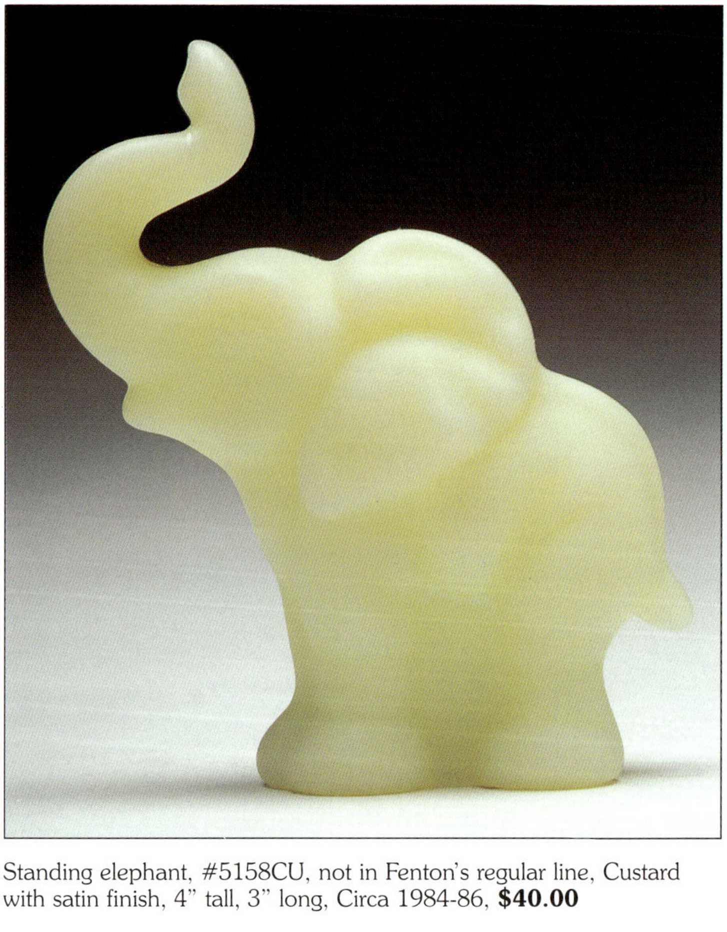

Standing elephant, #5158CU, not in Fenton's regular line, Custard with satin finish, 4" tall, 3" long, Circa 1984-86, **$40.00**

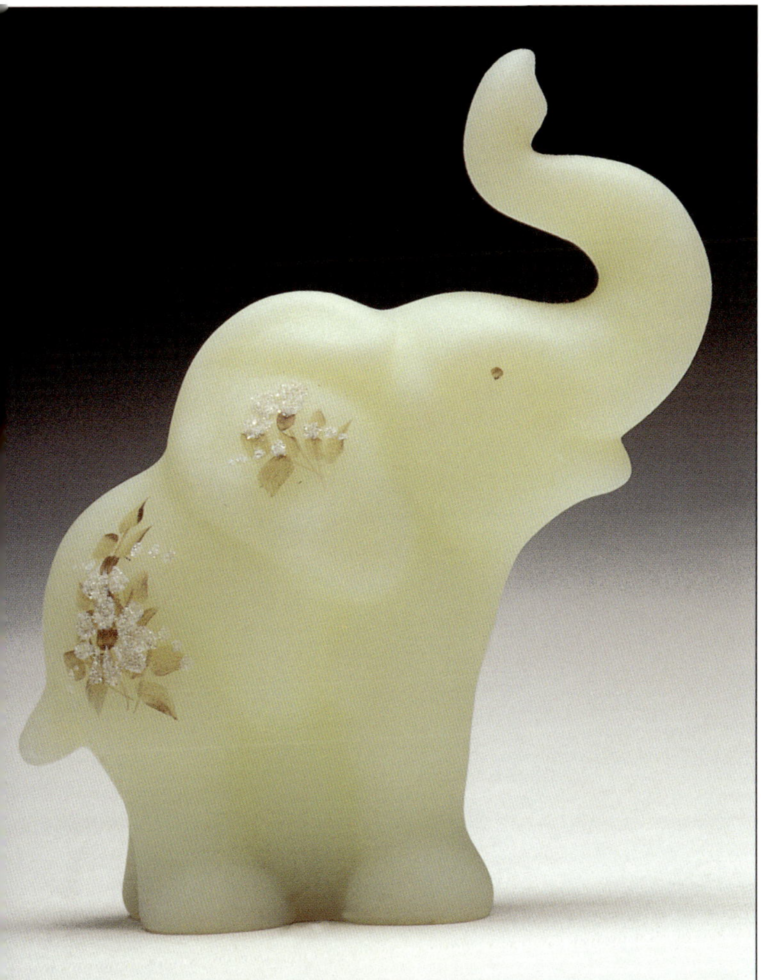

Standing elephant, #5158DC, Daisies on Custard, hand painted, 4" tall, 3" long, Circa 1984-86, **$45.00**

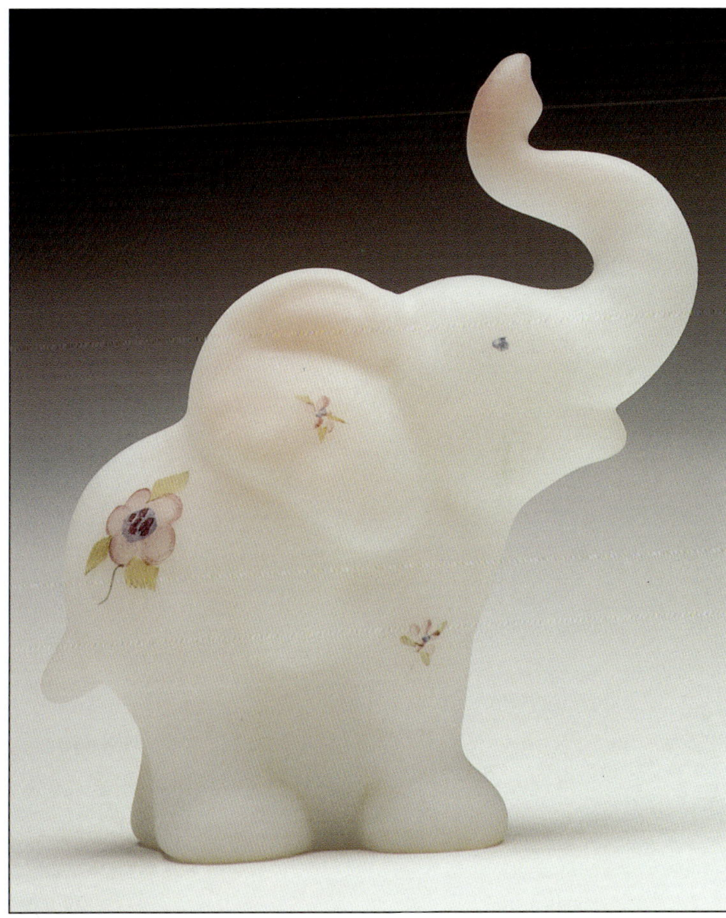

Standing elephant, right side view, #5158RK, Berries and Blossoms, hand painted, 4" tall, 3" long, Circa 1984-86, **$48.00**

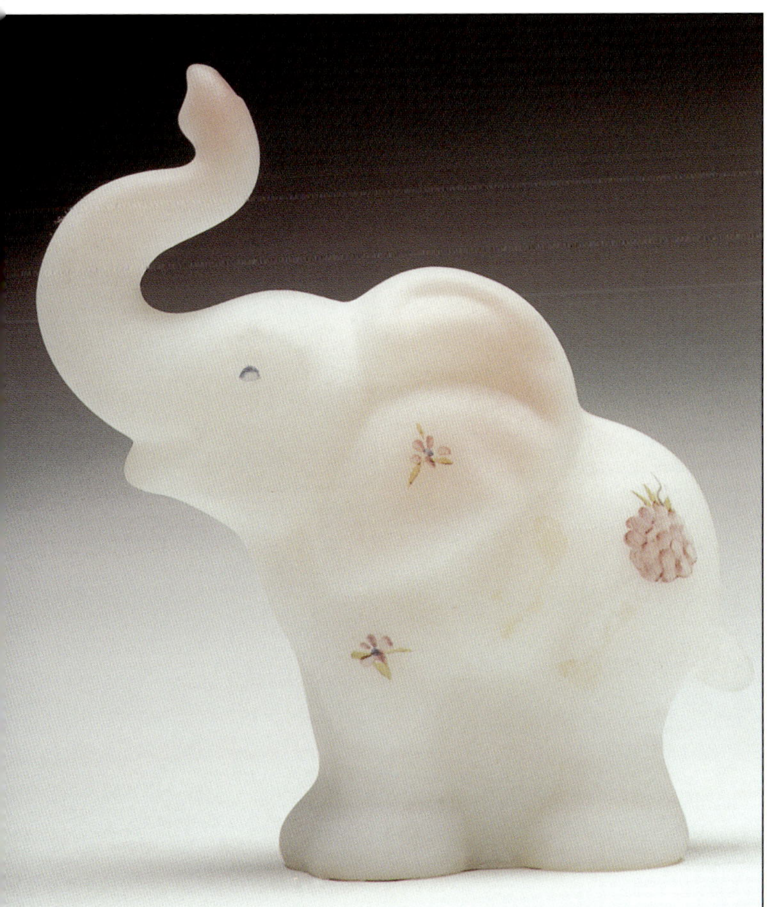

Standing elephant, left side view, #5158RK, Berries and Blossoms, hand painted, 4" tall, 3" long, Circa 1984-86, **$48.00**

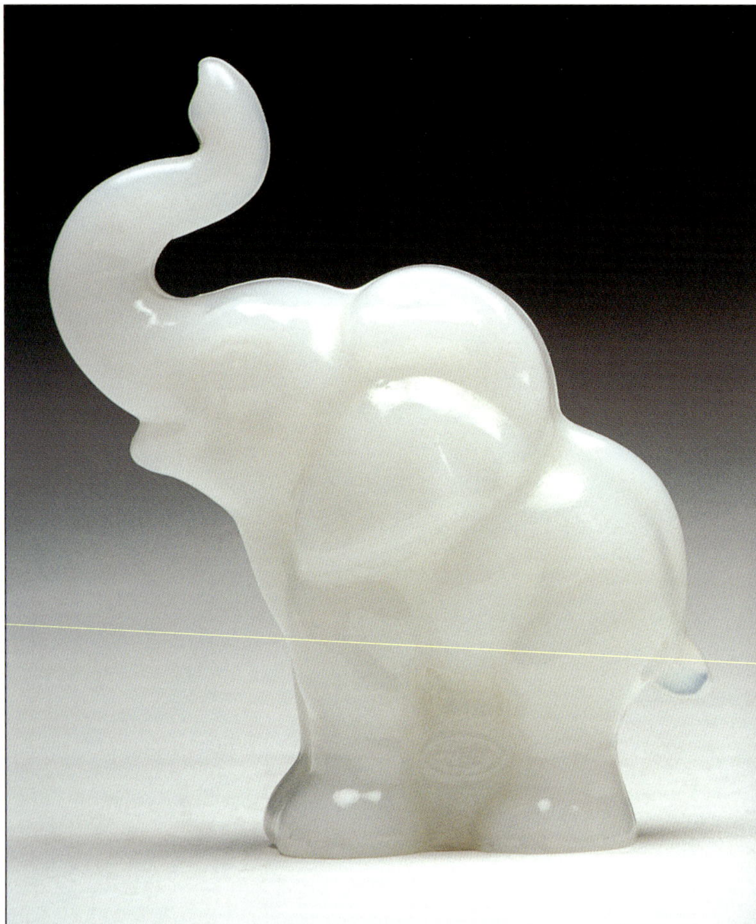

Standing elephant, #5158M4, not in Fenton's regular line, Opal, 4" tall, 3" long, Circa 1984-87, **$35.00**

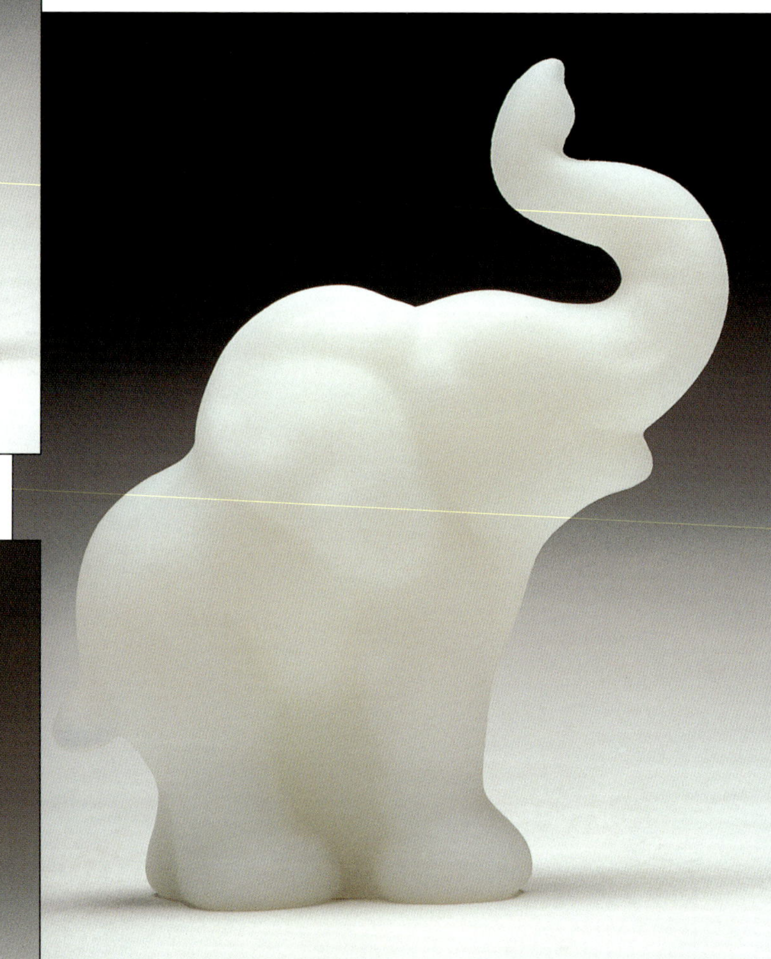

Standing elephant, #5158M4, not in Fenton's regular line, Opal with satin finish, 4" tall, 3" long, Circa 1984-87, **$25.00**

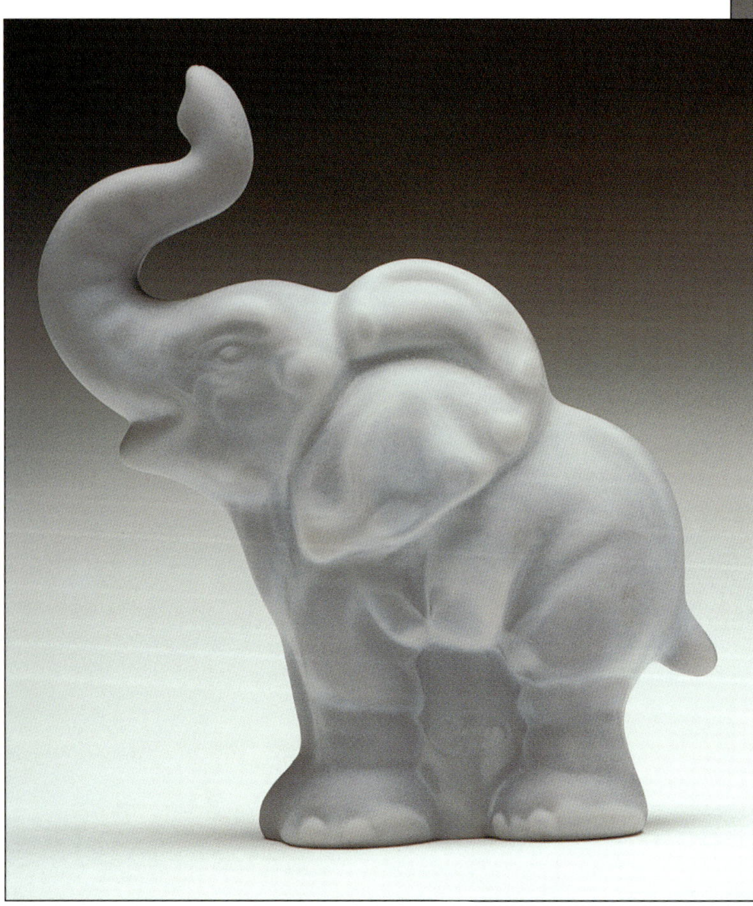

Standing elephant, #5158, not in Fenton's regular line, natural gray, hand painted, 4" tall, 3" long, Circa 1984-87, **$65.00**

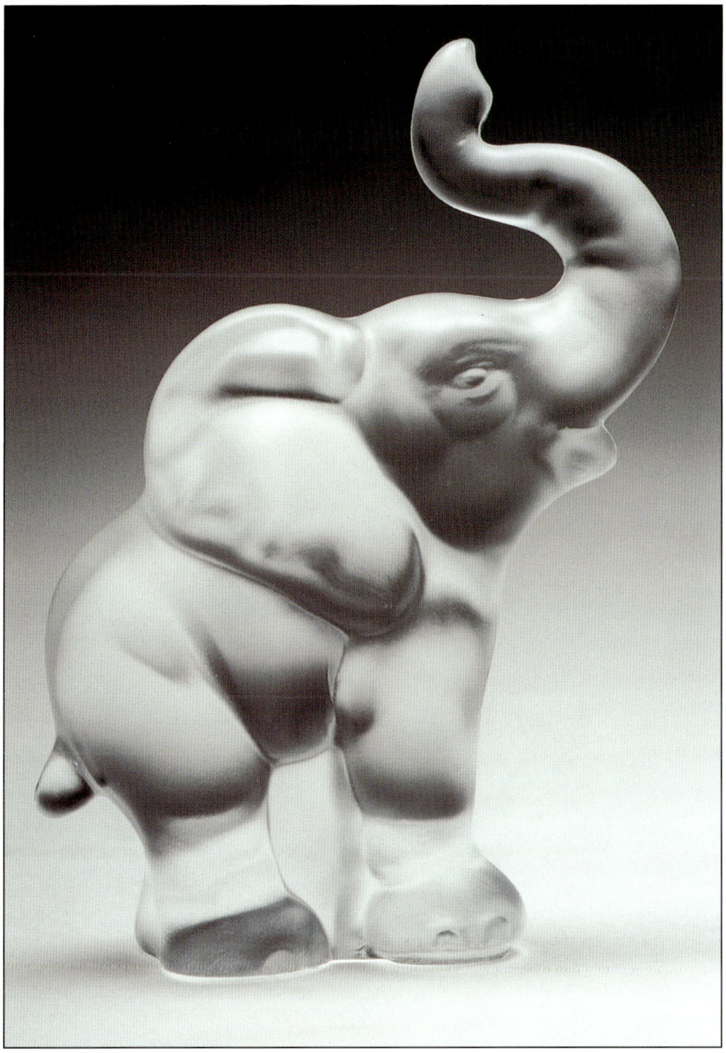

Standing elephant, #5158VE, Crystal Velvet, 4" tall, 3" long, Circa 1984-88, **$45.00**

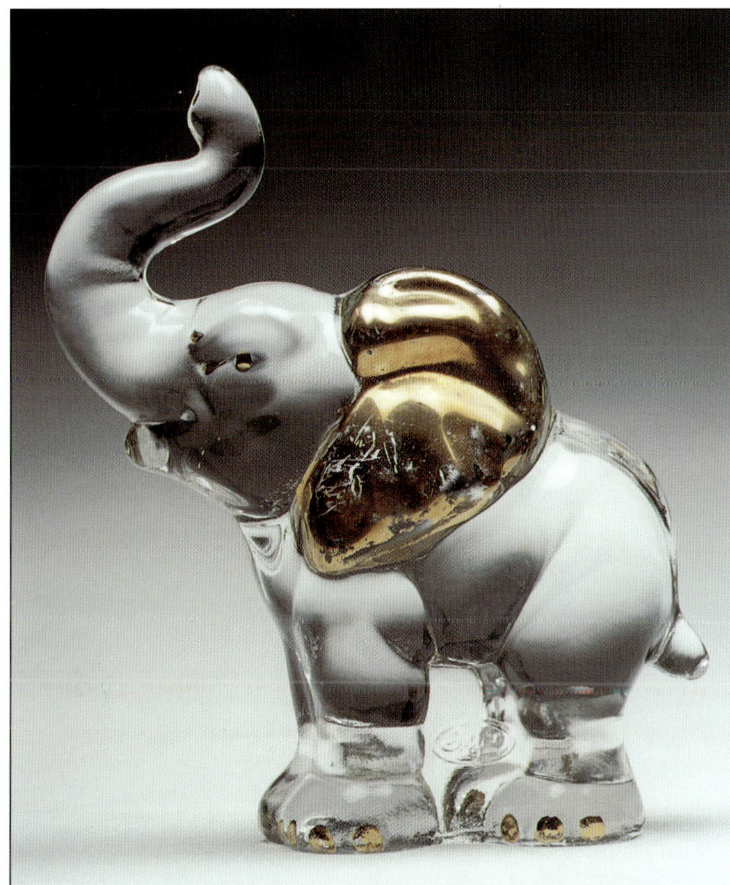

Standing elephant, #5158, not in Fenton's regular line, crystal with gold ears, 4" tall, 3" long, Circa 1984, **$55.00**

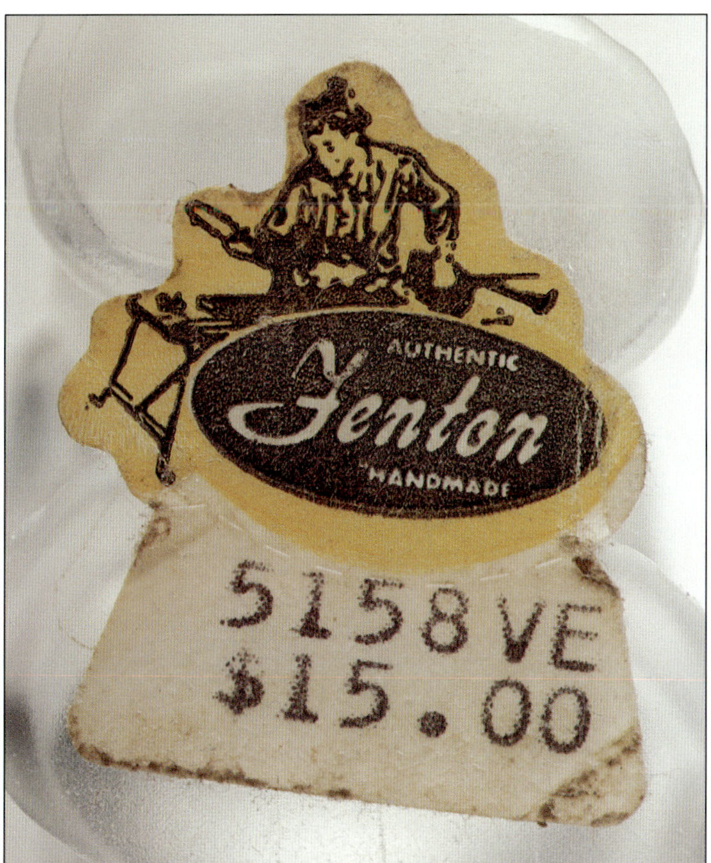

Original gold and black glass worker label

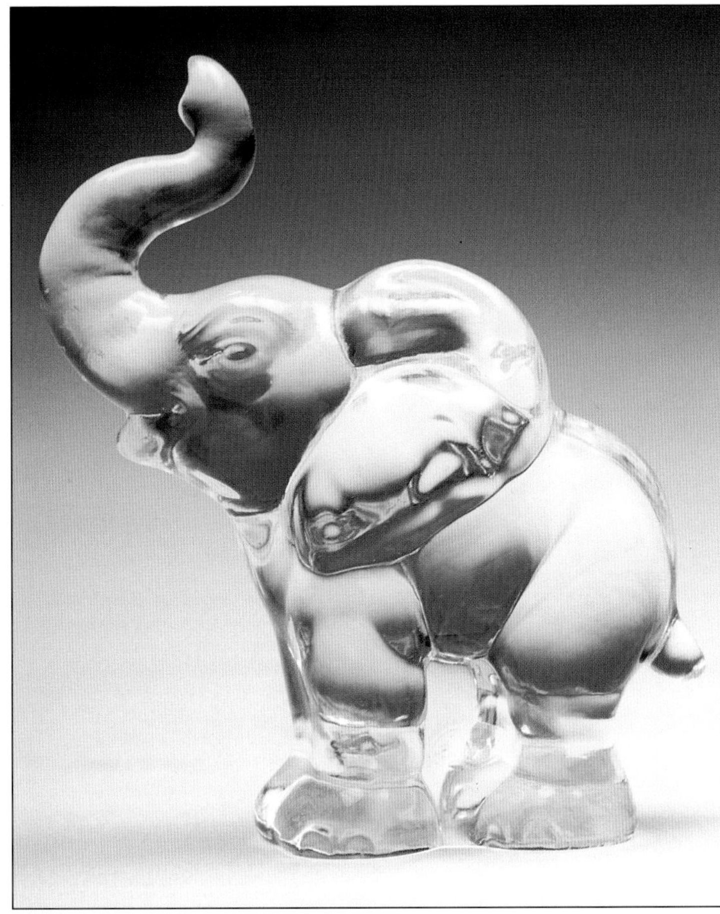

Standing elephant, #5158CY, Crystal, 4" tall, 3" long, Circa 1984-88 and also 1990-95, **$30.00**

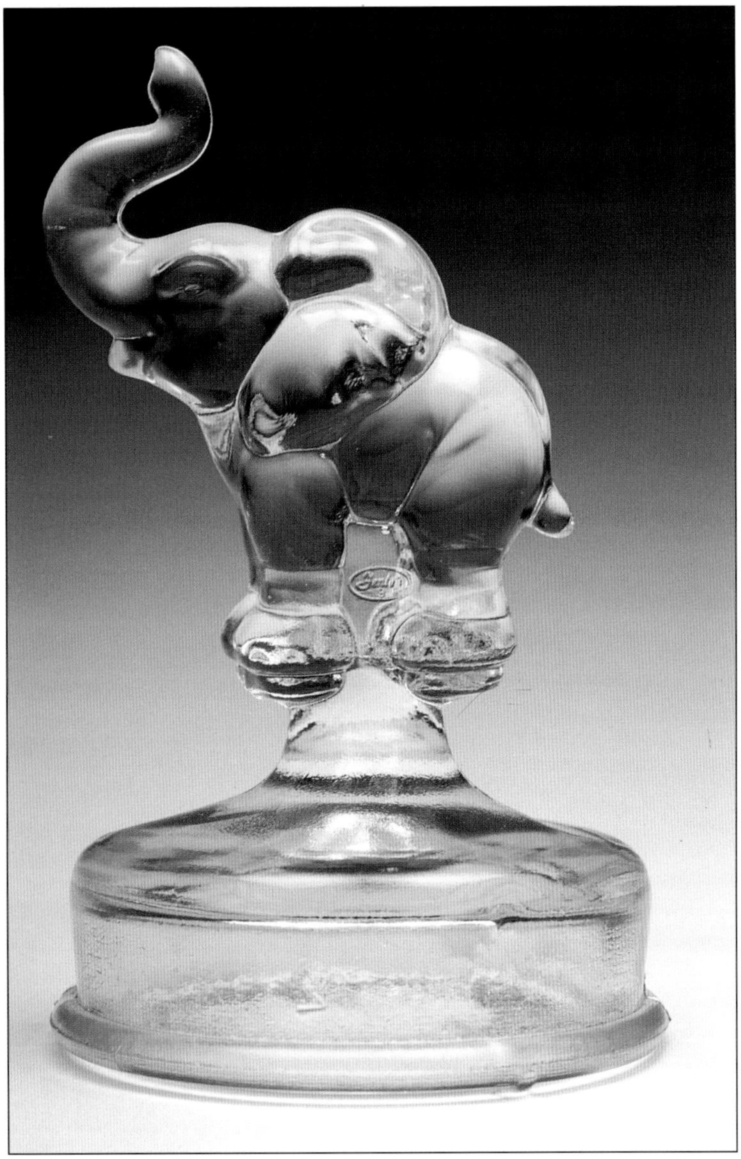

Standing elephant, #5158, not in Fenton's regular line, crystal on bust off base, 6" tall, 4" long, Circa 1984-89, **$75.00**

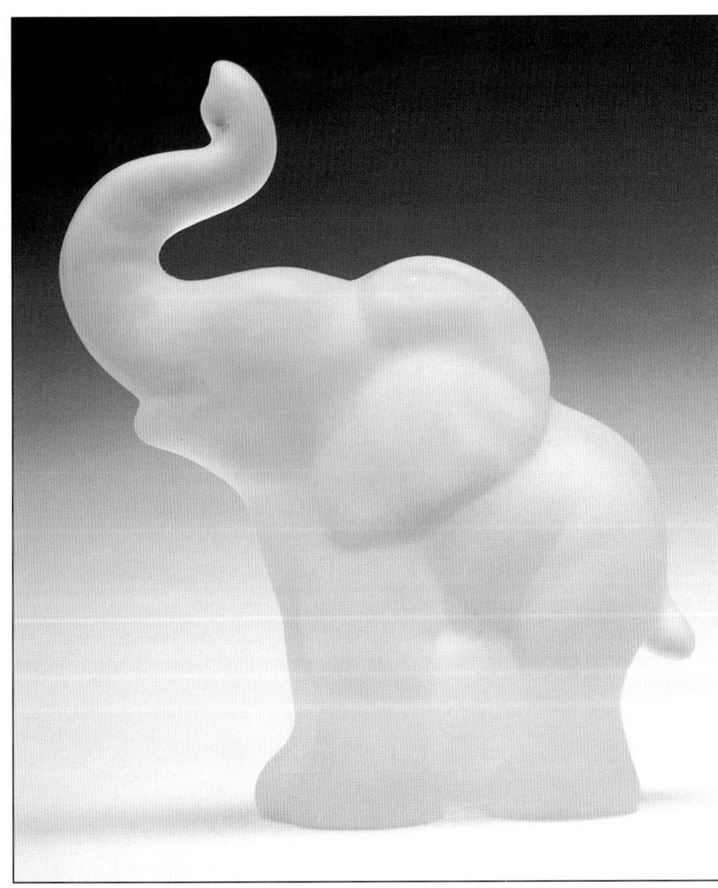

Standing elephant, #5158CY, not in Fenton's regular line, Crystal with satin finish, 4" tall, 3" long, Circa 1984-87 and also 1990-95, **$25.00**

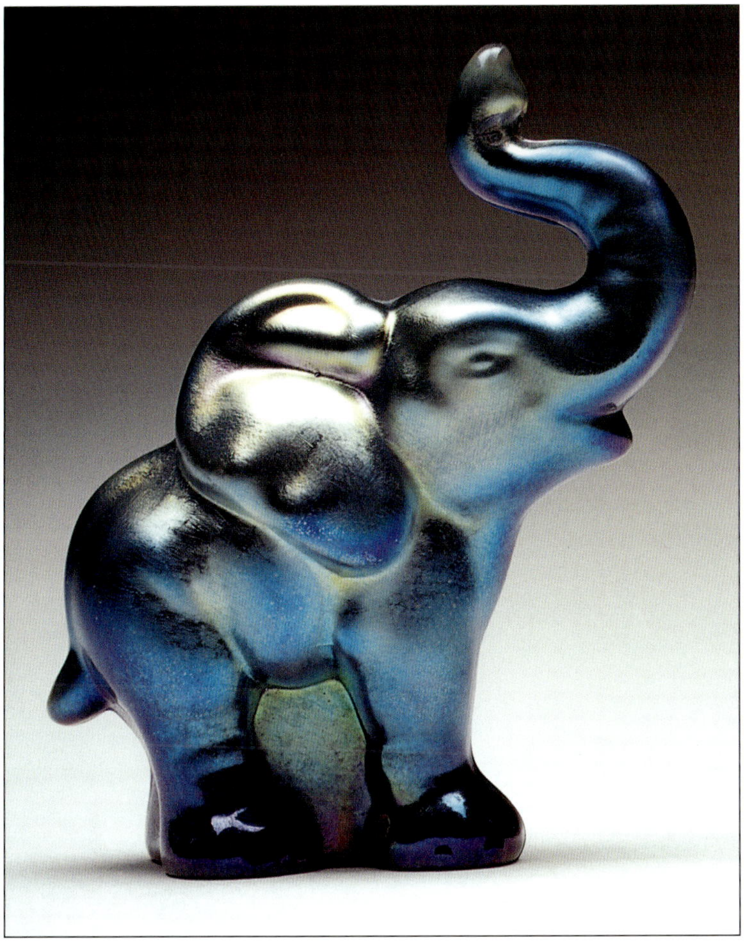

Standing elephant, #5158FN, not in Fenton's regular line, Favrene, 4" tall, 3" long, Circa 1987, **$85.00**

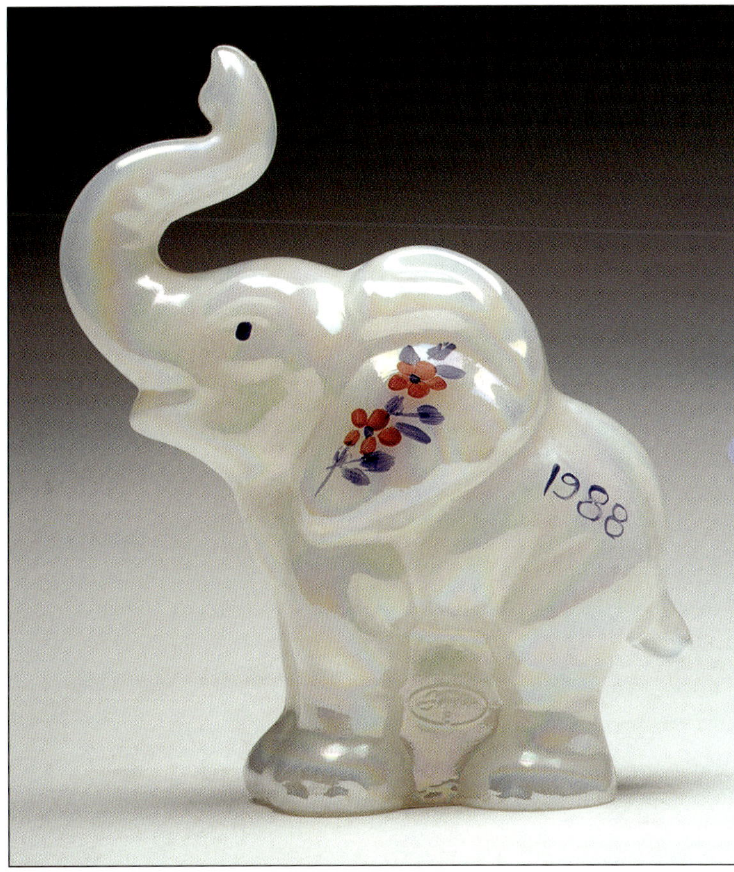

Standing elephant, #5158LQ, Pearlized finish, hand painted with red flowers, QVC item, 4" tall, 3" long, Circa 1988, **$45.00**

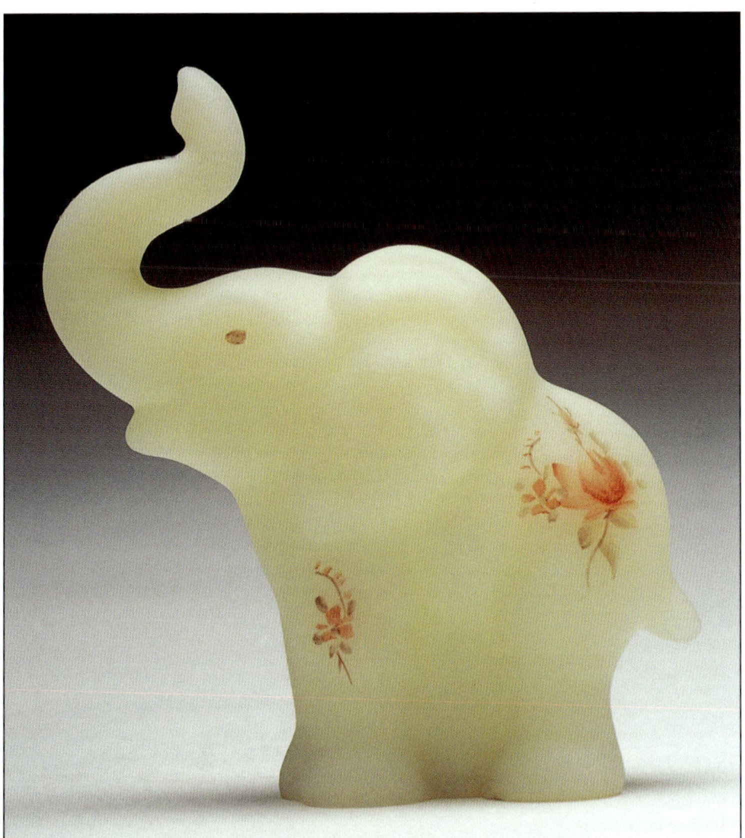

Standing elephant, #5158RC, Custard with Roses, Gracious Touch line, 4" tall, 3" long, Circa 1988, **$45.00**

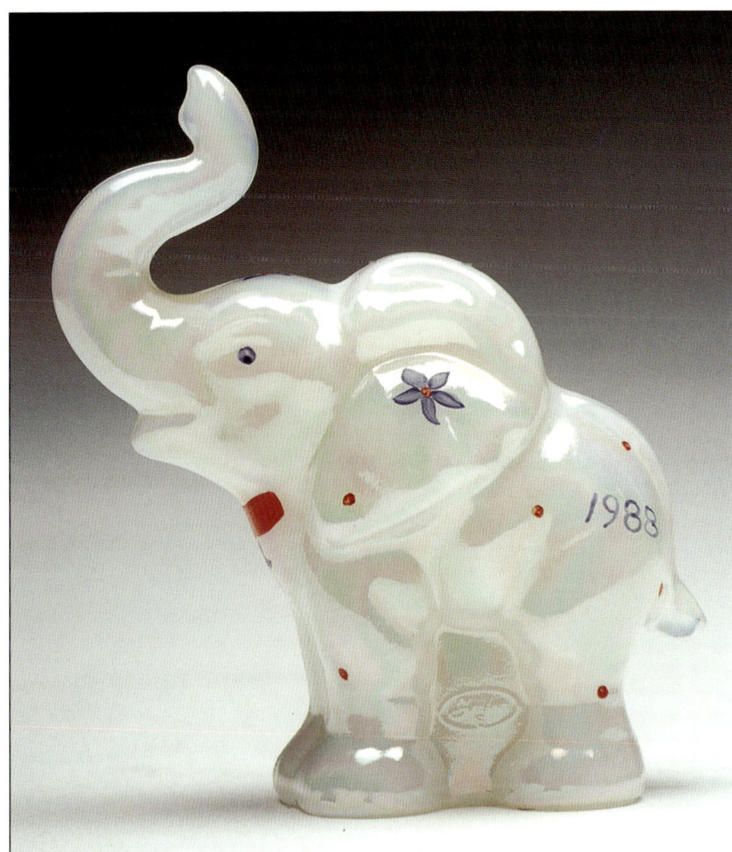

Standing elephant, #5158, Pearlized finish, hand painted star flowers, QVC item, 4" tall, 3" long, Circa 1988, **$48.00**

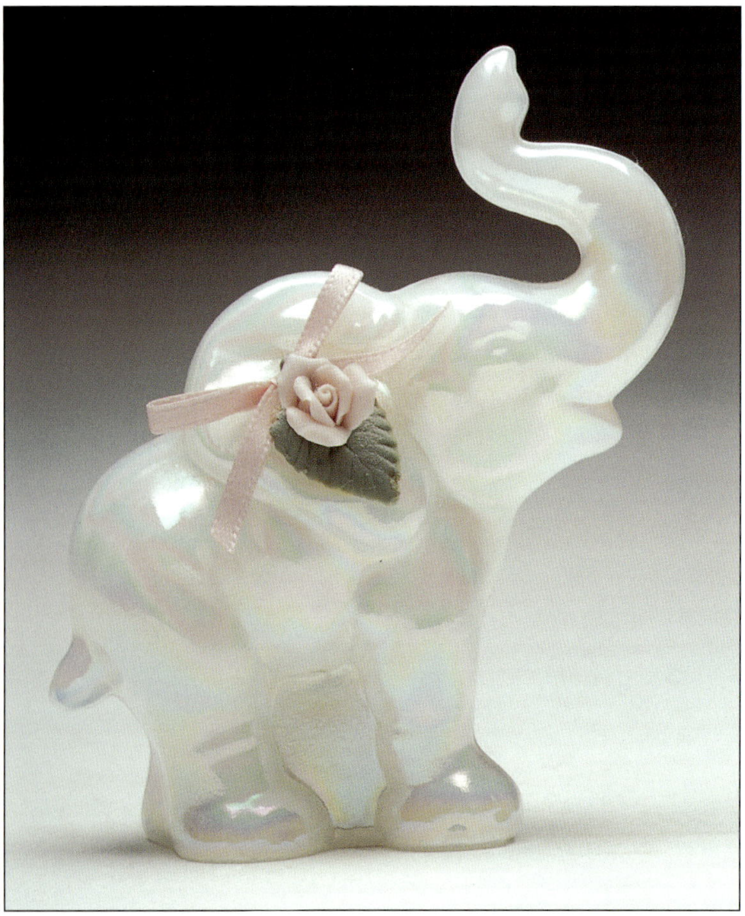

Standing elephant, #5158PT, Pearly Sentiments with applied pink porcelain rose, 4" tall, 3" long, Circa 1992-95, **$30.00**

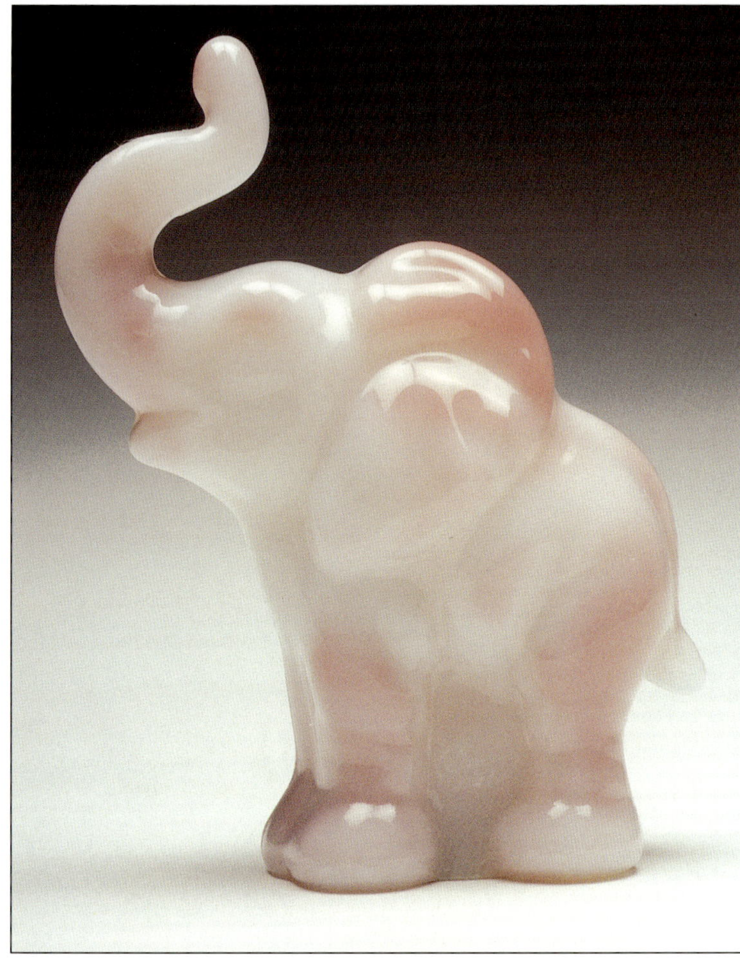

Standing elephant, #5158RE, Rosalene made for annual Fenton Gift Shop February sale, 4" tall, 3" long, Circa 1992, **$40.00**

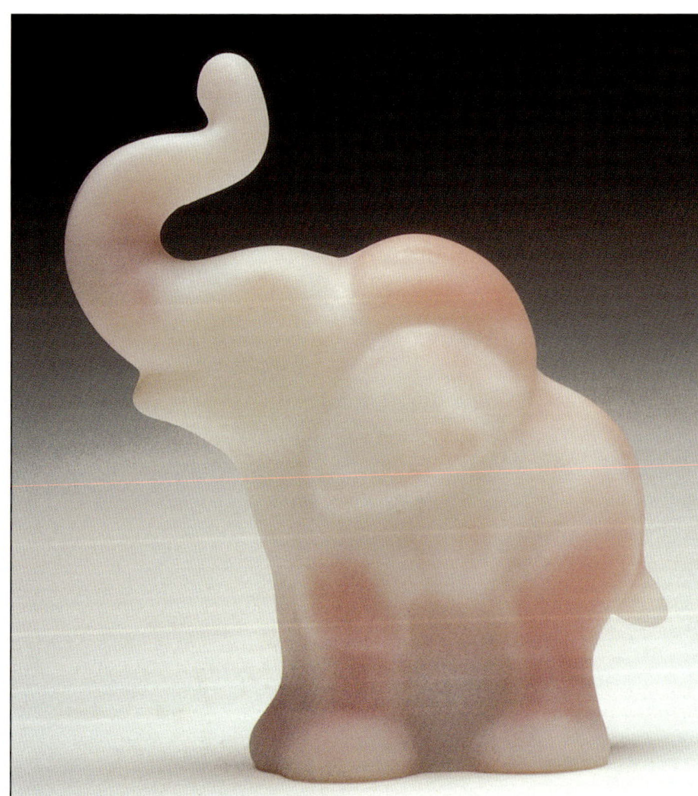

Standing elephant, #5158RE, not in Fenton's regular line, Rosalene with satin finish, made for Fenton Gift Shop, 4" tall, 3" long, Circa 1992, **$45.00**

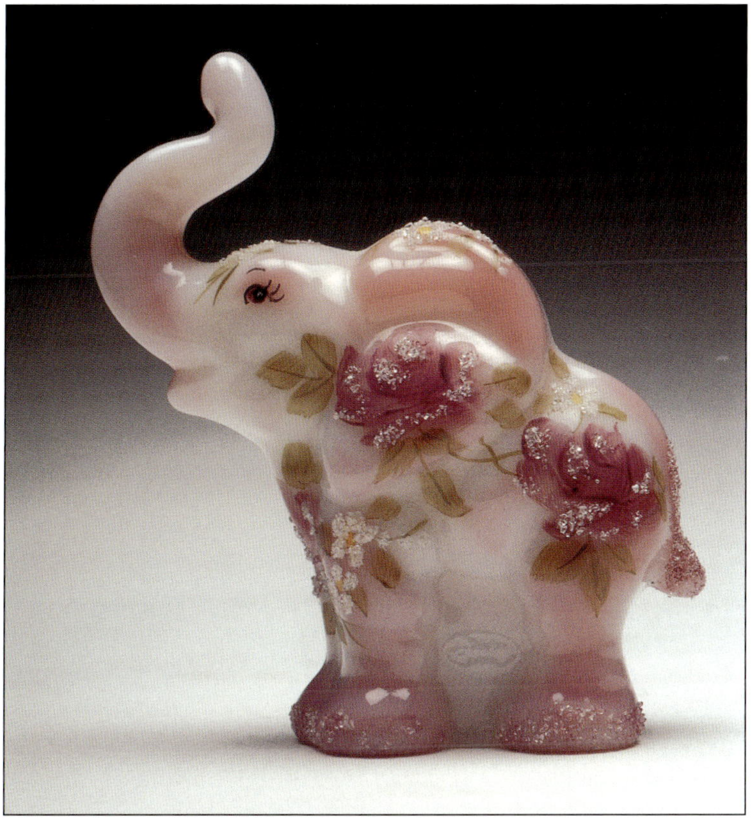

Standing elephant, #5158, not in Fenton's regular line, Rosalene hand painted, made for Fenton Gift Shop, 4" tall, 3" long, Circa 1992, **$75.00**

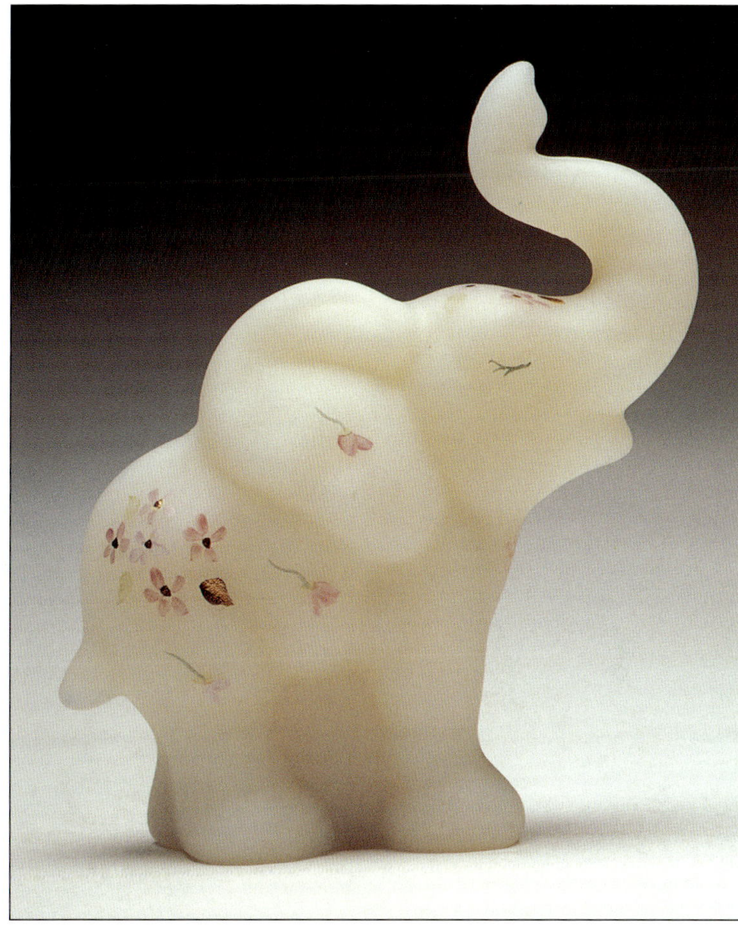

Standing elephant, #5158YB, Kristen's Floral, pink flowers with gold, 4" tall, 3" long, Circa 1995-96, **$45.00**

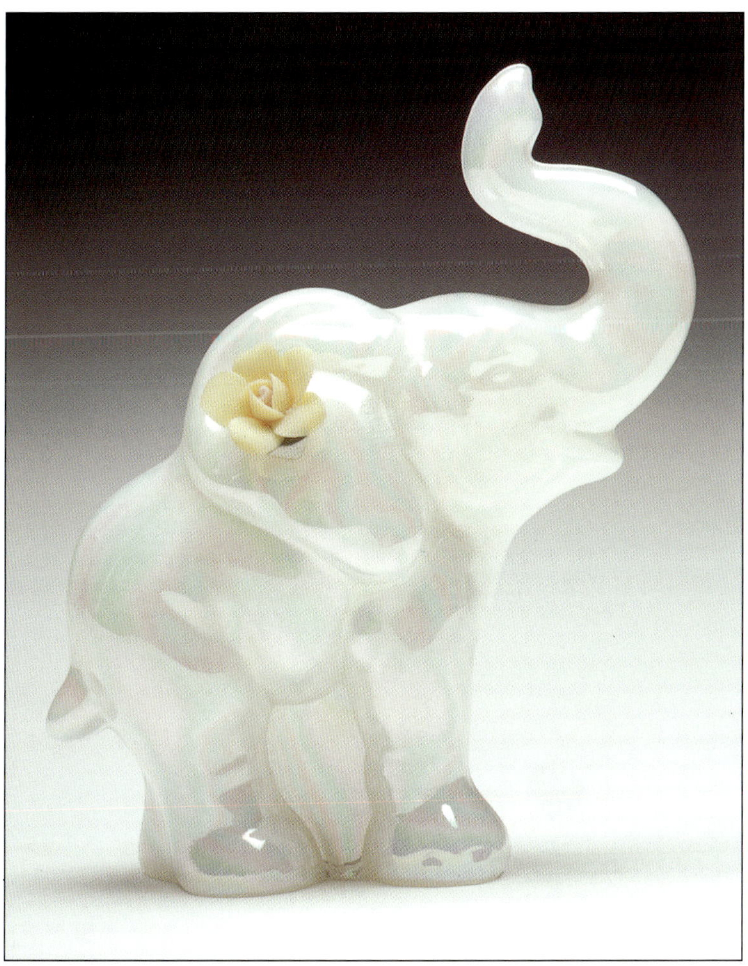

Standing elephant, #5158PT, Pearly Sentiments with applied yellow porcelain rose, 4" tall, 3" long, Circa 1994, **$38.00**

Standing elephant, #5158EG, Rose Garden, 4" tall, 3" long, Circa 1996-2001, **$35.00**

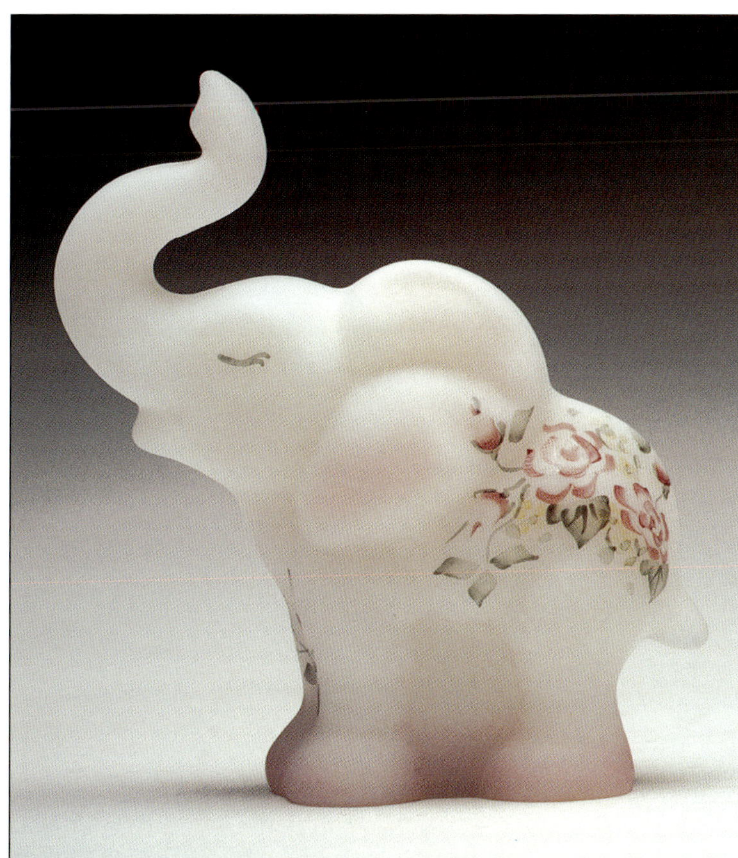

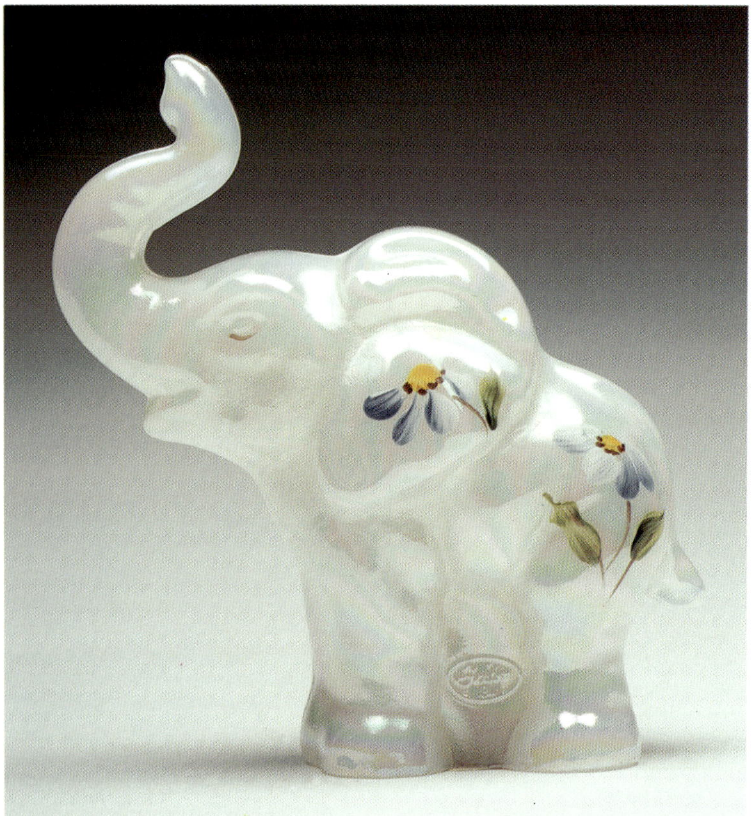

Standing elephant, #5158, not in Fenton's regular line, Pearlized finish hand painted with blue flowers (daisies), 4" tall, 3" long, Circa 1990's, **$48.00**

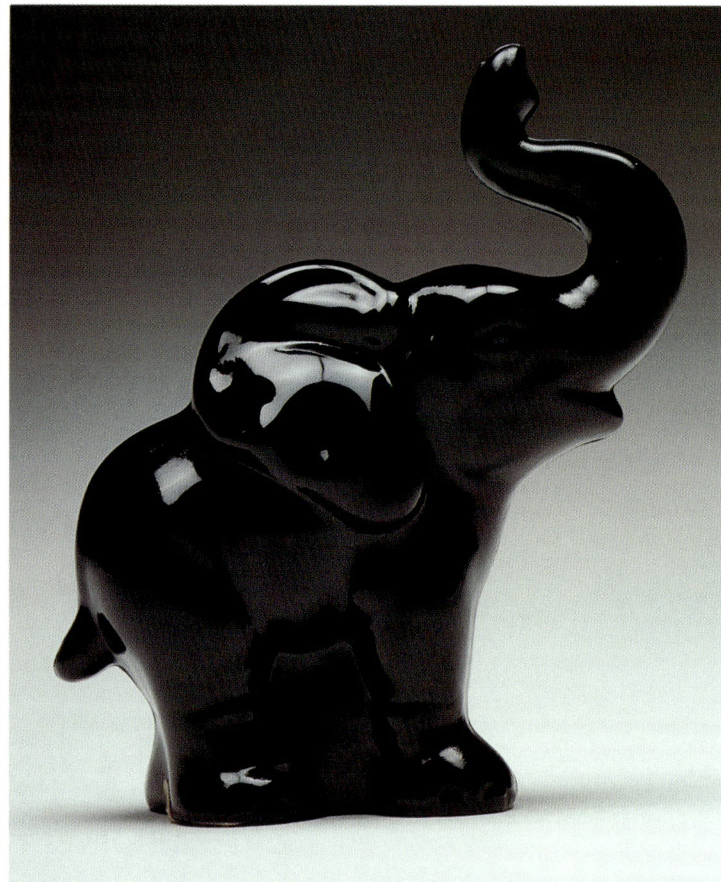

Standing elephant, #5158BK, not in Fenton's regular line, Ebony, 4" tall, 3" long, Circa 1990's, **$40.00**

Standing elephant, #5158JS, not in Fenton's regular line, Blue with satin finish and hand painted, 4" tall, 3" long, Circa 1990's, **$75.00**

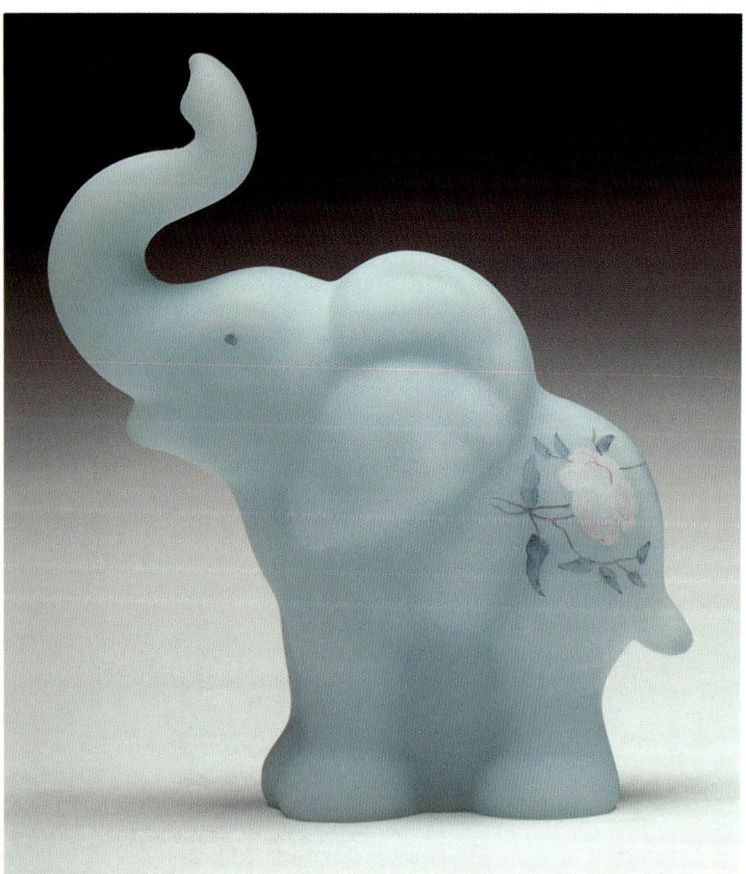

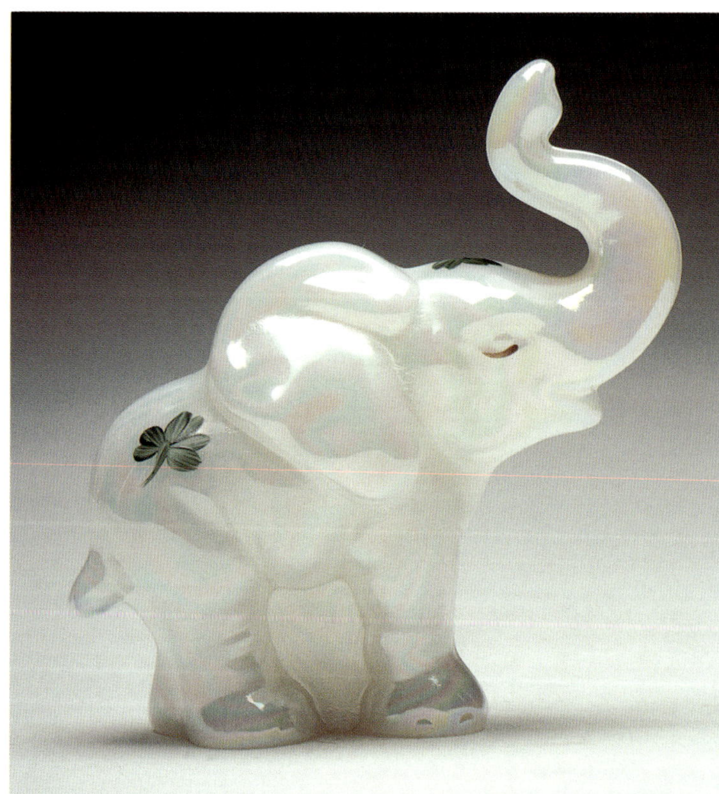

Standing elephant, #5158, not in Fenton's regular line, Pearlized finish, hand painted with shamrocks, 4" tall, 3" long, Circa 1990's, **$40.00**

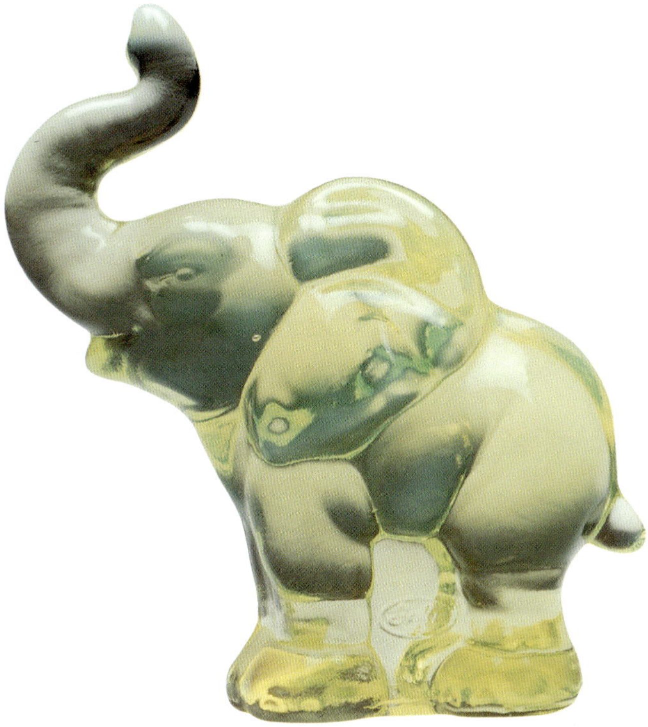

Standing elephant, #5158TO, Topaz (Vaseline), not in Fenton's regular line, made for Westmoreland Museum, 4" tall, 3" long, Circa 1997, **$35.00**

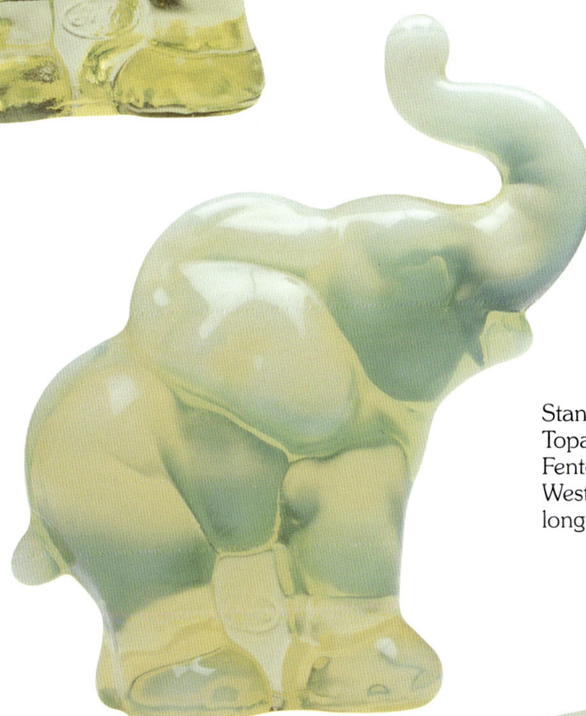

Standing elephant, #5158TO, Topaz (Vaseline) opalescent, not in Fenton's regular line, made for Westmoreland Museum, 4" tall, 3" long, Circa 1997, **$30.00**

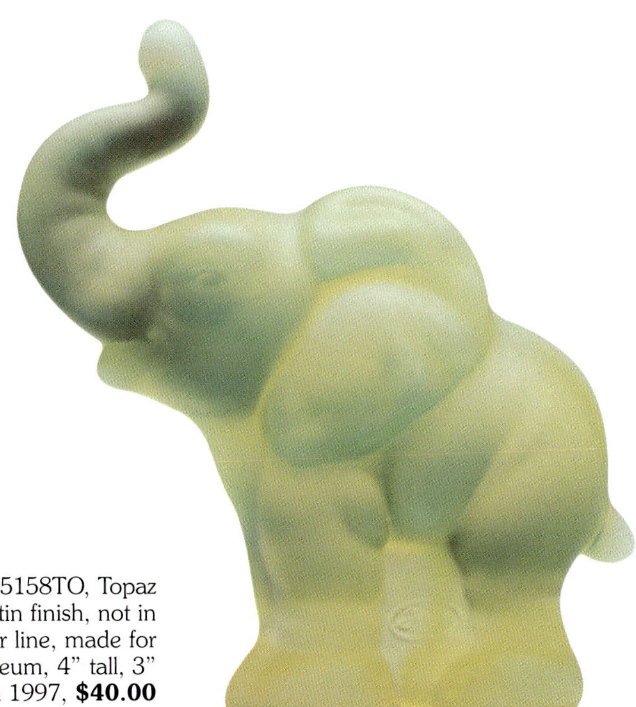

Standing elephant, #5158TO, Topaz (Vaseline) with satin finish, not in Fenton's regular line, made for Westmoreland Museum, 4" tall, 3" long, Circa 1997, **$40.00**

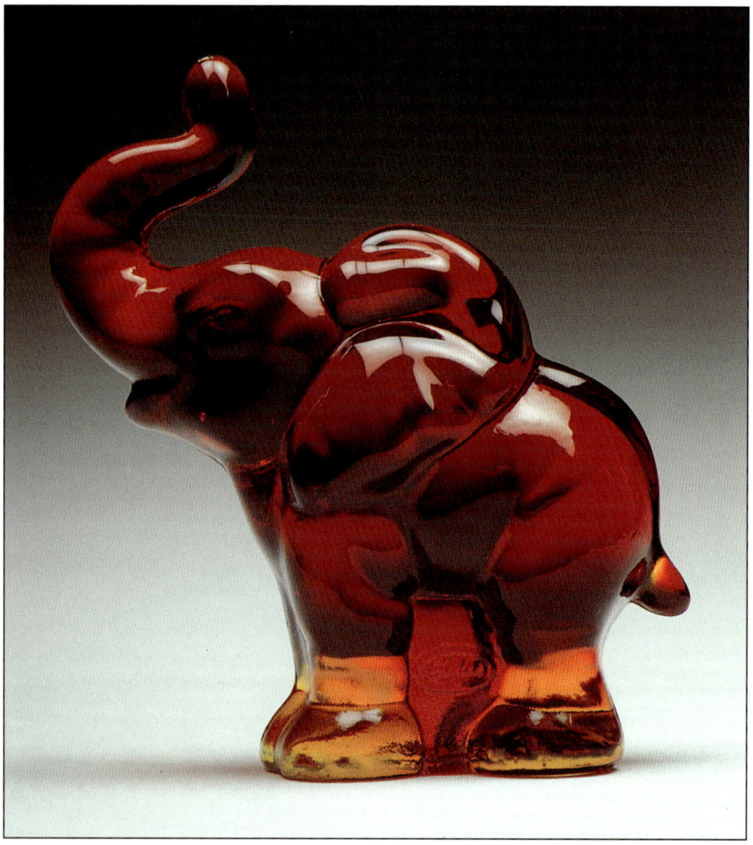

Standing elephant, #5158RU, Ruby, 4" tall, 3" long, Circa 1998-99, **$30.00**

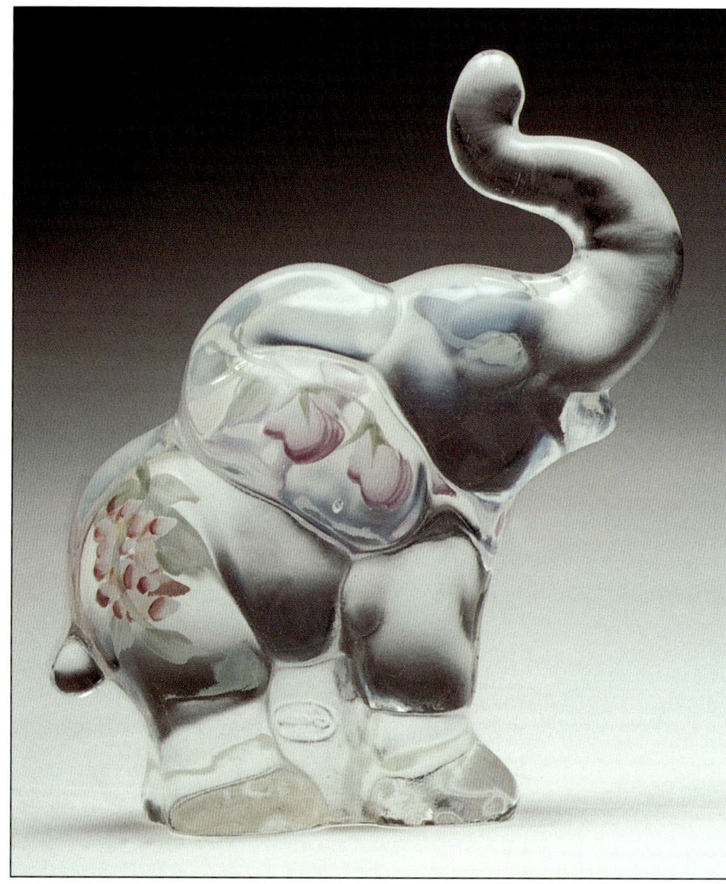

Standing elephant, #5158AZ, Martha's Rose, opalescent with pink and purple vine flowers, 4" tall, 3" long, Circa 1999, **$30.00**

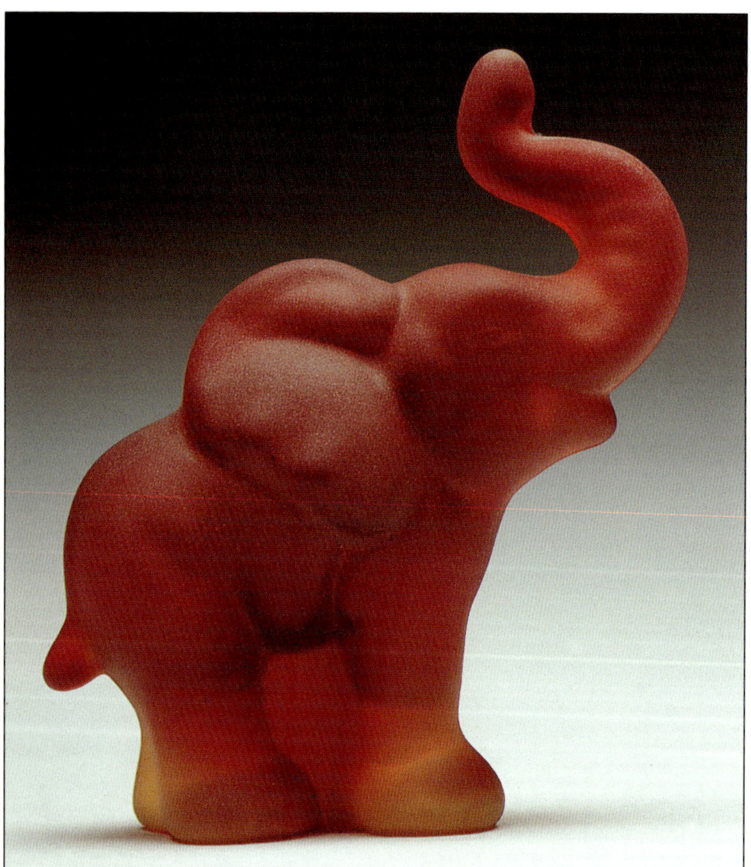

Standing elephant, #5158RU, Ruby with satin finish, 4" tall, 3" long, Circa 1998-99, **$38.00**

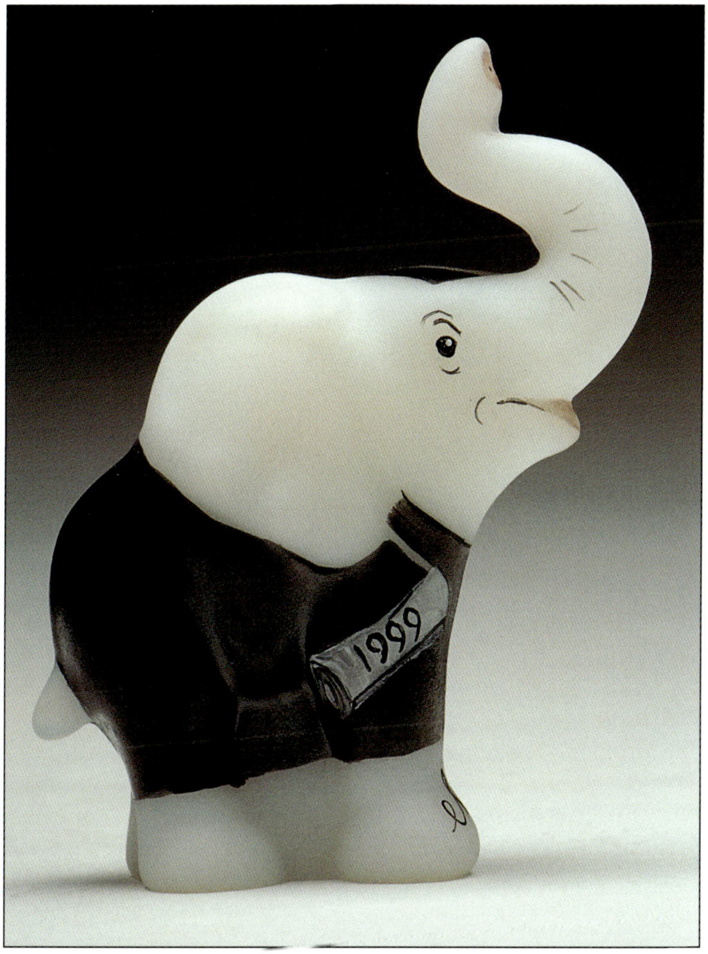

Standing elephant, #5158, not in Fenton's regular line, hand painted by Marten House, graduation decoration (only one done on a special order), 4" tall, 3" long, Circa 1999, **$75.00**

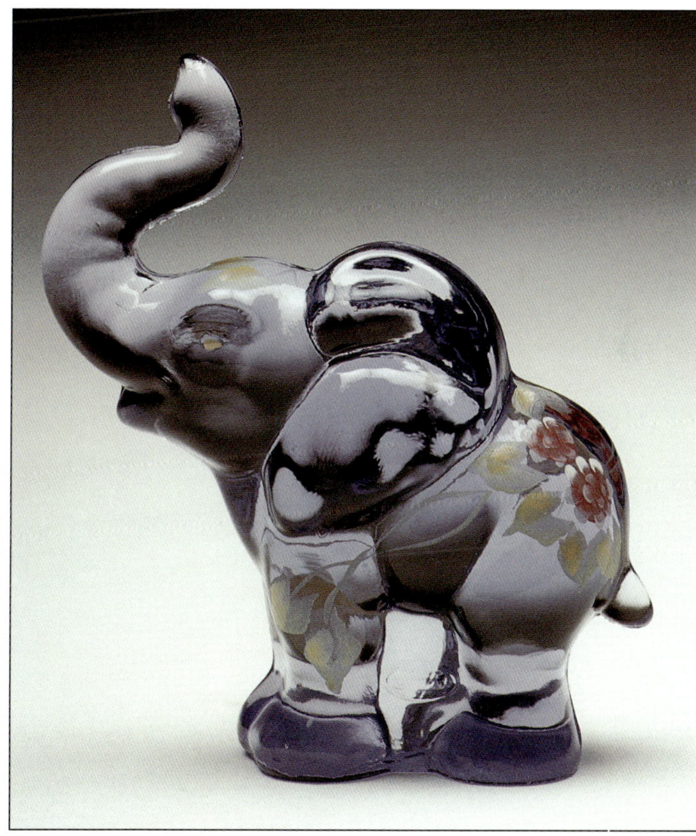

Standing Elephant, #5158L2, hand painted Lilacs on Violet, catalog exclusive, signed by Lynn Fenton Art Glass Company, 3.6" tall, 3" long, Circa 2001, **$45.00**

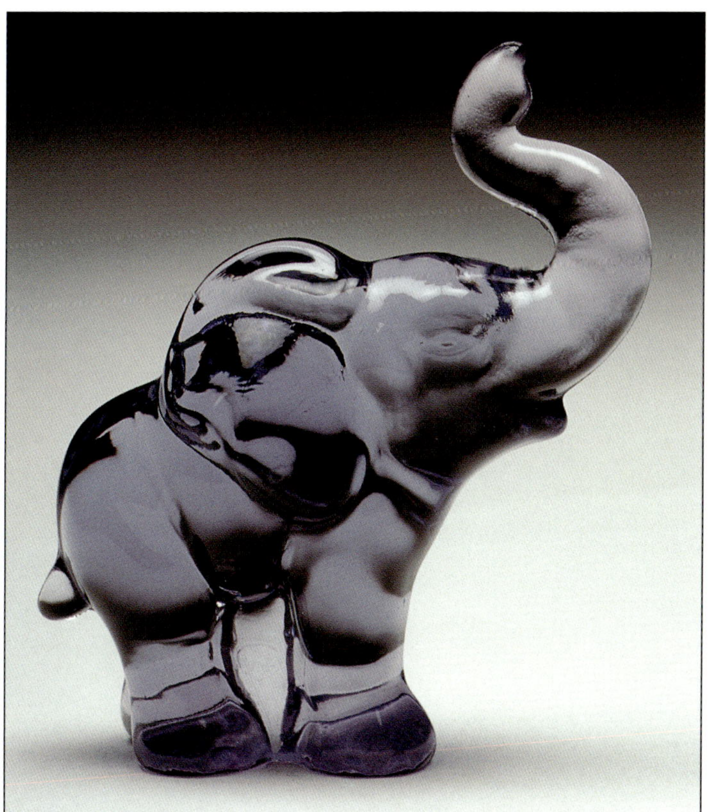

Standing Elephant #5158OE, not in Fenton's regular line, Violet, made for Fenton Gift Shop, 3.75" tall, 3.5" long, Circa 2001, **$30.00**

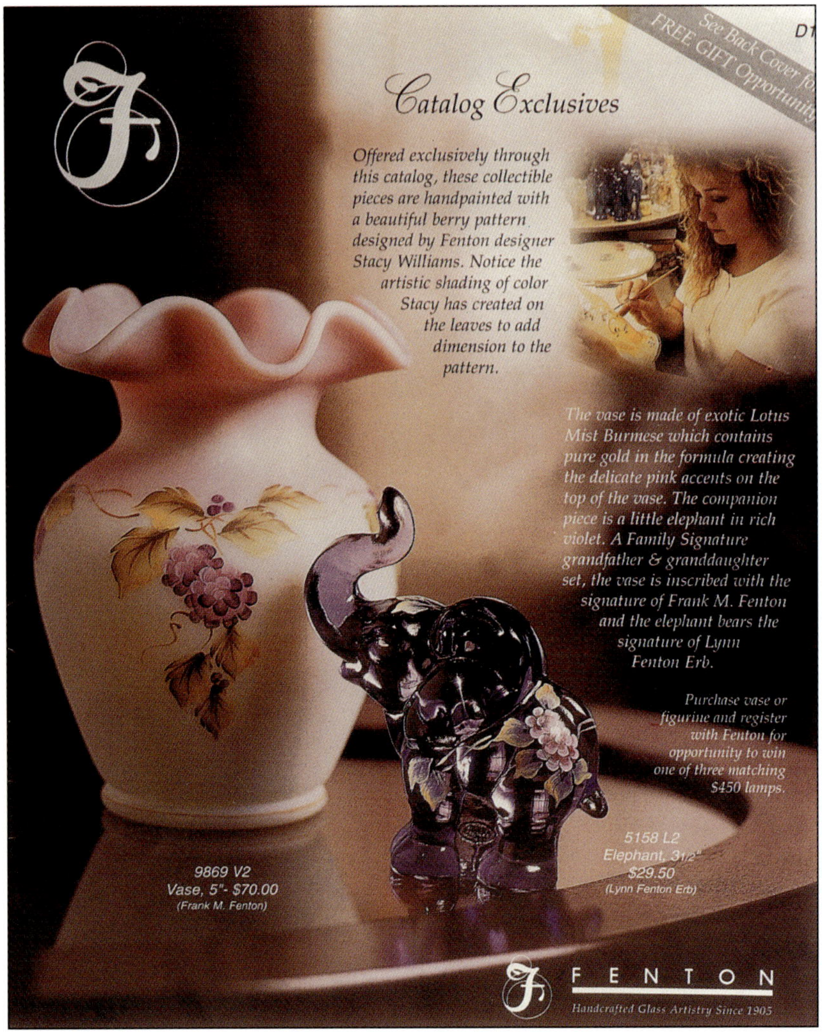

D1

See Back Cover for FREE GIFT Opportunity

Catalog Exclusives

Offered exclusively through this catalog, these collectible pieces are handpainted with a beautiful berry pattern designed by Fenton designer Stacy Williams. Notice the artistic shading of color Stacy has created on the leaves to add dimension to the pattern.

The vase is made of exotic Lotus Mist Burmese which contains pure gold in the formula creating the delicate pink accents on the top of the vase. The companion piece is a little elephant in rich violet. A Family Signature grandfather & granddaughter set, the vase is inscribed with the signature of Frank M. Fenton and the elephant bears the signature of Lynn Fenton Erb.

Purchase vase or figurine and register with Fenton for opportunity to win one of three matching $450 lamps.

9869 V2
Vase, 5"- $70.00
(Frank M. Fenton)

5158 L2
Elephant, 3 1/2"
$29.50
(Lynn Fenton Erb)

FENTON
Handcrafted Glass Artistry Since 1905

Original mini catalog cover page showing the two exclusive pieces, the Violet elephant and Lotus Mist vase. Reprinted with permission of Fenton Art Glass Company

Below left:
Standing Elephant, #5158SW, not in Fenton's regular line, Sunset, 3.6" tall, 3" long, Circa 2002, **$35.00**

Below:
Standing Elephant, #5158S6, Baroque Floral, hand painted on Sunset, 3.75" tall, 3.5" long, Circa 2002, **$48.00**

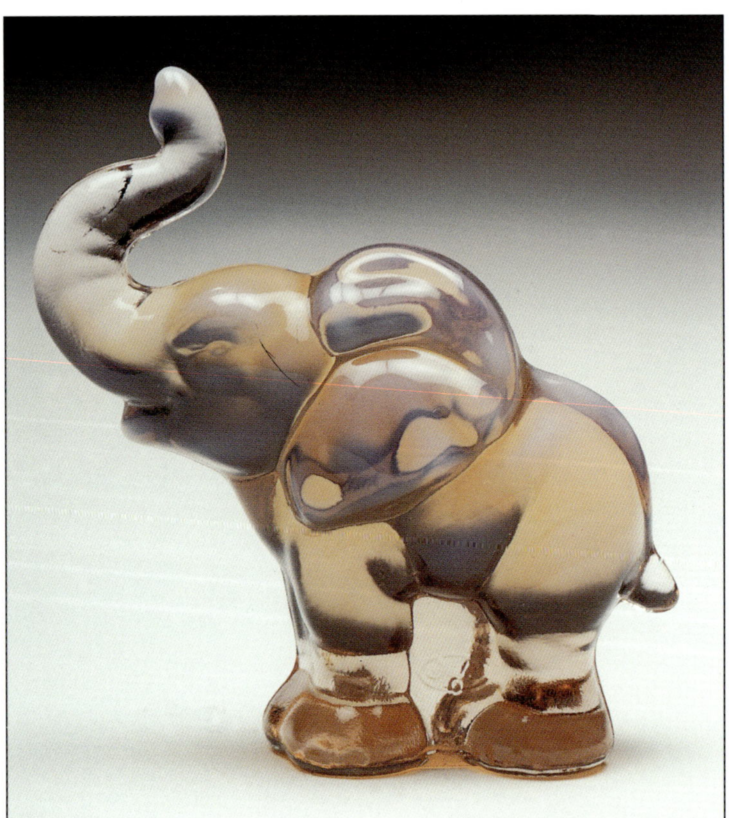

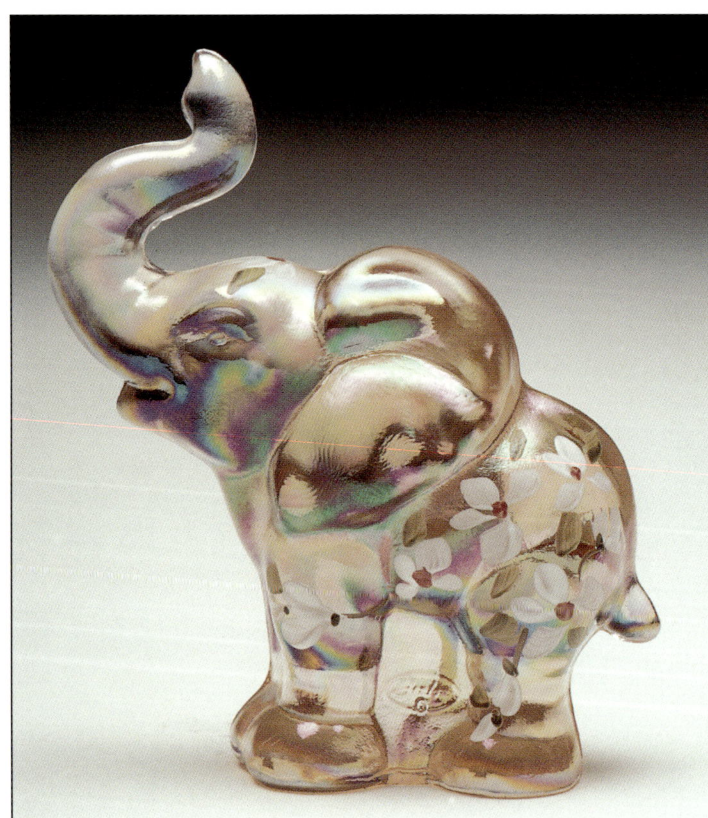

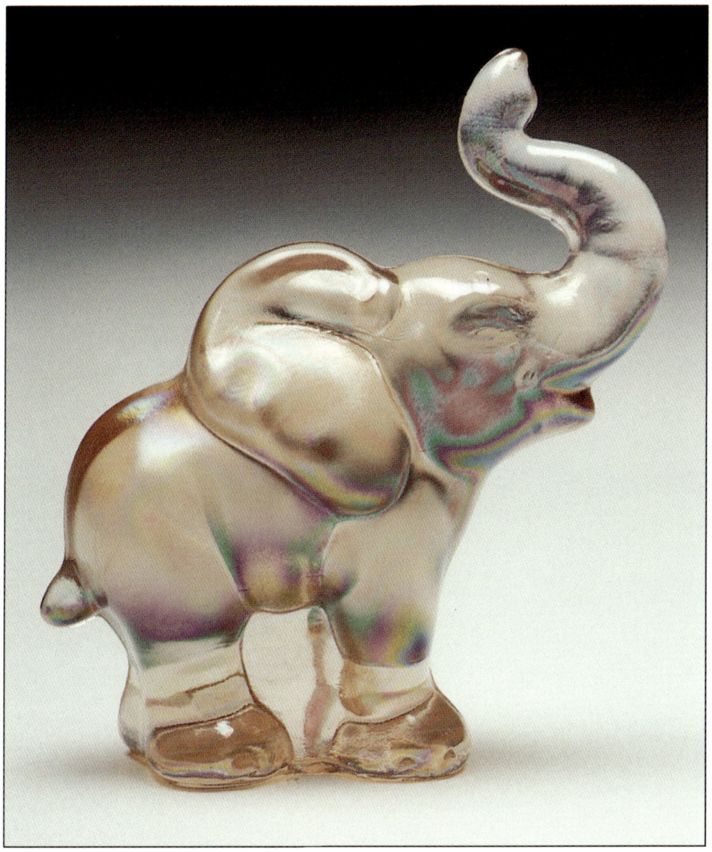

Standing Elephant, #5158SX, Sunset Iridized, 3.75" tall, 3.5" long, Circa 2002, **$38.00**

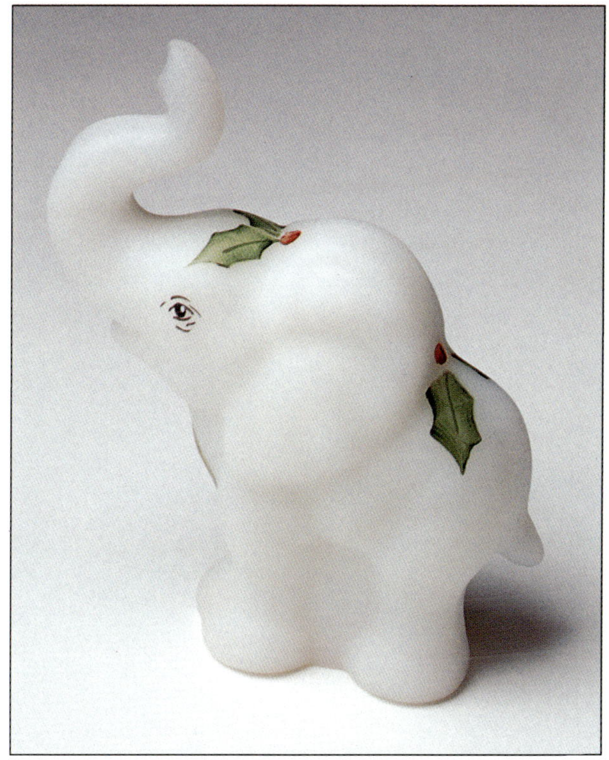

Standing Elephant, #5158, not in Fenton's regular line, Holly hand painted for a special order on Opal with satin finish, 3.75" tall, 3.5" long, Circa 2002, **$55.00**

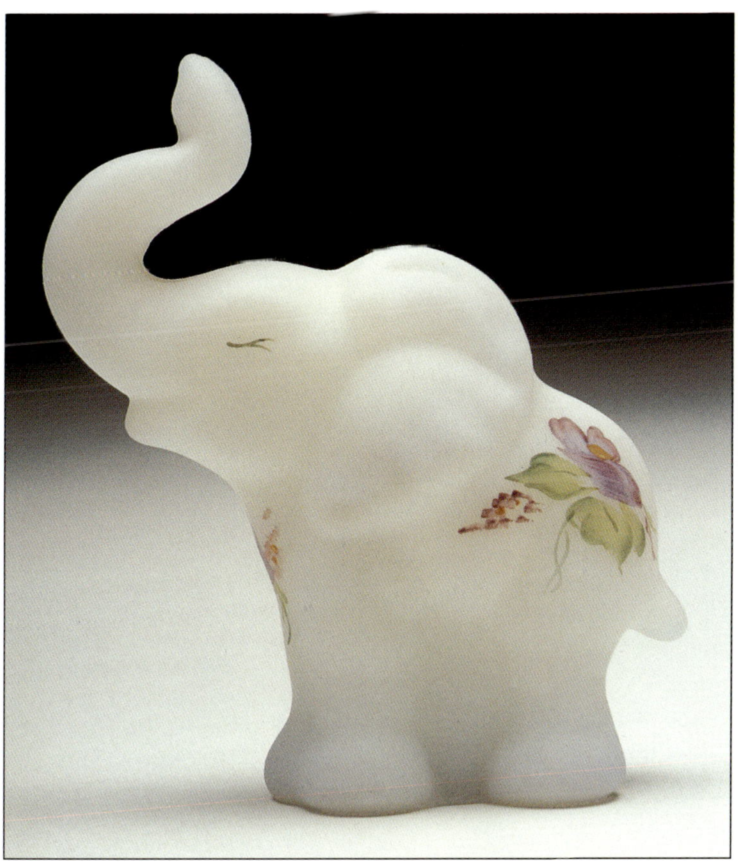

Standing Elephant, #5158, not in Fenton's regular line, Purple Flowers hand painted for a special order on Opal with satin finish, 3.75" tall, 3.5" long, Circa 2002, **$50.00**

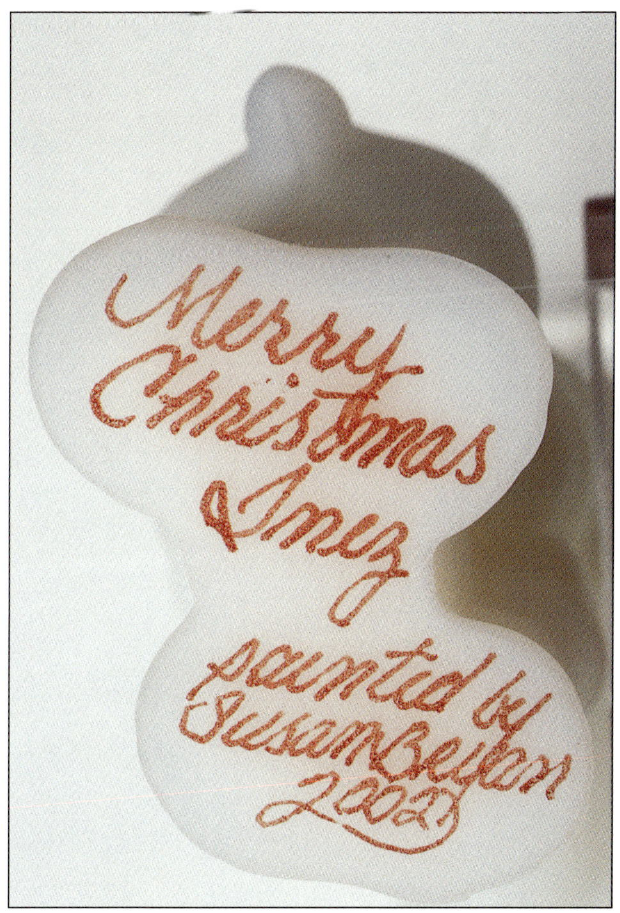

Standing Elephant, #5158, bottom of Holly decorated marked "Merry Christmas Inez Painted by Susan Bryan 2002"

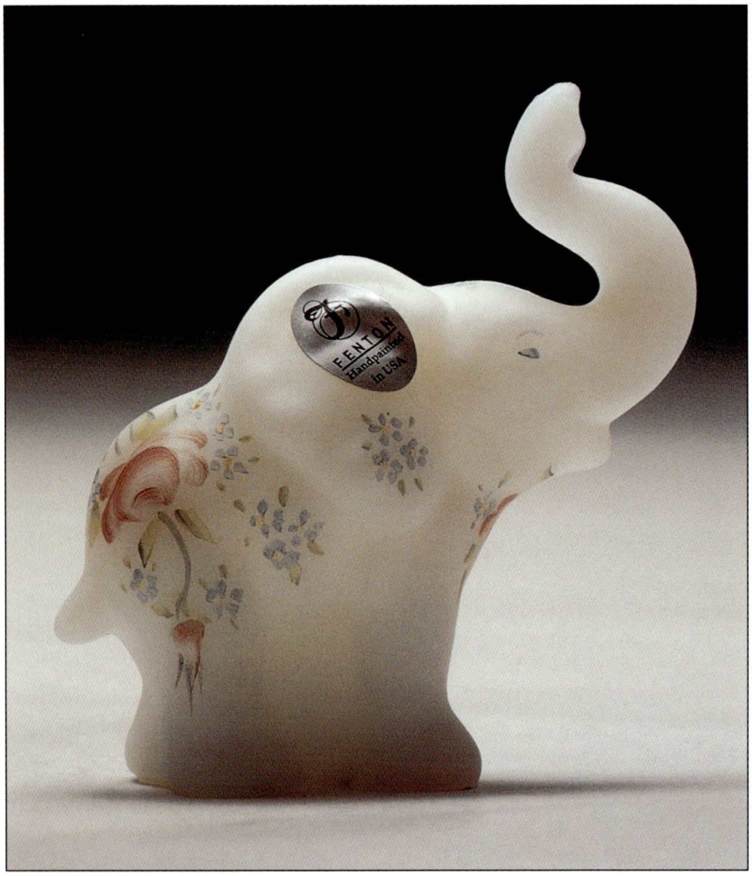

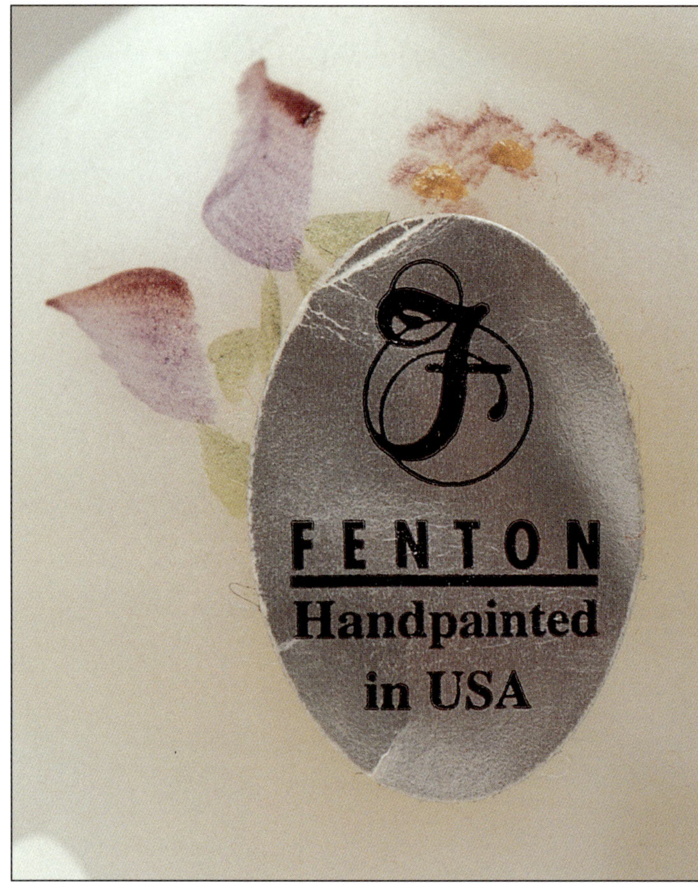

original oval silver label

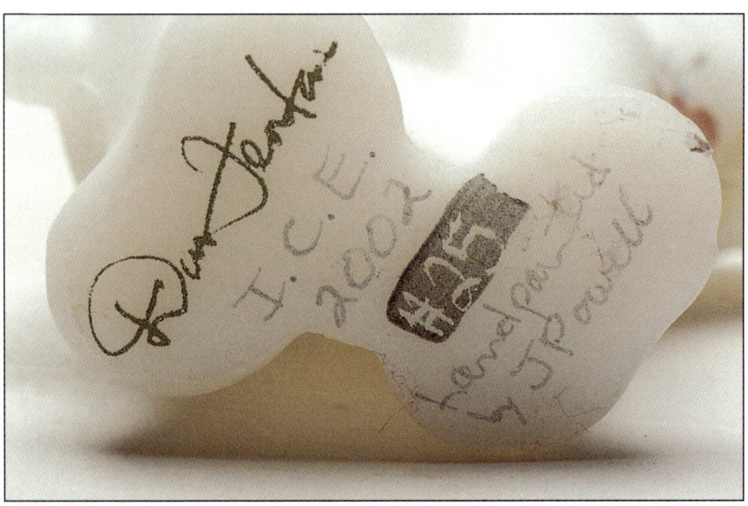

Standing elephant, #1518, flowers on opal, 3.75: tall, 3.5: long, lade for I. C. E., signed by Don Fenton, 2002. **$50.00**

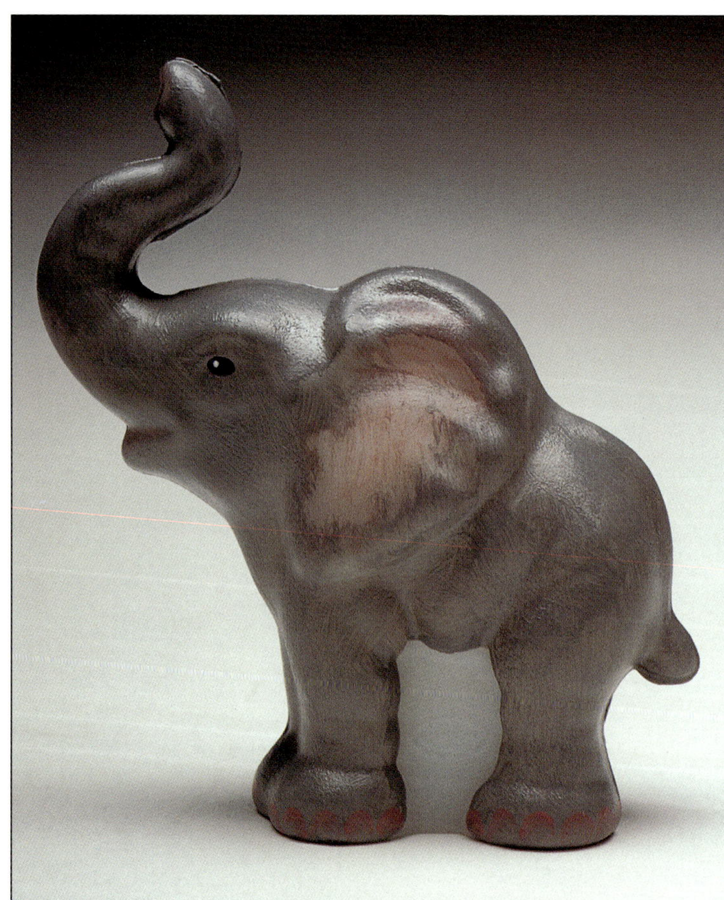

Standing Elephant, #5158, Natural gray with pink ears, made for Collectors Showcase, limited edition of 49, 3.8" tall, 3.5" long, Circa 2002, **$65.00**

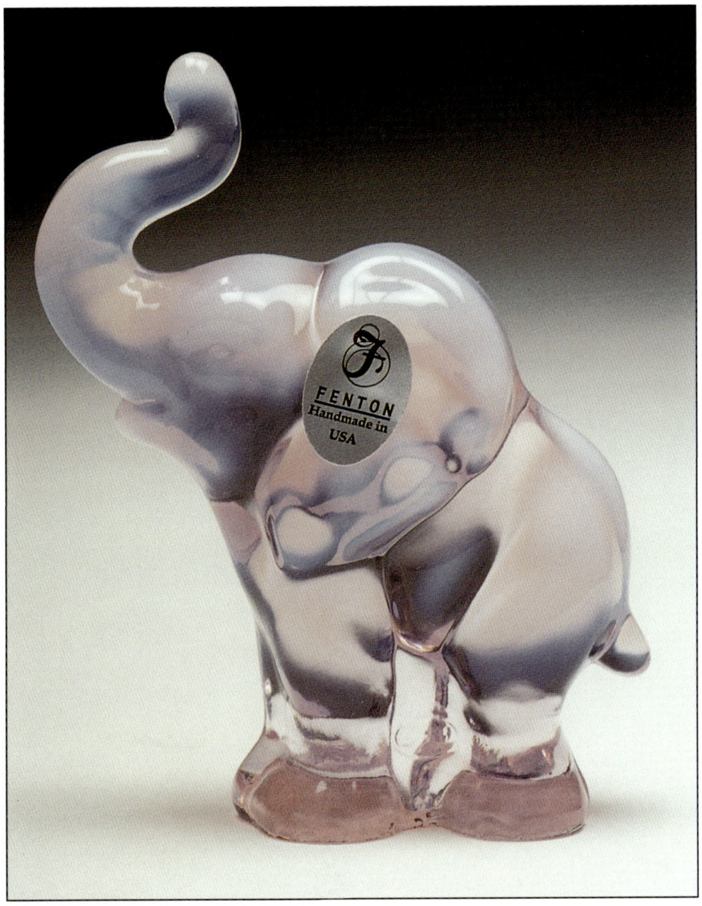

Standing Elephant, #5158NZ, Rose Milk Opalescent (note, variation in opalescent reheating effect), 3.75" tall, 3"long, Circa 2003, **$18.00**

Standing Elephant, #5158NZ, Rose Milk Opalescent (note, variation in opalescent reheating effect), 3.8" tall, 3.25" long, Circa 2003, **$18.00**

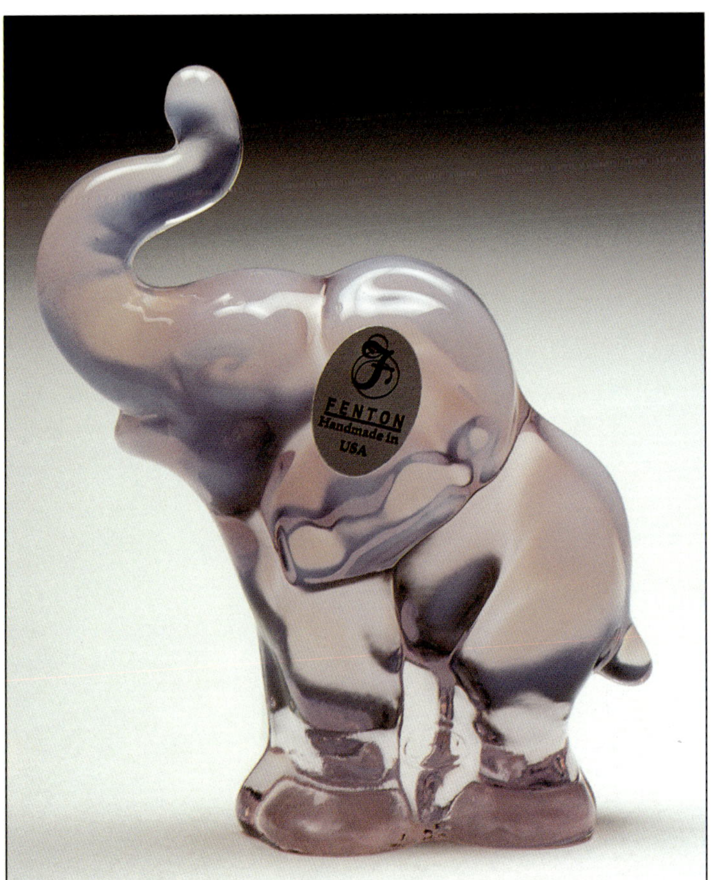

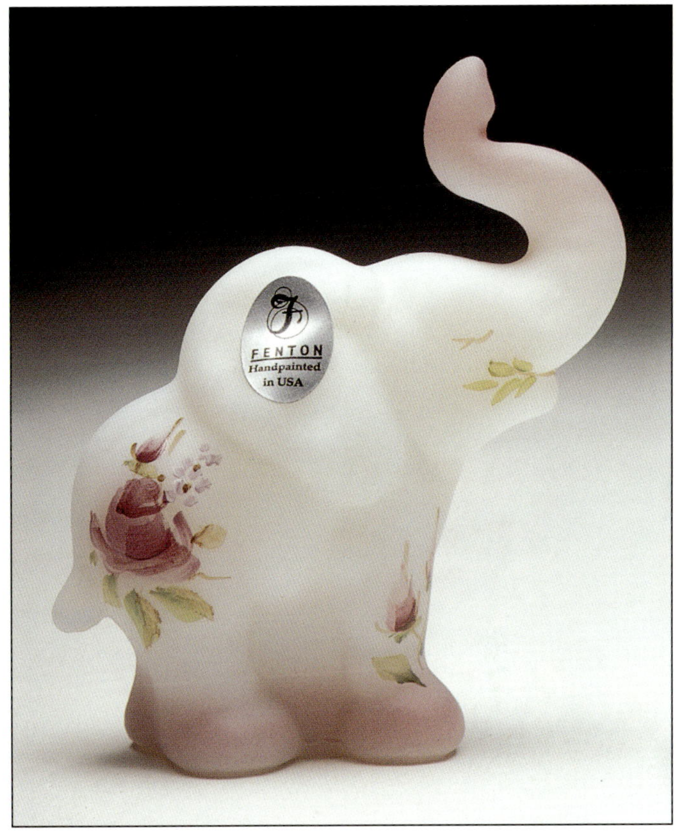

Standing elephant, #1518WP, Lilacs and Roses, 3.8" tall, 3.5" long, 2003 **$29.50**

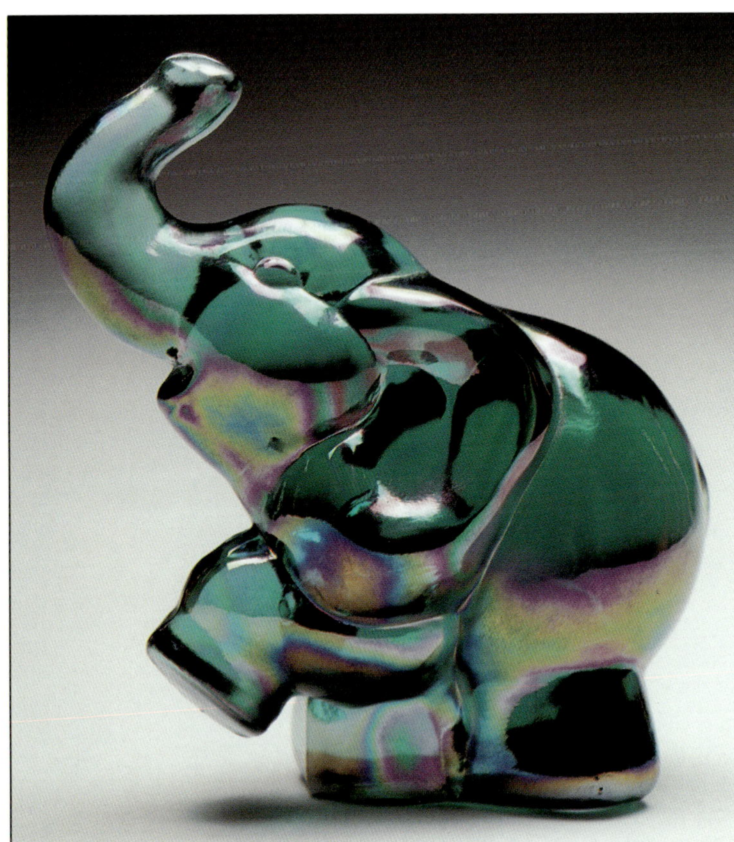

Circus Elephant, #5136SS, Spruce Green Carnival, 3.25" tall, 3.75" long, Circa 1995, **$18.00**

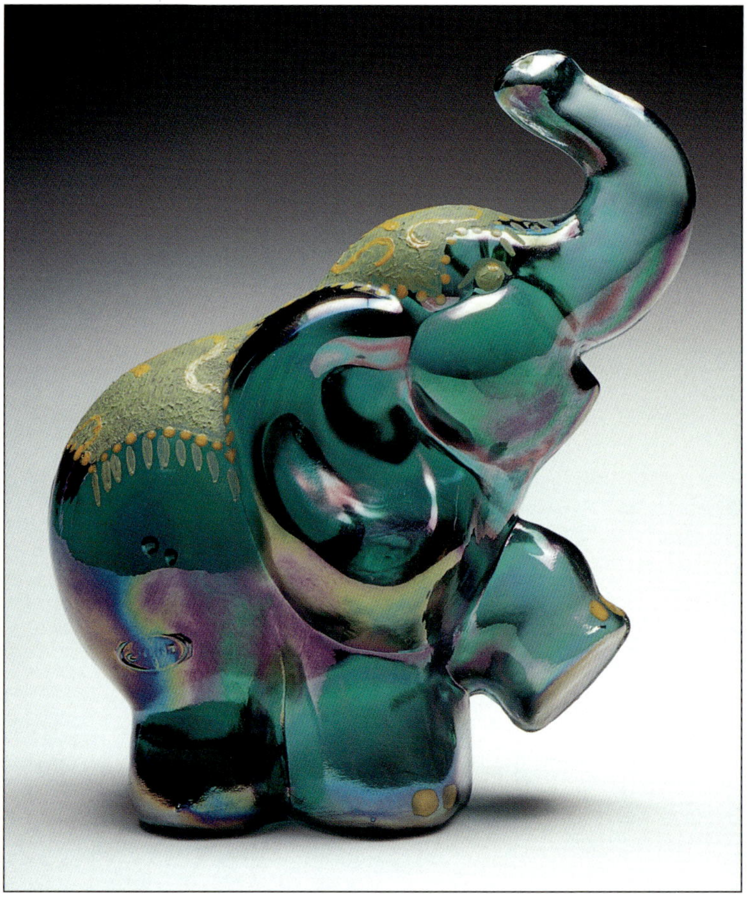

Circus Elephant, #5136SS, not in Fenton's regular line, Spruce Green Carnival hand painted with yellow and green blanket, 3.25" tall, 3.75" long, Circa 1995, **$45.00**

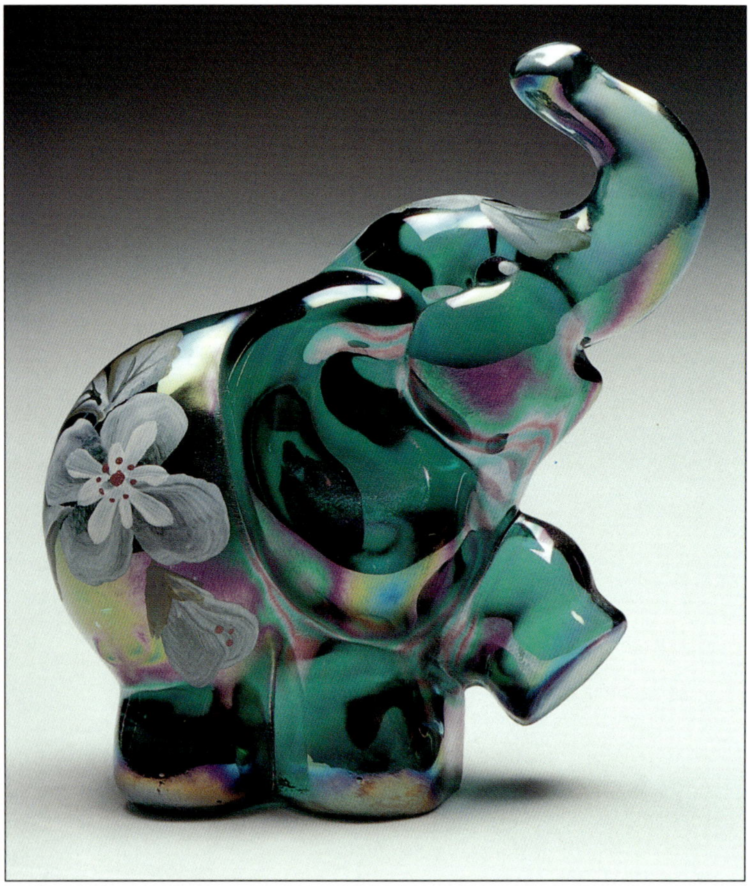

Circus Elephant, #C5136L6, Spruce Green Carnival hand painted, 3.25" tall, 3.75" long, QVC item June 1995, **$28.00**

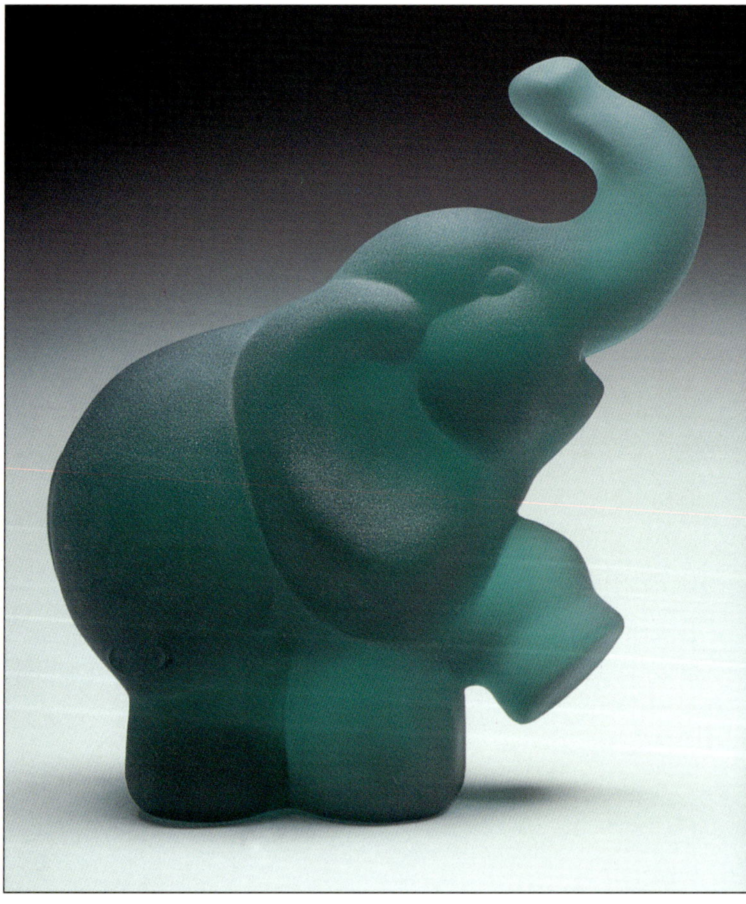

Circus Elephant, #5136SO, not in Fenton's regular line, Spruce Green with satin finish, 3.25" tall, 3.75" long, Circa 1995, **$30.00**

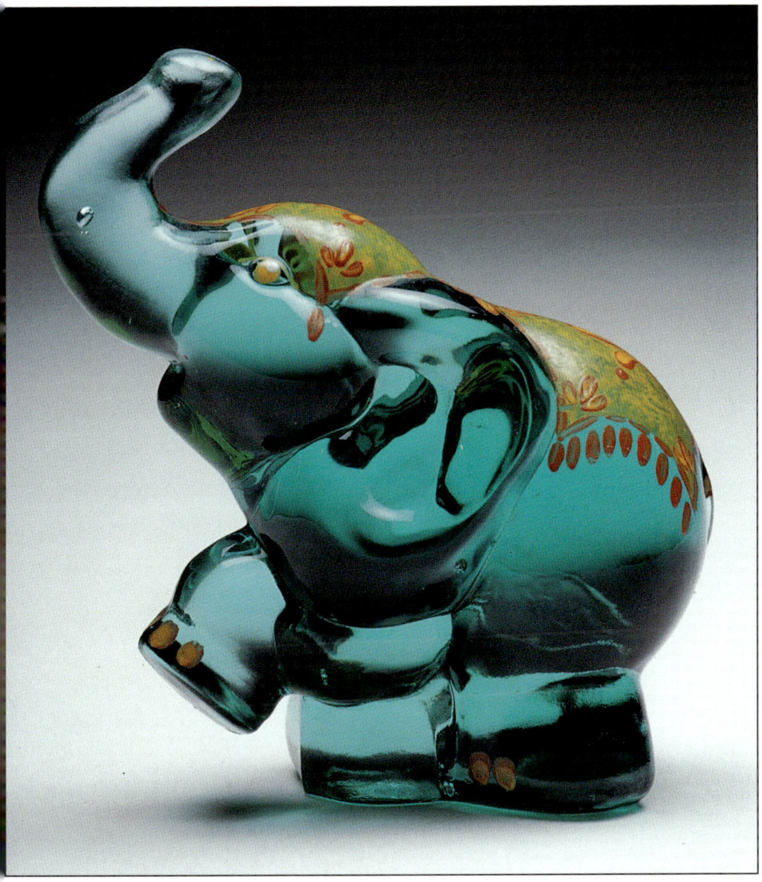

Circus Elephant, #5136, not in Fenton's regular line, Spruce Green, hand painted with orange and green blanket, #56, 3.25" tall, 3.75" long, Circa 1995, **$45.00**

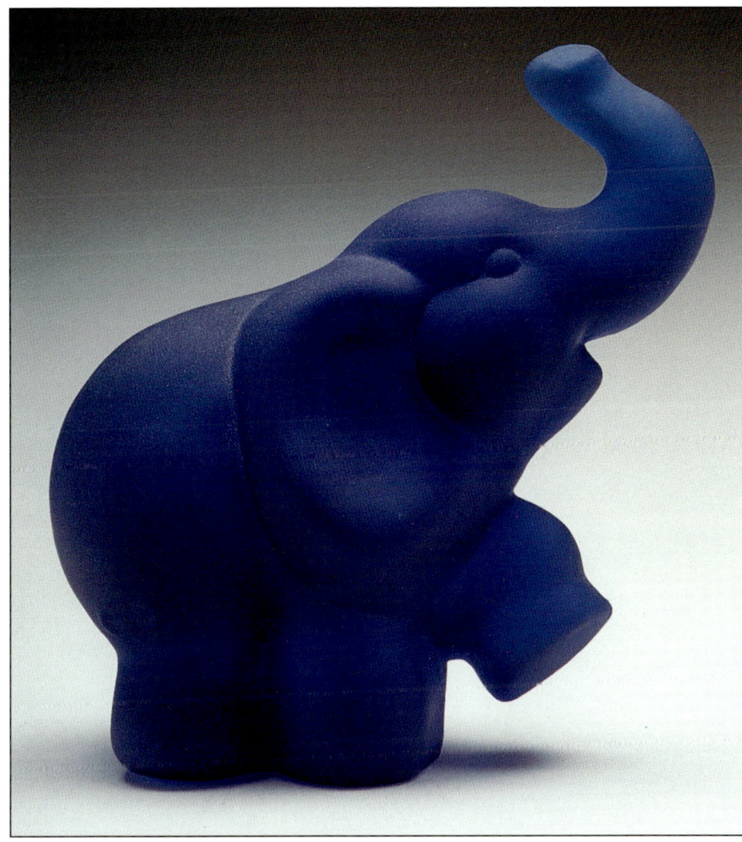

Circus Elephant, #5136KN, Cobalt with satin finish, 3.25" tall, 3.75" long, Circa 1995-96, **$24.00**

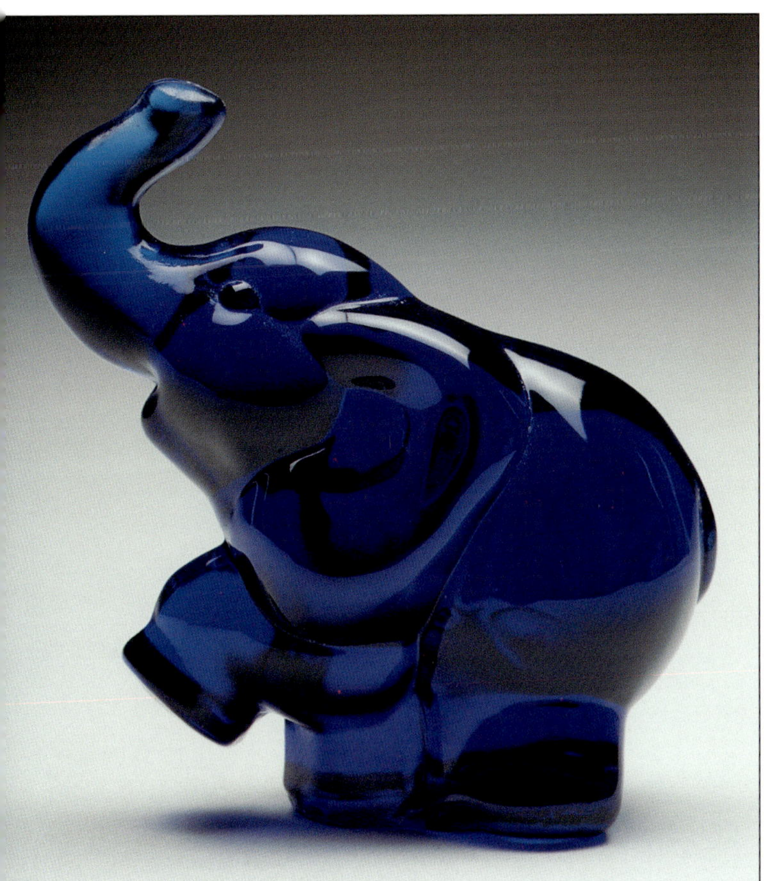

Circus Elephant, #5136KN, Cobalt, 3.25" tall, 3.75" long, Circa 1995-96, **$20.00**

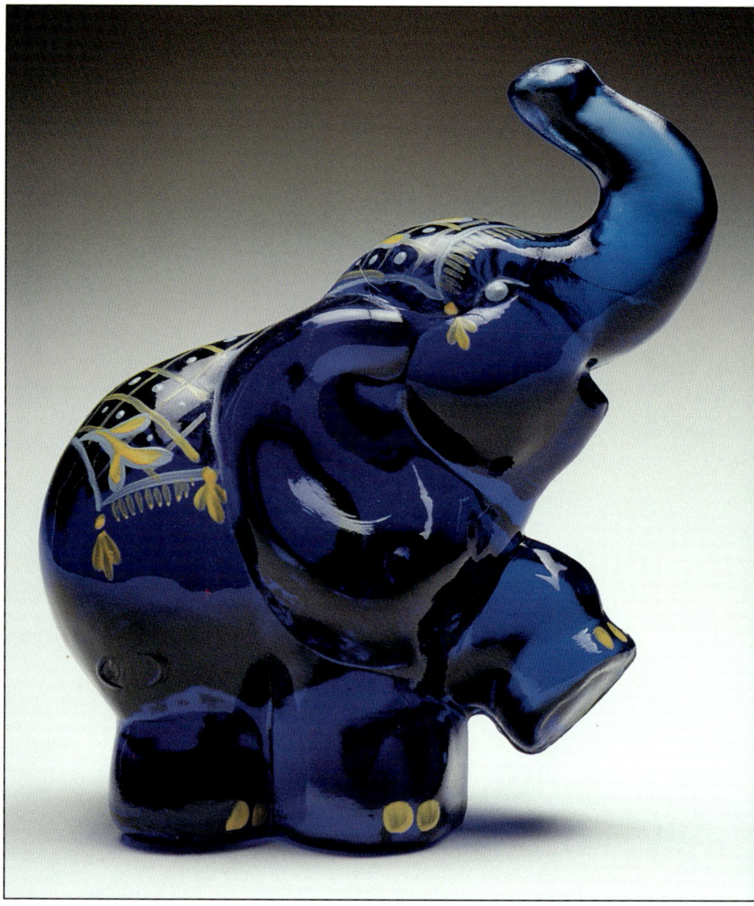

Circus Elephant, #5136, not in Fenton's regular line, Cobalt hand painted with yellow and blue checkered blanket, 3.25" tall, 3.75" long, Circa 1995-96, **$48.00**

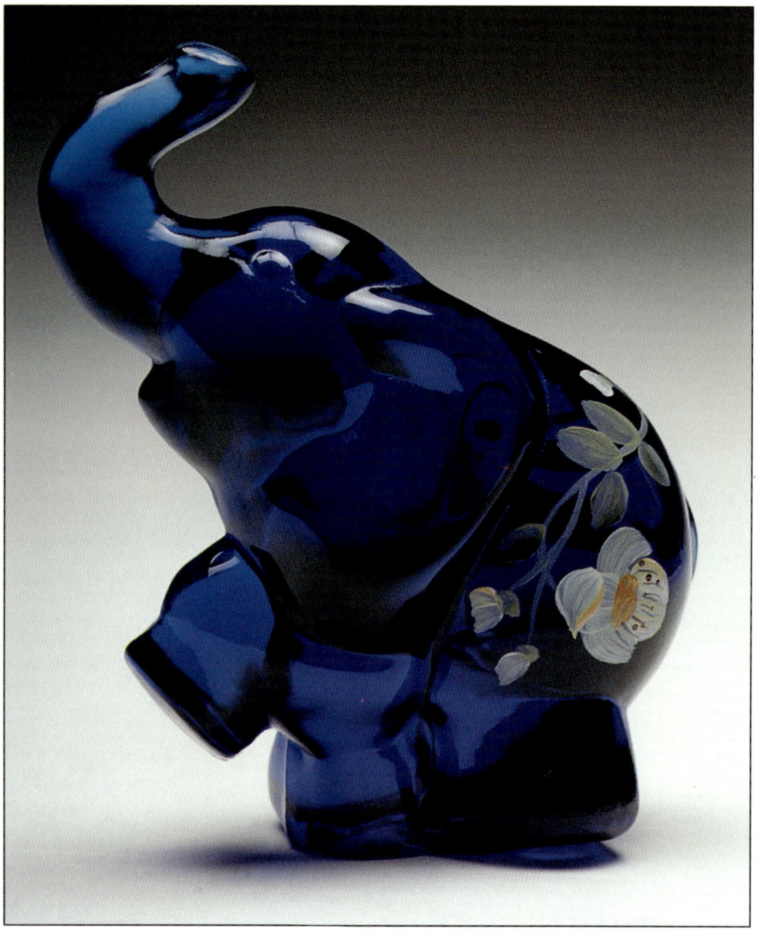

Circus Elephant, #5136KG, Golden Flax on Cobalt, 3.25" tall, 3.75" long, Circa 1995-96, **$35.00**

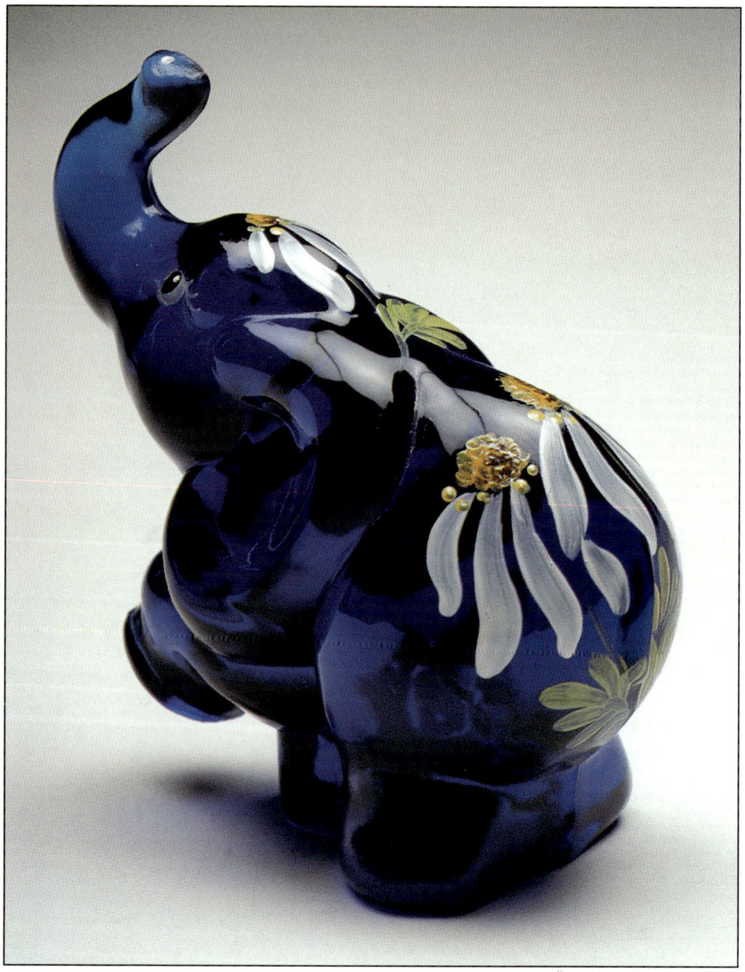

Circus Elephant, #5136, Cobalt, hand painted with white daisies, 3.25" tall, 3.75" long, Circa 1995-96, **$45.00**

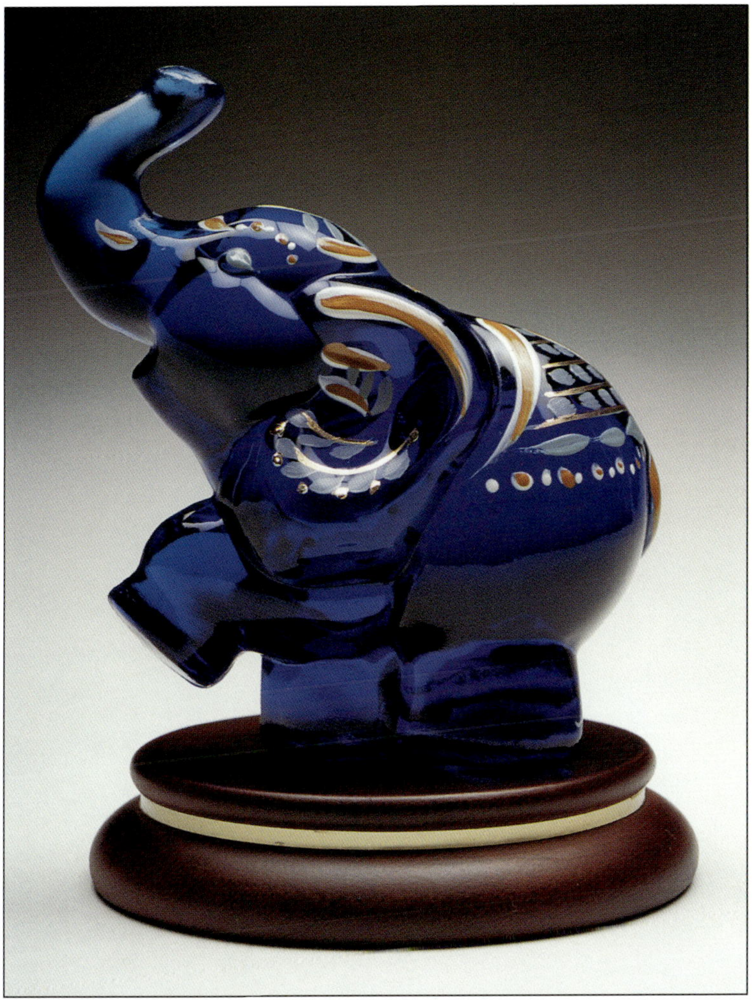

Circus Elephant, #5136X8, cobalt hand painted, Medallion collection, 3.25" tall, 3.75" long, Circa 1996-97, **$75.00**

Circus Elephant, #5136X8, cobalt hand painted, Medallion collection, view of Medallion label on base and back view

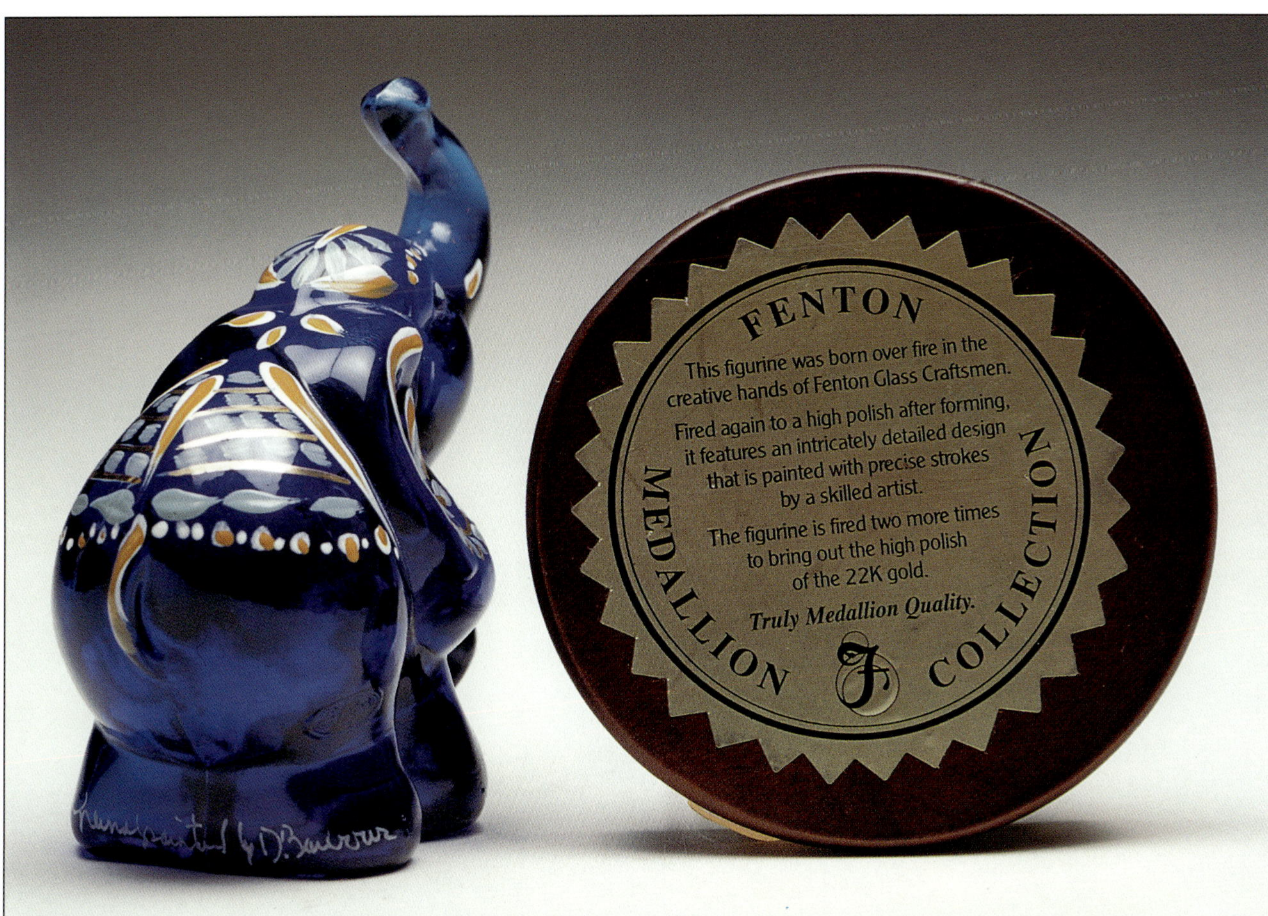

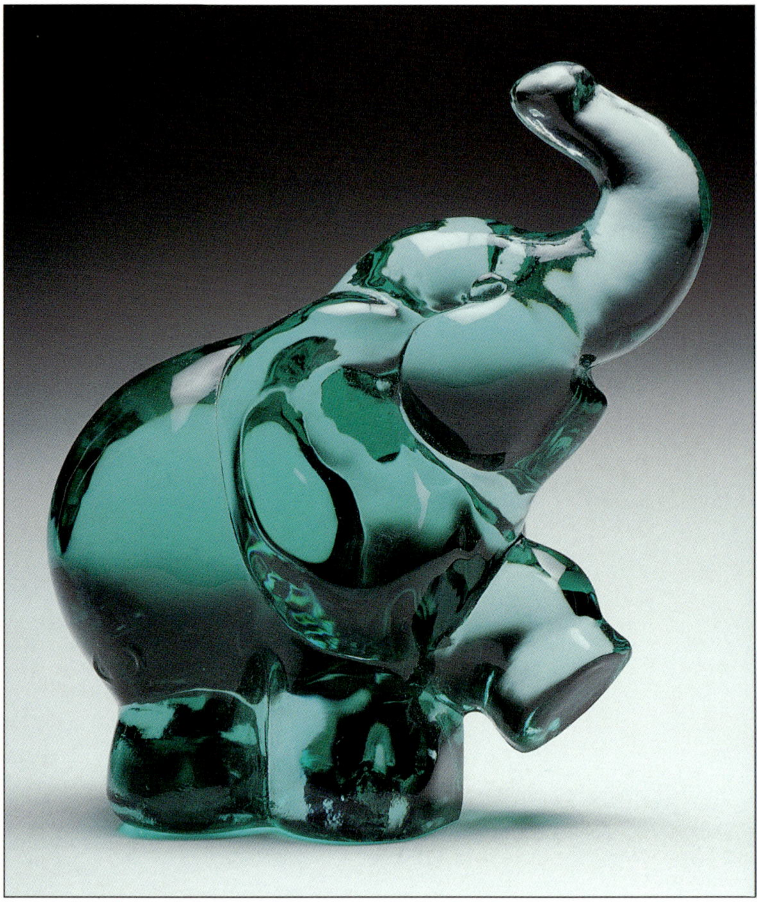

Circus Elephant, #5136LE, Sea Mist Green, 3.25" tall, 3.75" long, Circa 1996-97, **$20.00**

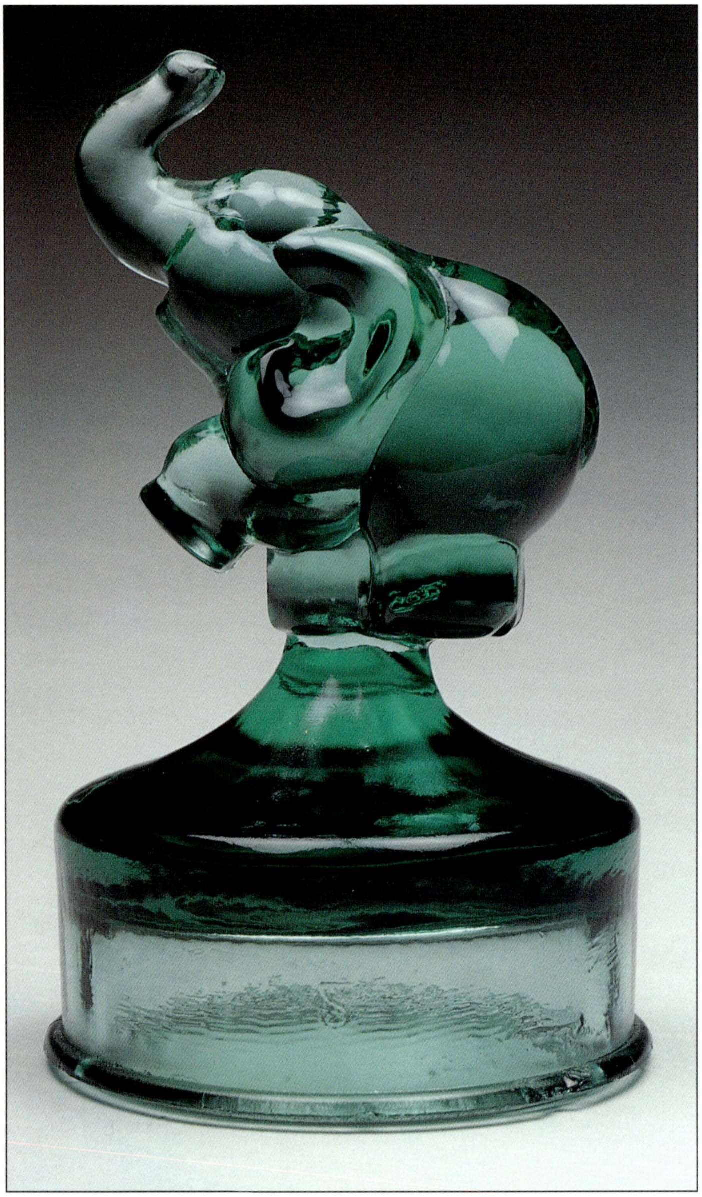

Circus elephant, #5136LE, Sea Mist Green on bust off base, 7" tall, 4" long, Circa 1997, **$75.00**

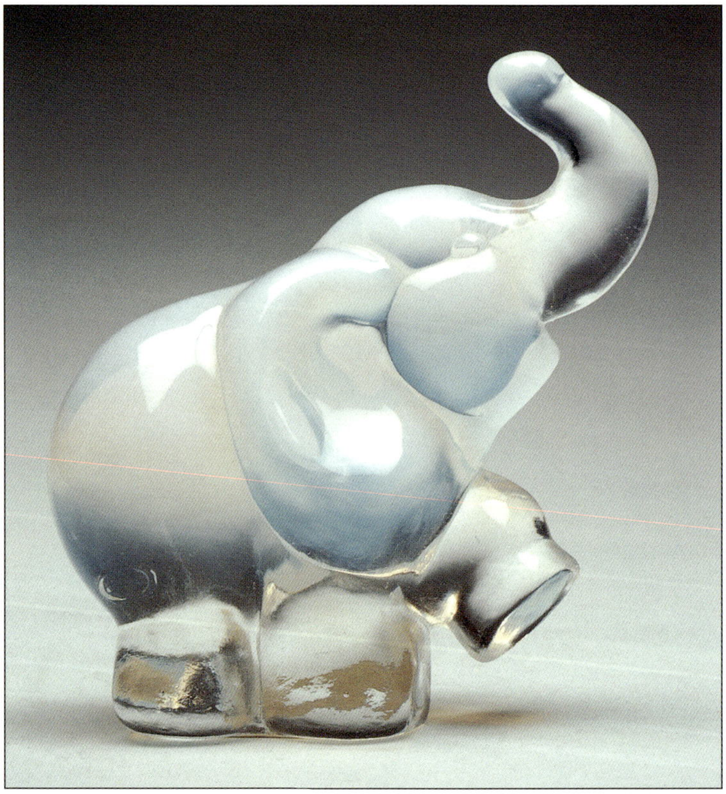

Circus elephant, #5136FO, not in Fenton's regular line, French Opalescent, 3.25" tall, 3.75" long, Circa 1997, **$30.00**

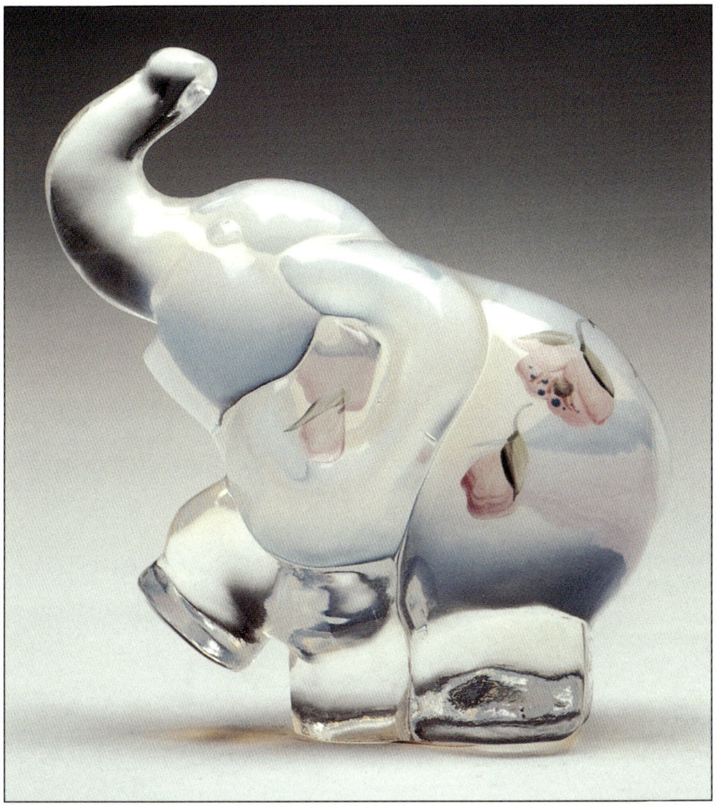

Circus elephant, #5136DX, Trellis, opalescent hand painted, 3.25" tall, 3.75" long, Circa 1997-99, **$35.00**

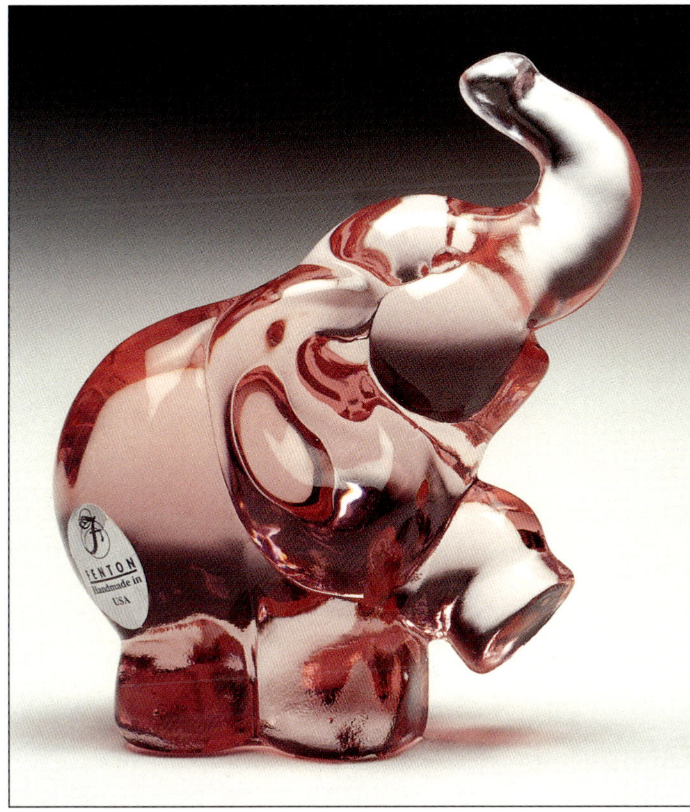

Circus Elephant #5136CP, Empress Rose, 3.25" tall, 3.75" long, Circa 1998-2000, **$18.00**

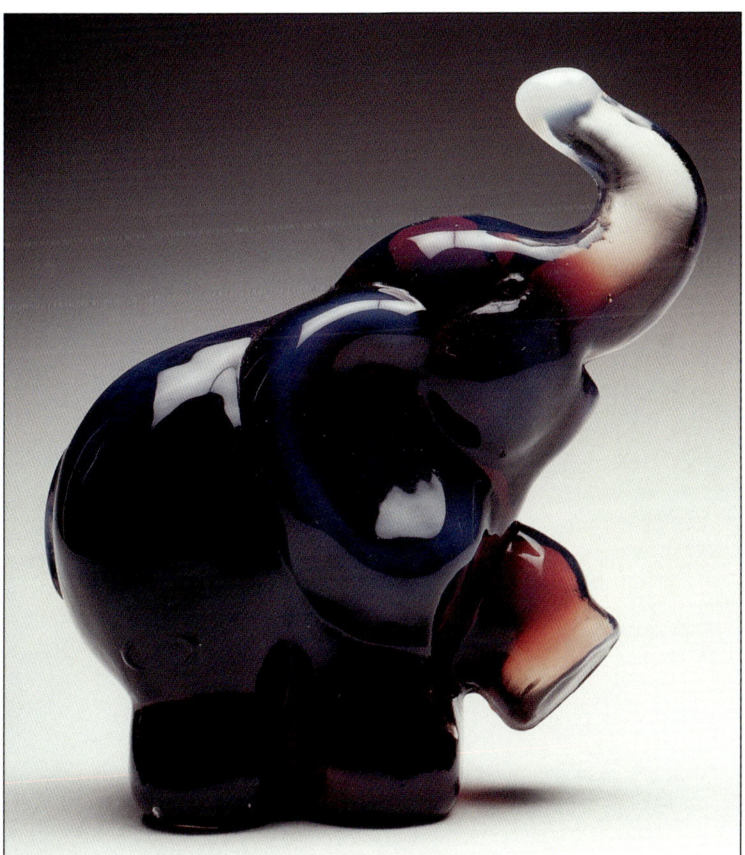

Circus Elephant, #5136PO, not in Fenton's regular line, Plum Opalescent, 3.25" tall, 3.75" long, Circa 1998, **$85.00**

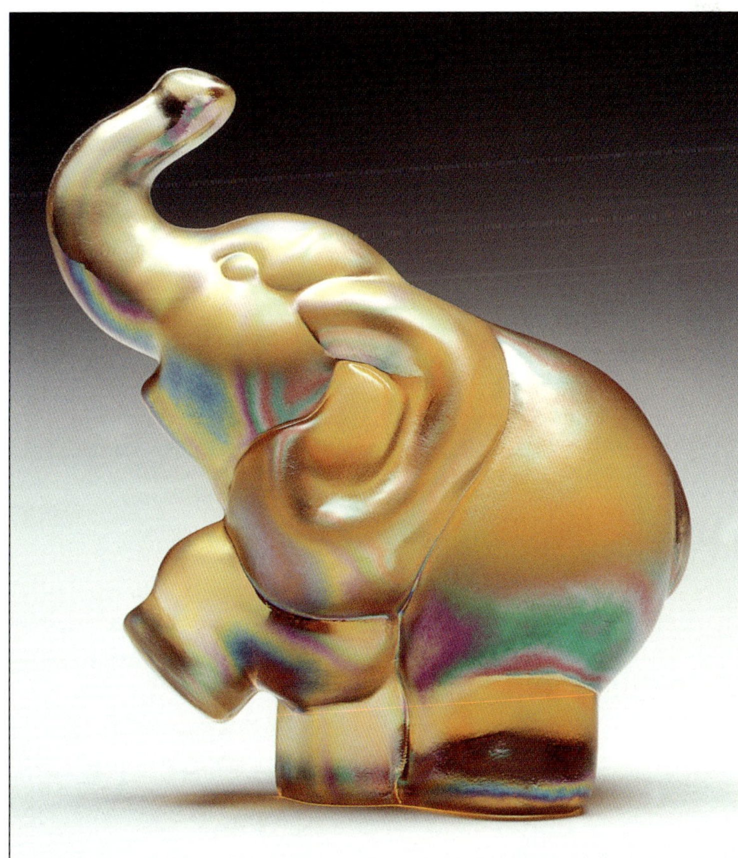

Circus elephant, #C5136CV, Iridized Gold, 3.25" tall, 3.75" long, QVC item, Circa 1998, **$30.00**

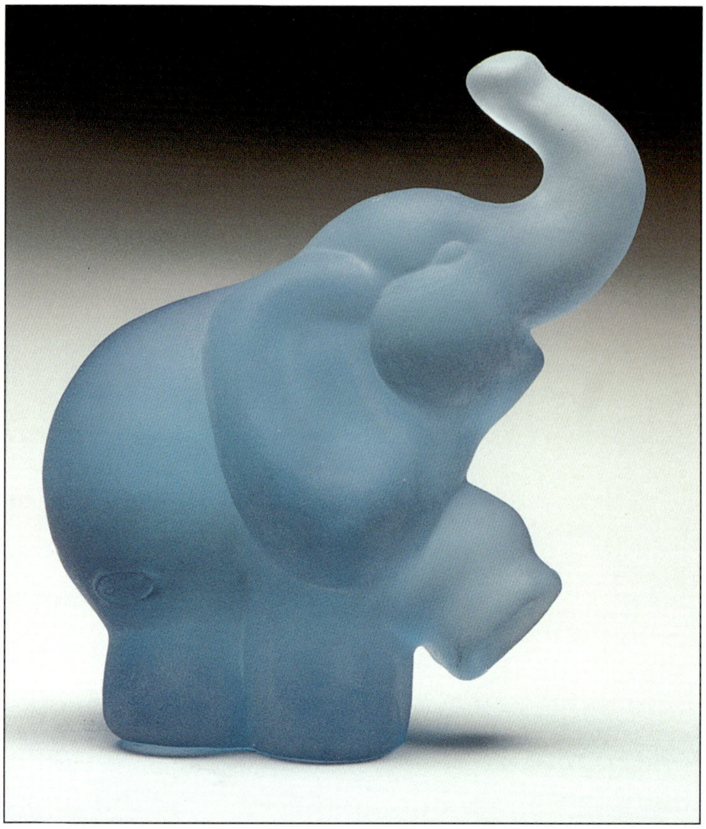

Circus Elephant #5136LC, not in Fenton's regular line, Ice Blue with satin finish, 3.25" tall, 3.75" long, Circa 2000, **$24.00**

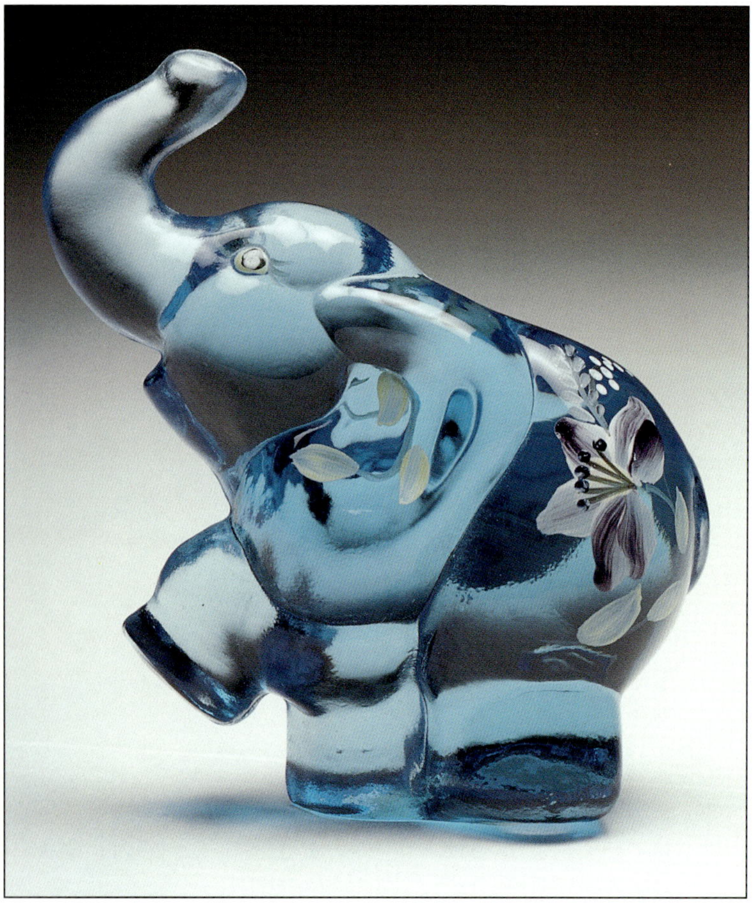

Circus elephant, #5136LH, Bell Flowers on Ice Blue, 3.25" tall, 3.75" long, Circa 1999, **$30.00**

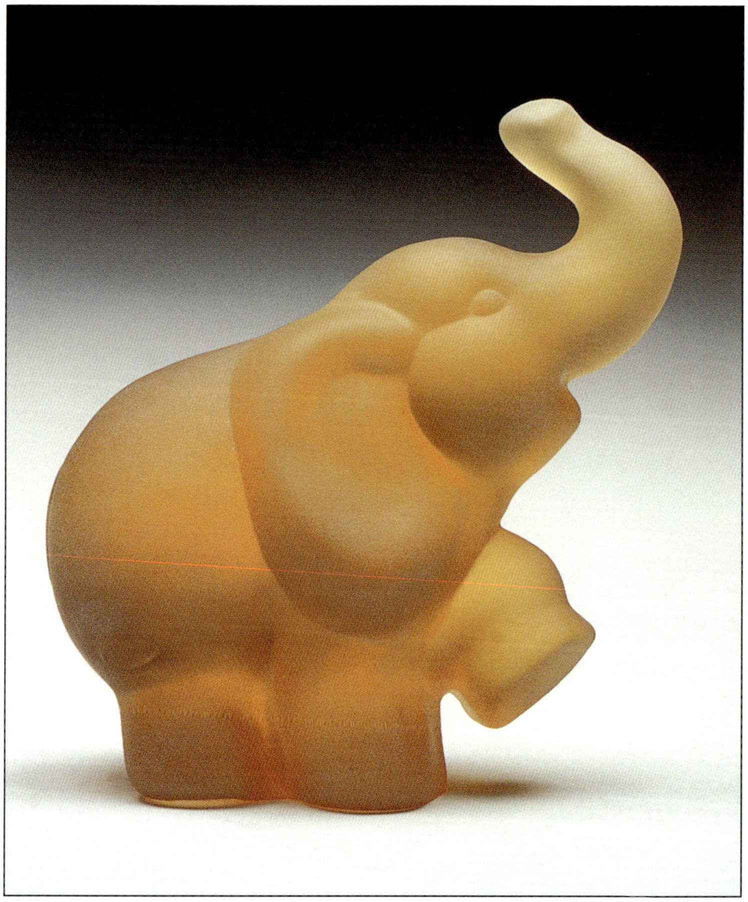

Circus Elephant #S5136GX, not in Fenton's regular line, Amber with satin finish, 3.25" tall, 3.75" long, Circa 2000. **$22.00**

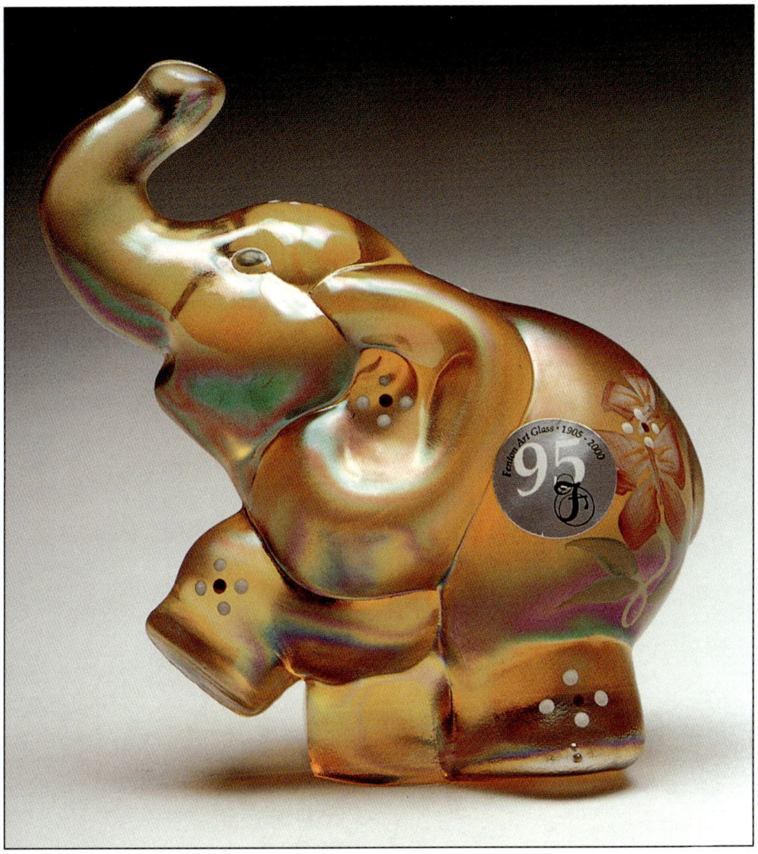

Circus Elephant #5136, Butterfly Garden on Gold, exclusive piece for Fenton Art Glass Company open house with Shelly Fenton signature, 3.25" tall, 3.75" long, Circa 2000, **$45.00**

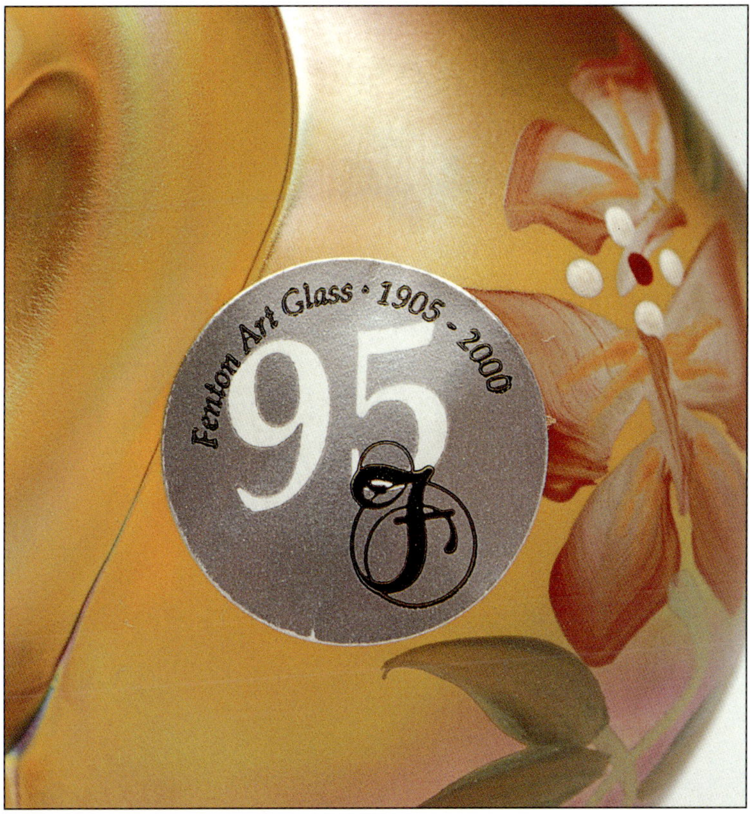

original label of 95th anniversary 1905 -2000

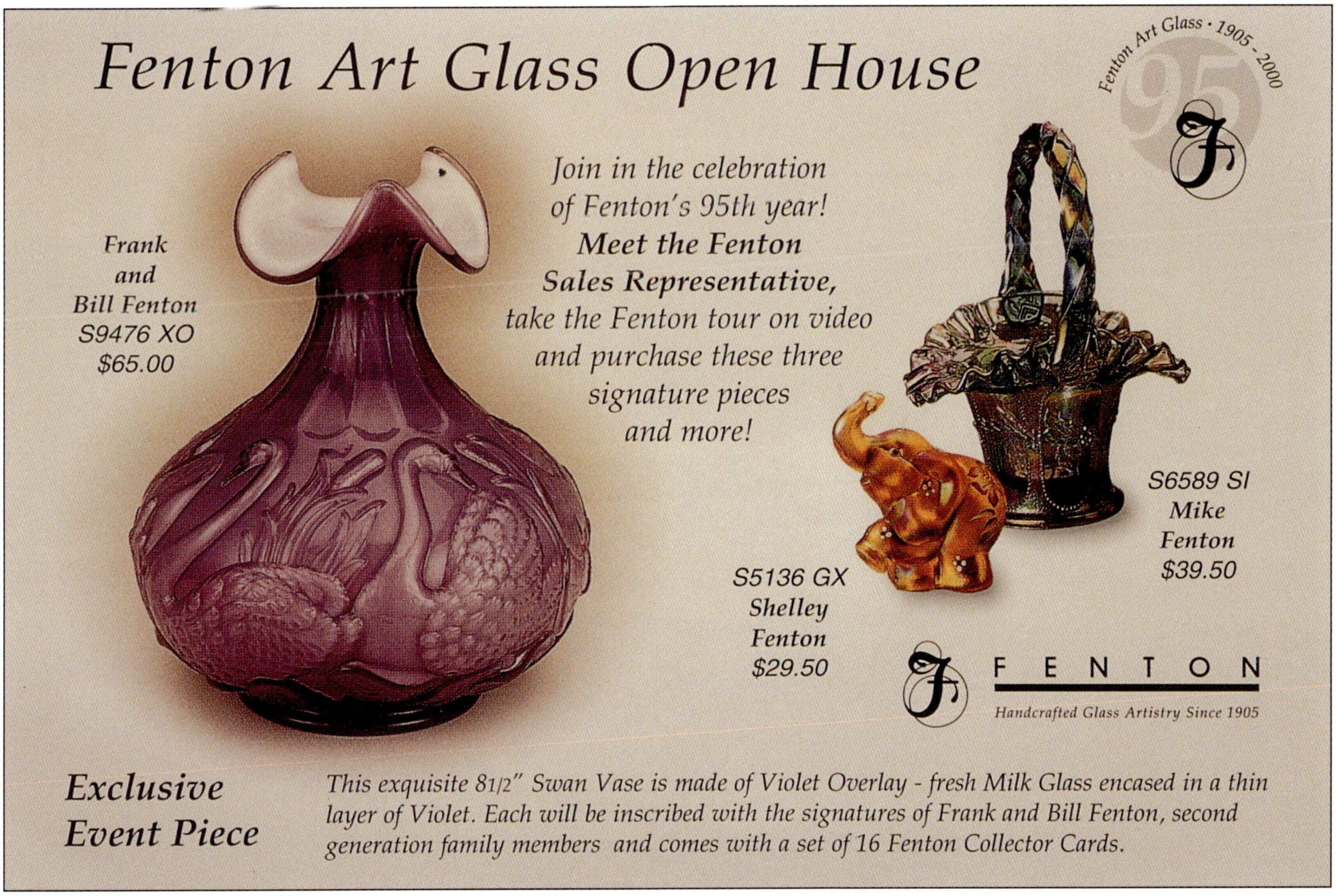

Original brochure of Fenton Open House showing the elephant. Reprinted with permission of Fenton Art Glass Company

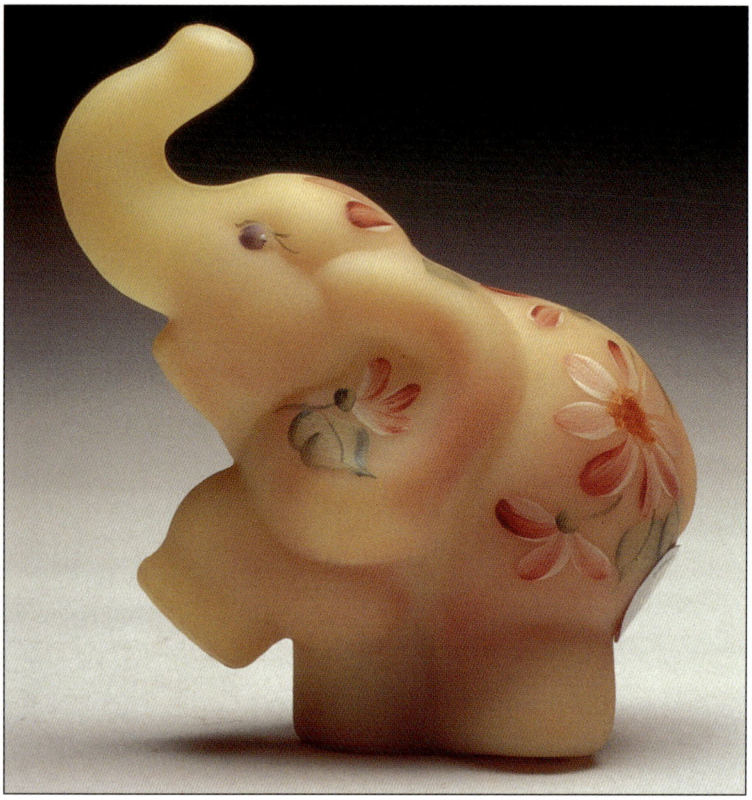

Circus Elephant #C51364N, Burmese hand painted with Daisies for QVC, 3.75" tall, 3.5" long, Circa 2000, **$45.00**

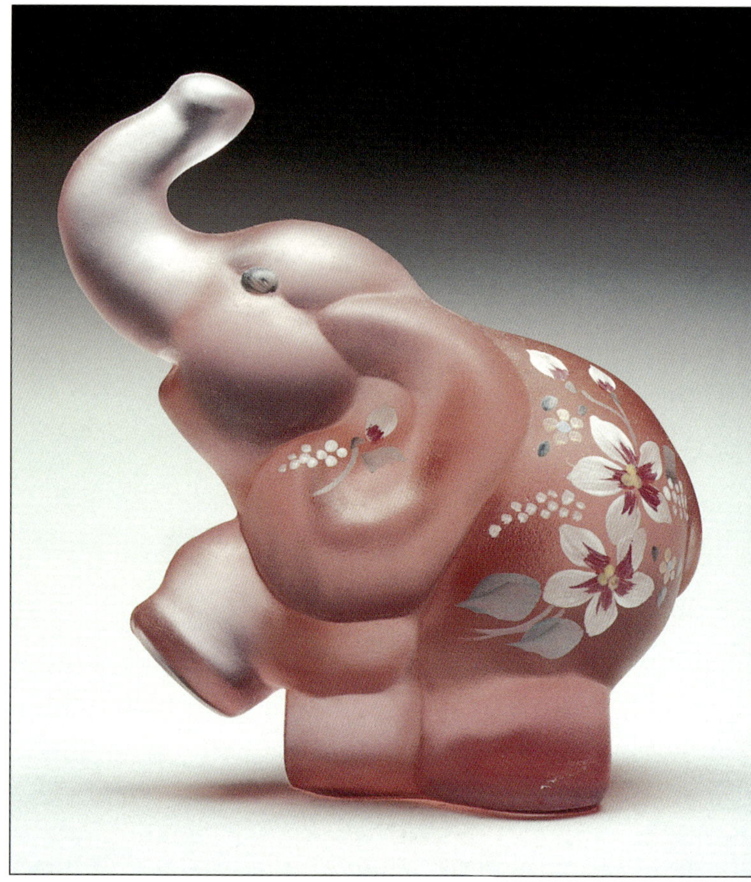

Circus Elephant #5136CD, hand painted Daisies on Empress Rose with satin finish, 3.25" tall, 3.75" long, Circa 2001, **$28.00**

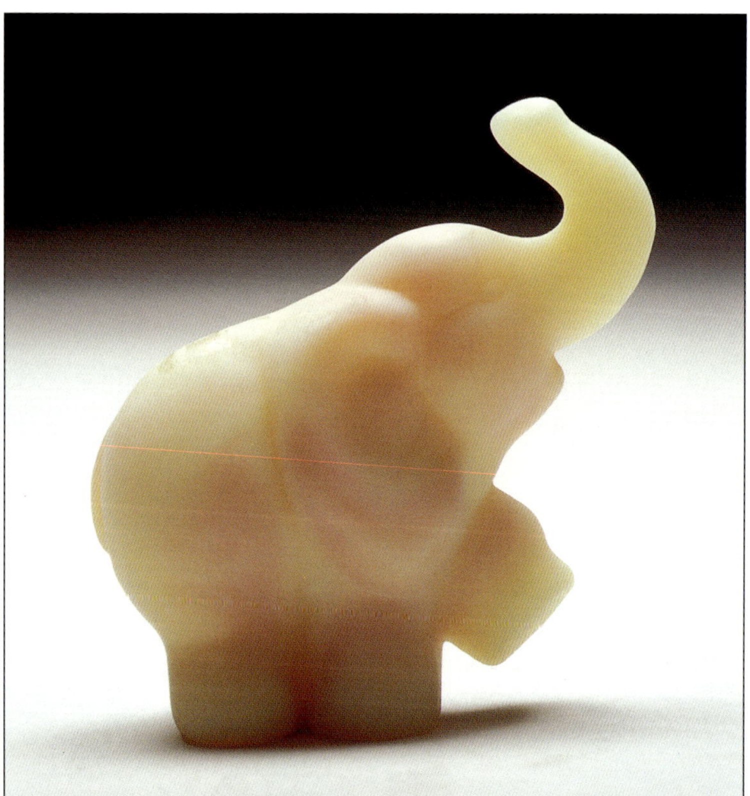

Circus elephant, #5135BR, Burmese, 3.75" tall, 3.5" long, Fenton gift shop, 2002. **$35.00**

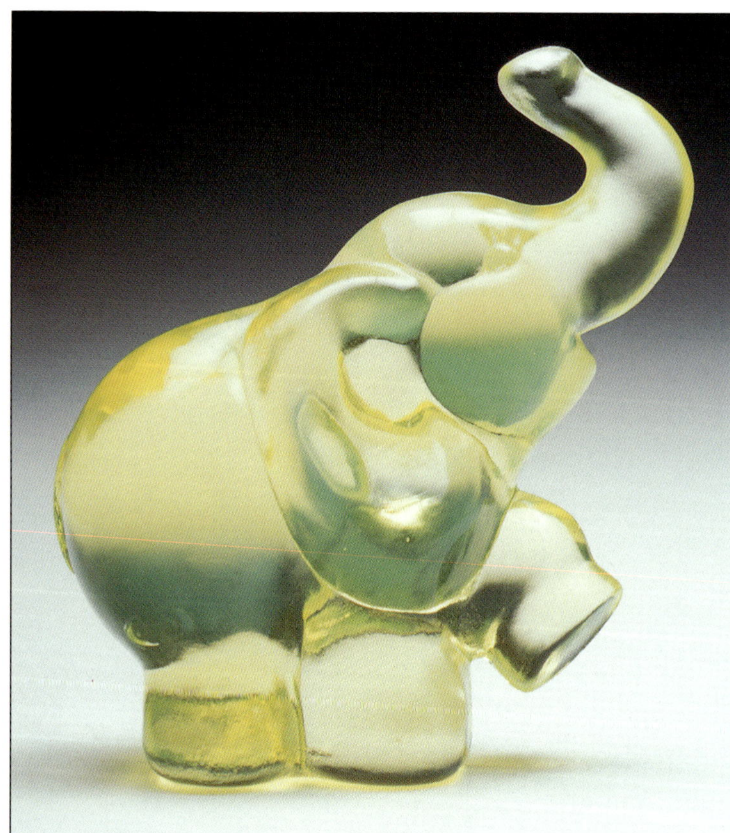

Circus elephant, #5136TO, Topaz (Vaseline) Opalescent, not in Fenton's regular line, made for Westmoreland Museum, 3.25" tall, 3.75" long, Circa 2001, **$25.00**

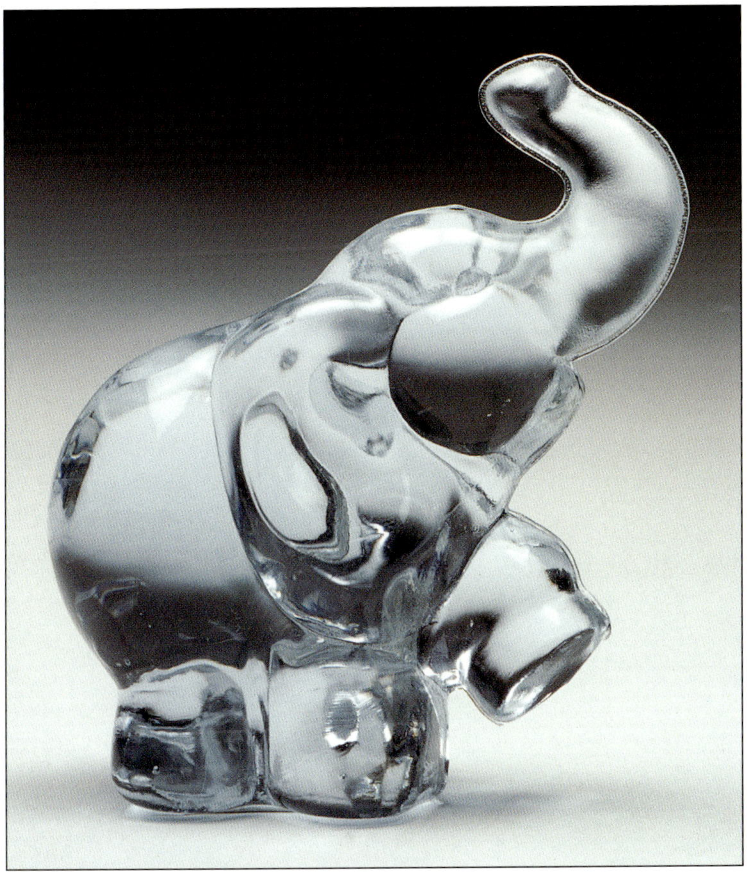

Circus Elephant #5136YR, Pink Chiffon (diachromatic color changes under different types of lighting), 3.25" tall, 3.75" long, Circa 2001, **$19.50**

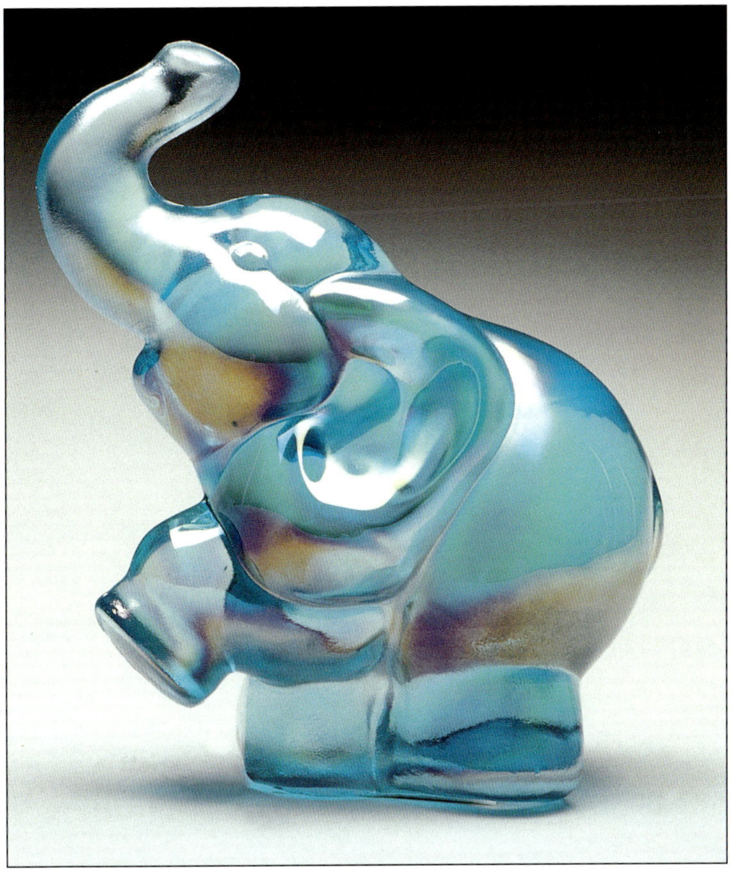

Circus Elephant #5136IZ/SY, Blue Topaz Iridized, 3.25" tall, 3.75" long, Circa 2002, **$24.00**

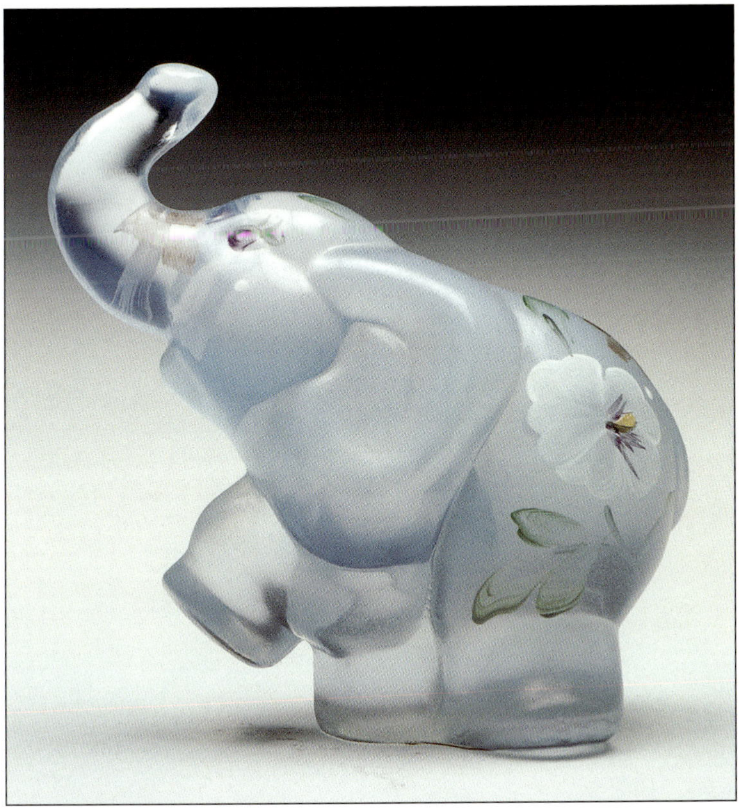

Circus Elephant #5136X9, "Spring Splendor" hand painted on Pink Chiffon (diachromatic color changes under different types of lighting), 3.25" tall, 3.75" long, Circa 2002, **$27.50**

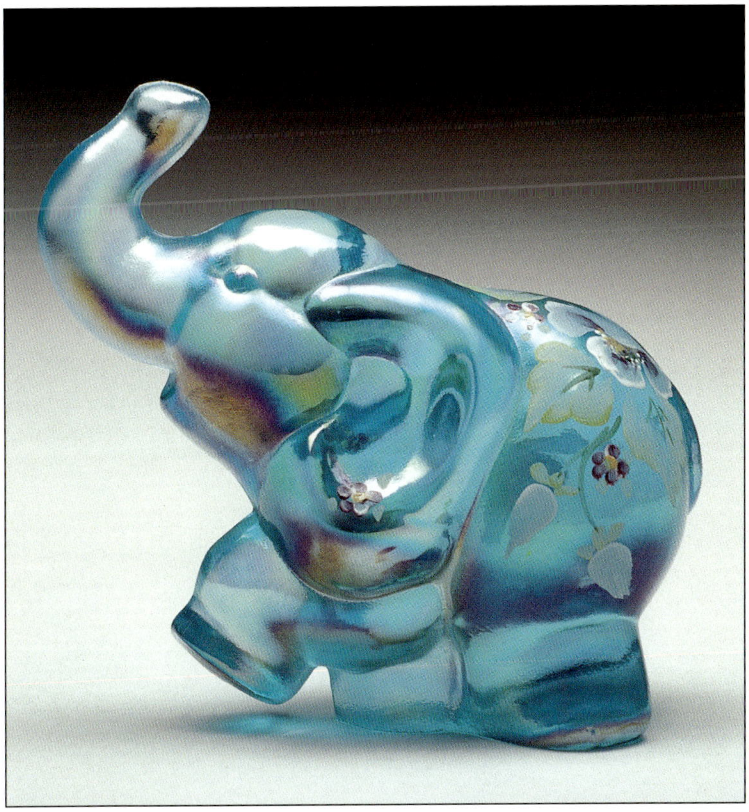

Circus Elephant #5136A4, hand painted Blue Topaz Iridized for QVC, 3.25" tall, 3.75" long, Circa 2002, **$35.00**

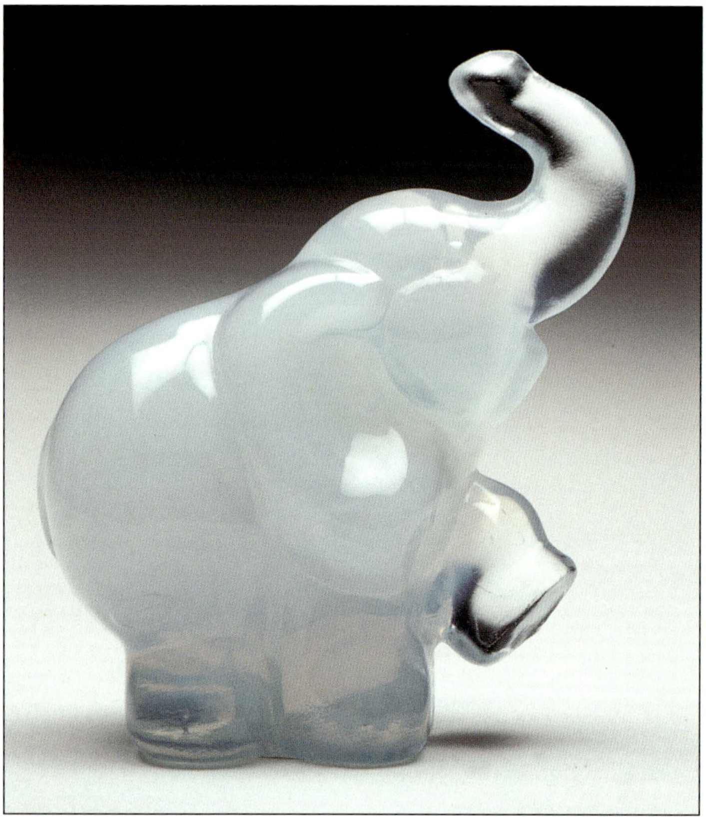

Circus Elephant #5136FQ, not in Fenton's regular line, Opal Mist, made for Fenton Gift Shop, 3.25" tall, 3.75" long, Circa 2002, **$25.00**

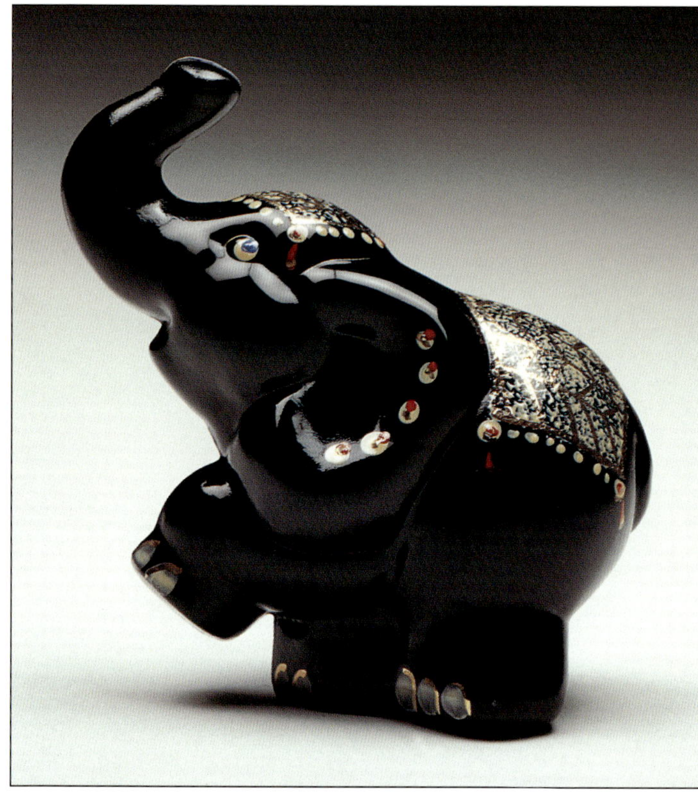

Circus Elephant #C5136D5, hand painted Black for QVC, 3.25" tall, 3.75" long, Circa 2002, **$38.00**

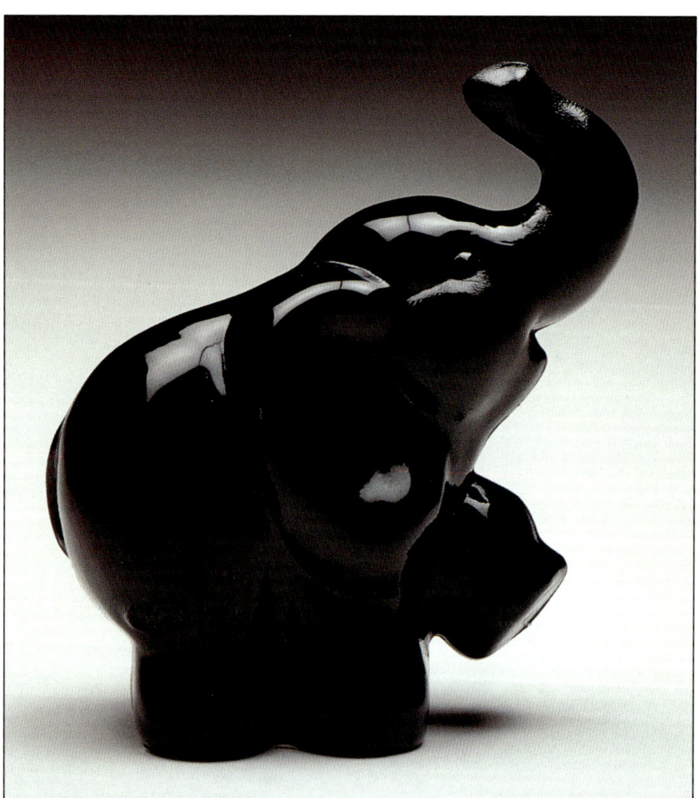

Circus Elephant #5136BK, not in Fenton's regular line, Black, made for Fenton Gift Shop, 3.25" tall, 3.75" long, Circa 2002, **$24.00**

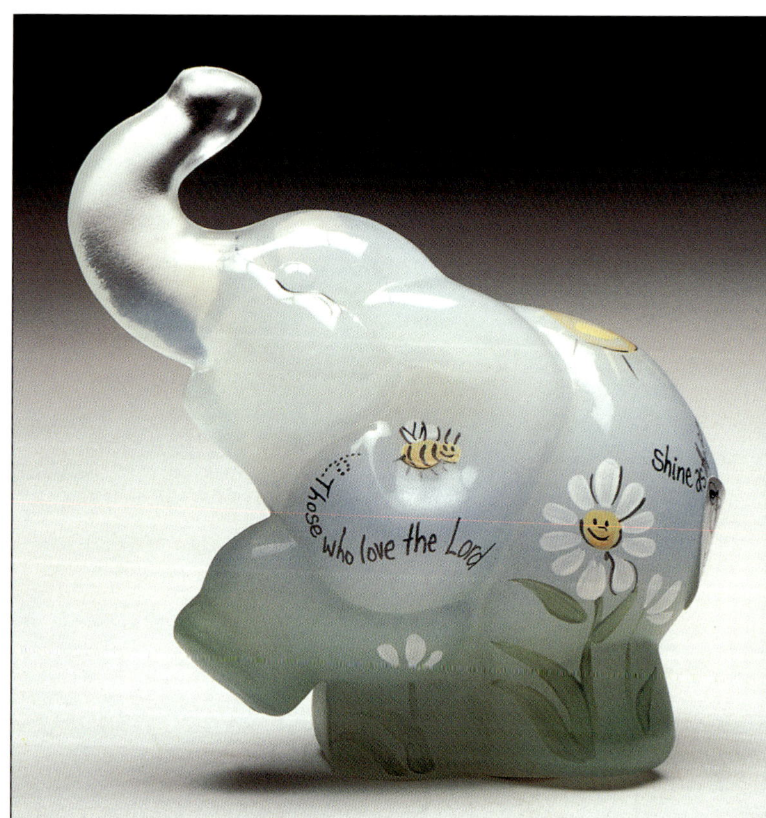

Circus Elephant, #5136Q4, Inspirations, Opal accented with green and blue with saying on it, hand painted by S. Capshaw, 3.75" tall, 3.5" long, Circa 2003, **$29.50**

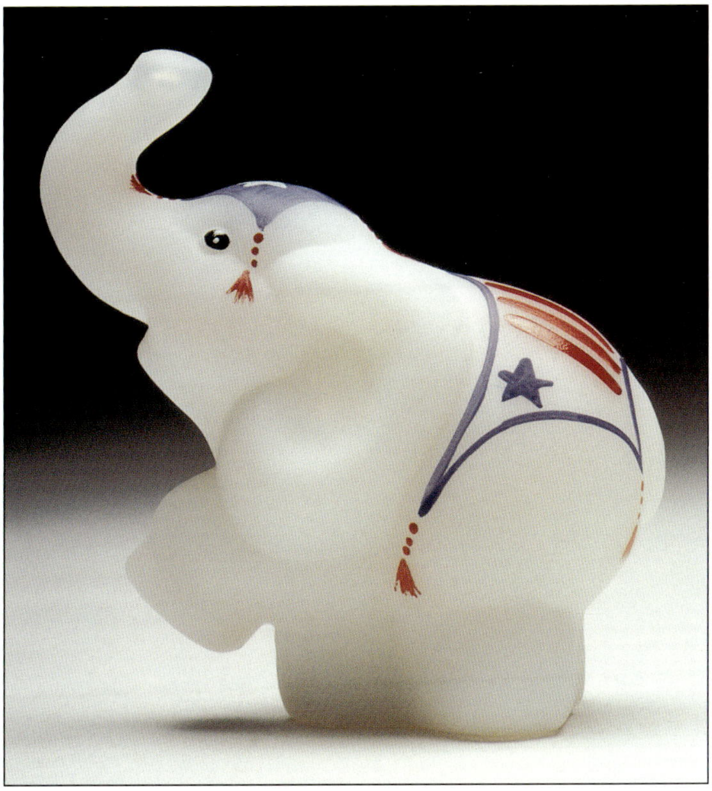

Circus Elephant, #5136, Opal with satin finish and hand painted with red and blue, made exclusively for annual Fenton Art Glass Company Gift Shop February sale, limited issue, 4" tall, 3.5" long, Circa 2003, **$65.00**

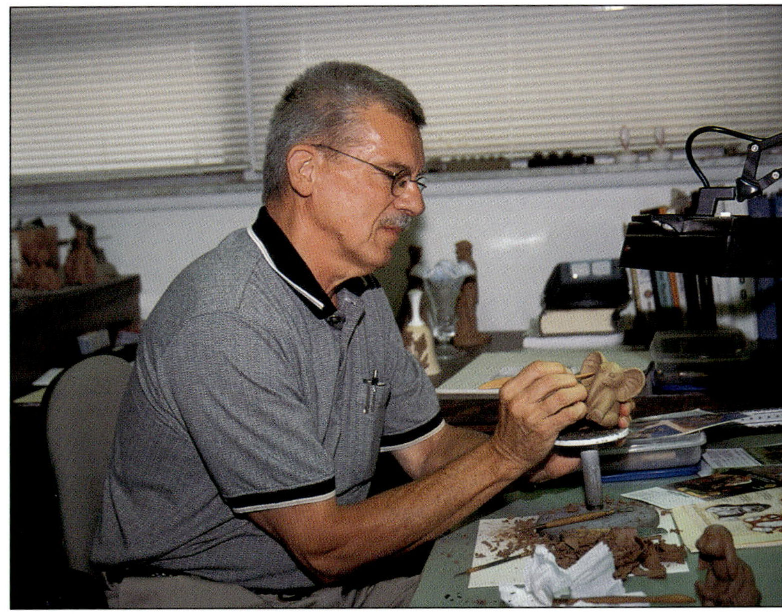

Jon Saffell sculpting a new Fenton elephant, with trunk down

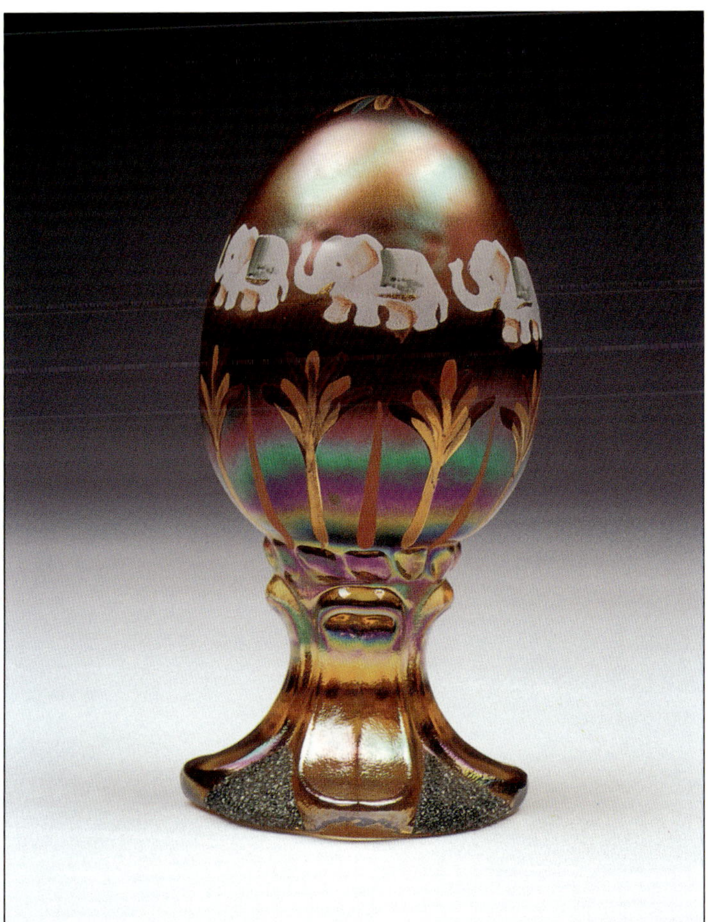

Egg, #5146, not in Fenton's regular line, Amber iridized hand painted with white elephants, 3.75" tall, Circa 2000, **$35.00**

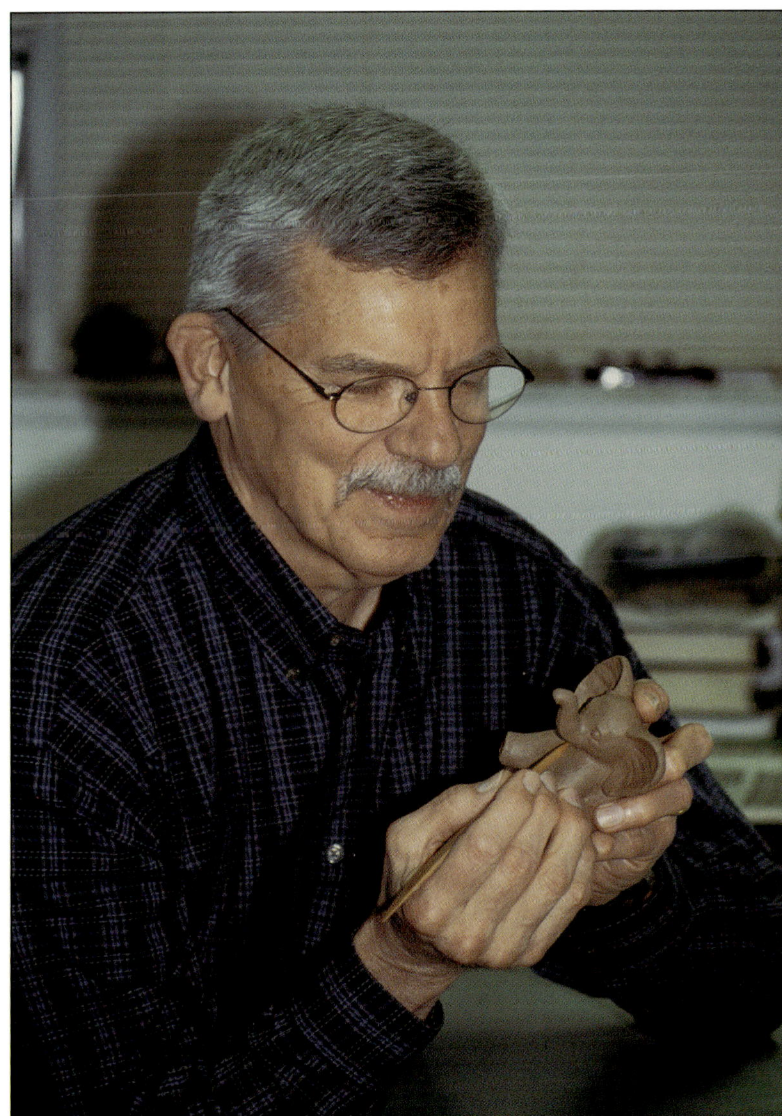

Jon Saffell sculpting the revised new Fenton elephant, with trunk up

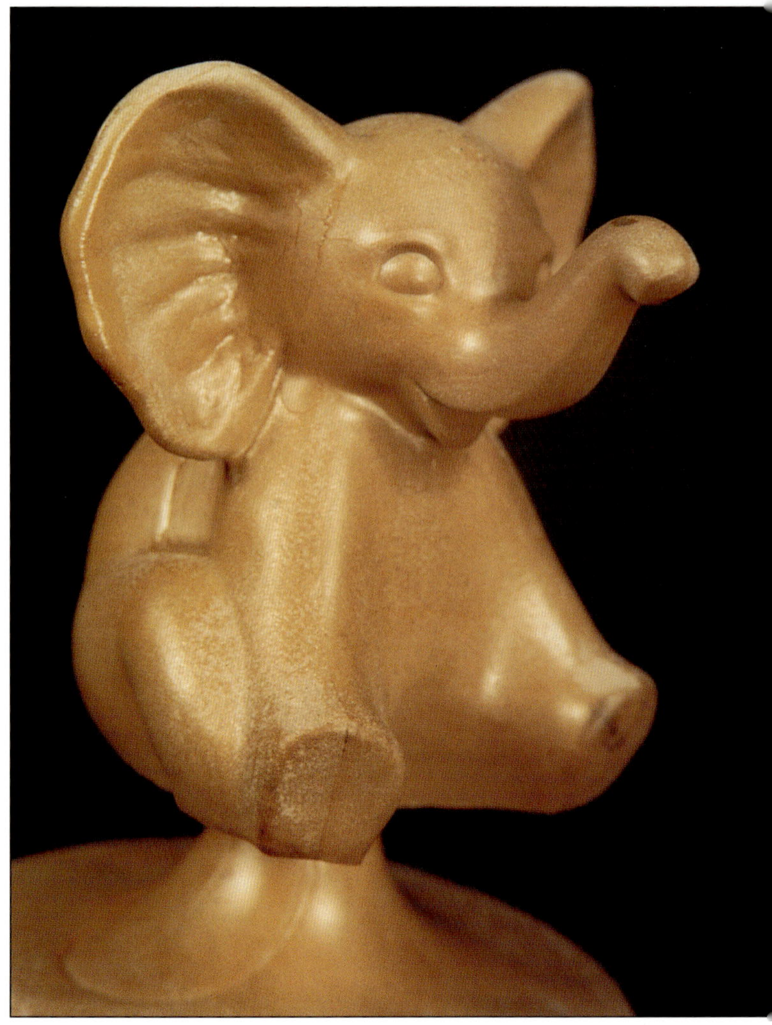

New elephant, plastic (used to test mould), Circa 2003

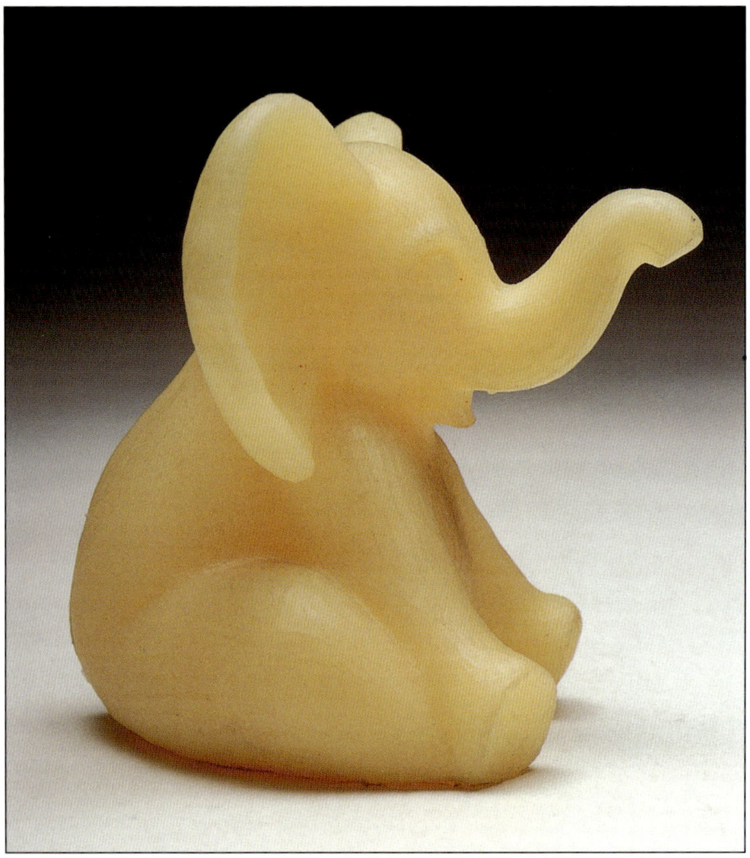

New elephant, wax (used to test mould), Circa 2003

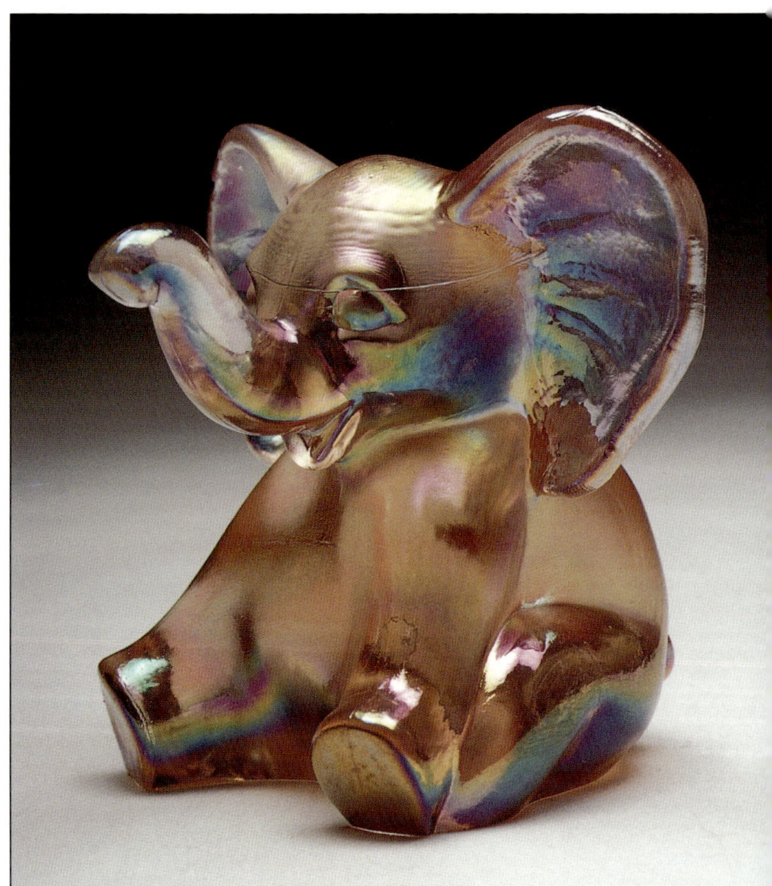

New elephant of glass, sample, not in Fenton's regular line, Sunset Iridized, 3.25" tall, 3.5" wide, Circa 2003

Fostoria Glass Company 1887-1983

The Fostoria Glass Company was founded in Fostoria, Ohio. Lucien Martin and W.S. Brady were the founders. In 1891, they experienced a glitch in their production when their inexpensive supply of gas had pretty much disappeared. A decision was made to move the factory to Moundsville, West Virginia, since the investors lived there.

In 1901, W. Dalzell, who had extensive experience with Dalzell Brothers and Gilmore & Findaly, came to work at Fostoria. About a year later, he became Fostoria's president and began a new direction for the company. After W. Dalzell died in 1928, Calvin Roe became the company's president. Under Roe's guidance and knowledge the majority of their glass animals were made, however it is not known who designed them.

For a brief time, William Dalzell, who was son of W. Dalzell, became the company's president after the passing of Roe in 1945. William watched sales continue to climb, before finally peaking in 1950. He contracted with Ann Donahue Studios of New York, to create some animals. In about 1957, about a year prior to William's retirement in 1958, Fostoria obtained a new designer, Jon Saffell, who created several lines of stemware and a few animals.

Robert Hannum was the company's president from 1958 to 1968. His talent shined in difficult management situations and his competence was proven dealing with labor problems and solutions. When Hannum died in 1968, David Dalzell, son of William, took his place. David was the president until Fostoria closed in 1983.

Fostoria ultimately closed because of their inability to compete. There were large costs associated with their etched tableware lines, and this made it difficult to survive against cheaper imports on the market. The company was sold to Lancaster Colony.

The Fostoria elephant was designed at the Ann Donahue Studios in New York. The moulds themselves were created at the Fostoria mould shop. The initial offering was only done in crystal, and later the elephant was reissued in black. Today Fostoria's black elephant is more valuable, since it was made for such a short period of time.

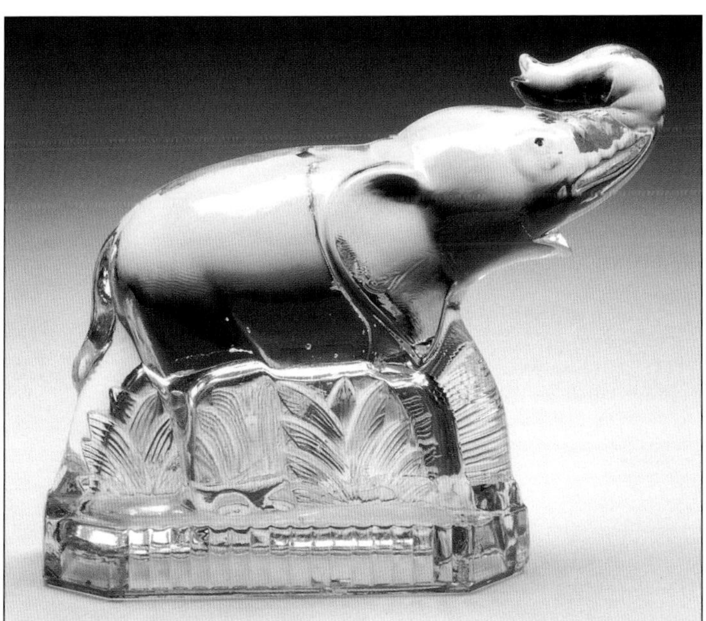

Elephant book end, Crystal, 6.25" tall, 7.5" long, Circa 1940-43, **$125.00**

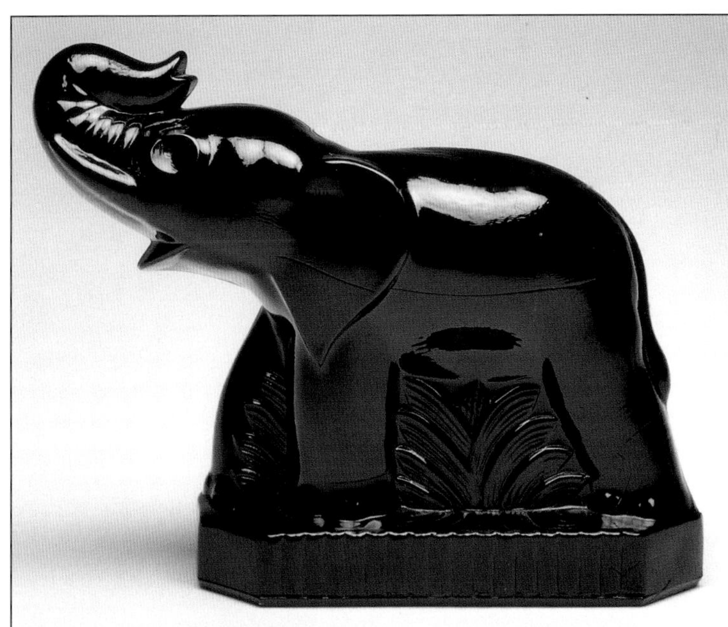

Elephant book end, Ebony, 6.25" tall, 7.5" long, Circa 1980, **$175.00**

Franklin Mint
1964-Present

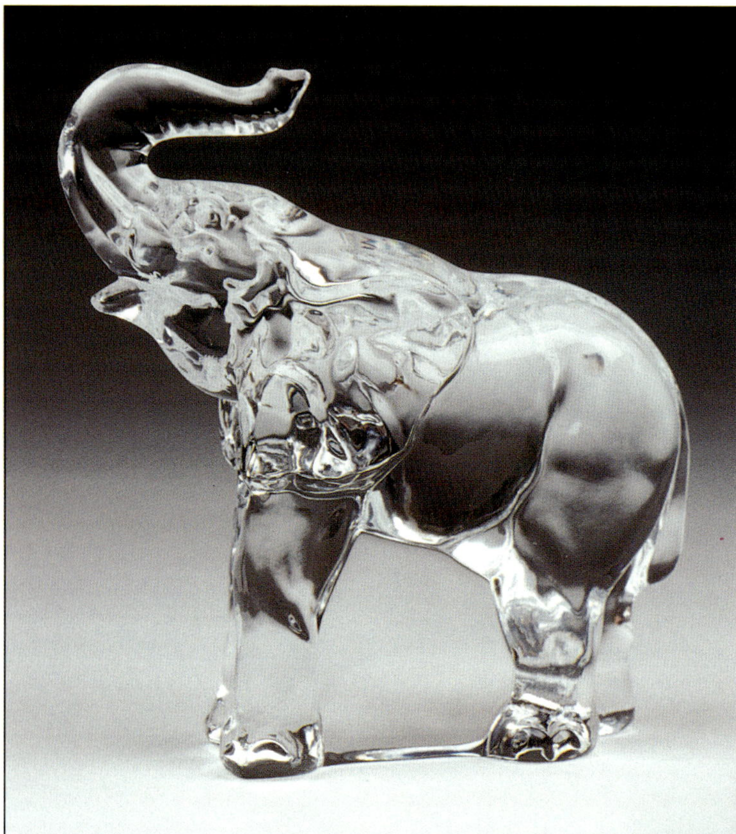

Elephant with trunk up, "Animals of Ark Crystal" series, crystal, male, 5" tall, 3.5" long, Circa 1980's, **$55.00**

The Franklin Mint is located in Lima, Pennsylvania, with world headquarters in Philadelphia. At their own museum they display original treasured masterpieces of the heirlooms they create. They sell excellent replicas. Their mission is to serve the collector and preserve cultural art heritage.

The "Animals of the Ark" was the first crystal sculpture series issued by the Franklin Mint. This limited edition was available only by advance subscription ordered by November 30, 1976; delivery began in January, 1977. Each pair of seven animals, a male and female, was issued every three months until the set was complete. The elephants were issued in February of 1978. The complete set included camels, elephants, giraffes, horses, kangaroos, lions, and polar bears.

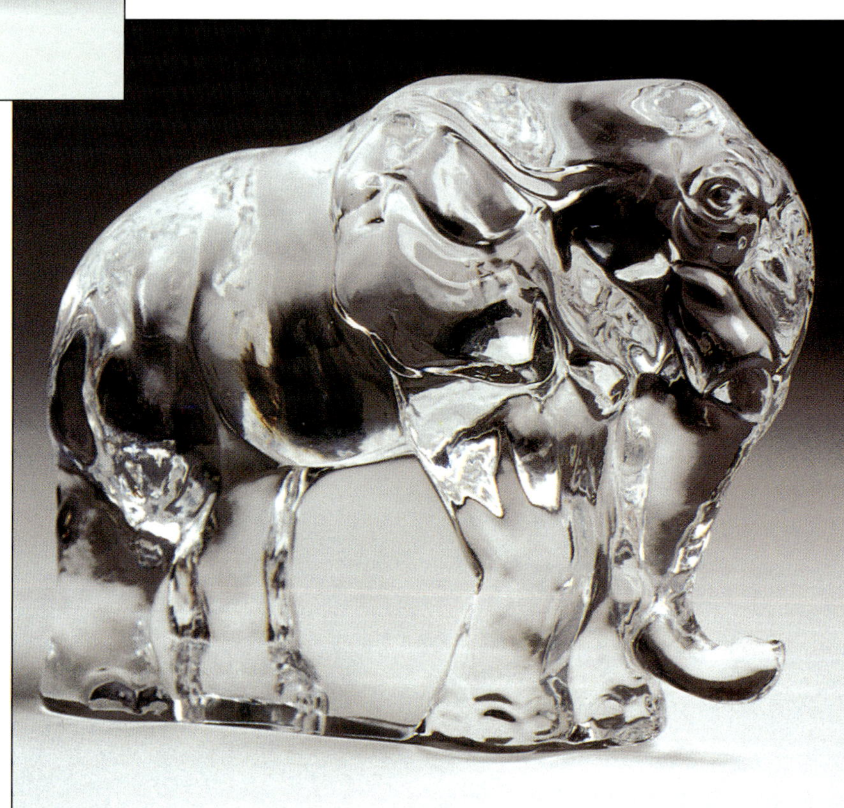

Elephant with trunk down, "Animals of Ark Crystal" series, crystal, female, 3.5" tall, 4.5" long, Circa 1980's, **$55.00**

Guernsey Glass Company 1967-Present

In 1967, the Guernsey Glass Company was founded, through the dreams of the Bennett brothers, in Cambridge, Guernsey County, Ohio. This company is located near the Boyd Glass facility. The Guernsey trademark, found on all their glass, is a B inside a triangle. The B comes from the name Bennett.

Harold Bennett began his career, not in the glass business but in the grocery business. However, he was a collector with a passion for glass. He had a huge collection of Cambridge glass and to further his joy created a museum that could display his 5000-plus pieces. Further, he had briefly worked for Cambridge Glass, and through them he gained access to their glass formulas.

Currently, Harold Bennett contracts with Mosser Glass, also located in Cambridge, Ohio, to make the glass utilizing his moulds.

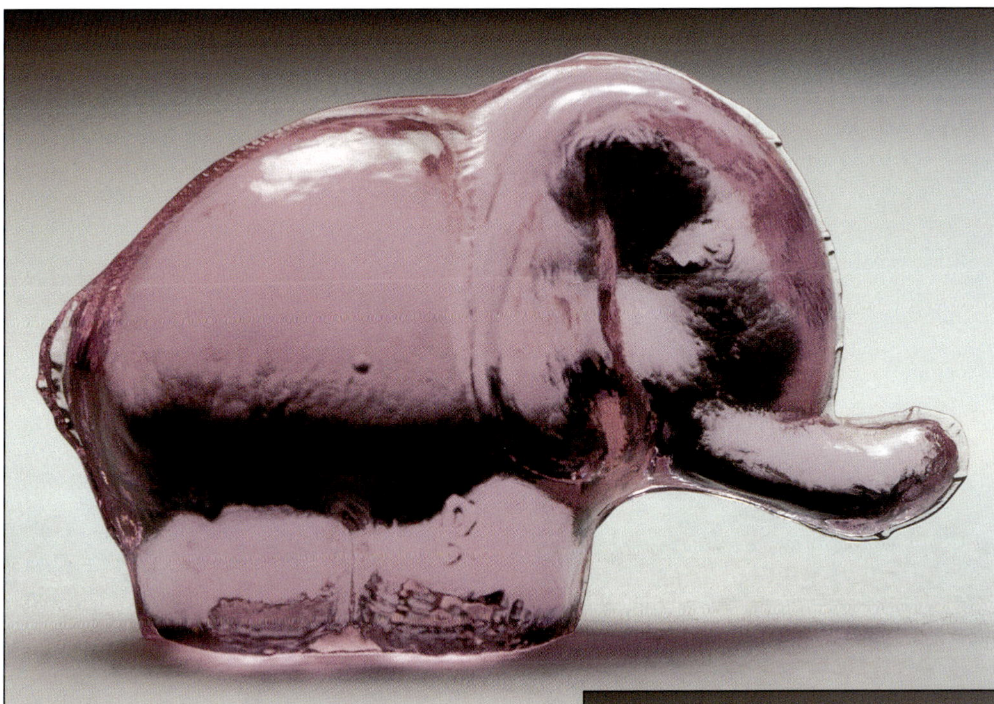

Standing with trunk out, Alexandrite, B above front shoulder, 1.3" tall, 2.1" long, Circa 1990's, **$9.50**

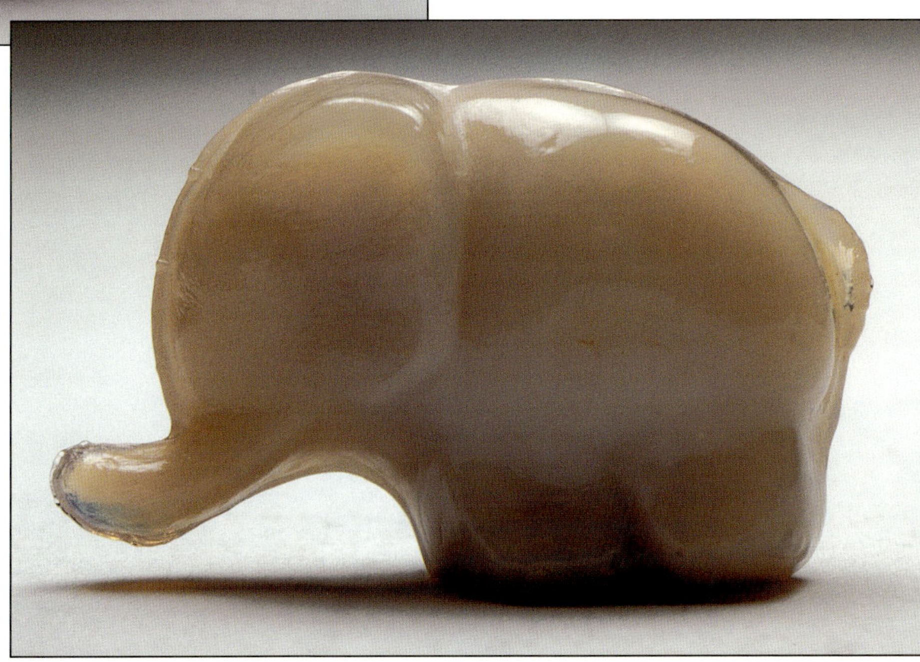

Standing with trunk out, Crown Tuscan, 1.3" tall, 2.1" long, Circa 1990's, **$8.00**

A.H. Heisey & Company 1895-1957

Augustus H. Heisey had immigrated to America from Germany. He worked for Cascade Glass and then King Glass, in 1861, and served in the military during the Civil War. After his military service, Heisey worked for Ripley & Company. With work experience in glass behind him, he ventured out on his own and began his own business in 1895. He located the factory in Newark, Ohio, and in 1896 the first glass was made.

His company became a success and he wanted to display a kind of recognition, so Augustus developed a trademark logo which had an H inside a diamond. Heisey worked to advertise their glass as high quality, and the logo would ensure its being distinct.

Royal Hickman, who had once been with Royal Haeger Pottery, joined the Heisey company in 1941. This is important because he designed the vast number of Heisey animals. Tennessee William's play "The Glass Menagerie" was on Broadway in 1946 and the glass animals of Heisey and Viking were prominent features. When this play was turned into a movie, their exposure was further enhanced, since only Heisey animals were used. To encourage sales, advertisements tied together the movie and store displays, which led customers to buy their favorite Heisey glass animals.

The 1950s were hard times for glass companies and imports were taking sales away from Heisey's business. They responded by making an agreement with designer Eva Zeisel, in 1953, and the Holophane Company, owner of Verlys designs, in 1955, to create and produce a variety of new products to bring the company through their financial slump. Yet these efforts did not prove successful for sales.

Tragically, Heisey became another victim of low finances and factory closure. They had closed just for December, 1957, but they never reopened. To keep the Heisey name and spirit alive, Imperial Glass purchased all of the Heisey moulds, in 1958, and Heisey's famous diamond-H trademark.

The letters of HCA stand for the Heisey Club of America. After the closure of the Imperial Glass Company, the HCA worked hard to purchase back most of the Heisey moulds.

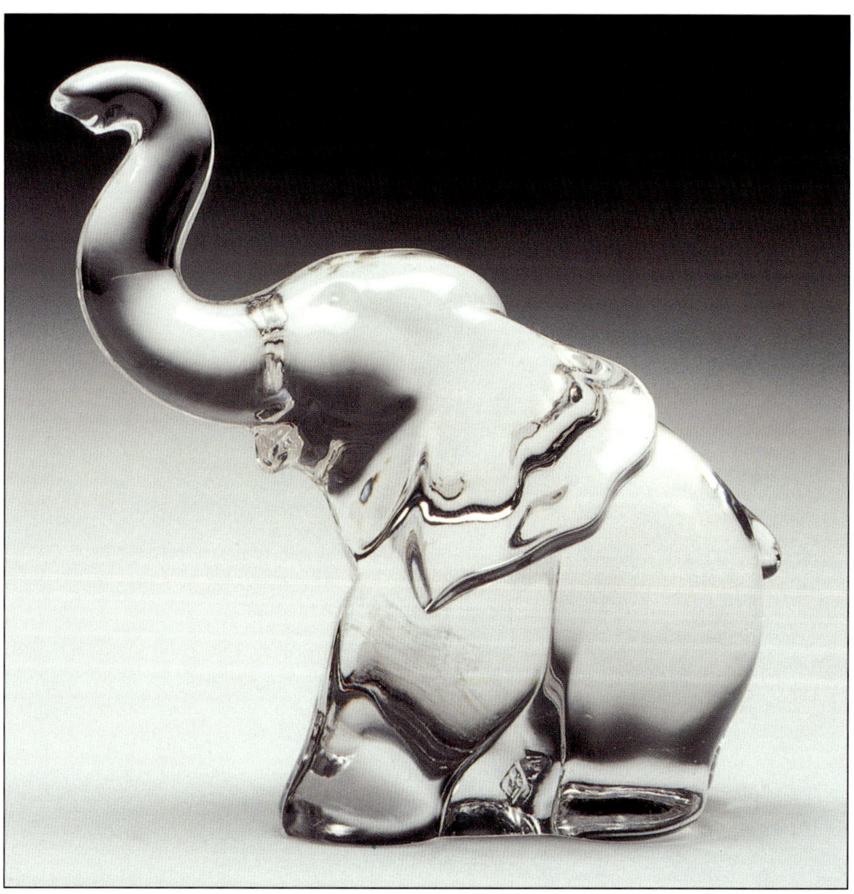

Small Elephant, Crystal, 4.5" tall, 5" long, Circa 1944-53, **$295.00**

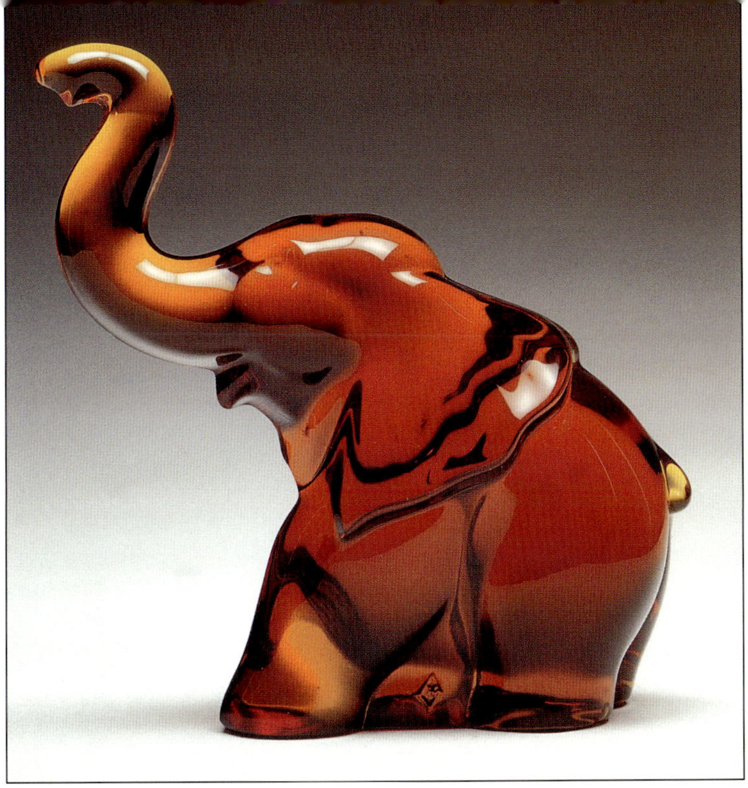

Small elephant, Sultana, marked H in diamond (for Heisey) between legs, 4.6" tall, 4.5" long, Circa early 1950's, **$1,500.00**

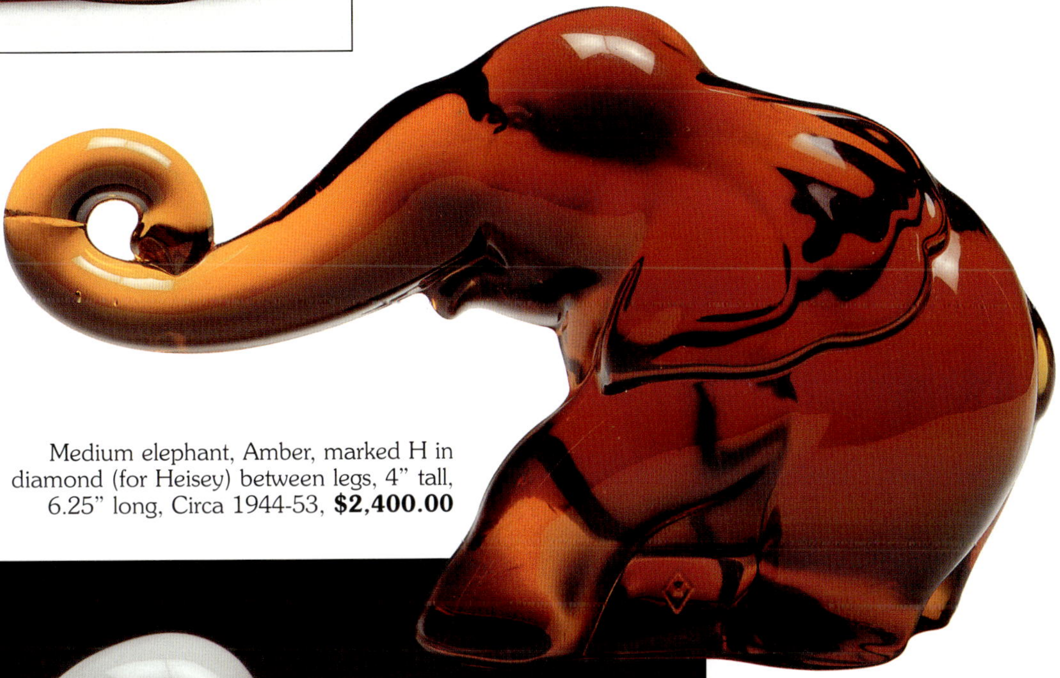

Medium elephant, Amber, marked H in diamond (for Heisey) between legs, 4" tall, 6.25" long, Circa 1944-53, **$2,400.00**

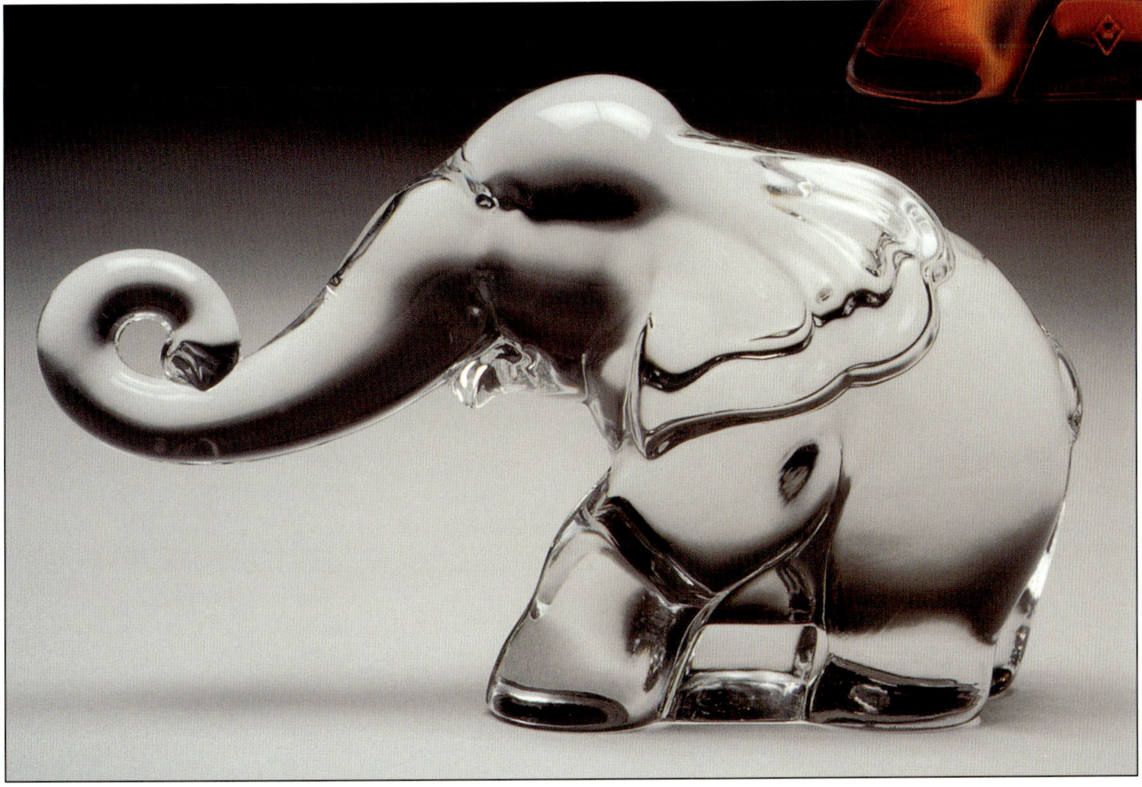

Medium Elephant, Crystal, long trunk out, 4" tall, 6.25" long, Circa 1944-55, **$375.00**

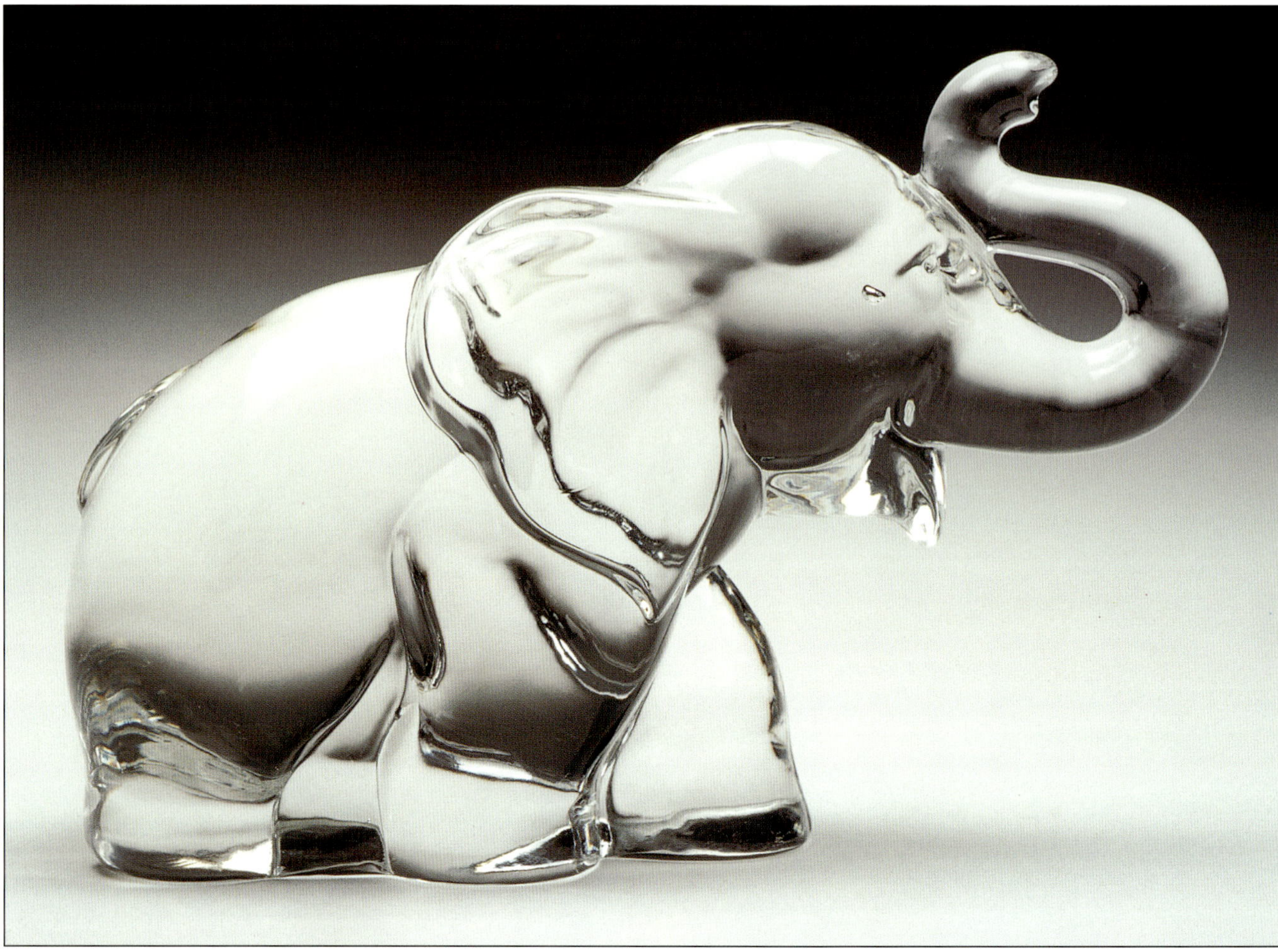

Large Elephant, Crystal, 4.5" tall, 6.25" long, Circa 1944-53, **$495.00**

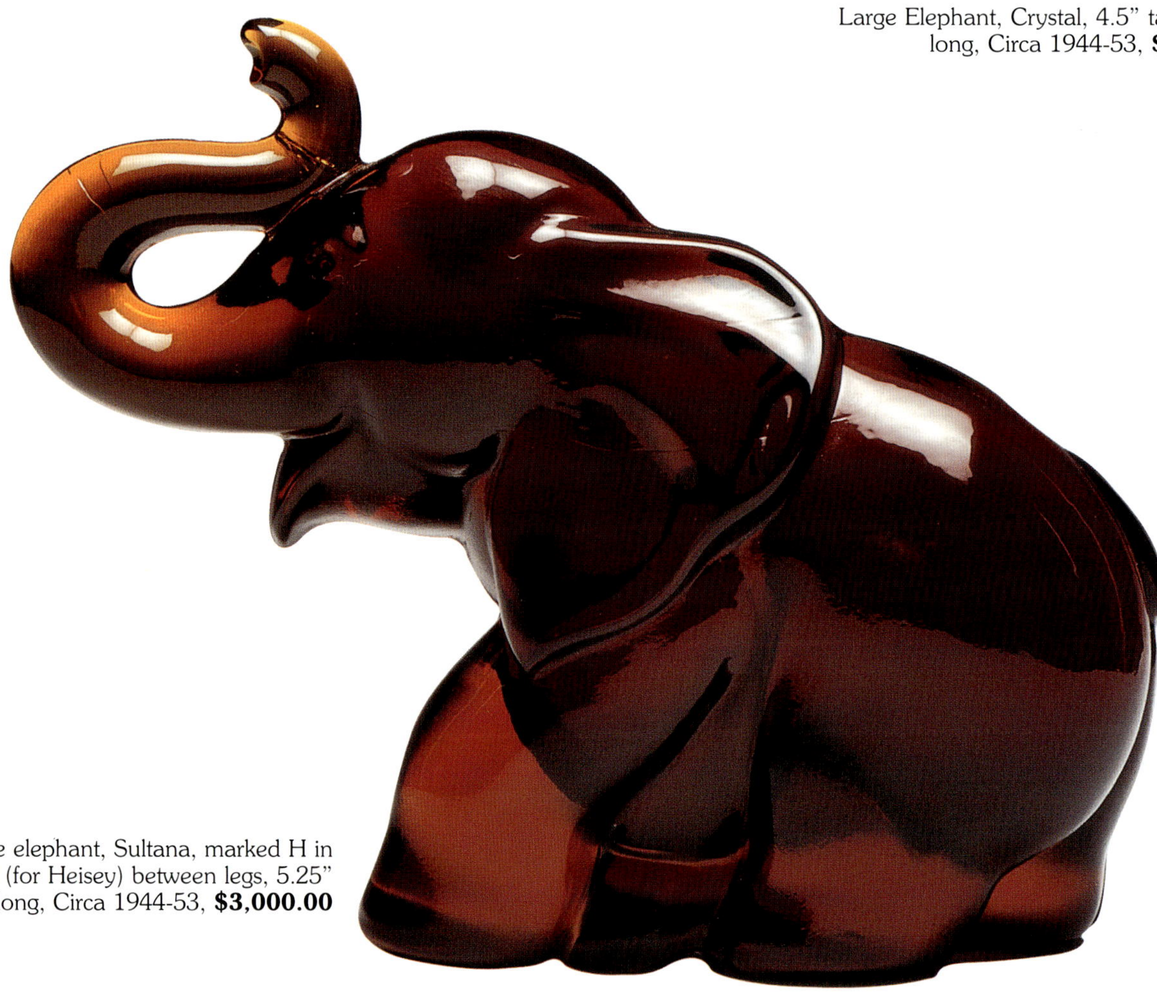

Large elephant, Sultana, marked H in diamond (for Heisey) between legs, 5.25" tall, 6.5" long, Circa 1944-53, **$3,000.00**

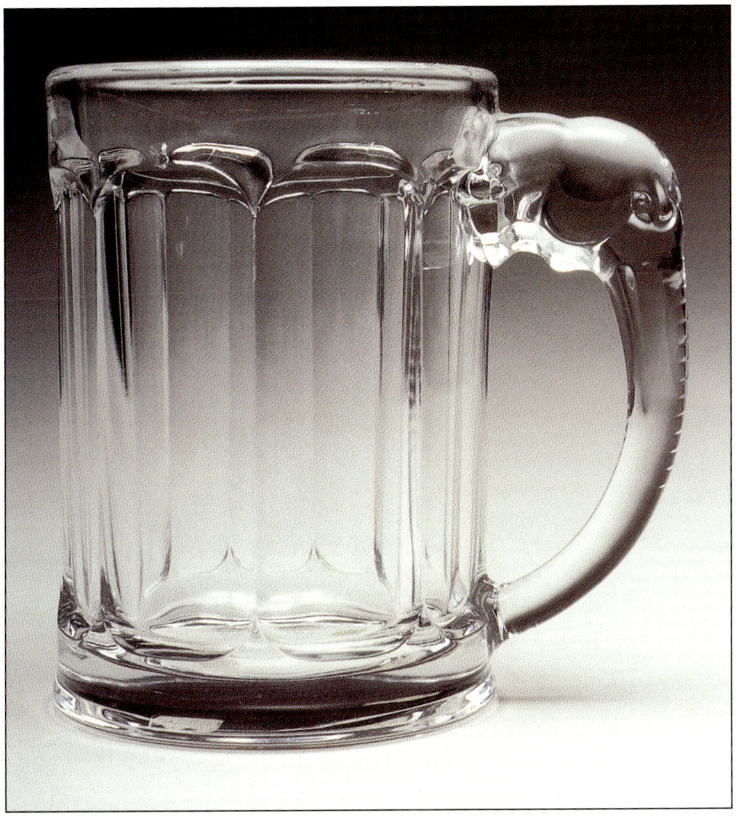

Beer Mug #1591A (designed by Horace King), elephant head mug, Crystal, 12 fluid ounces, 5" tall, 3.5" wide (5" wide including handle), Circa 1947, **$450.00**

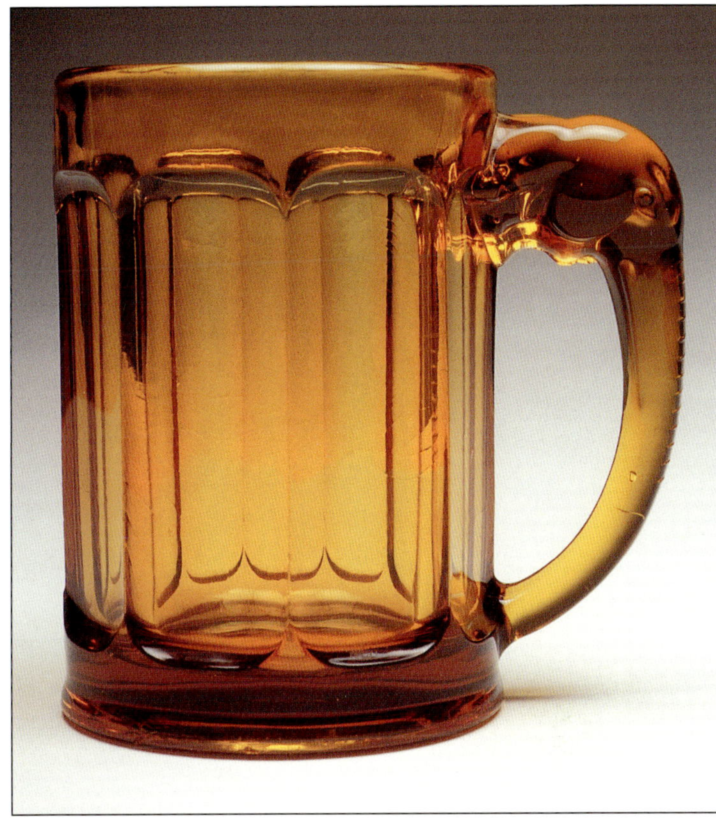

Beer Mug #1591A (designed by Horace King), elephant head mug holds 12 fluid ounces, Amber,5" tall, 3.5" wide (5" wide including handle), Circa 1947, **$900.00**

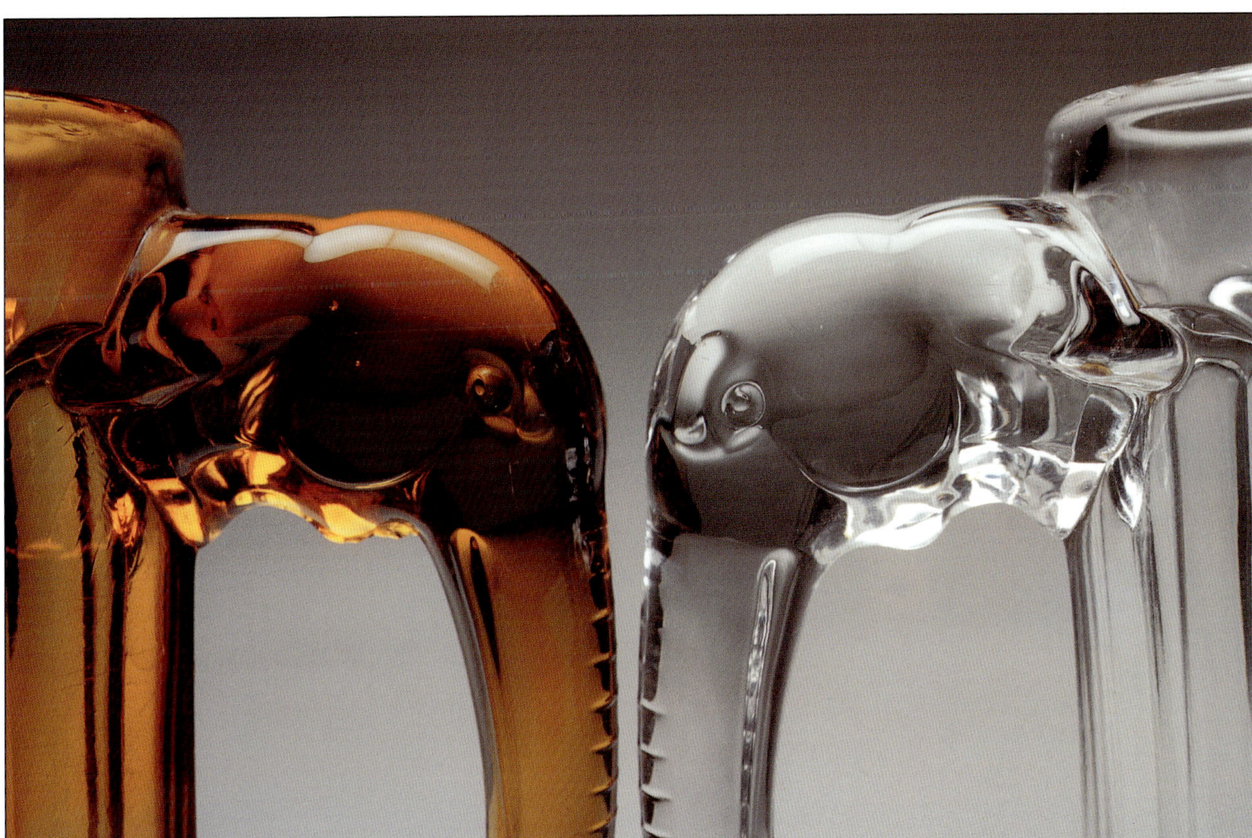

Detail of handles on Beer Mug #1591A (designed by Horace King), elephant head mug

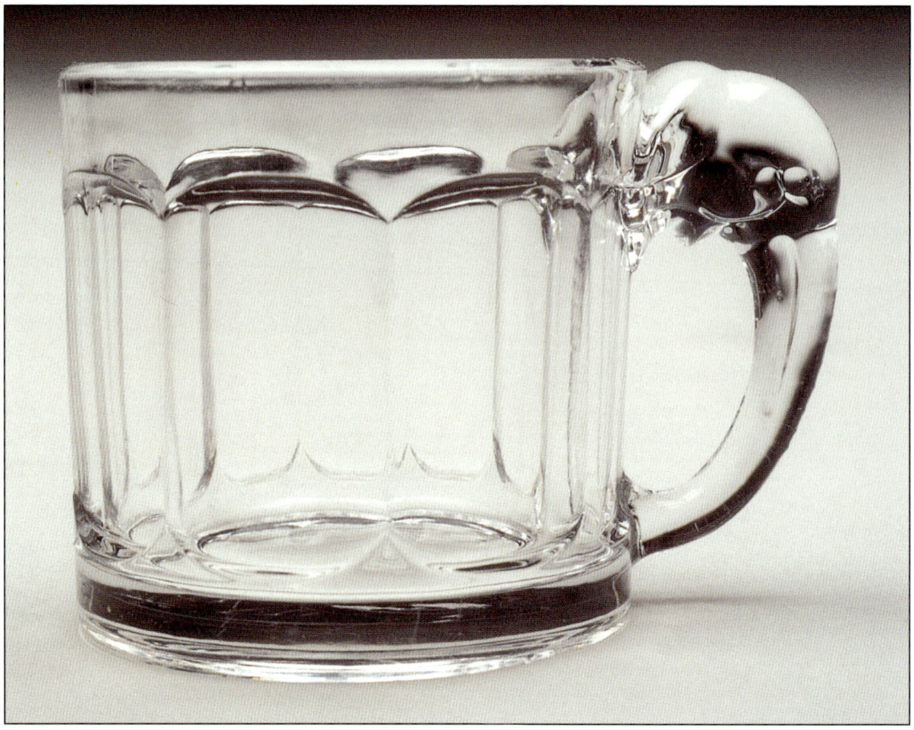

Mug with elephant head, looks like storybook mug except with plain panels, Crystal, 3" tall, 3" wide, Circa 1946, **$900.00**

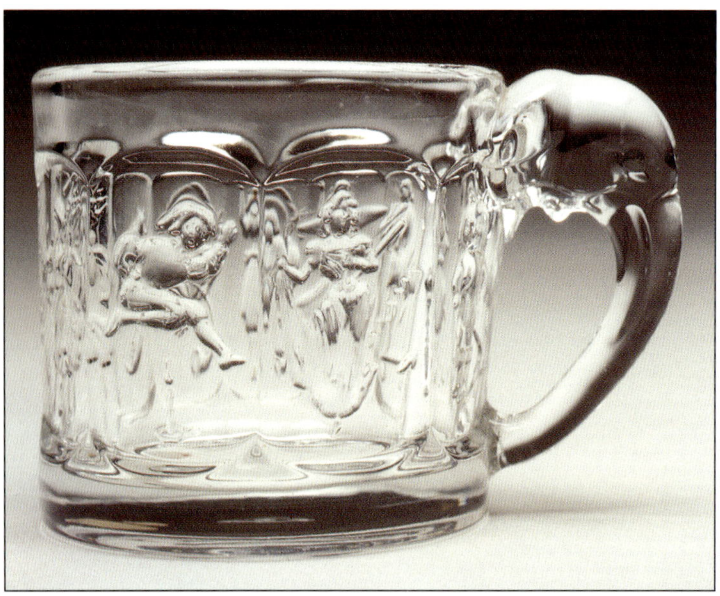

Storybook mug, Crystal, marked H in diamond (for Heisey), 2.8" tall, 3" wide (4.25" wide including elephant head), Circa 1947-50, **$600.00**

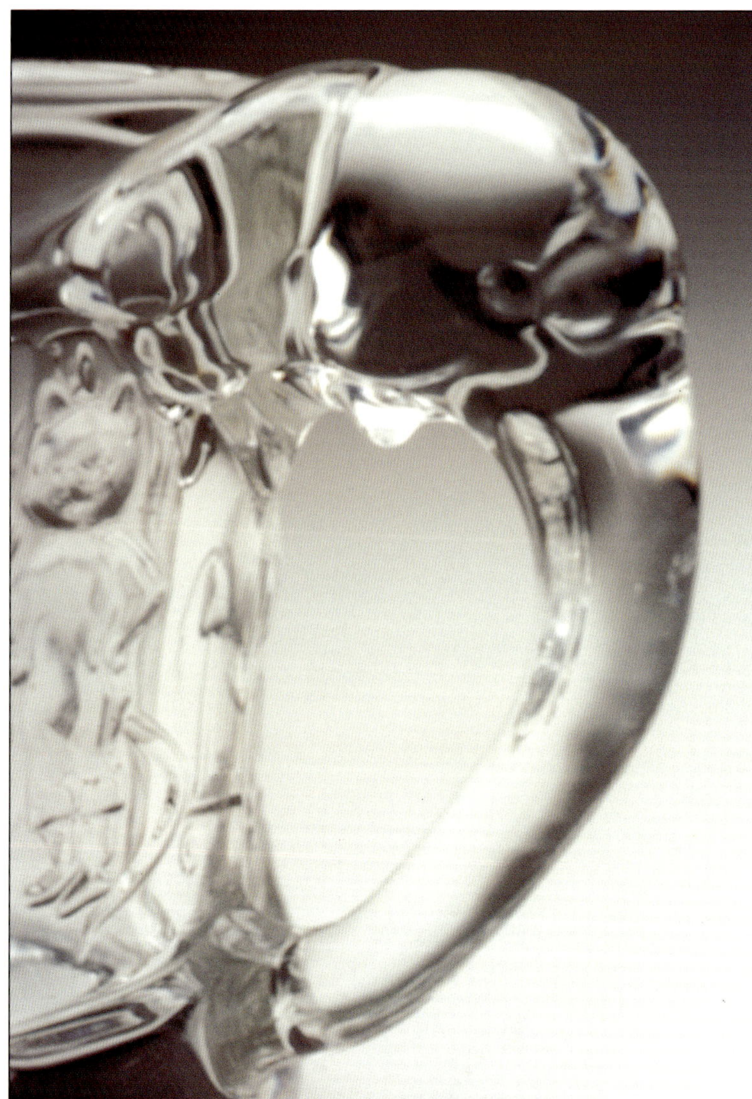

Detail of elephant head handle on Storybook Mug

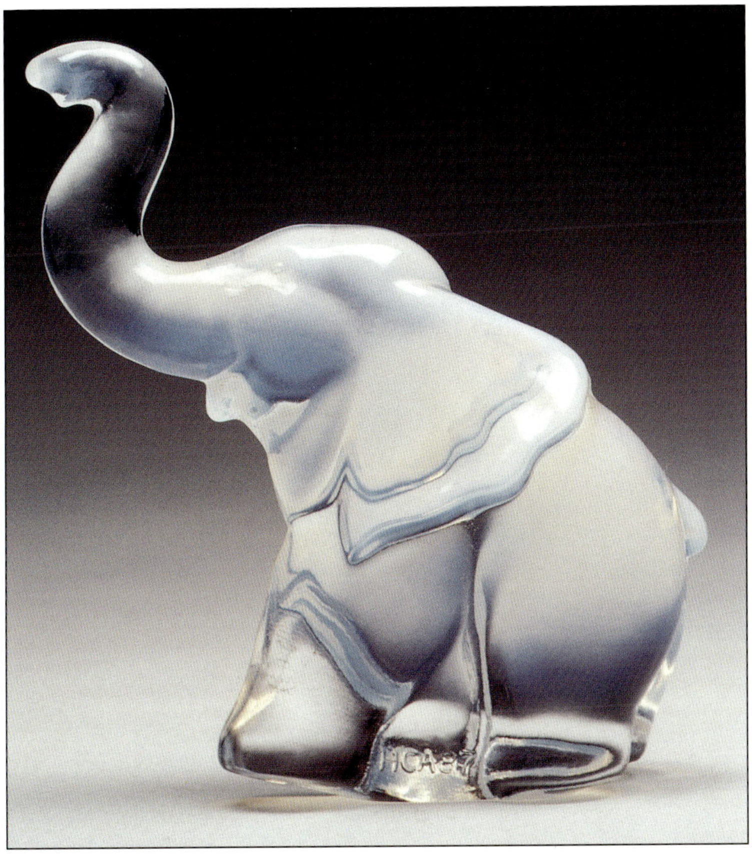

Small elephant, French Opalescent, marked "HCA 87" for Heisey Club of America between legs, Made by Fenton Art Glass Company Art Glass Company, 5" tall, 4.5" long, Circa 1987, **$65.00**

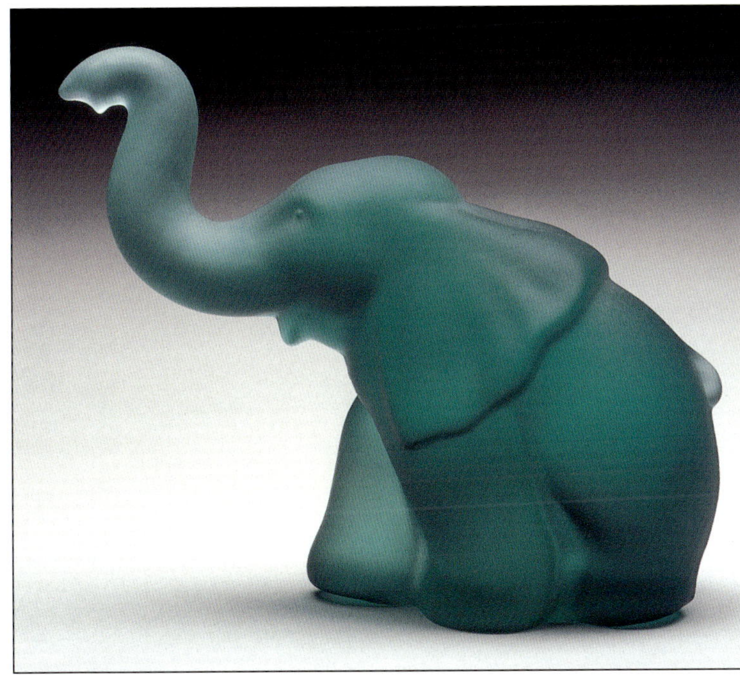

Small elephant, Sea Mist Green with satin finish, marked script F for Fenton and marked "HCA 93" for Heisey Club of America between legs, Made by Fenton Art Glass Company Art Glass Company, 4.4" tall, 5" long, Circa 1993, **$48.00**

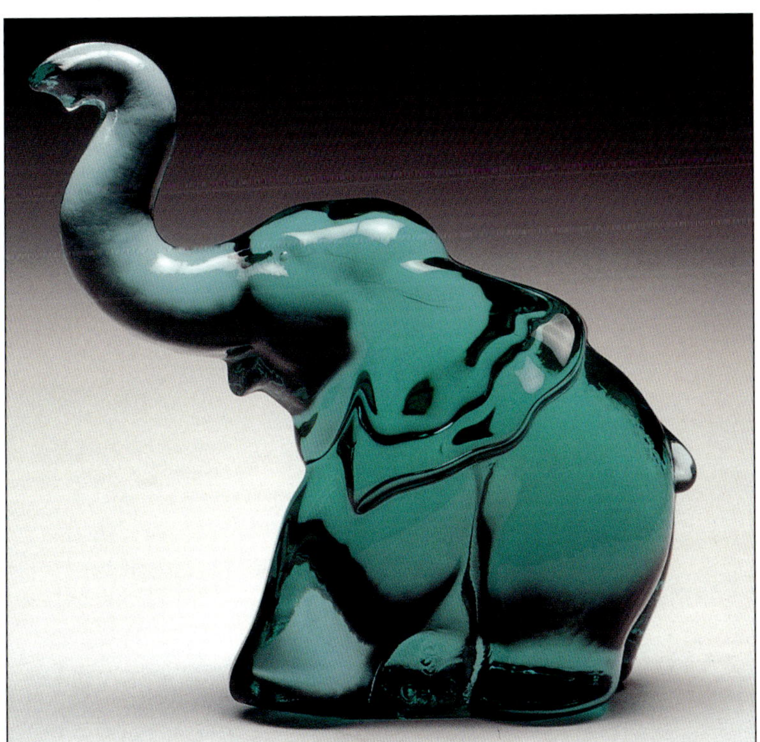

Small Elephant, Sea Mist Green, Made by Fenton Art Glass Company, 4.5" tall, 5" long, Circa 1992, **$45.00**

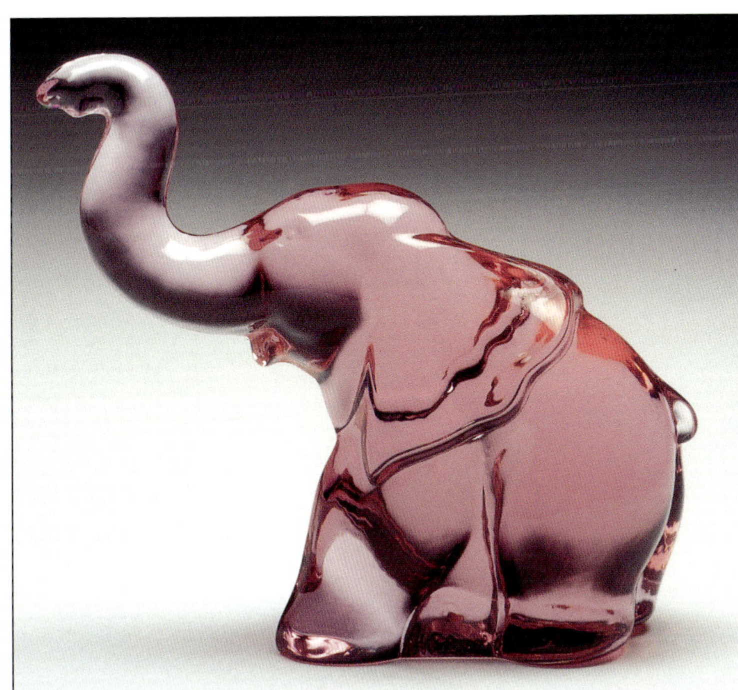

Small Elephant, Lavender Ice, Made by Dalzell Viking, 4.5" tall, 5" long, Circa 1993, **$60.00**

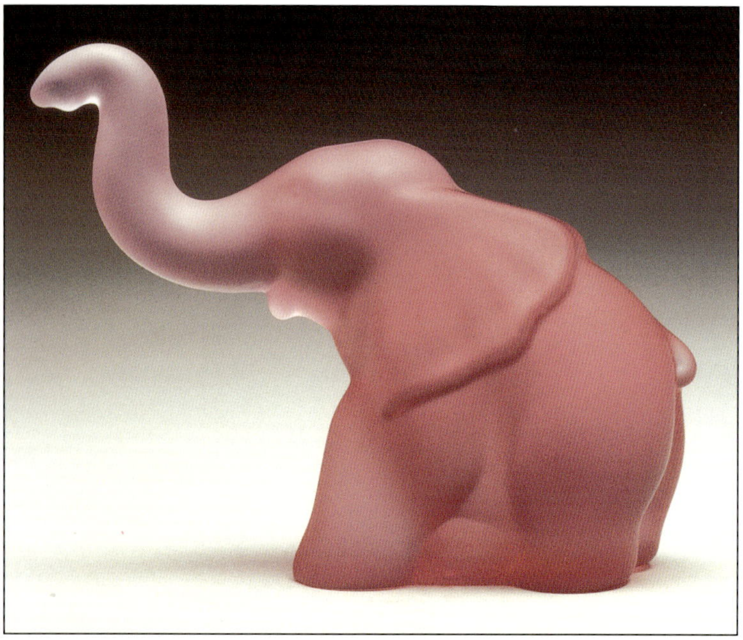

Small elephant, Lavender Ice with satin finish, marked "D" for Dalzell Viking and marked "HCA 93" for Heisey Club of America, 4.25" tall, 5" long, Circa 1993, **$50.00**

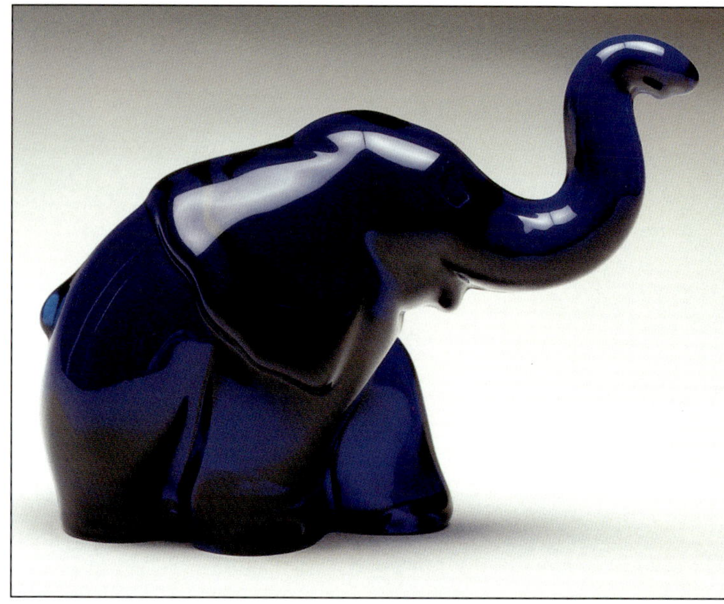

Small Elephant, Cobalt, Made by Mosser Glass, 4" tall, 5" long, Circa 2000, **$65.00**

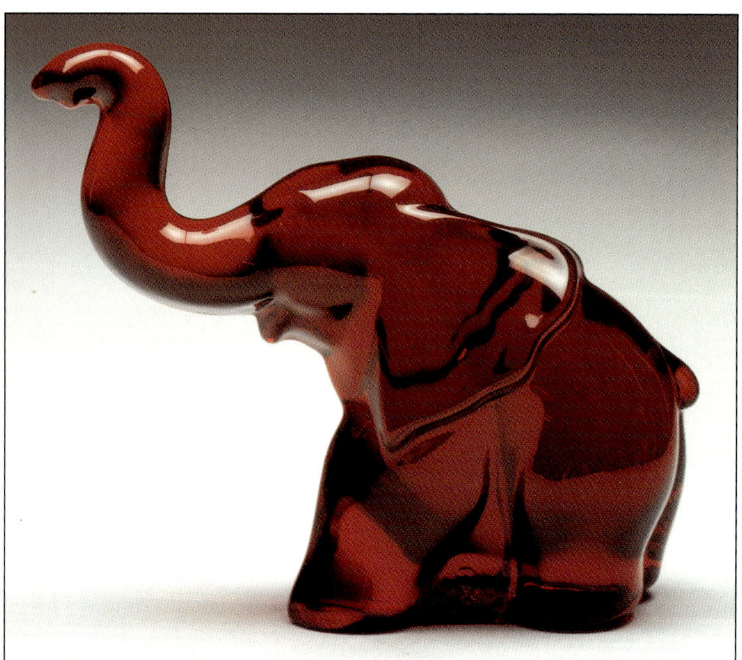

Small Elephant, Ruby, Made by Dalzell Viking, 4.25" tall, 5" long, Circa 1998, **$85.00**

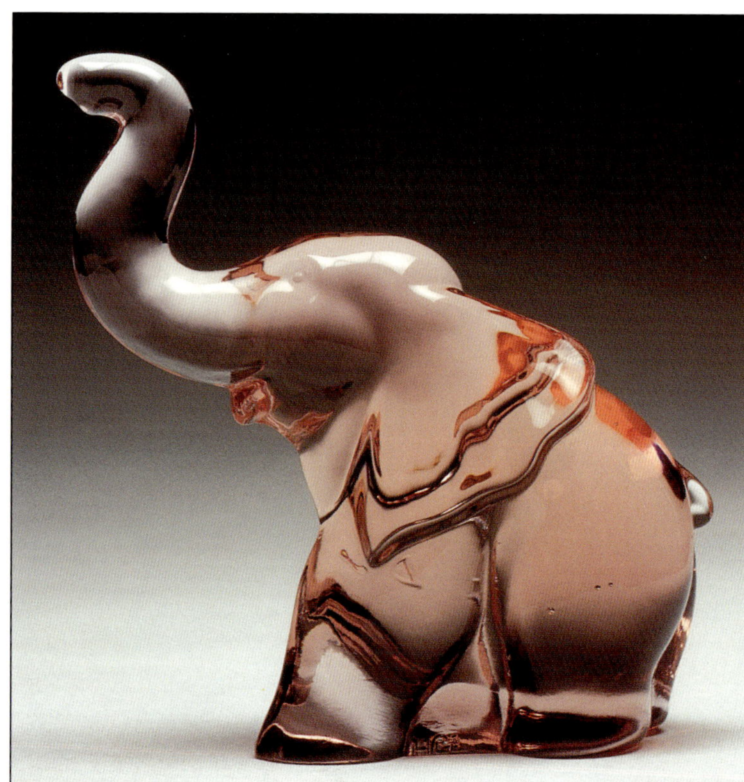

Small elephant, Pink, marked "D" on the shoulder for Dalzell Viking and "HCA" for Heisey Club of America between legs, sample item, 4.75" tall, 5" long, Circa 1997, **$245.00**

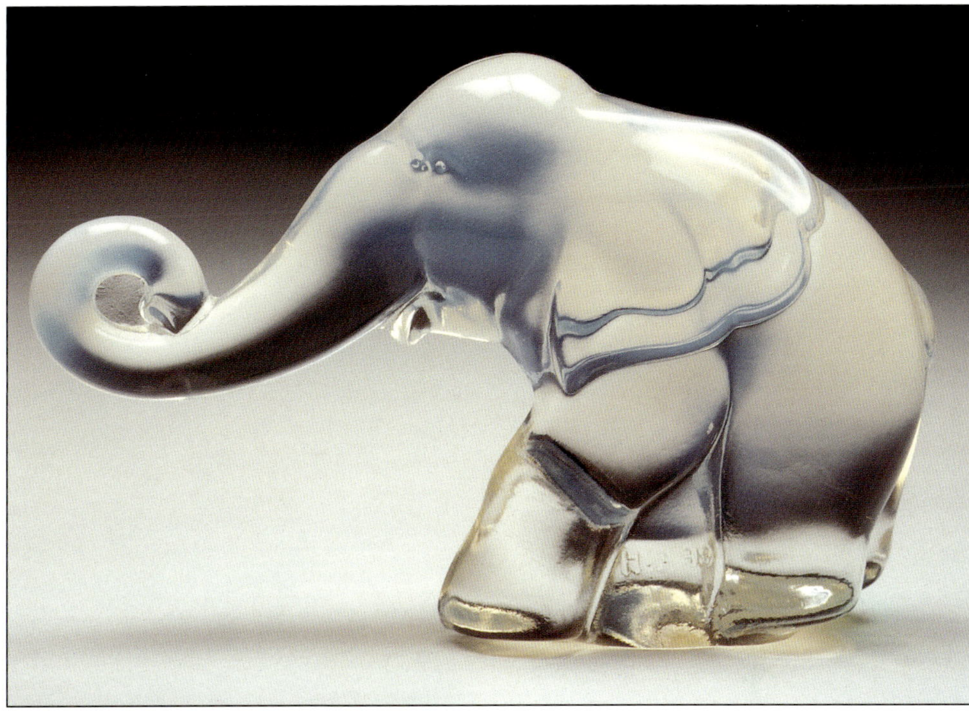

Medium Elephant, French Opalescent, Made by Fenton Art Glass Company, 3.75" tall, 6.25" long, Circa 1988, **$75.00**

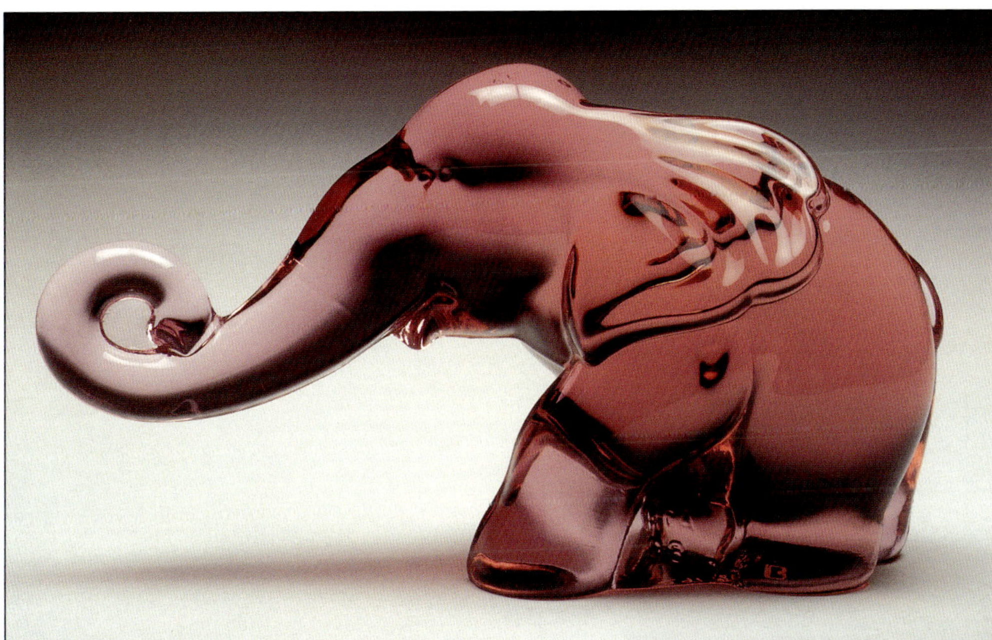

Medium Elephant, Lavender Ice, Made by Dalzell Viking, Limited to 450, 3.75" tall, 6.25" long, Circa 1993, **$75.00**

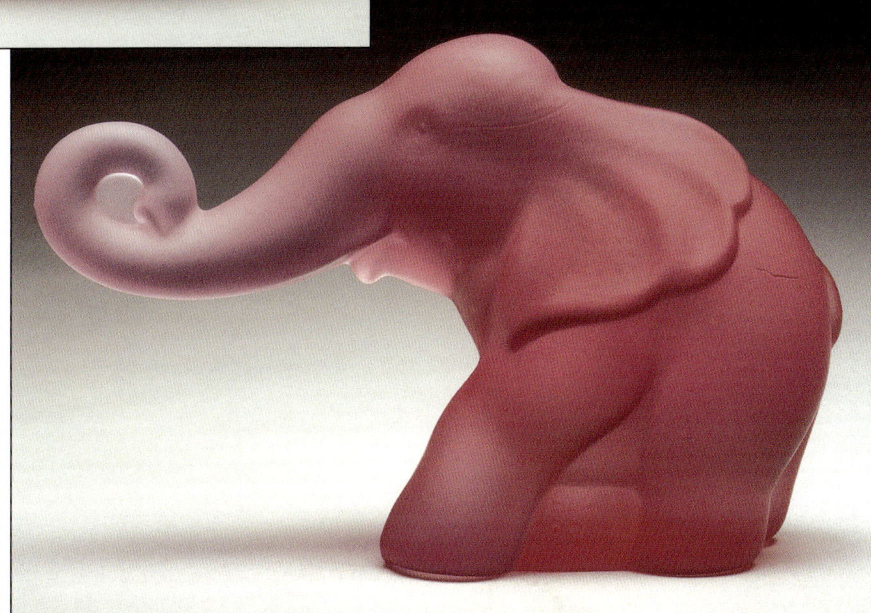

Medium elephant, Lavender Ice with satin finish, marked "D" for between legs for Dalzell Viking and "HCA 93" for Heisey Club of America, 4.25" tall, 6.25" long, Circa 1993, **$65.00**

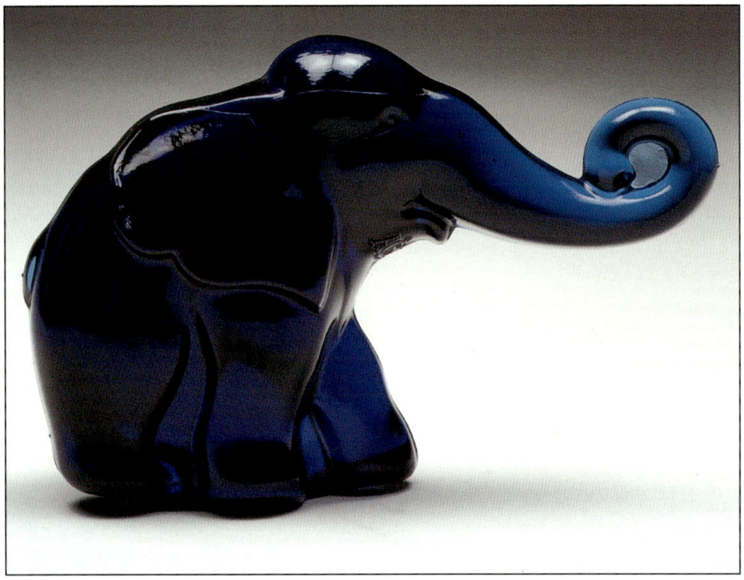

Medium elephant, Cobalt, Made by Mosser Glass, 4.25" tall, 6.25" long, Circa 2000, **$95.00**

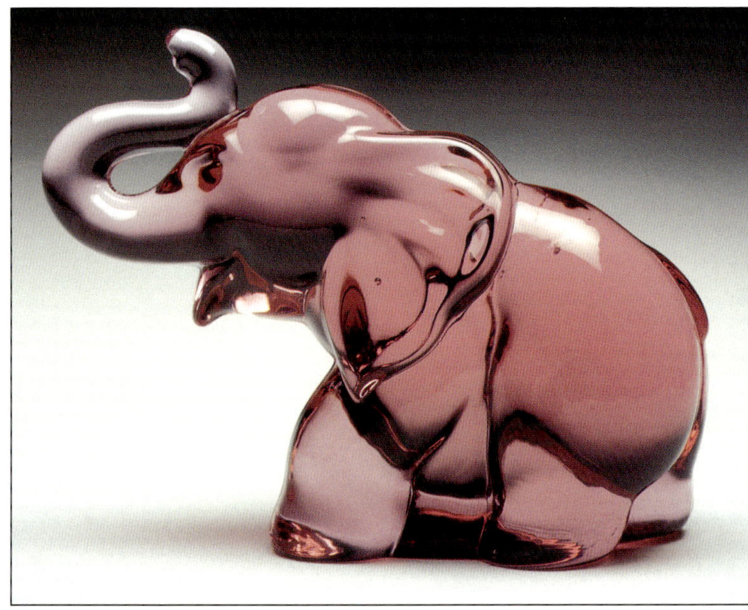

Large Elephant, Lavender Ice, Made by Dalzell Viking, Limited to 450 made, 5" tall, 6.25" long, Circa 1993, **$85.00**

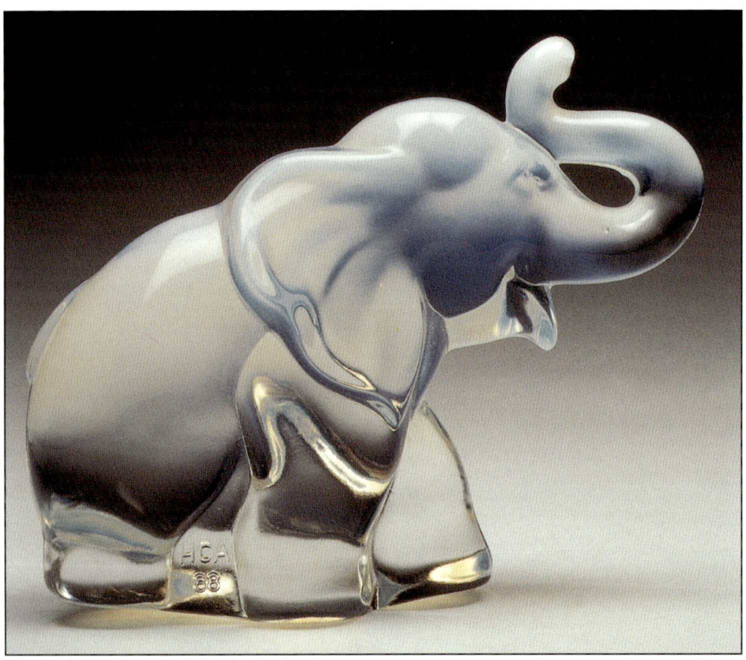

Large elephant, French Opalescent, marked "HCA 88" for Heisey Club of America between legs, Made by Fenton Art Glass Company Glass, 5.25" tall, 6.5" long, Circa 1988, **$85.00**

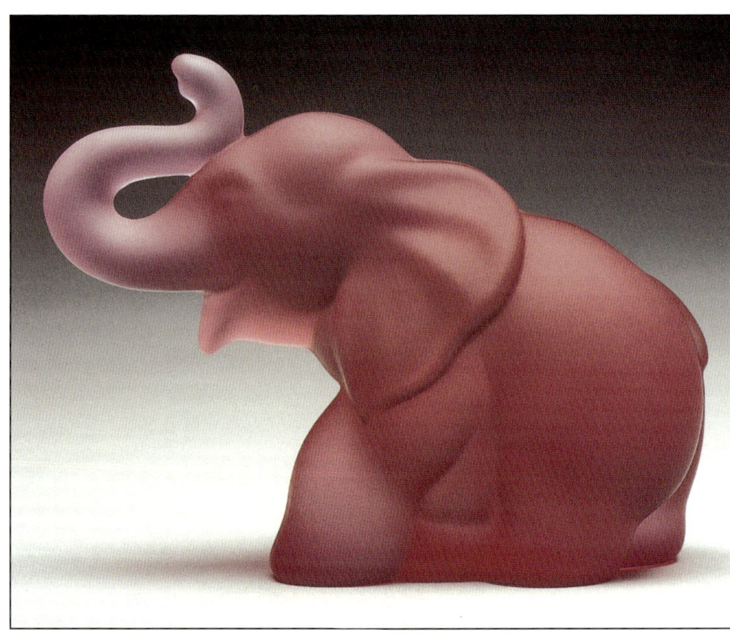

Large elephant, Lavender Ice with satin finish, marked "D" between legs for Dalzell Viking and "HCA 93" for Heisey Club of America, 5.1" tall, 6.5" long, Circa 1993, **$75.00**

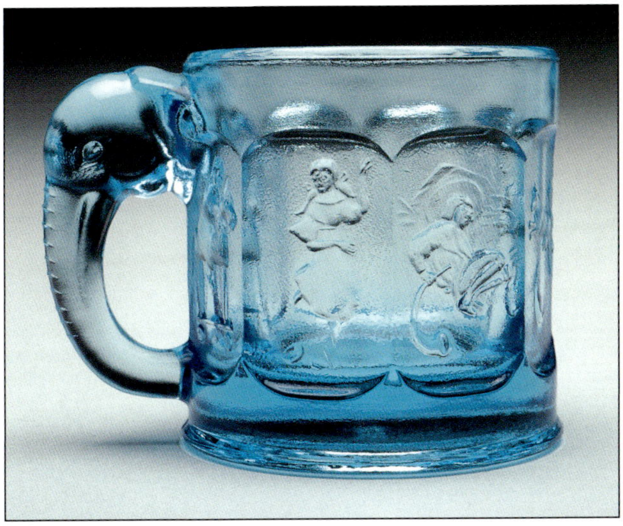

Storybook Mug, Pink, marked "HCA" for Heisey Club of America, Made by Dalzell Viking, 3" tall, 6 fluid ounces, Circa 1997, **$18.00**

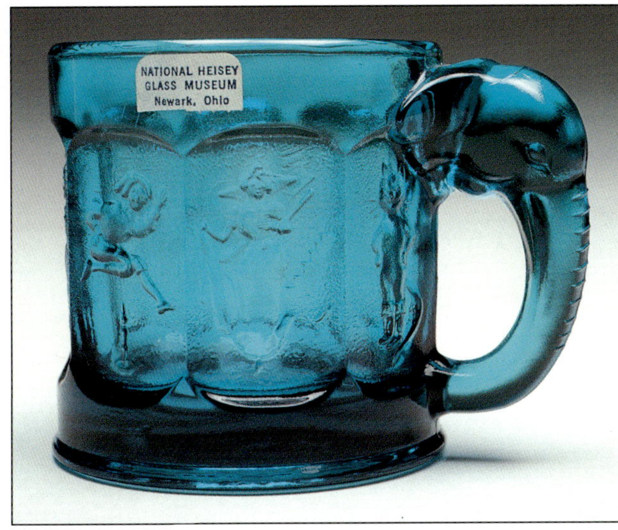

Storybook mug, Teal, marked "HCA 89" for Heisey Club of America, 3.1" tall, 3" wide, Circa 1989, **$30.00**

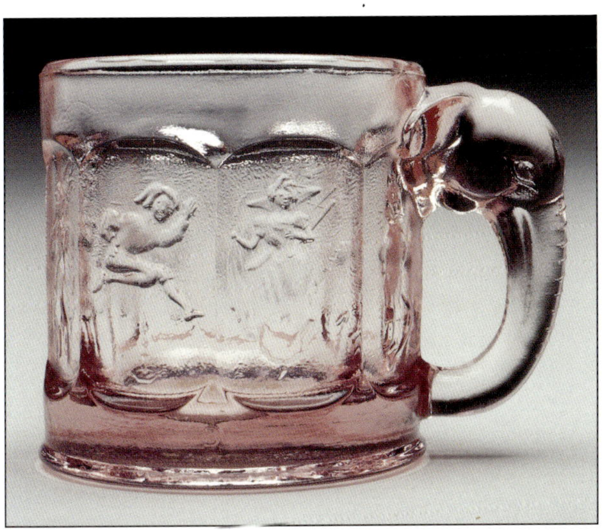

Storybook Mug, Blue, marked "HCA" for Heisey Club of America, 3" tall, 6 fluid ounces, Circa 1987, **$24.00**

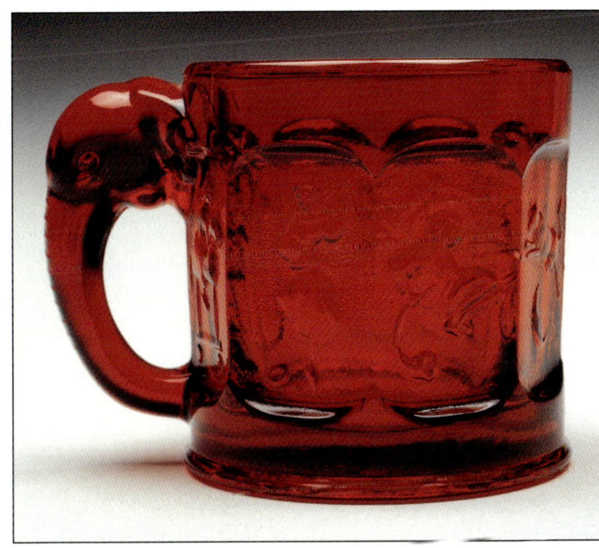

Storybook Mug, Ruby, marked "HCA" for Heisey Club of America, 3" tall, 6 fluid ounces, Circa 1989, **$35.00**

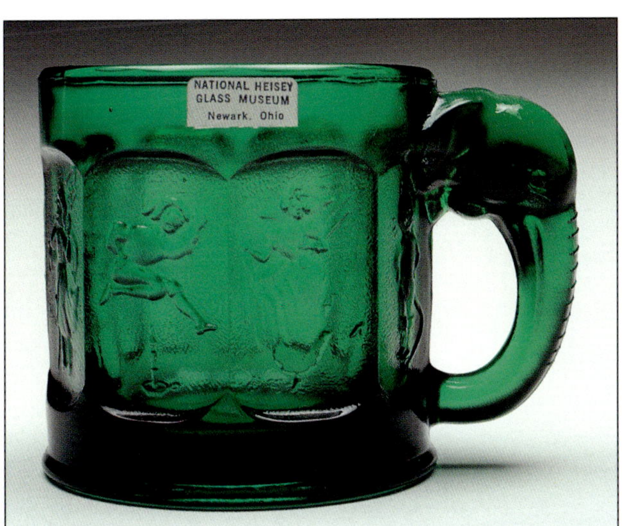

Storybook Mug, dark transparent green for Heisey Club of America, 3" tall, 6 fluid ounces, Circa 1989, **$28.00**

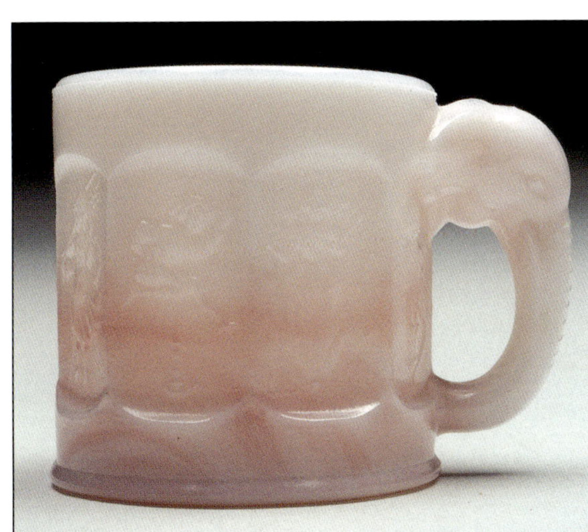

Story book mug, Rosalene, made by Fenton Art Glass Company Art Glass, 3" tall, 6 fluid ounces, Circa 1990, **$28.00**

Hocking Glass Company 1905-Present

The Hocking Glass Company started in 1905, in Lancaster, Ohio. Their roots were with jelly jars, lamp chimneys, and globes, and they expanded with tableware and novelty items in the 1920s.

The crystal-covered elephant was first made in 1928, when 36 pieces were sold to the California Perfume Company, the predecessor of the Avon Products Company. These glass elephants were intended to be gifts for top sales representatives, filled with Vernafleur bath salts. It is speculated that after the special promotion pieces were made for California Perfume Company, Hocking created their own pieces for retail sales. Additionally, elephants were produced in these four colors: crystal, crystal satin, pink, and green. It seems they were pleased with the result of these realistic elephants. This covered elephant was referred to as a pachyderm, but if you look at it closely, you see it resembles the Fenton "Jumbo," but is smaller in size. The Fenton "Jumbo" was not covered.

The Hocking Glass Company purchased Lancaster Glass in 1924 and Monongah Glass in 1930. Hocking combined with Anchor Cap & Closure Corporation, in 1937, and became Anchor Hocking. Standard Glass Company was absorbed by Anchor Hocking in 1940, and finally Phoenix Glass was purchased in 1970. This expansion created a highly diverse company, and Anchor Hocking is today's largest American producer of glass tableware.

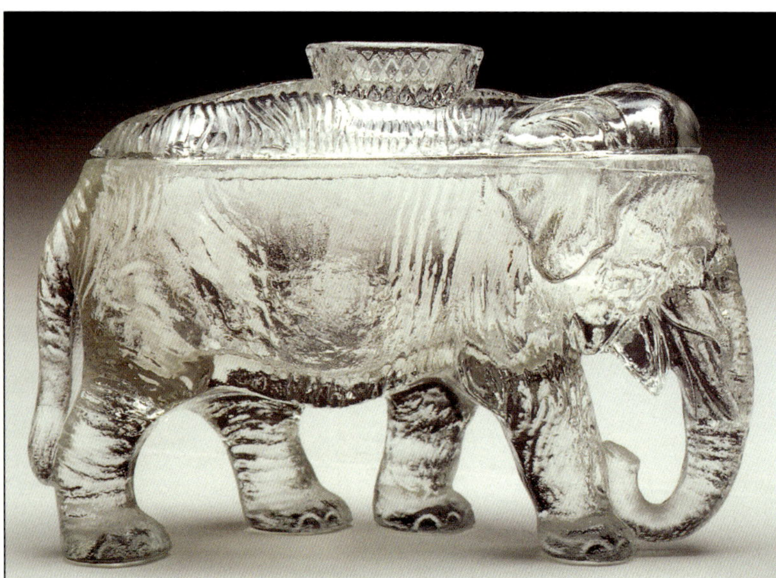

Elephant (Pachyderm) candy dish, Crystal, 4.4" tall, 6" long, Circa 1920's, **$85.00**

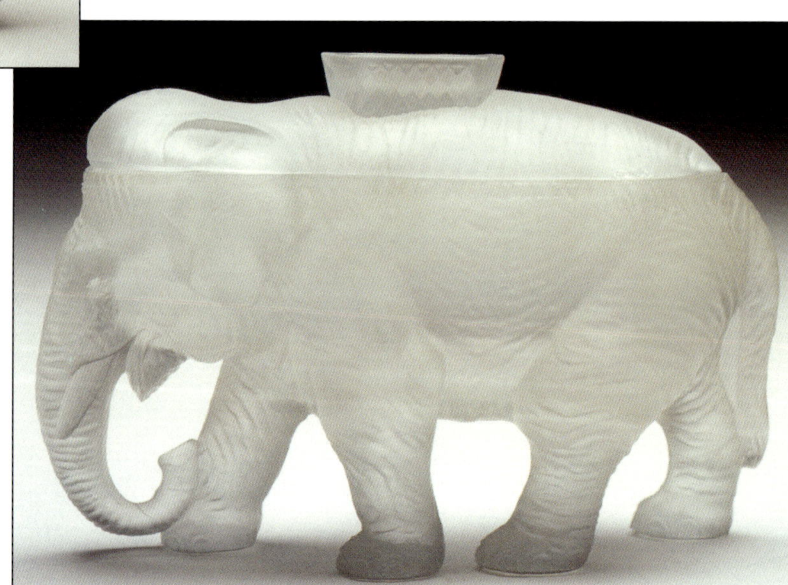

Elephant (Pachyderm) candy dish, Crystal with satin finish, 4.4" tall, 6" long, Circa 1920's, **$95.00**

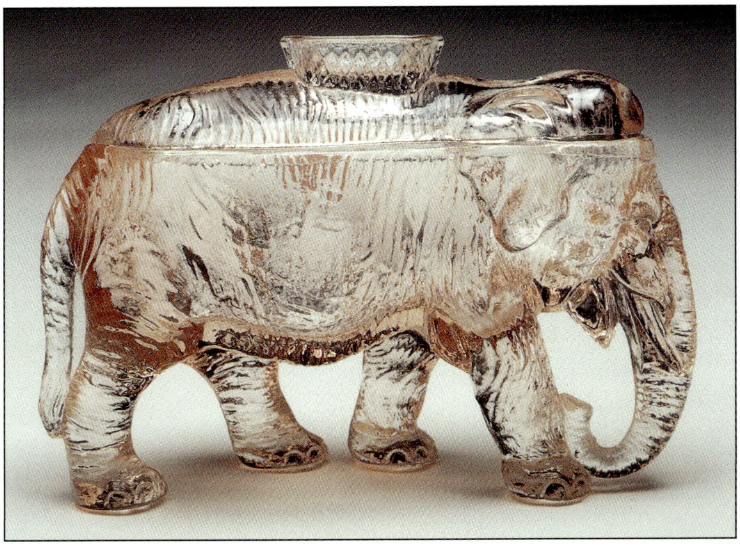

Elephant (Pachyderm) candy dish, Pink, 4.4" tall, 6" long, Circa 1920's, **$175.00**

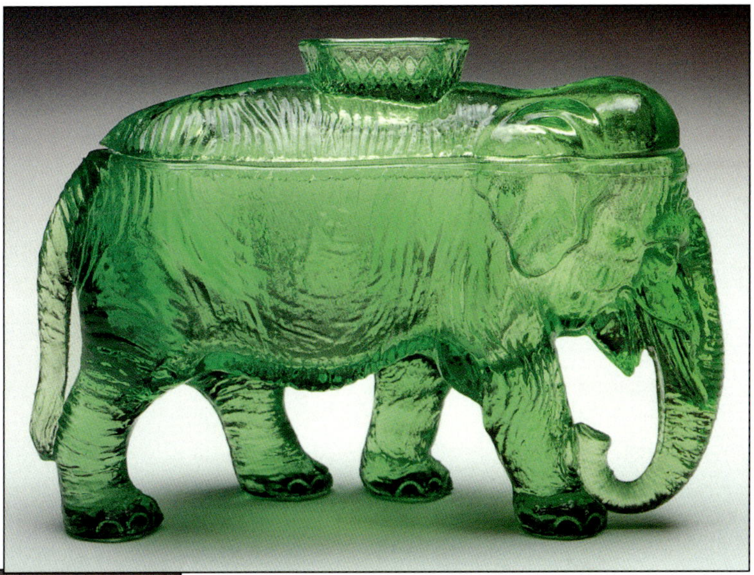

Elephant (Pachyderm) candy dish, Green, 4.4" tall, 6" long, Circa 1920's, **$175.00**

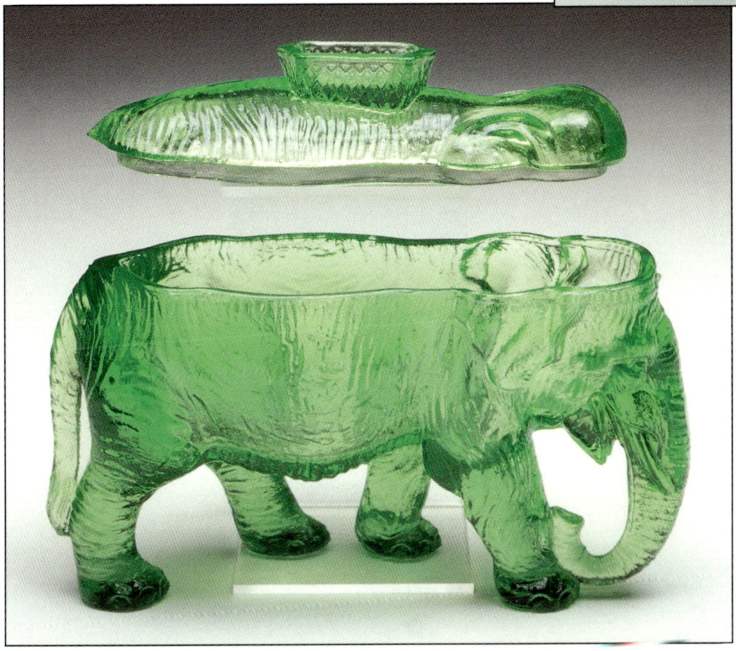

Left:
Elephant (Pachyderm) candy dish, Green, shown with back off

Comparison of Green Hocking elephant on the left and Fenton Rose colored elephant on the right

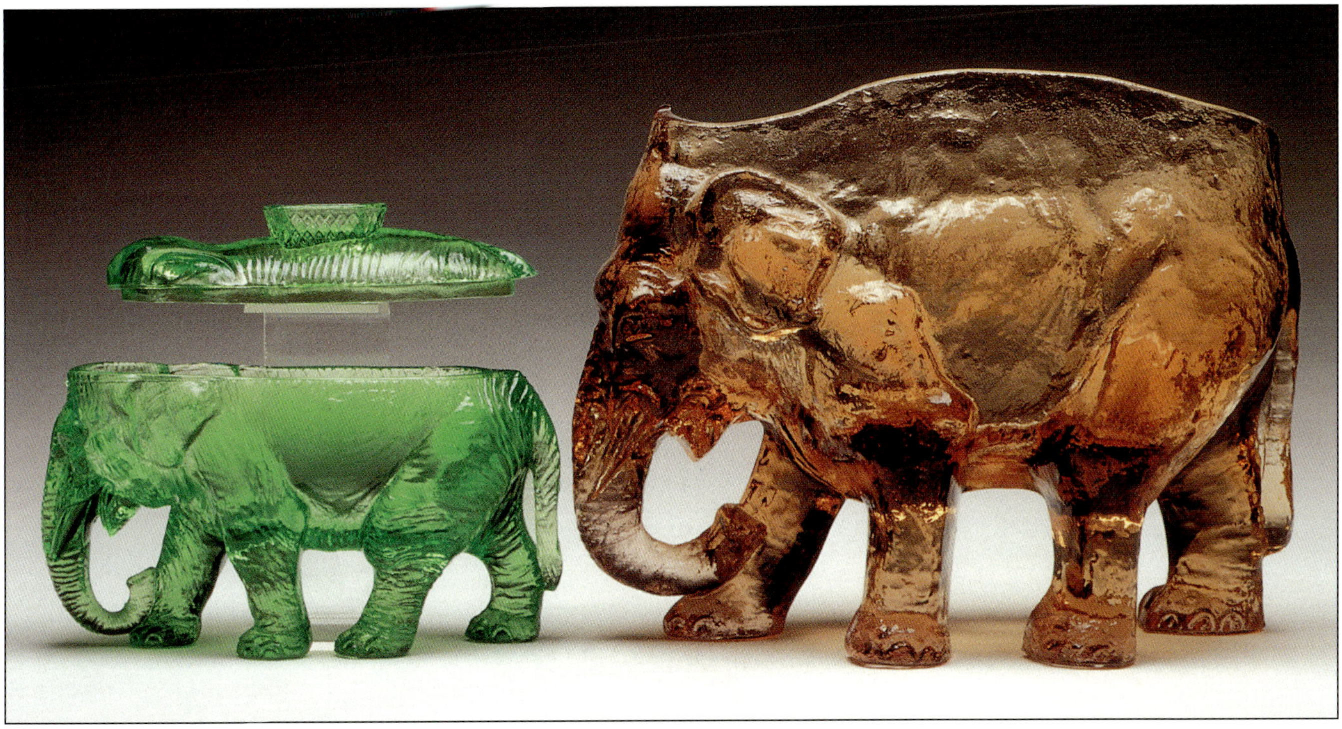

Houze Glass Company 1902-Present

Leon J. Houze, a Belgian immigrant, founded the L. J. Houze Convex Glass Company, in 1902, in Point Marron, Pennsylvania, which is just north of Morgantown, West Virginia.

The company's roots were in window glass and formerly had been named Federated Glass Company. The new company specialized in glass lamps, smoking sets, and desk items, including a variety of glass ink blotters that were animal shapes; one was an elephant. The elephant was designed by Garrett Thew in 1931. Donkey (for Democrats) and elephant (for Republicans) glass forms were issued for political campaigns.

This company's unique work is distinguished. For example, they made all the glass windows for the White House renovation for Harry Truman. The company has been very versatile, their variety including sun glass lenses and perfume bottles. Houze has been in business for over a 100 years, which is an incredible record.

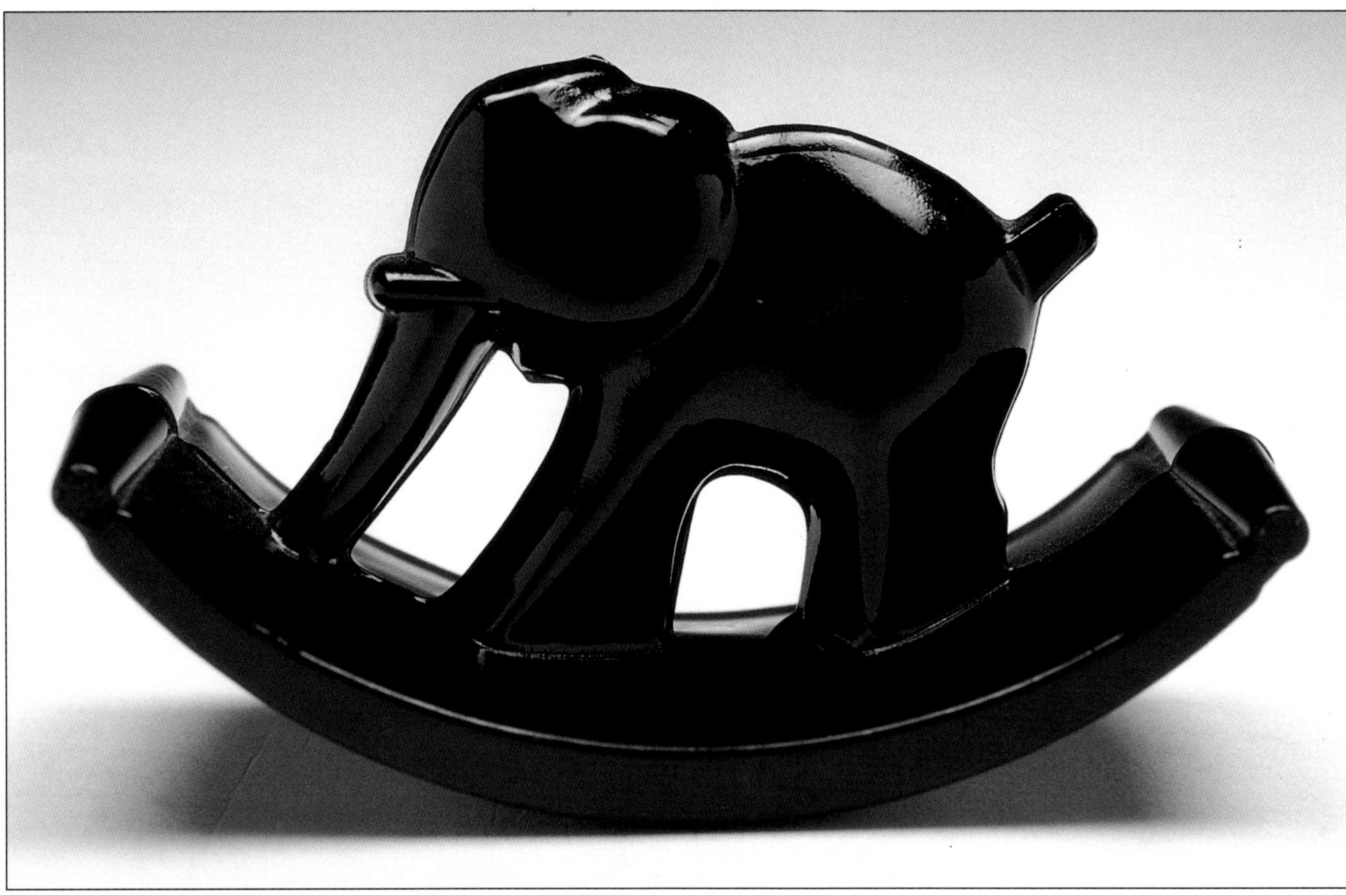

Elephant ink blotter, Black, marked on back copyright THEW-31, **$45.00**

Imperial Glass Company 1901-1982

Imperial Glass Company had its beginnings with Muhleman's Crystal Glass Company, which was organized in 1901 by Edward Muhleman, an investor who had been in search of some promising business ventures. Muhlman contacted other investors within the Bellaire area of Ohio and they agreed to build a glass factory there. Production started in 1904, and it was not long after that Imperial grew to be a major manufacturer.

Imperial company markings on some of their glass have been I.G. since the 1950s. Further, the Heisey company and Cambridge company were bought to be part of Imperial in 1958. Heisey had had glass animals already, and when they were made in new and exciting colors, Imperial's sales soared. Among these animals were elephants. To further their success and boost sales, Imperial workers experimented with old formulas, such as slag glass and carnival glass. Their new versions did help the company's sales.

Lenox Incorporated purchased the Imperial Glass Company in 1973. With this change, the mark on the glass had to be changed as well, so it became L.I.G. (Lenox Imperial Glass). However, this company was short lived, since Lenox sold the plant just a few years later. Next, Arthur Lorch purchased the company in 1981. and the mark became A.L.I.G. (Arthur Lorch Imperial Glass). However, Lorch kept the company only a short time, less time than Lenox, and sold the company to Robert Stahl in 1982. Stahl identified the answers to the company's financial strife, yet no local banks would front the finances. Hence, the company filed for bankruptcy and the court sold it all to Lancaster Colony in 1984. To complete the transaction, there was a liquidation sale at which the Heisey Collectors of America and the National Cambridge Collectors Club took the opportunity to purchase many of the moulds left in the factory.

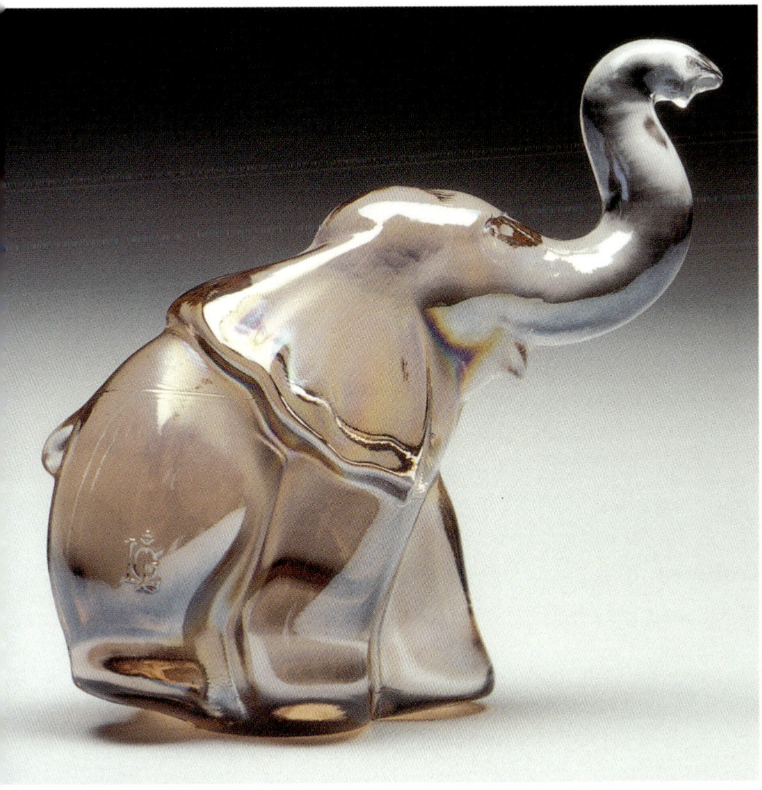

Small elephant, Pink Iridized (only 300 made), 4.6" tall, 4.6" long, Circa 1980 **$85.00**

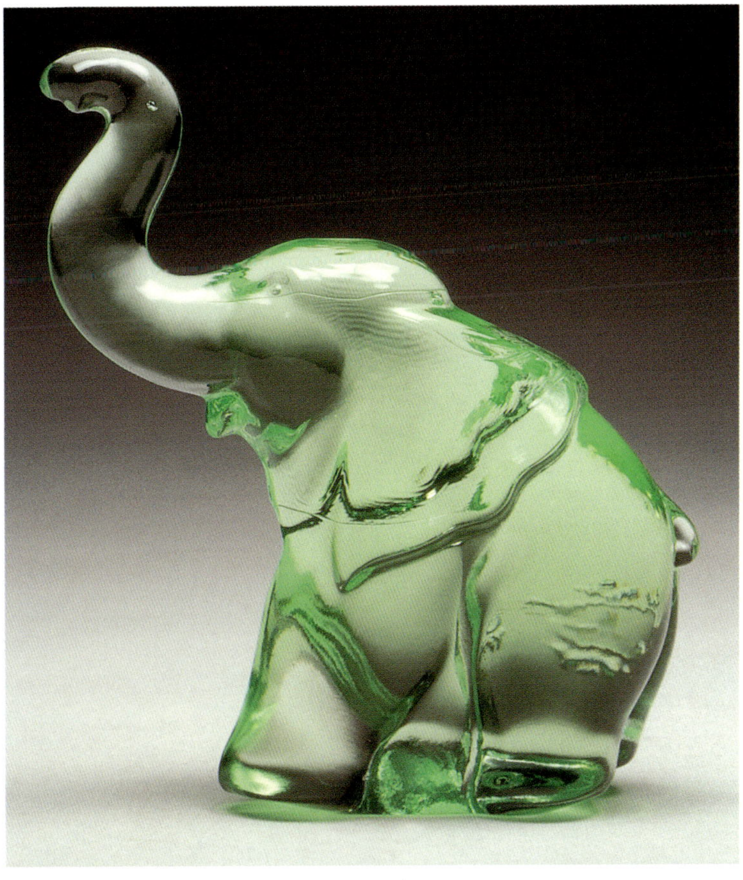

Small elephant, Meadow green, (only 25 made), marked on hind leg "ALIG" for (Arthur Lorch) Imperial, 5" tall, 5" long, Circa 1980, **$250.00**

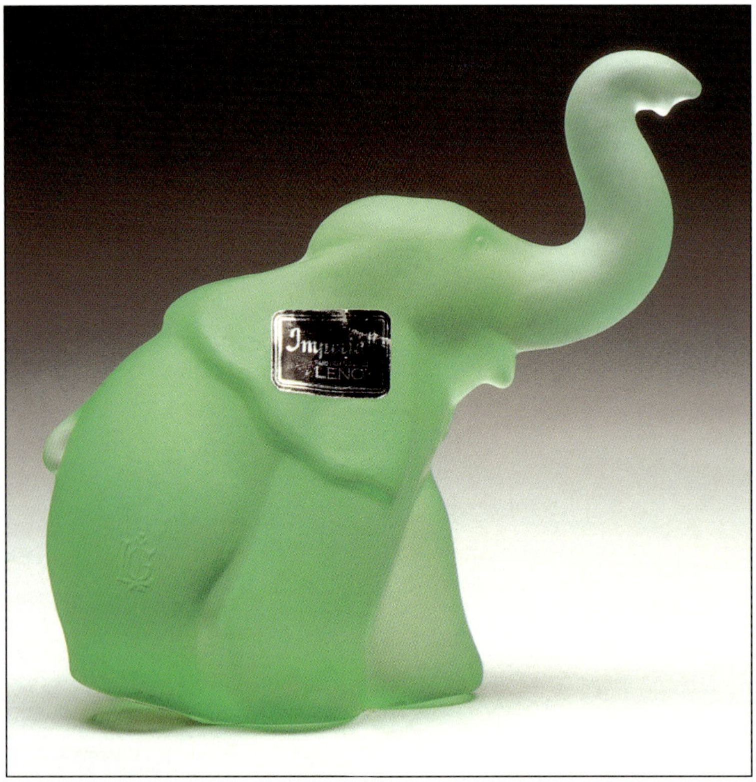

Small elephant, Meadow Green with satin finish, (only 200 made), marked on hind leg “LIG” for Imperial Lenox, original black and silver label Imperial Lenox, 4.7” tall, 5” long, Circa 1980, **$100.00**

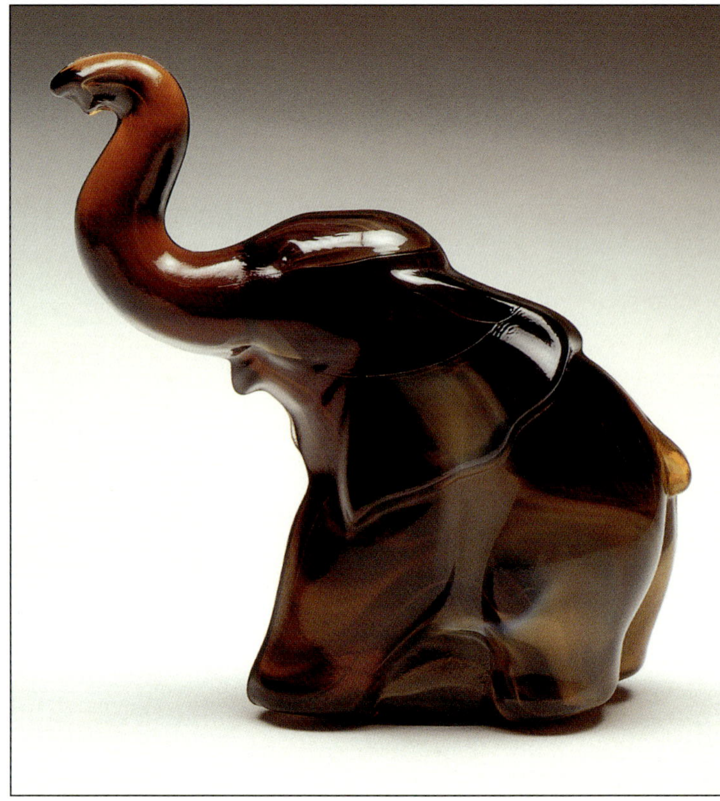

Small Elephant, Carmel Slag, (only 500 made) marked “ALIG” for (Arthur Lorch) Imperial, 4.75” tall, 5” long, Circa 1982-83, **$85.00**

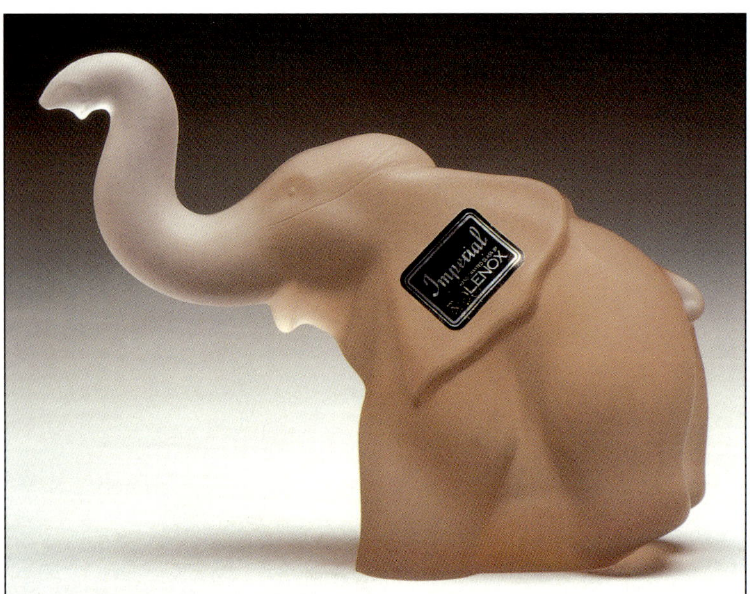

Small elephant, Pink with satin finish, (only 500 made), marked on hind leg “LIG” for Imperial Lenox, original black and silver label Imperial Lenox, 4” tall, 5” long, Circa 1980, **$65.00**

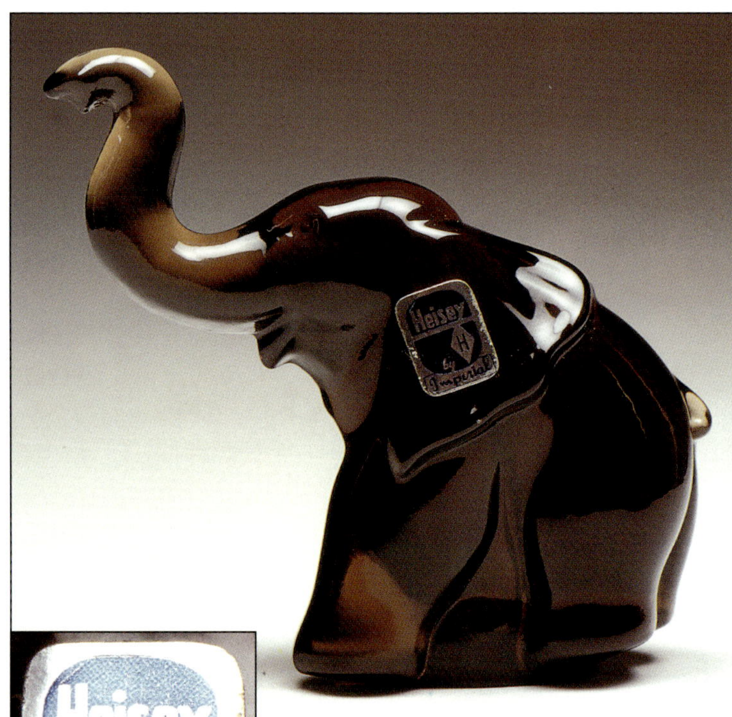

Small elephant, Nut Brown, (only 185 made) marked on hind leg “ALIG” for (Arthur Lorch) Imperial, original blue and silver label marked “Heisey by Imperial”, 4.6” tall, 5” long, Circa 1983, **$145.00**

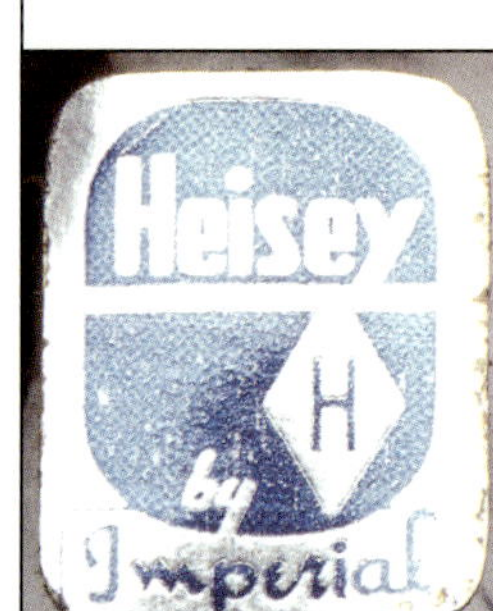

Detail of “Heisey by Imperial” blue and silver foil label

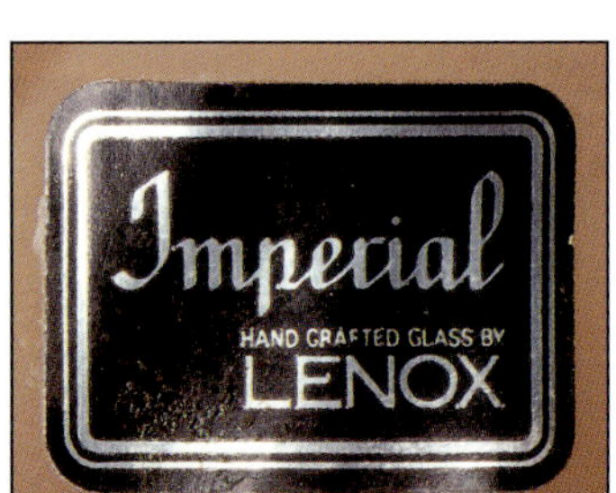

Detail of Imperial Lenox black and silver label on Pink with satin finish small elephant

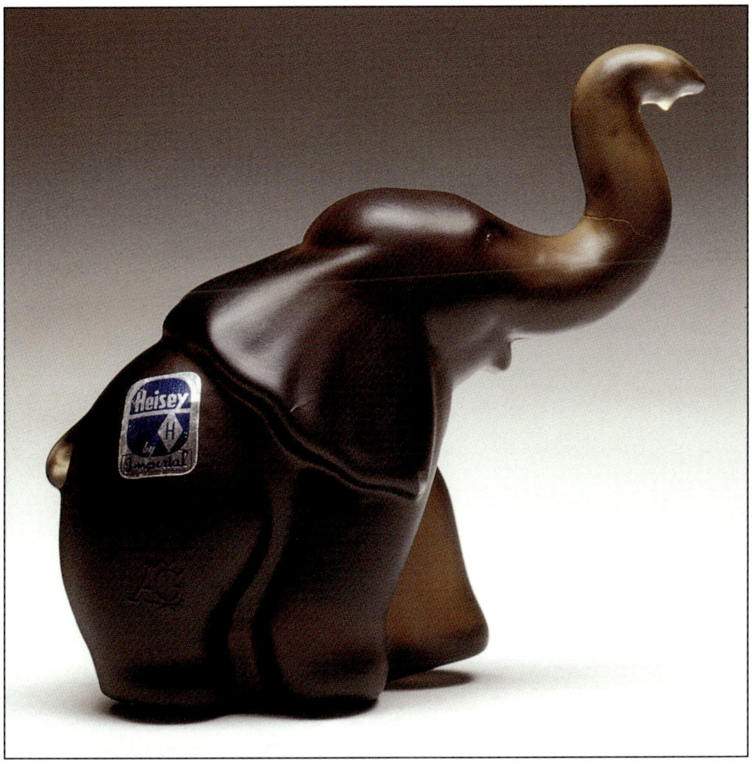

Small elephant, Nut Brown with satin finish, (only 185 made) marked on hind leg "ALIG" for (Arthur Lorch) Imperial, also has original blue and silver label saying Heisey by Imperial, 4.6" tall, 5" long, Circa 1983, **$125.00**

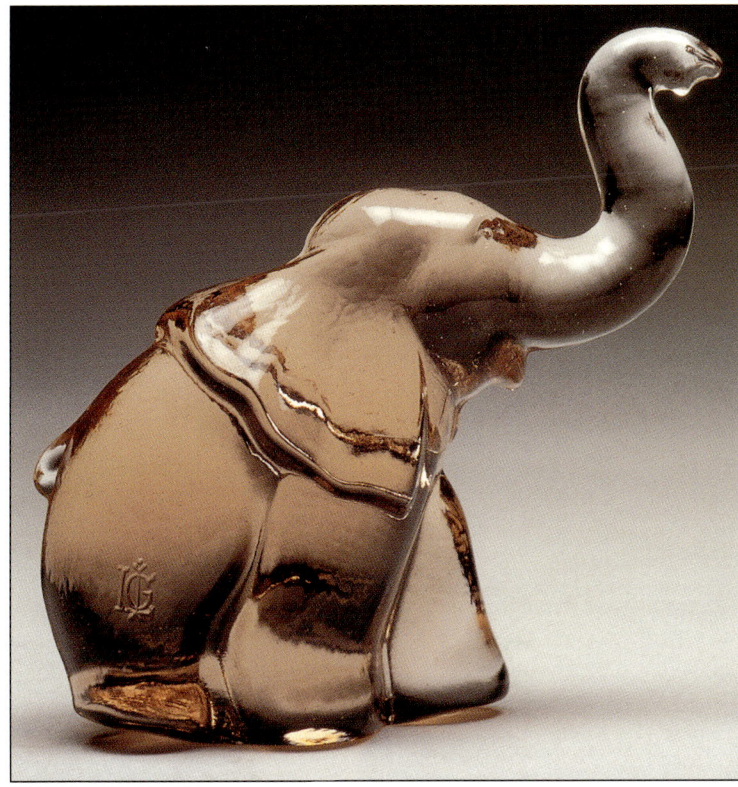

Small elephant, Salmon, (only 20 made) marked on hind leg "LIG" for Imperial Lenox, 4.6" tall, 5" long, Circa 1984, **$250.00**

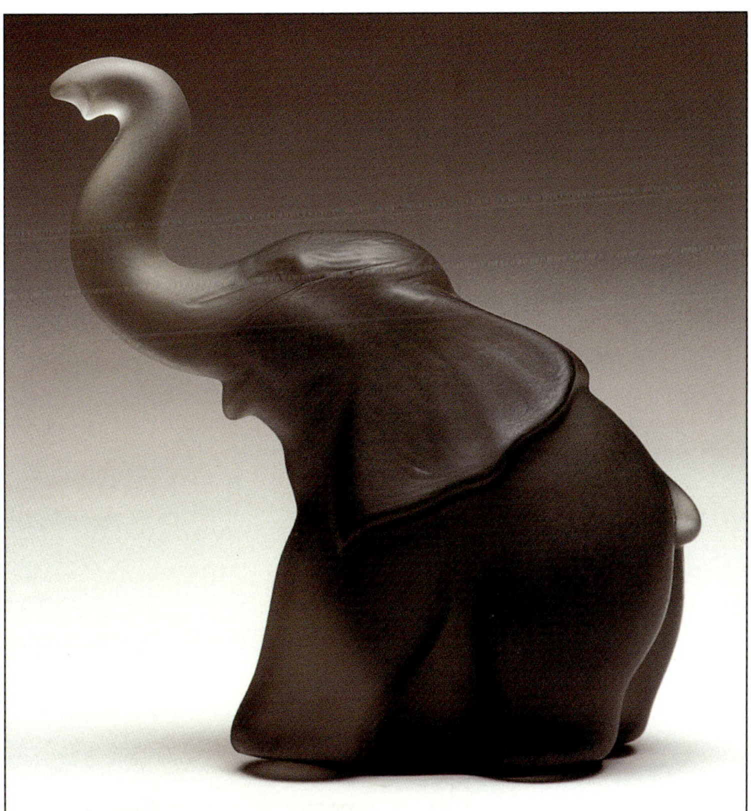

Small elephant, Charcoal with satin finish, (only 15 made) marked on hind leg "IG" for Imperial, 4.8" tall, 5" long, Circa 1983, **$350.00**

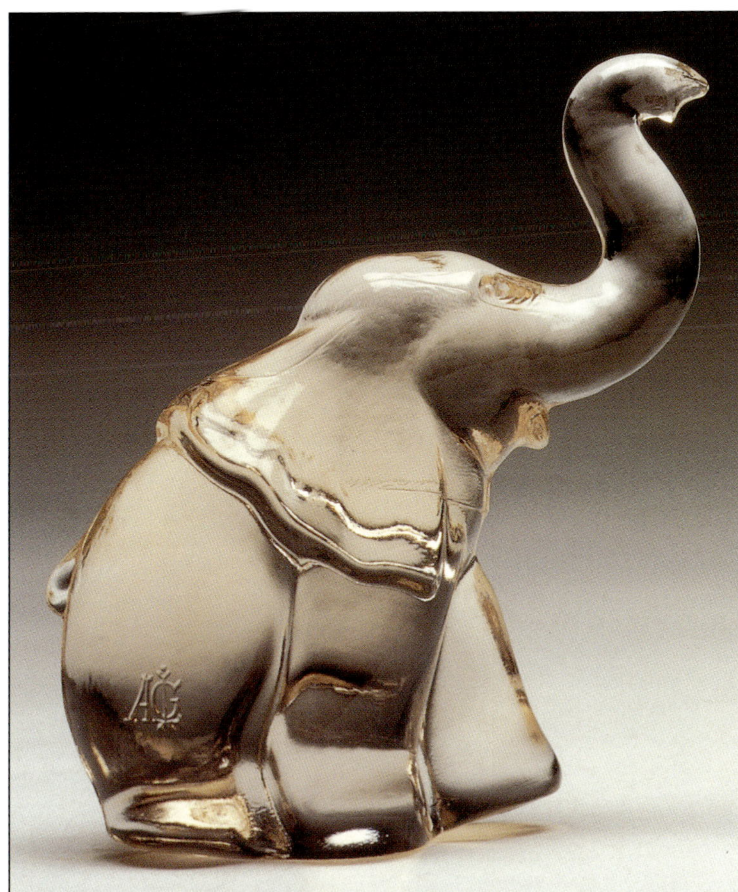

Small elephant, Light pink, (only 25 made) marked on hind leg "ALIG" for (Arthur Lorch) Imperial, 5" tall, 4.75" long, Circa 1984, **$250.00**

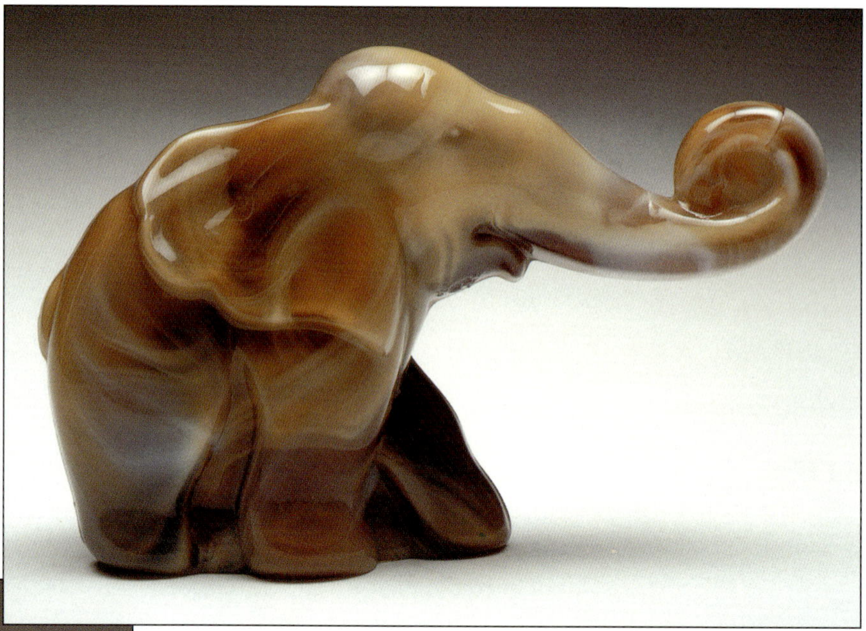

Medium Elephant, #3942, Carmel Slag, (1,500 made) marked under lip "IG" for Imperial, 4.1" tall, 6.25" long, Circa 1969-77, **$95.00**

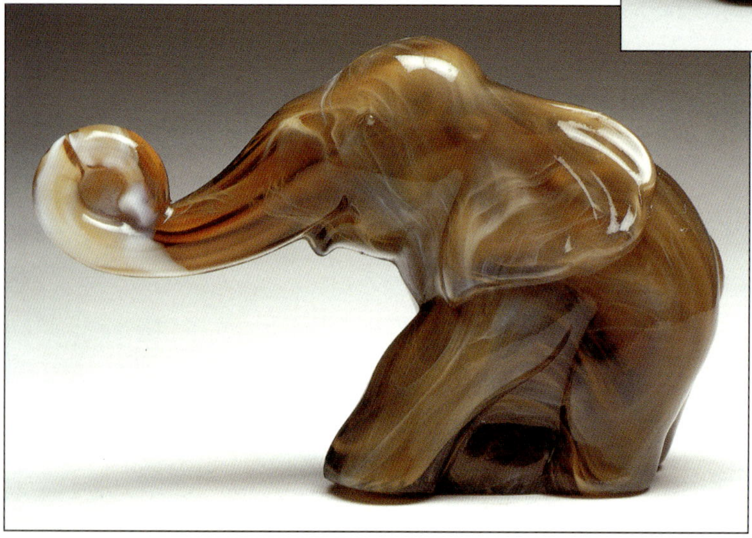

Medium Elephant, #3942, Carmel Slag, comparison to show strong variation in colors of this slag glass color, **$95.00**

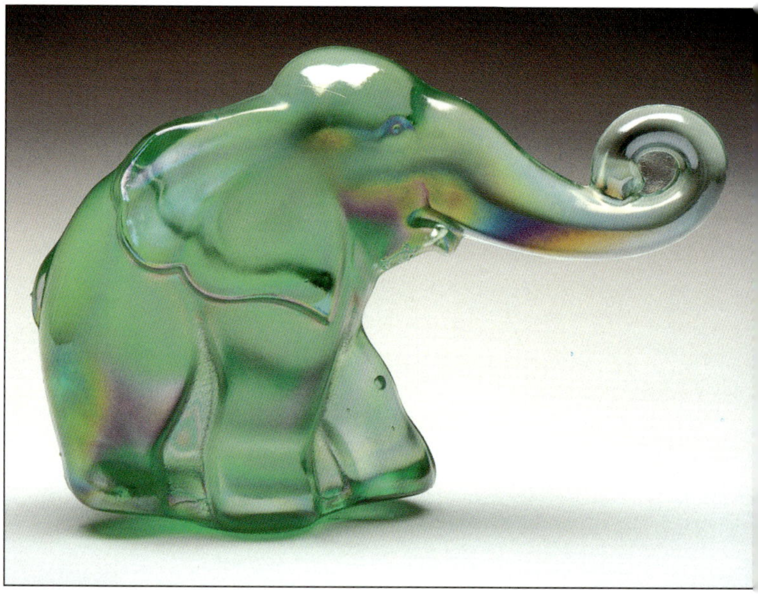

Medium Elephant, marked "LIG" for Imperial Lenox, Meadow Green Carnival, (only 750 made), 4.5" tall, 6.25" long, Circa 1980, **$75.00**

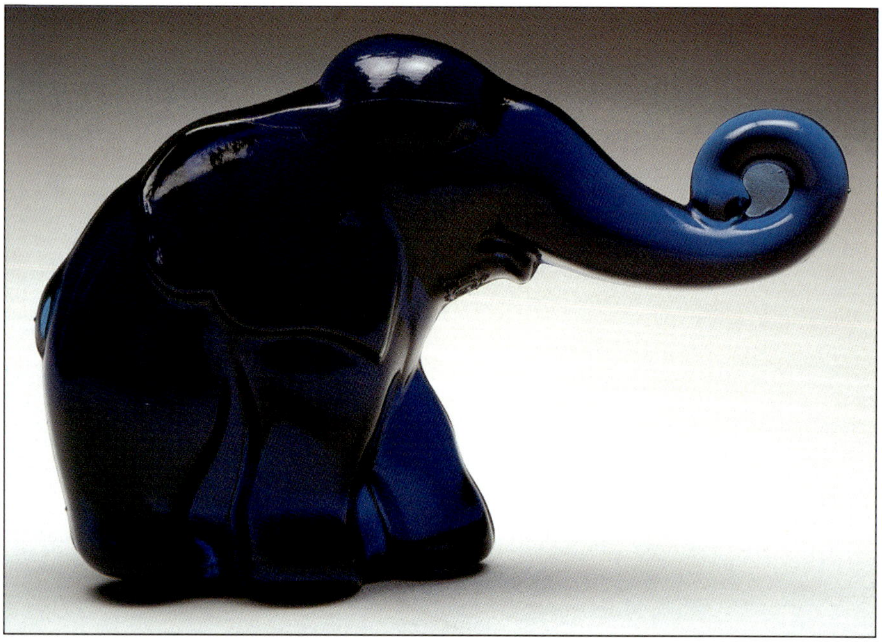

Medium Elephant, marked "ALIG" for (Arthur Lorch) Imperial, Ultra Blue (cobalt), only 569 made, 4.25" tall, 6.25" long, Circa 1982 **$125.00**

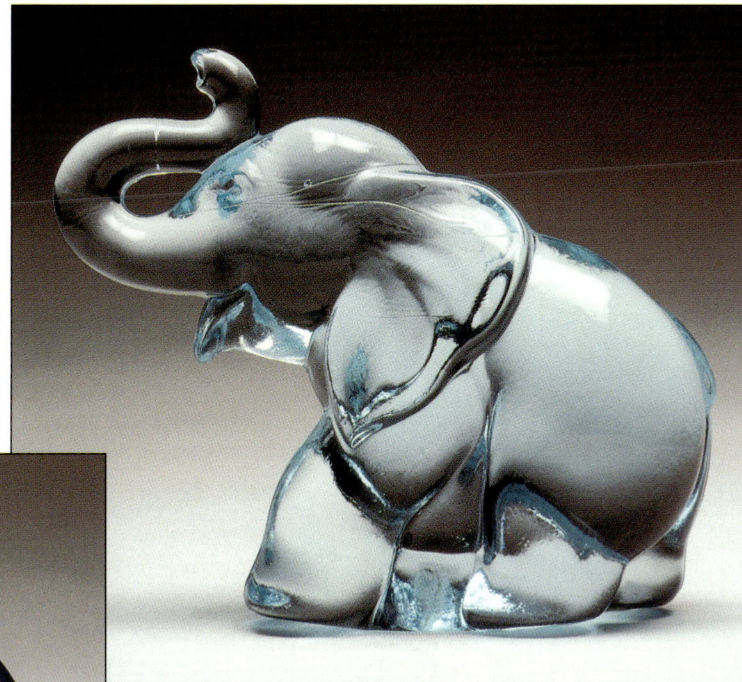

Large elephant, Horizon Blue, (only 16 made) no mark, 5.4" tall, 6.5" long, Circa 1984, **$450.00**

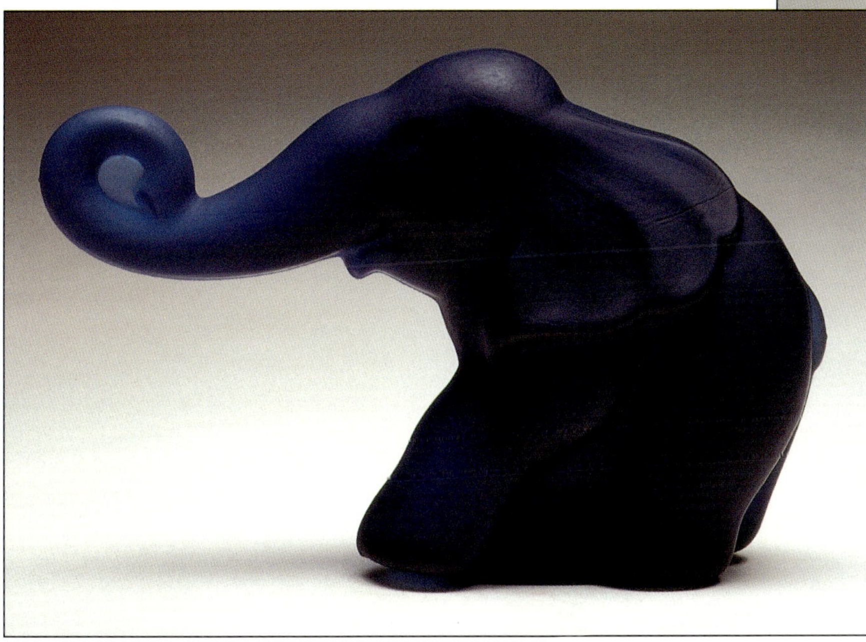

Medium elephant, Ultra Blue with satin finish, marked under lip "ALIG" for (Arthur Lorch) Imperial, 4.5" tall, 6.4" long, Circa 1982, **$100.00**

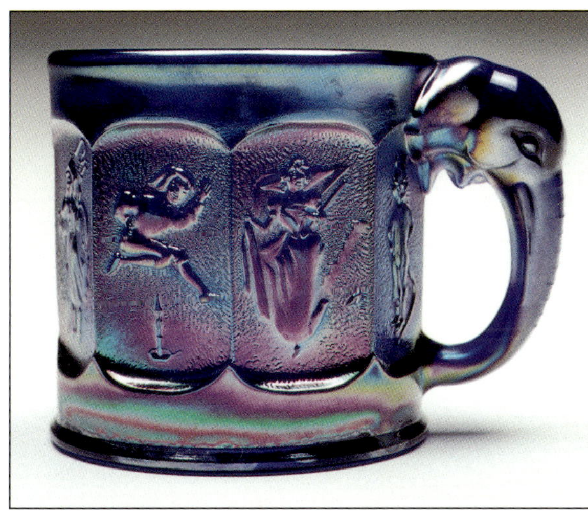

Storybook Mug, Aurora Jewels (carnival finish), marked "IG" for Imperial, 3" tall, 6 fluid ounces, Circa 1971-72, **$30.00**

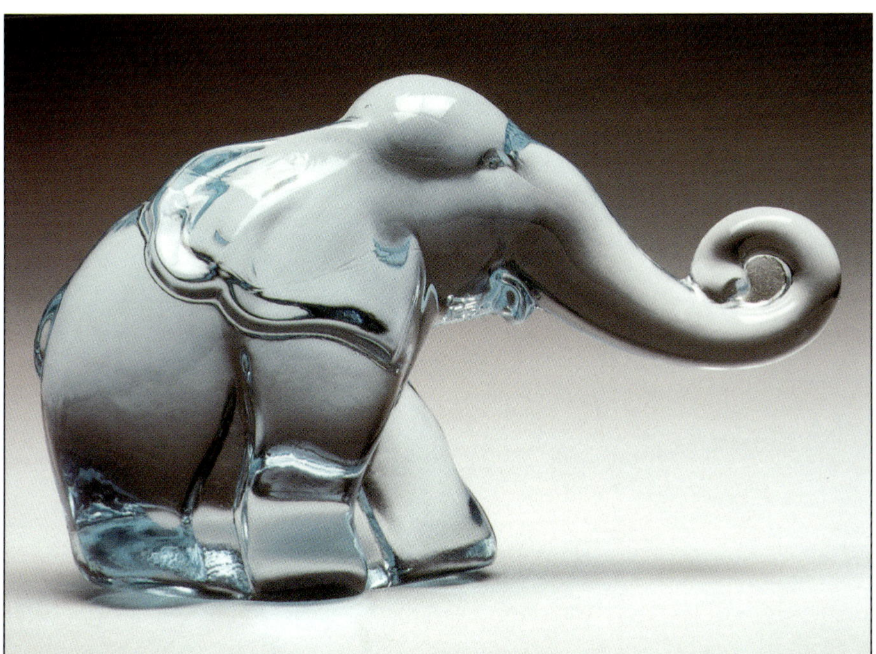

Medium elephant, Horizon Blue, (only 32 made) marked under lip "ALIG" for (Arthur Lorch) Imperial, 4.25" tall, 6.25" long, Circa 1984, **$250.00**

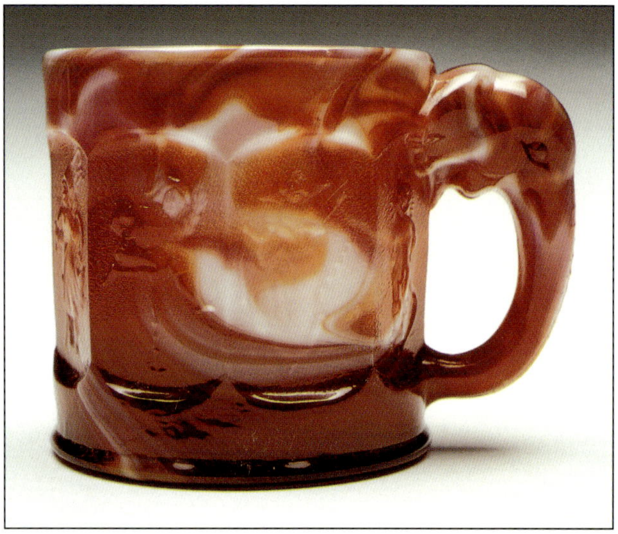

Storybook Mug, Red Slag, marked "IG" for Imperial, 3" tall, 6 fluid ounces, Circa 1975-77, **$35.00**

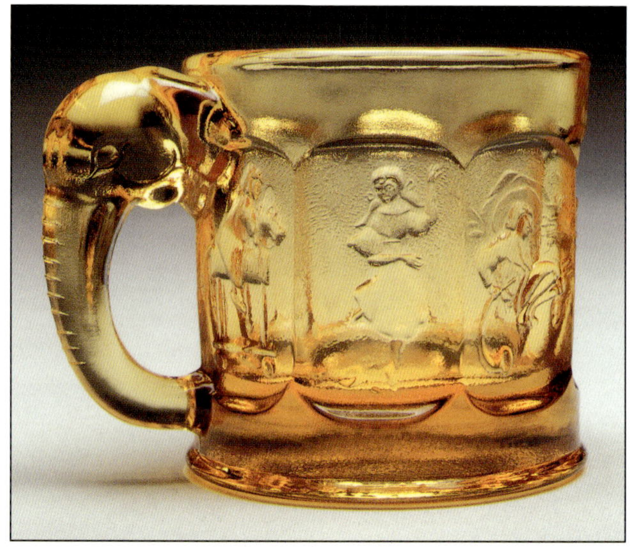

Storybook mug, Sunshine Yellow, marked "ALIG" for (Arthur Lorch) Imperial, 3.1" tall, 3" wide, Circa 1981, **$25.00**

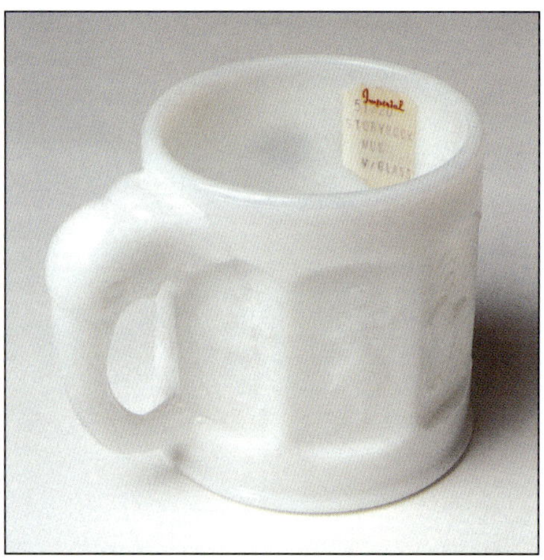

Storybook Mug, Milk Glass, marked "IG" for Imperial, 3" tall, 6 fluid ounces, Circa 1975-77, **$20.00**

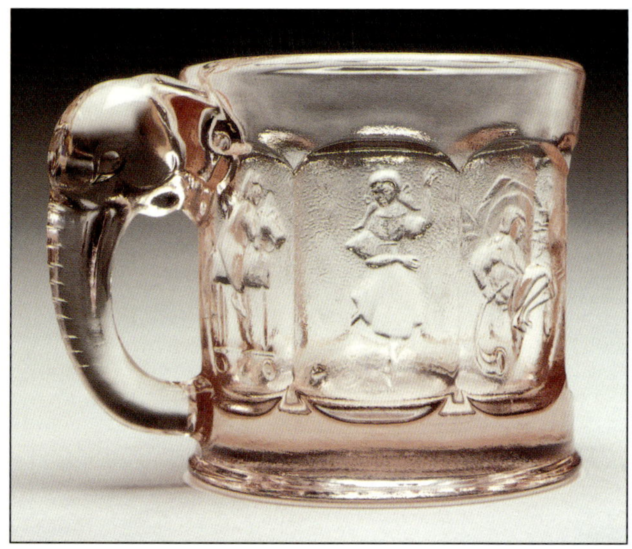

Storybook Mug, Pink, marked "ALIG" for (Arthur Lorch) Imperial, 3.1" tall, 3" wide, Circa 1984, **$25.00**

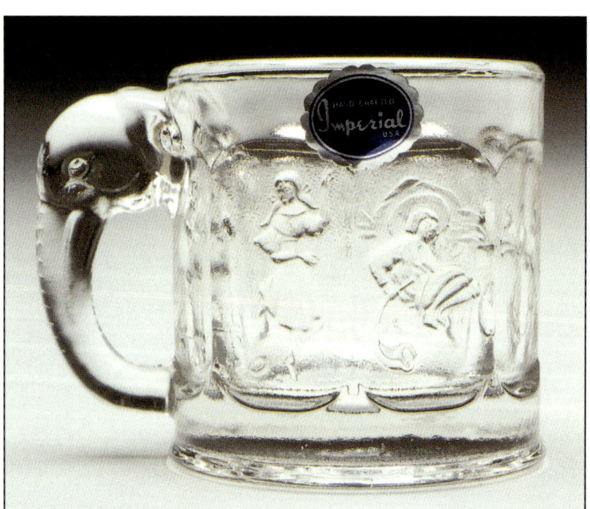

Storybook Mug, Crystal, marked "ALIG" for (Arthur Lorch) Imperial, 3" tall, 6 fluid ounces, Circa 1980, **$25.00**

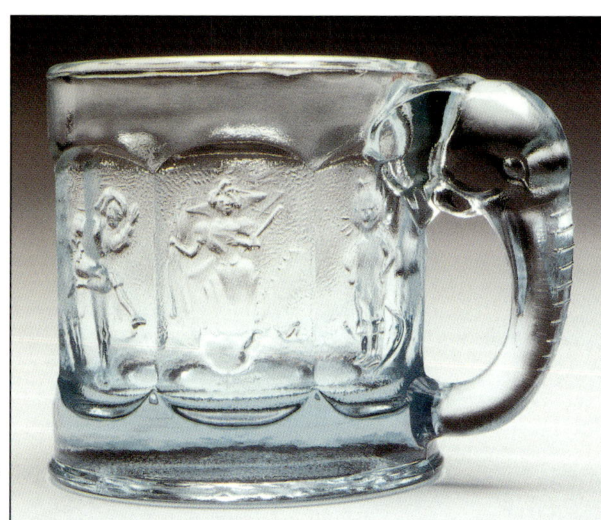

Storybook mug, Light Blue, marked "ALIG" for (Arthur Lorch) Imperial, 3.1" tall, 3" wide, Circa 1984, **$25.00**

Jeannette Glass Company 1920s-Present

Jeannette Glass Company was named for their location in Jeannette, Pennsylvania. The company's roots were in bottle making, but in the 1920s the company made a wise investment into machinery that brought about their production of glass tableware. They became one of the top producers of their time. By 1927, all hand production came to an end there, since it was not an efficient production method.

In 1950s, Jeannette Glass Company was still making traditional glassware, but they were interested in branching out to the gift and novelty items business. As a way to expand, Jeannette purchased the McKee Glass Company, which had been owned by Thatcher Glass, in 1961. Just a year later, Jeannette moved into the former McKee facility. Jeannette Glass is still creating glassware for the home.

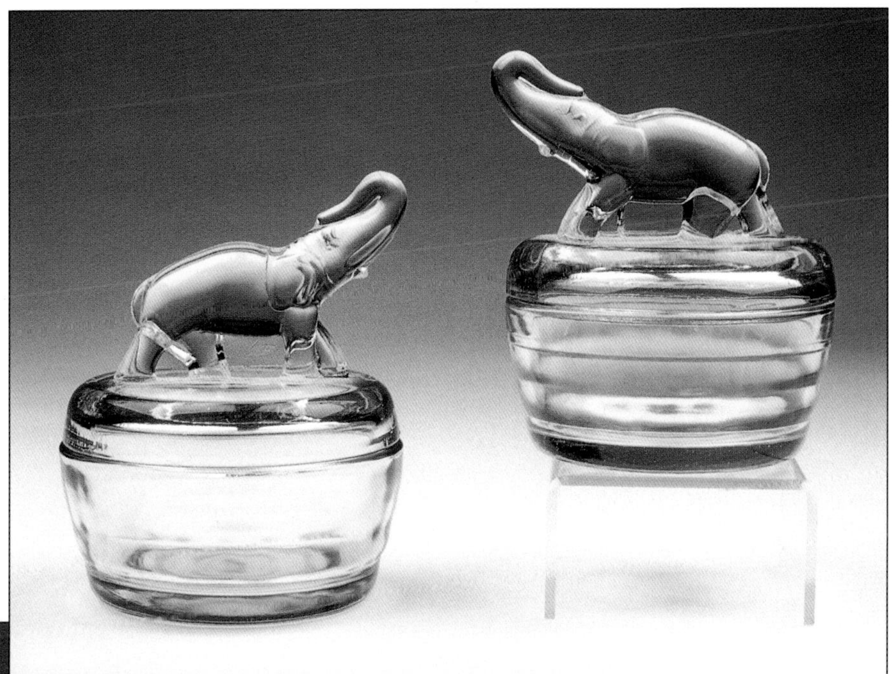

Flephant covered powder dishes, Crystal, 5" tall, 4" wide, Circa 1930's, **$25.00** each

Below:
Elephant covered powder dishes, shown with cover on and off

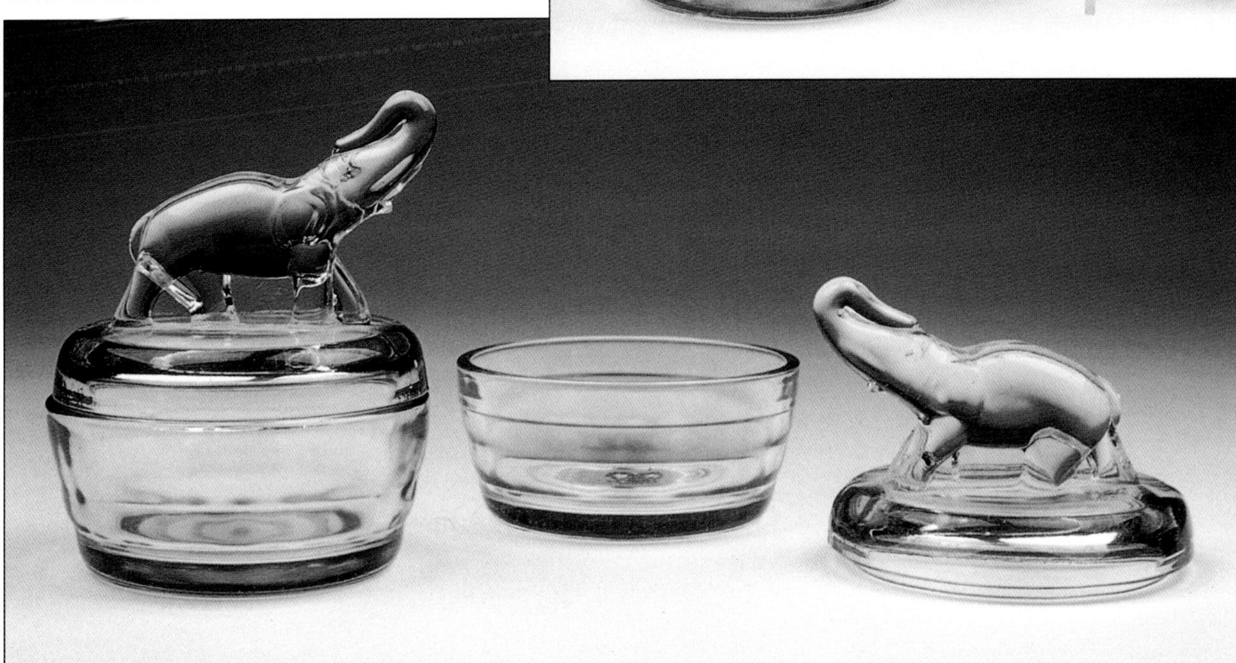

King Glass Company 1859-1891

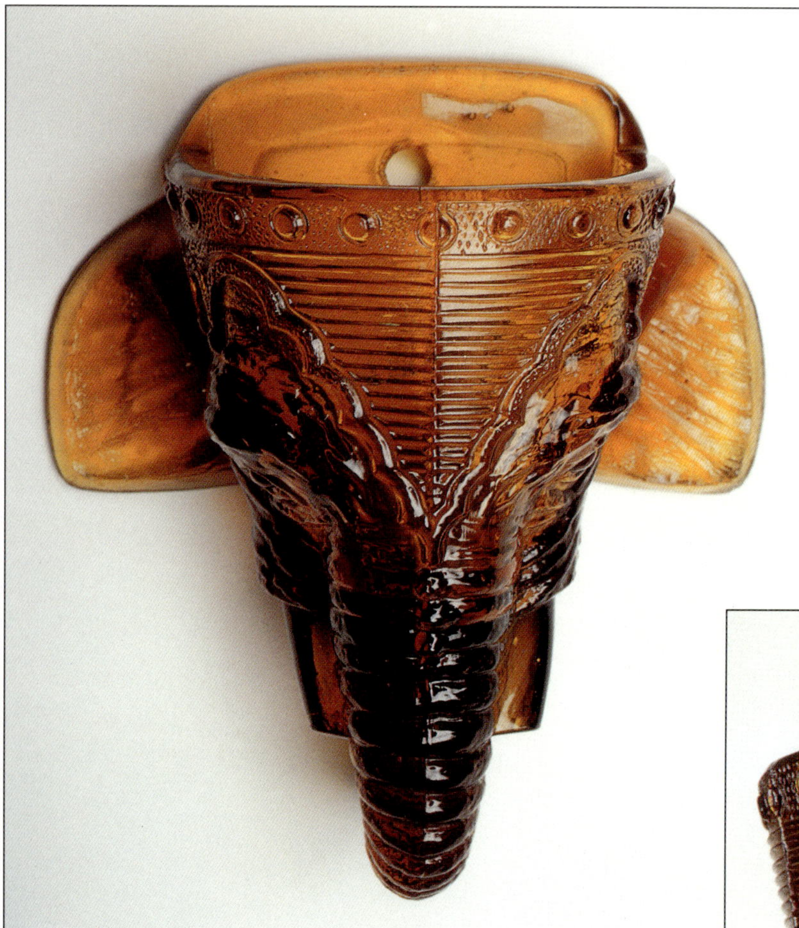

Elephant Head - match safe, Amber, 4.5" tall, 4.6" wide, Circa 1889, **$60.00**

Previously known as Cascade Glass Works, this company opened in 1859 and was founded by business partners Johnson and King. They were located in Pittsburgh, Pennsylvania. There were numerous name changes, but eventually the company would be called King Glass in 1888. Three years later, when King Glass Company became a part of the United States Glass organization, their identity became just Factory K. There is little concrete information about the company after this.

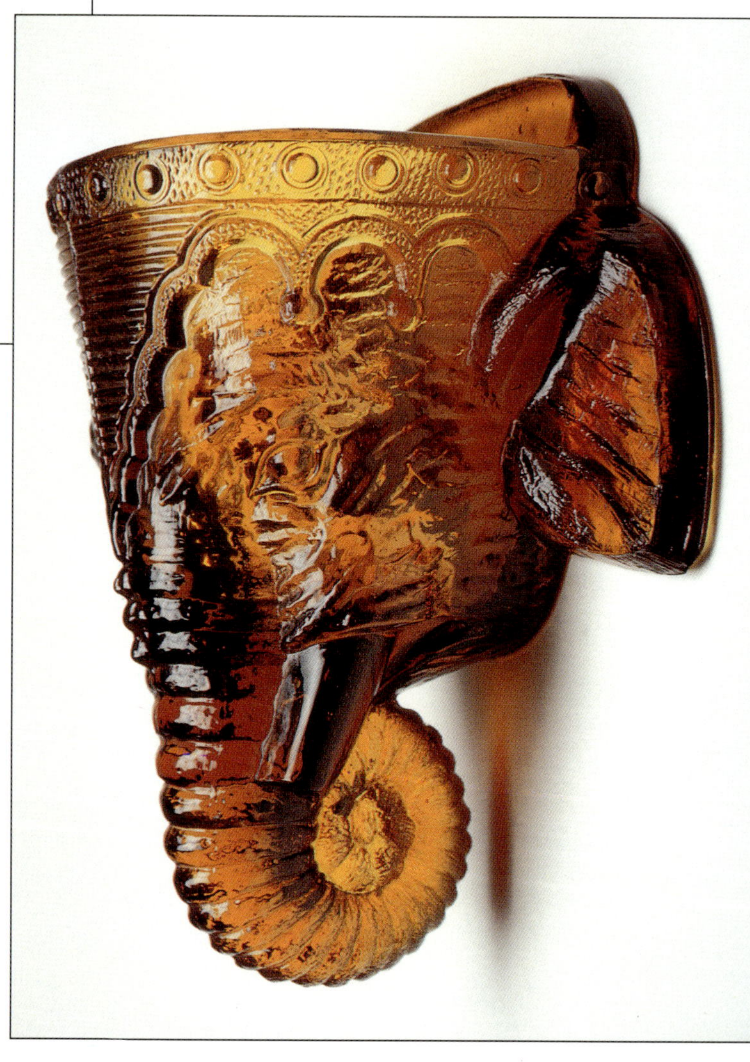

Elephant Head - match safe, Amber, shown for side view

Lenox Incorporated 1889-Present

Originally called The Ceramic Art Company, this firm was founded May 18th, 1889, by Jonathan Coxon Sr. and Walter Scott Lenox. It is presumed that Coxon left the company around 1894. In 1906, the company name was changed to Lenox Incorporated.

The roots of the business were producing decorative ceramic wares, with a strong emphasis on giftware, instead of dinnerware. Lenox Incorporated expanded its dinnerware production and lessened the hand-painting emphasis. When World War II occurred, they had produced over 3,000 various shapes, and with each of these they could make over 1,000 separate designs. After World War I, Lenox brought crystal, bone china, and ovenware into their lines, as they have today.

Lenox Inc. purchased glassmakers Bryce Brothers in 1965, to have their own glass division. In 1973, Lenox purchased the Imperial Glass Company (see above), held it only a few years, and sold it to Arthur Lorch.

Today the Lenox Incorporated corporate headquarters are located in Lawrenceville, New Jersey.

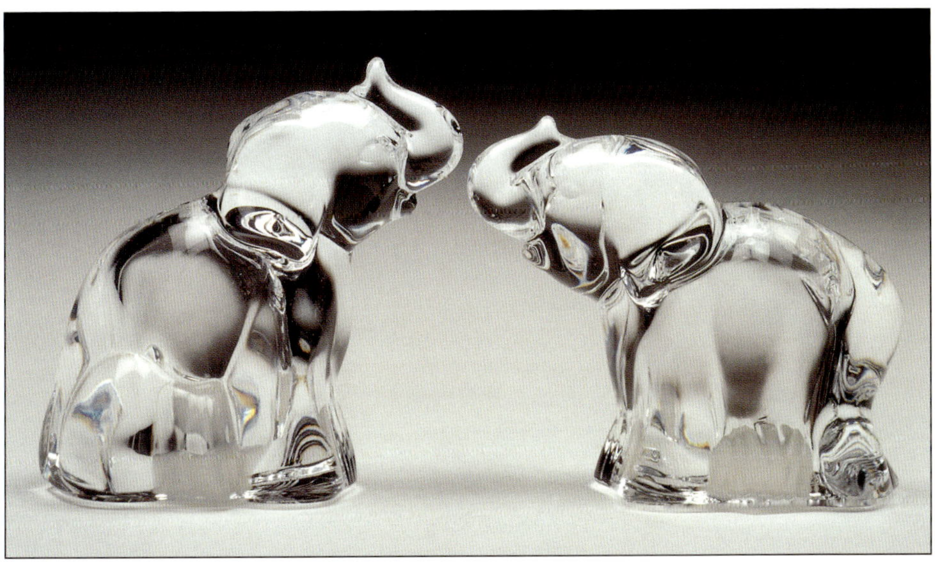

Standing Elephant Shakers, 3" tall, 3" long, Circa 1990's, **$35.00** pair

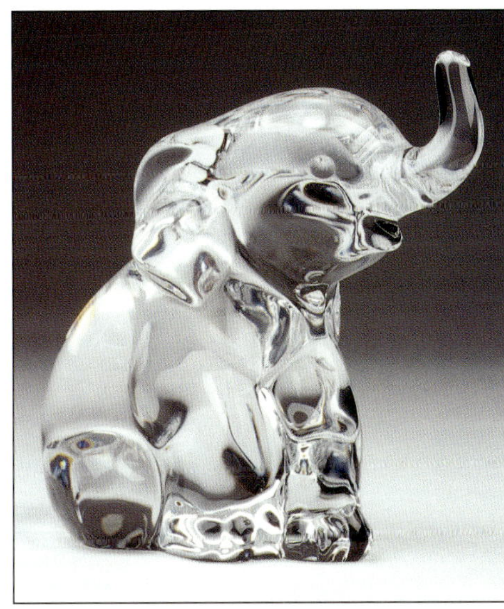

Elephant with trunk up, Crystal, 4.25" tall, 2" long, Circa 1990's, **$30.00**

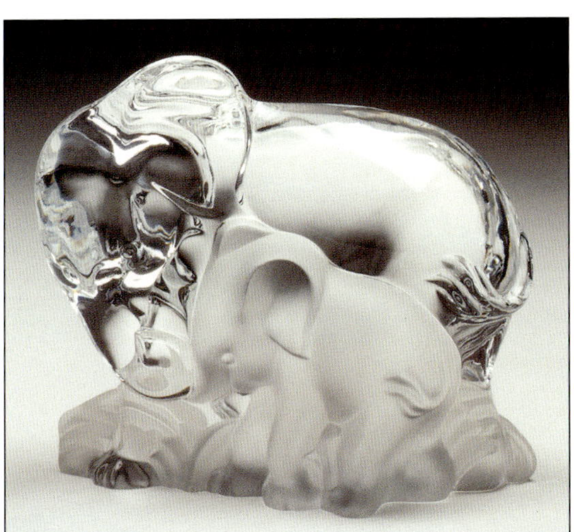

Elephant, 5.1" tall, Crystal, Mother with baby, 5.5" long, Circa 1990's, **$85.00**

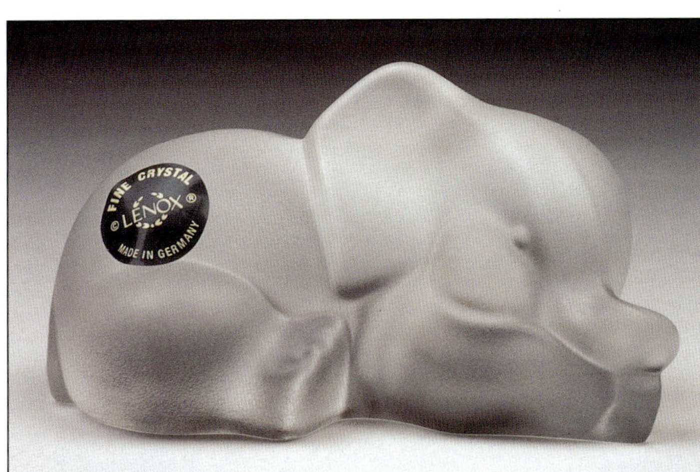

Elephant baby, Crystal with satin finish, 2" tall, 4.25" long, Circa 1990's, **$30.00**

Mosser Glass Company 1971-Present

Tom Mosser's glass career started at a very early age. He was 16 when he began working for Cambridge Glass Company and he stayed there until it closed in closed in 1959. Mosser then worked for Variety Glass Company, in 1959, later becoming its sole owner. Variety Glass was not making collectible glass, their business was medical and scientific glassware.

Mosser had a continuing interest in collectables and giftware, and wanted to produce his own designs. To achieve this goal, he purchased land in 1971 in Cambridge, Ohio, and built a new factory where the whole Mosser family could be involved together. Currently Mosser produces giftware and novelty items in a wide variety of colors. Only a few Mosser items are marked with their trademark, which is a capital M by itself, or a capital M inside the outline of the state of Ohio.

Robert T. Henry, President of Henry's Bimbah Collectible Art Glass Inc., Fort Wayne, Indiana, contracted Mosser to make a series of 25 limited-edition glass elephants. They were called "Henry's Bimbah Elephant" and consisted of a standing elephant on an oval base. The following is a list of the dates, colors, and number produced:

#1 July 1980, Autumn Amber, 978
#2 August 1980, Royal Custard, 983
#3 September 1980, Sunflower (vaseline), 987
#4 October 1980, Pink Petunia, 968
#5 November 1980, Taffy (slag), 994
#6 December 1980, Blue Horizon (iridescent), 993
#7 January 1981, Black Knight (iridescent), 938
#8 February 1981, Jungle Grey, 971
#9 March 1981, Shamrock (green), 990
#10 April 1981, April Gem (iridescent crystal), 991
#11 May 1981, Honey Comb (slag), 995
#12 June 1981, Lilac (heatherbloom), 960
#13 July 1981, Glowing Ember (iridescent), 992
#14 August 1981, Toby (slag blue/white), 962
#15 September 1981, Rose Bud (cranberry), 975
#16 October 1981, Snowy Pine (slag green/white), 988
#17 November 1981, Blue Boy (cobalt), 978
#18 December 1981, Gold Nugget, 969
#19 January 1982, Sheba (slag amethyst/milk glass), 970
#20 February 1982, Susie (red), 986
#21 March 1982, Shawn (iridized green), 944
#22 April 1982, Starlite (crystal), 987
#23 May 1982, Cocoa (Greentown chocolate), 927
#24 June 1982, Henry's Dream (vaseline opalescent), 944
#25 July 1982, Henry's Surprise, only 260

The mould was retired in July, 1982, and placed in the Fort Wayne, Indiana, Historical Museum.

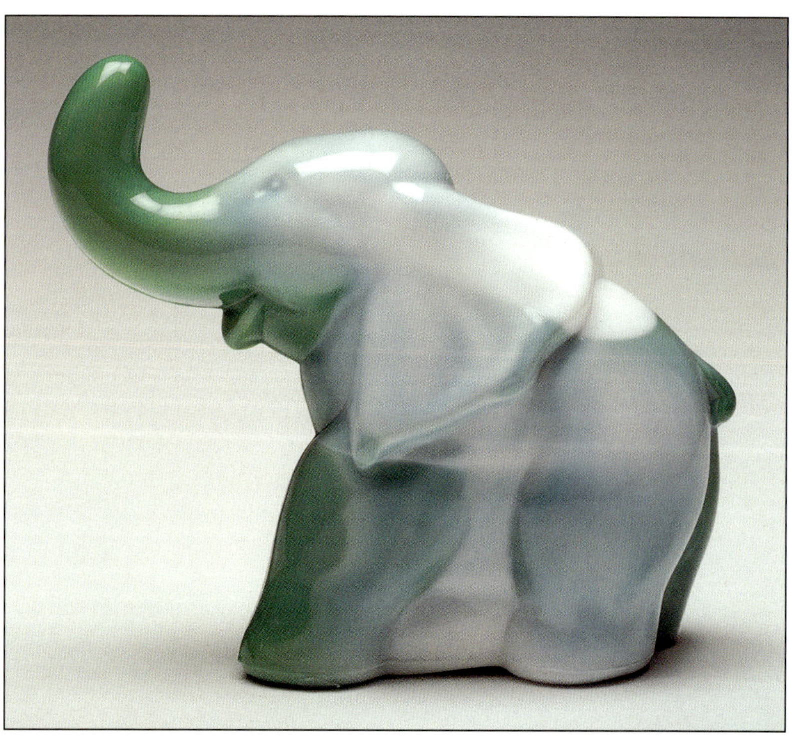

Elephant with trunk up #129, Green Slag, 3.3" tall, 4" long, Circa 1995, **$28.00**

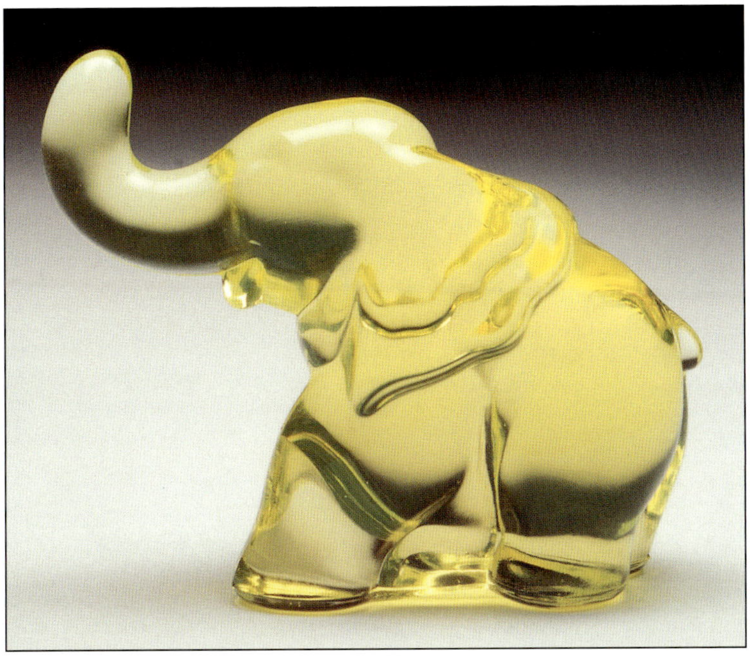

Elephant with trunk up #129, Vaseline, 3.3" tall, 4" long, Circa 1995 to present, **$19.50**

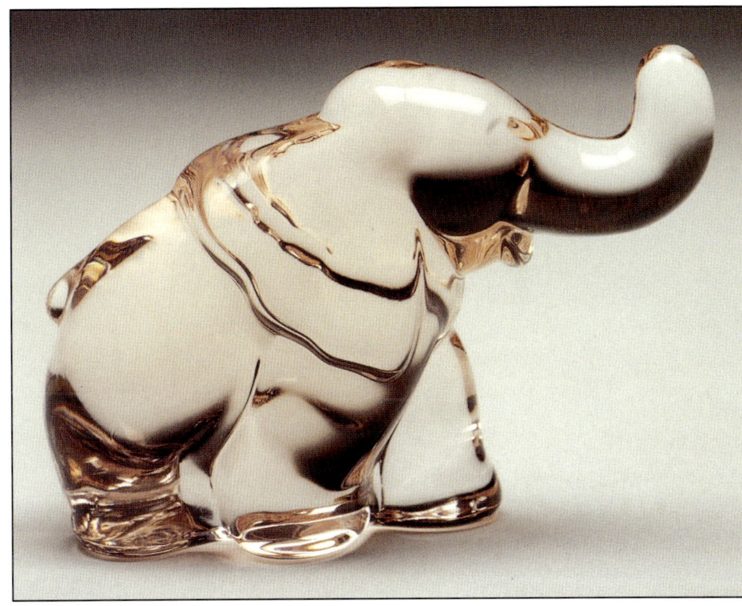

Elephant with trunk up #129, Rose, 3.25" tall, 4" long, Circa 1995 to present, **$17.50**

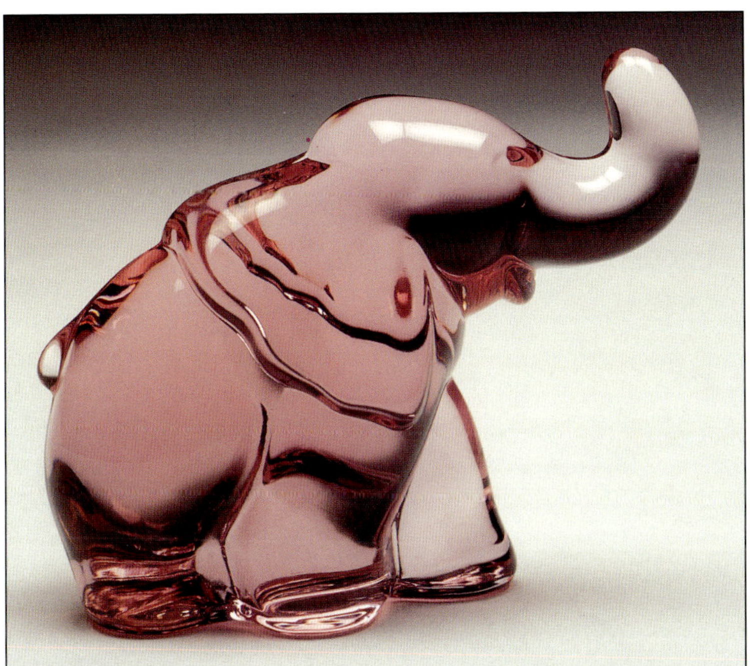

Elephant with trunk up #129, Cranberry Ice, 3.25" tall, 4" long, Circa 1995 to present, **$17.50**

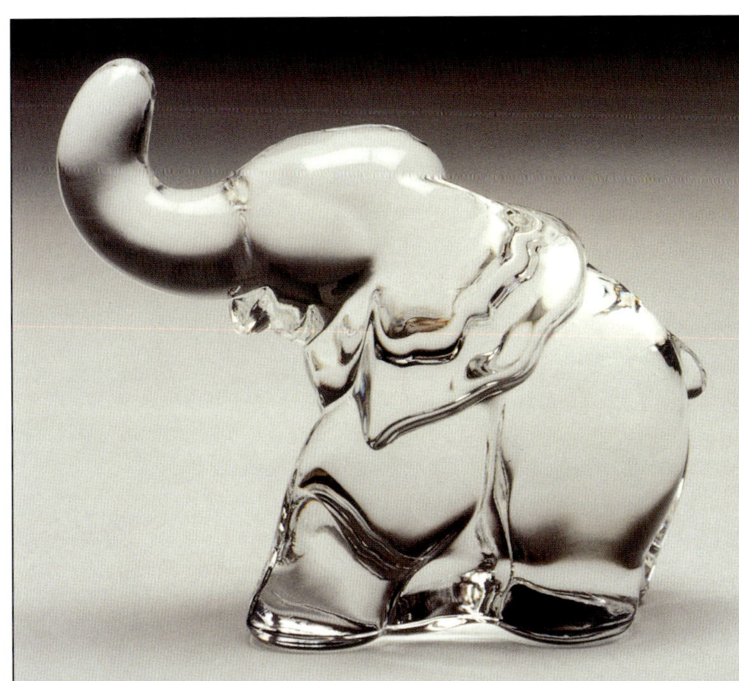

Elephant with trunk up #129, Crystal, 3.25" tall, 4" long, Circa 1995 to present, **$17.50**

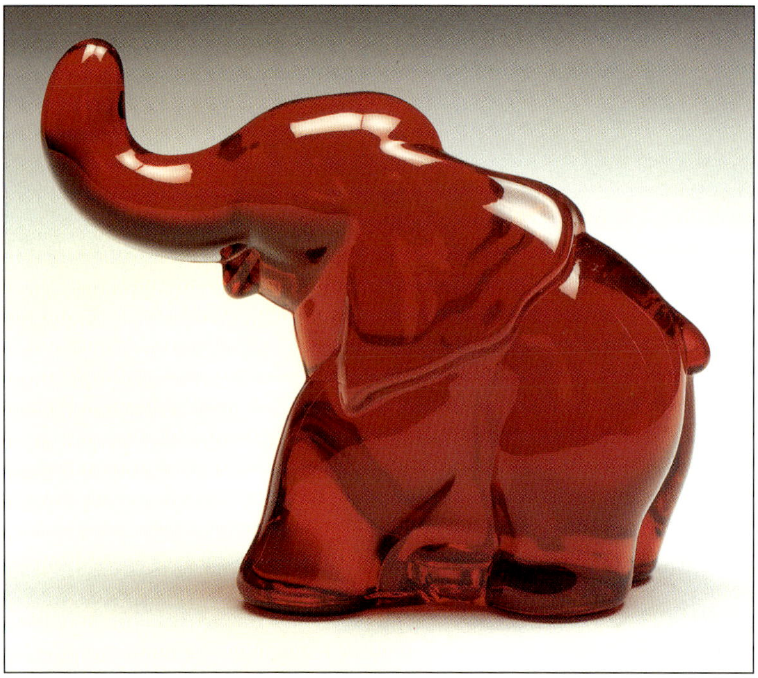

Elephant with trunk up #129, Ruby, 3.25" tall, 4" long, Circa 1995 to present, **$19.50**

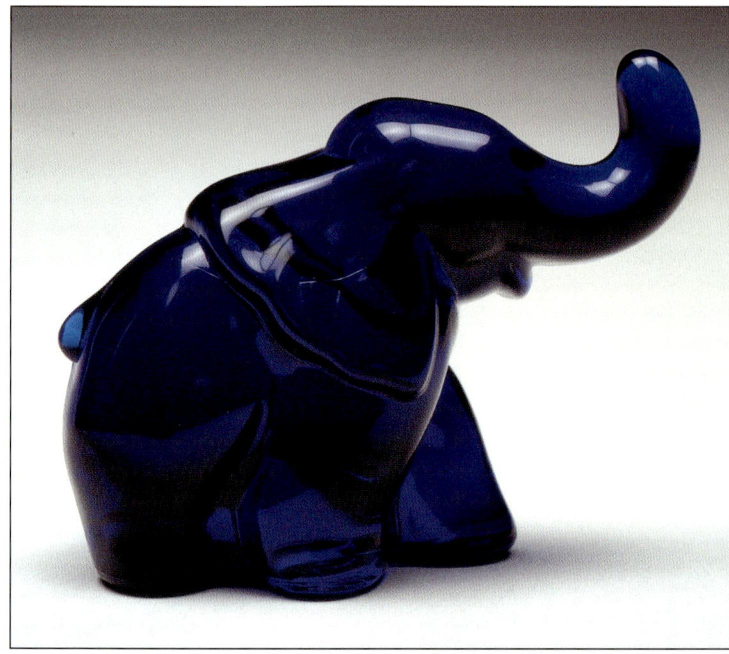

Elephant with trunk up #129, Cobalt, 3" tall, 4" long, Circa 1995 to present, **$17.50**

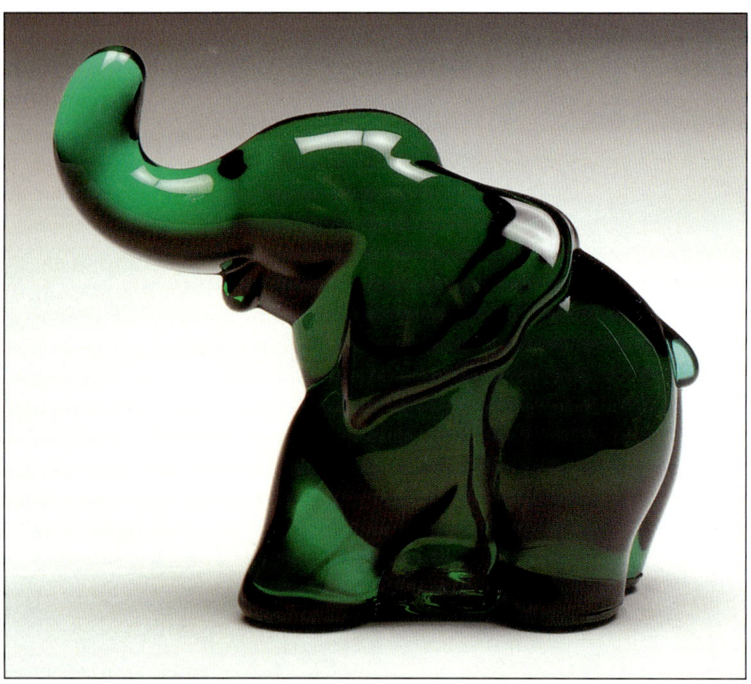

Elephant with trunk up #129, Hunter Green, 3.25" tall, 4" long, Circa 1995 to present, **$17.50**

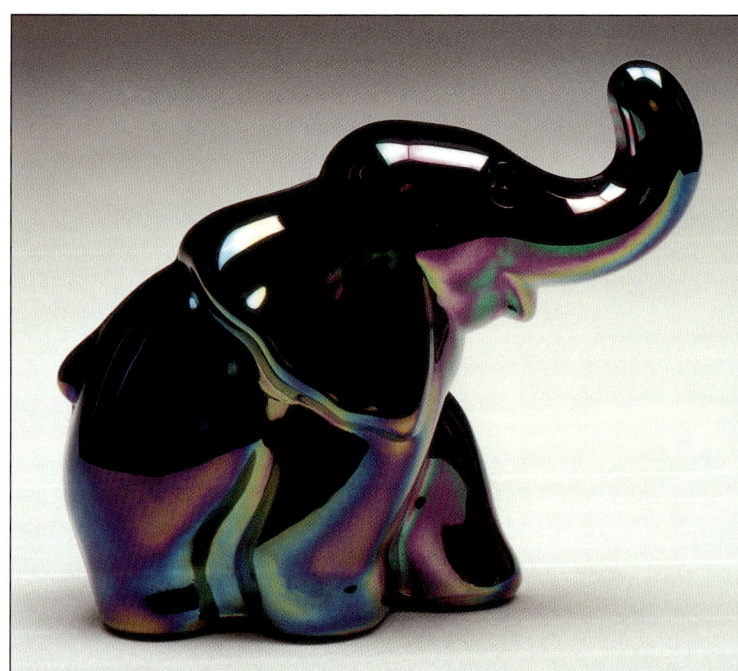

Elephant with trunk up #129, Amethyst Carnival, 3.25" tall, 4" long, Circa 1995 to present, **$18.50**

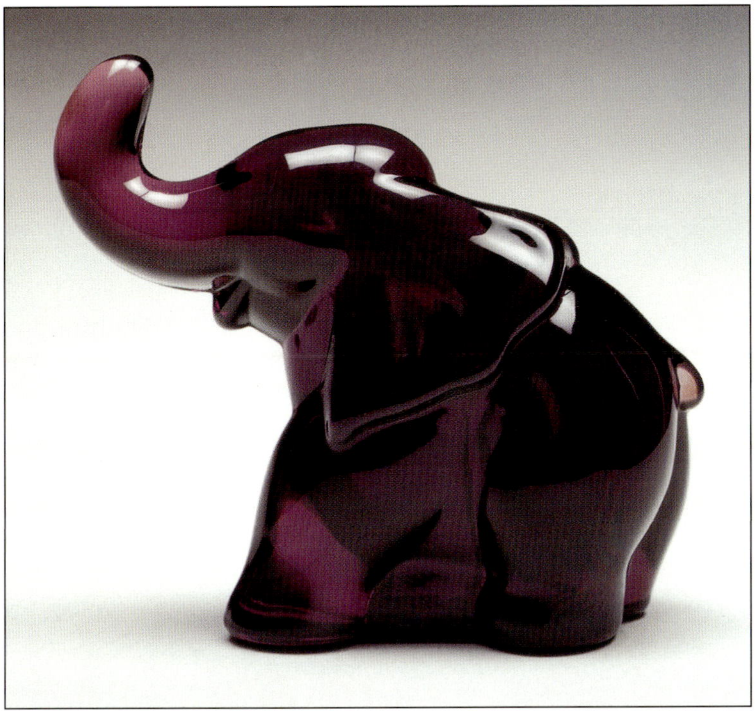

Elephant with trunk up #129, Amethyst, 3.25" tall, 4" long, Circa 1995 to present, **$17.50**

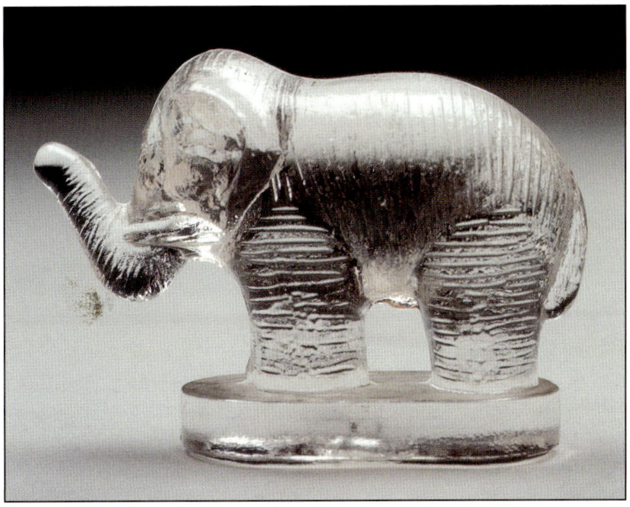

Small elephant with trunk out #166, Pink with an oval base, 1.8" tall, 2.5" long, Circa 1975-99, **$5.00**

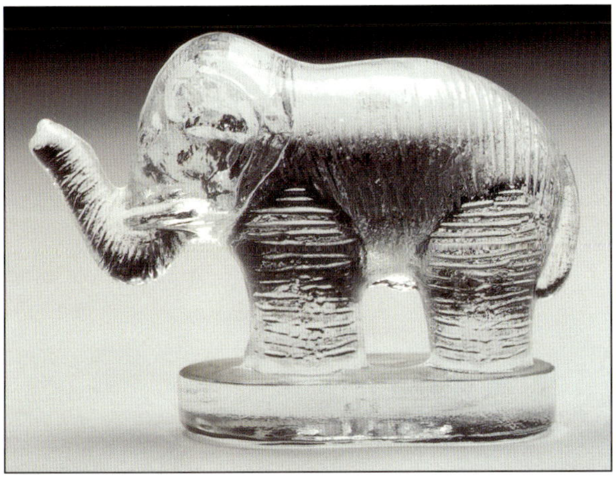

Small elephant with trunk out #166, Crystal with an oval base, 1.8" tall, 2.5" long, Circa 1975-99, **$6.00**

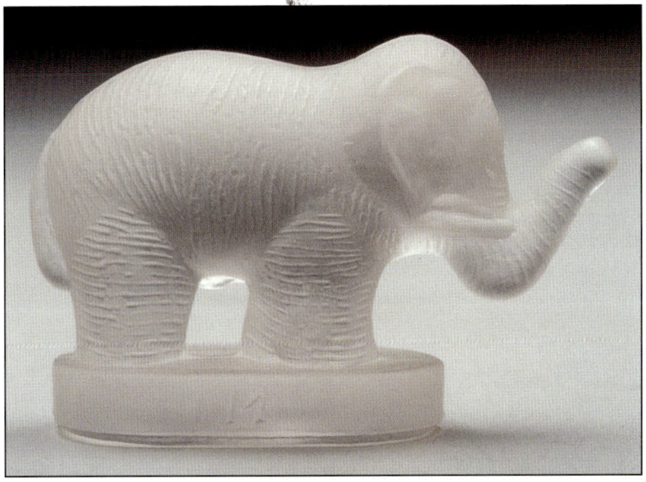

Small elephant with trunk out #166, Pink with satin finish, oval base,1.8" tall, 2.5" long, Circa 1975-99, **$5.50**

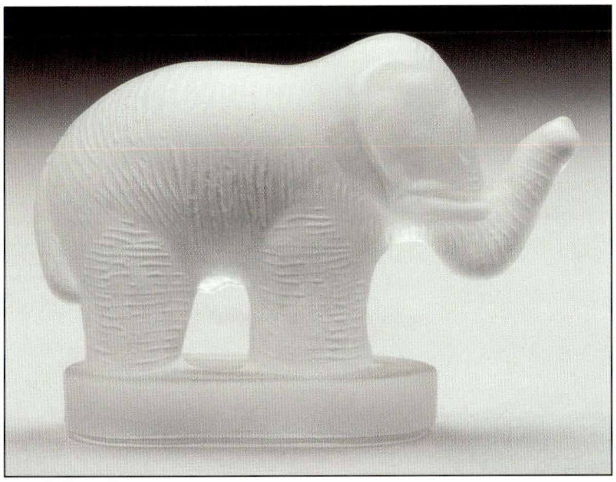

Small elephant with trunk out #166, Crystal with satin finish, oval base, 1.8" tall, 2.5" long, Circa 1975-99, **$6.50**

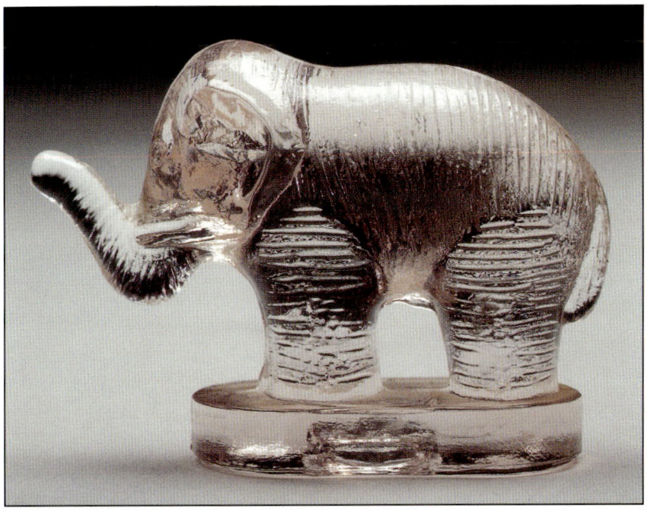

Small elephant with trunk out #166, Rose with an oval base,1.8" tall, 2.5" long, Circa 1975-99, **$6.00**

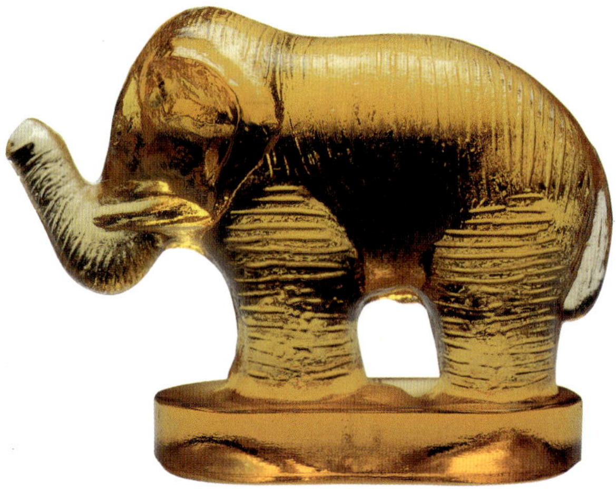

Small elephant with trunk out #166, Amber with an oval base,1.8" tall, 2.5" long, Circa 1975-99, **$5.00**

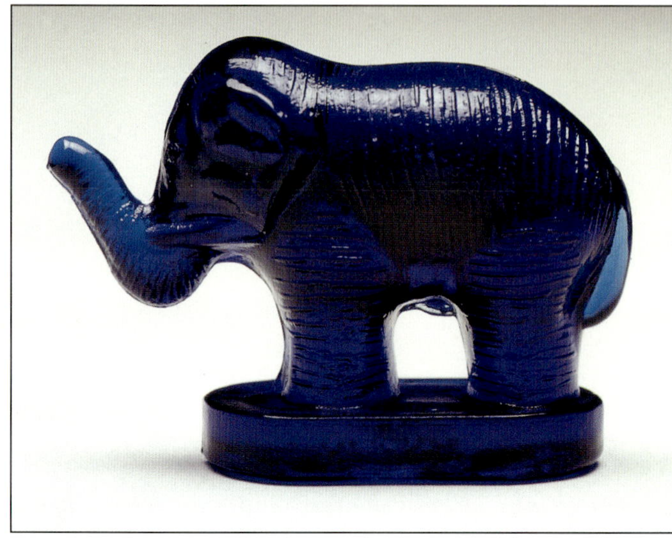

Small elephant with trunk out #166, Cobalt with an oval base,1.8" tall, 2.5" long, Circa 1975-99, **$6.50**

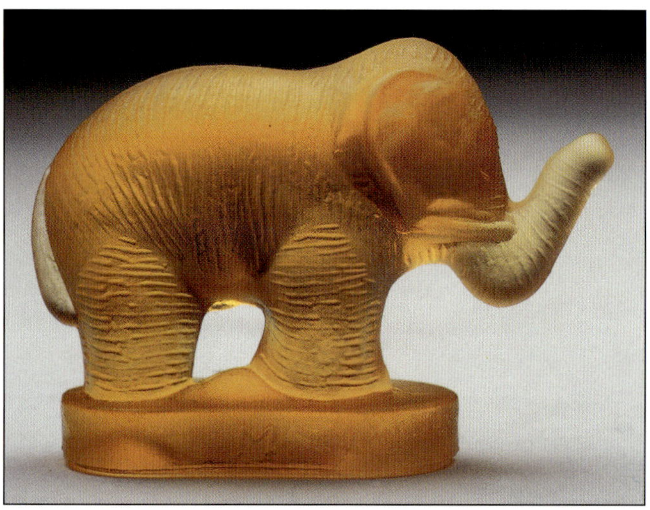

Small elephant with trunk out #166, Amber with satin finish, oval base,1.8" tall, 2.5" long, Circa 1975-99, **$5.50**

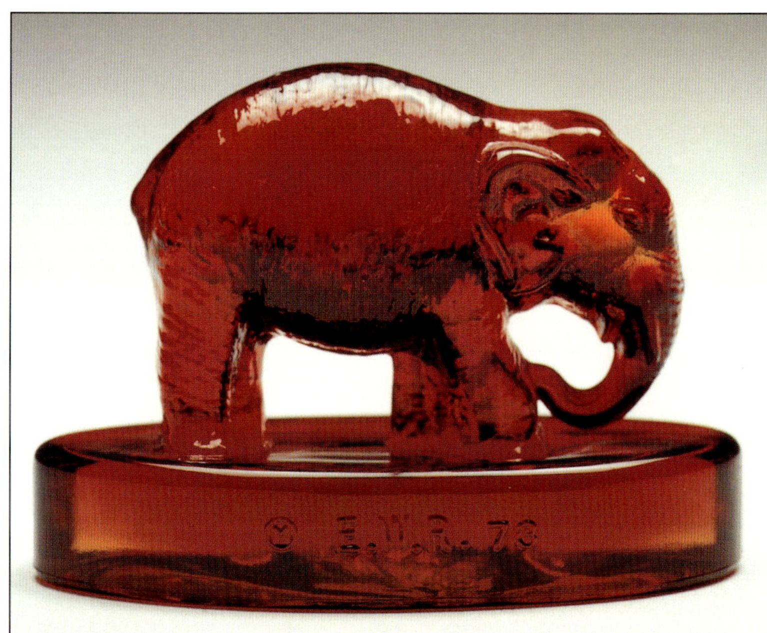

Contract work: Elephant with trunk down, Red on oval base, marked with M inside a circle for Mosser followed by the initials M E.W.R. 73, 2.4" tall, 3" long, Circa 1973, **$24.00**

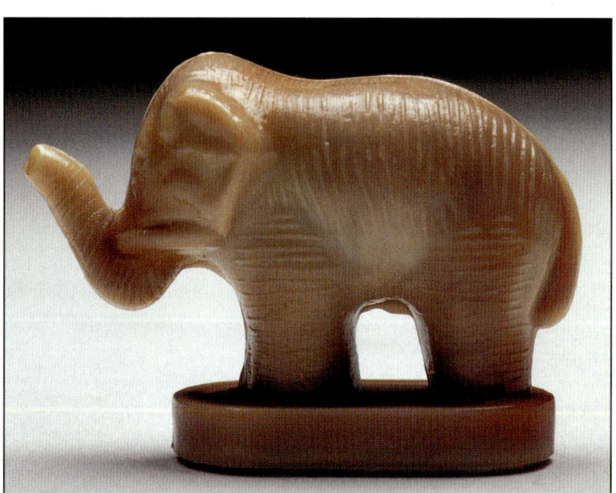

Small elephant with trunk out #166, Chocolate with an oval base,1.8" tall, 2.5" long, Circa 1975-99, **$6.50**

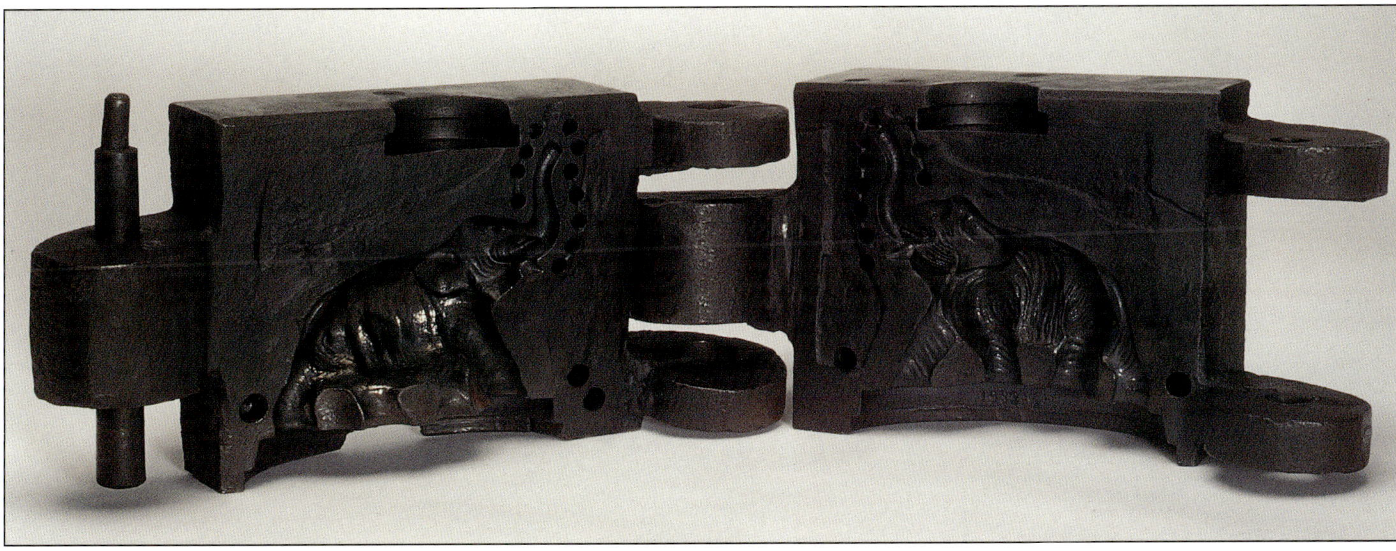

Original cast iron mould used for Bimbah elephants

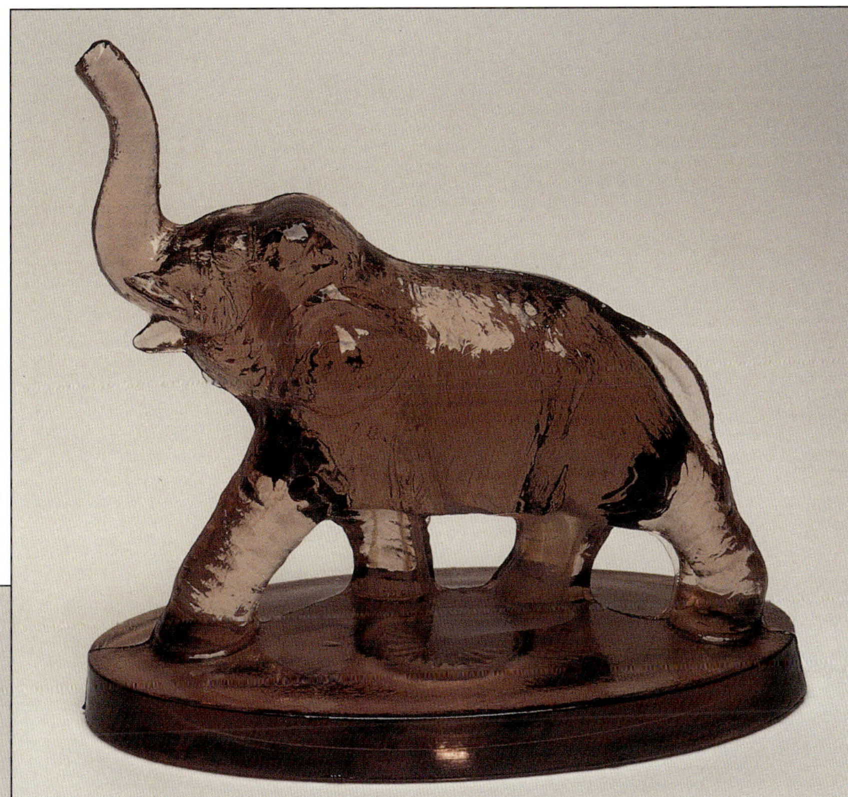

Contract work: Bimbah Elephant, Lilac (Heatherbloom), made for Robert T. Henry, 4.5" tall 5" long, only 960 made, June, 1981, **$24.00**

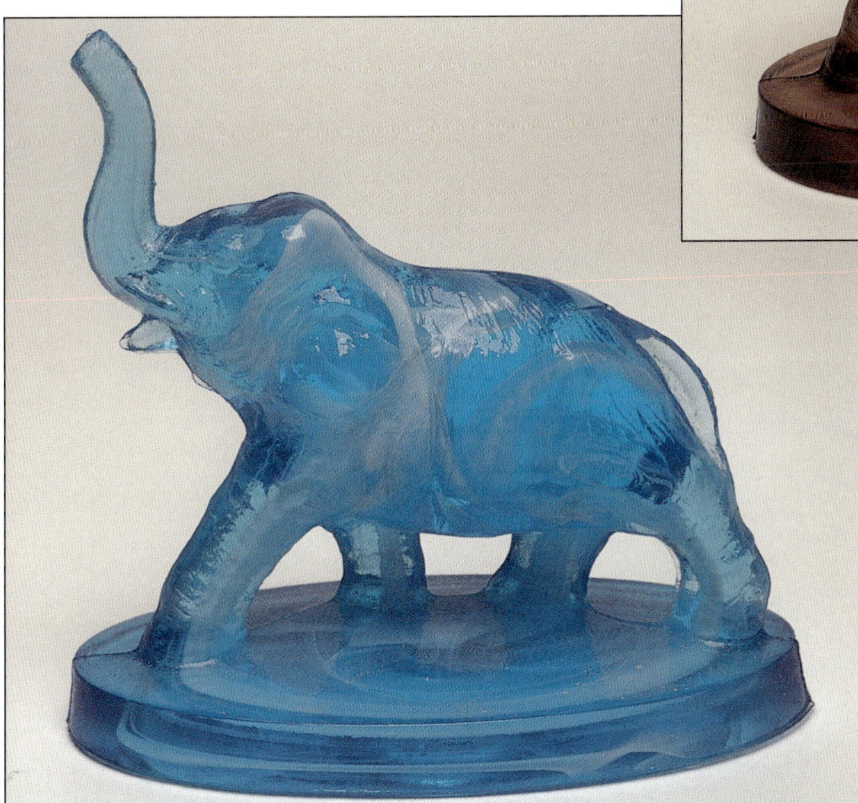

Contract work: Bimbah Elephant, Toby (slag blue and white), made for Robert T. Henry, 4.5" tall 5" long, only 962 made, August, 1981, **$29.50**

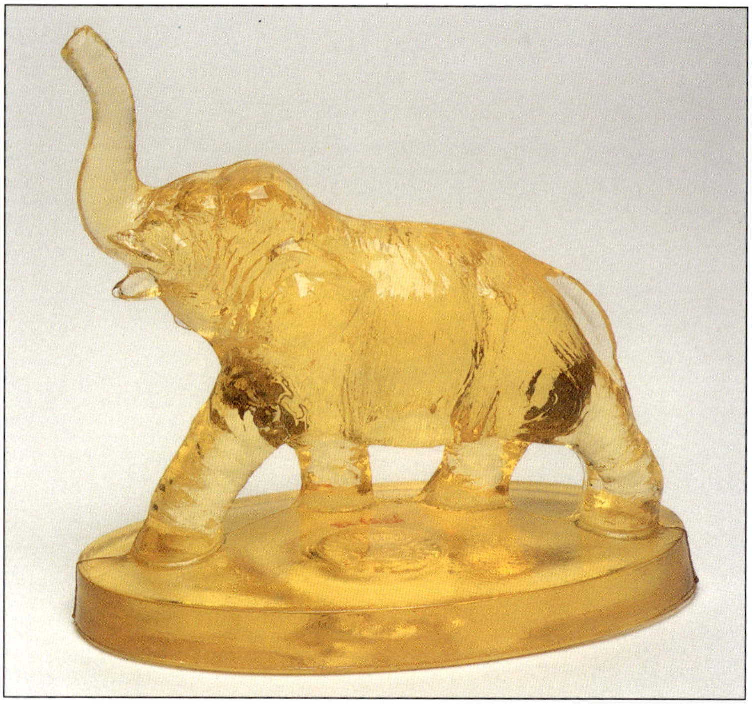

Contract work: Bimbah Elephant, Golden Nugget (yellow), made for Robert T. Henry, 4.5" tall 5" long, only 969 made, December, 1981, **$24.00**

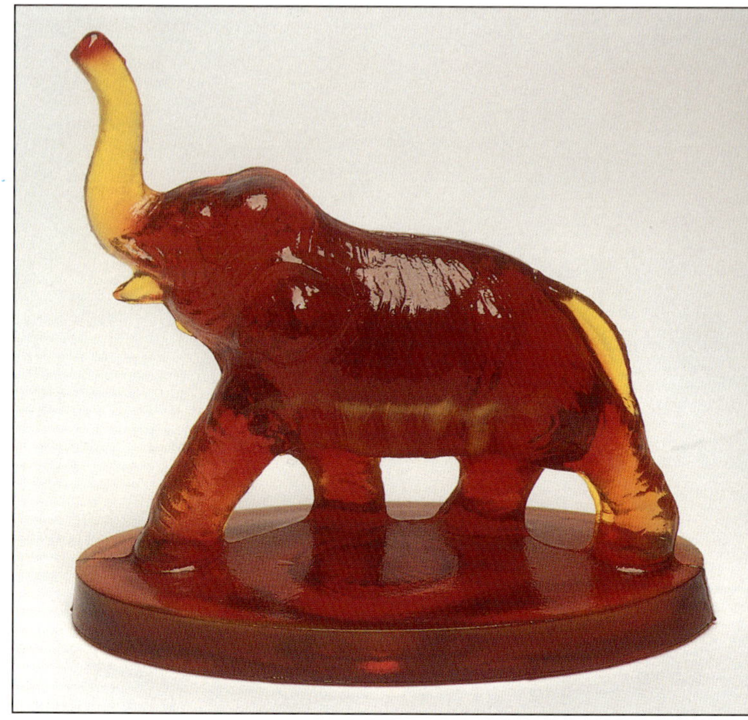

Contract work: Bimbah Elephant, Susie (red), made for Robert T. Henry, 4.5" tall 5" long, only 944 made, March, 1982, **$29.50**

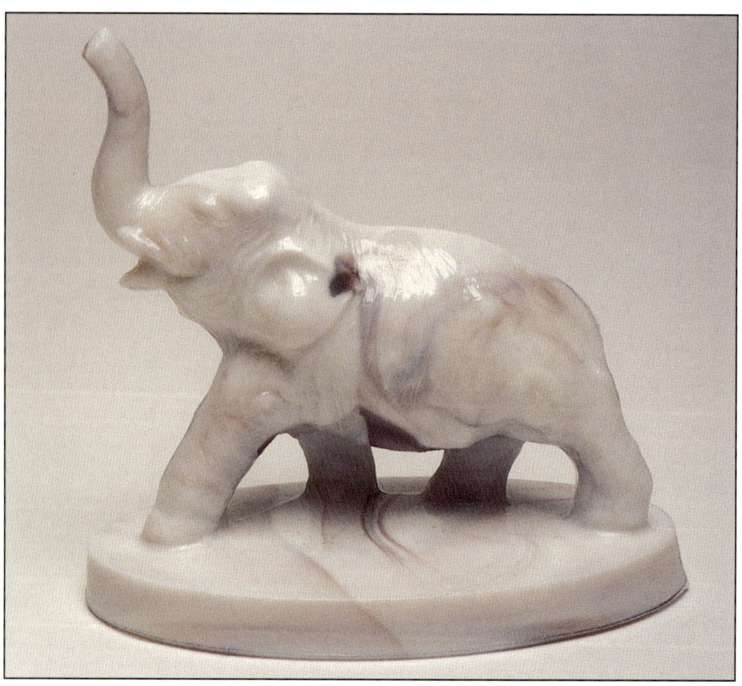

Contract work: Bimbah Elephant, Sheba Slag (amethyst and melk glass), made for Robert T. Henry, 4.5" tall 5" long, only 970 made, January, 1982, **$25.00**

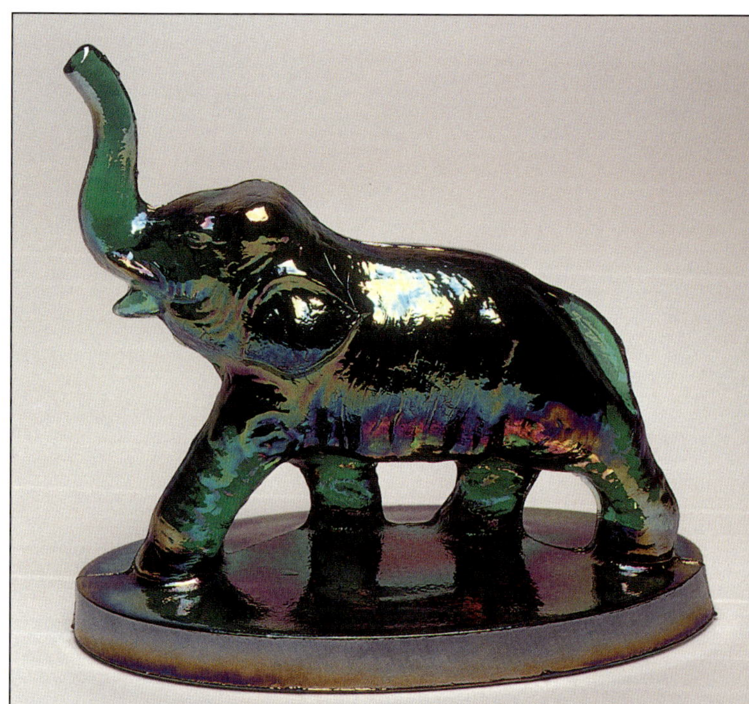

Contract work: Bimbah Elephant, Shawn (green iridized), made for Robert T. Henry, 4.5" tall 5" long, only 944 made, March, 1982, **$29.50**

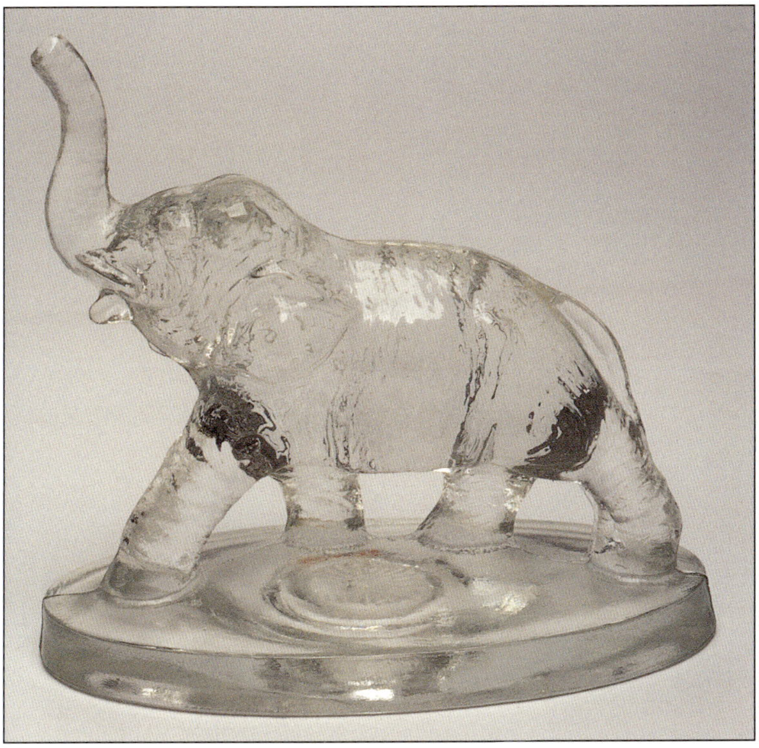

Contract work: Bimbah Elephant, Starlight (crystal), made for Robert T. Henry, 4.5" tall 5" long, only 987 made, April, 1982, **$24.00**

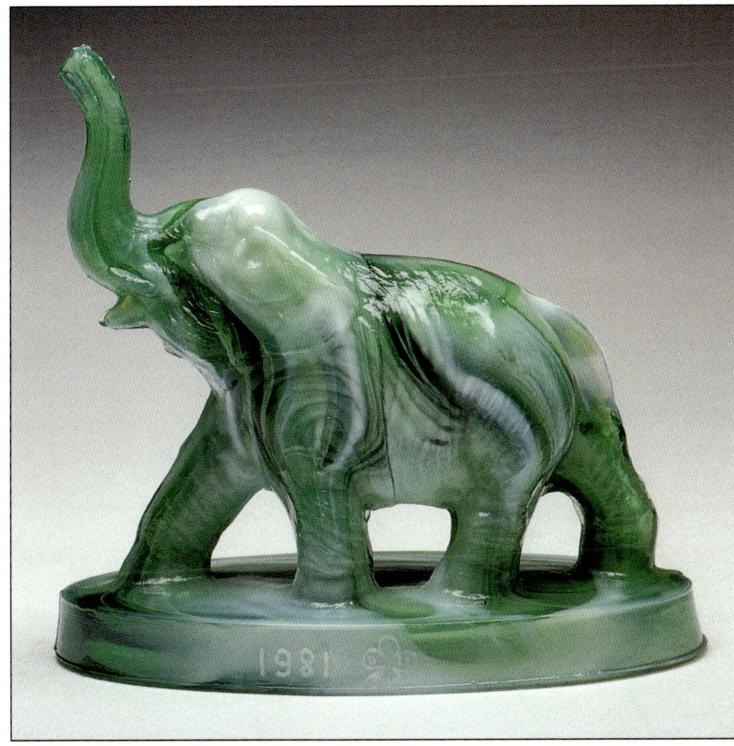

Contract work: Bimbah Elephant, "Snowy Pine" a green slag color, made for Robert T. Henry, 4.5" tall 5" long, only 988 made, October 1981, **$24.00**

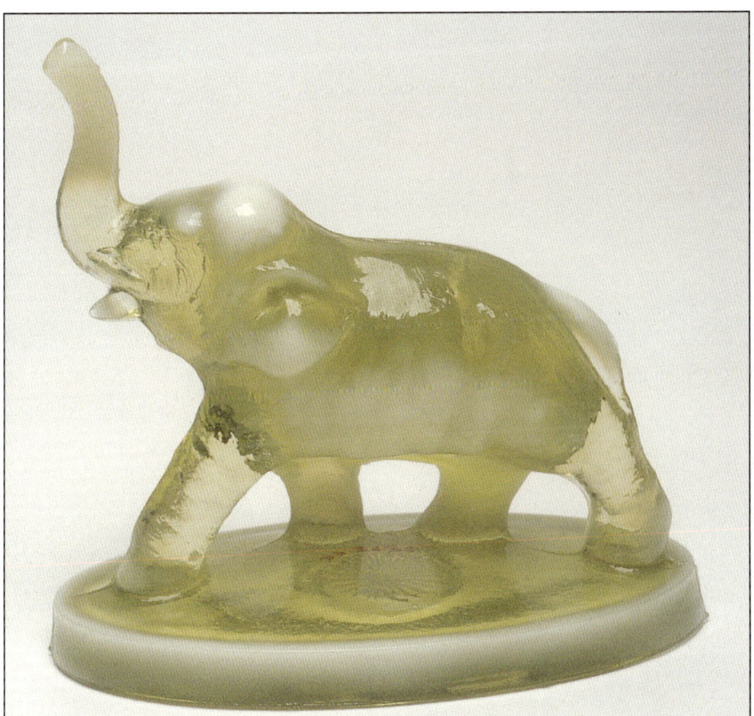

Contract work: Bimbah Elephant, Henry's Dream, made for Robert T. Henry, 4.5" tall 5" long, only 944 made, June, 1982, **$25.00**

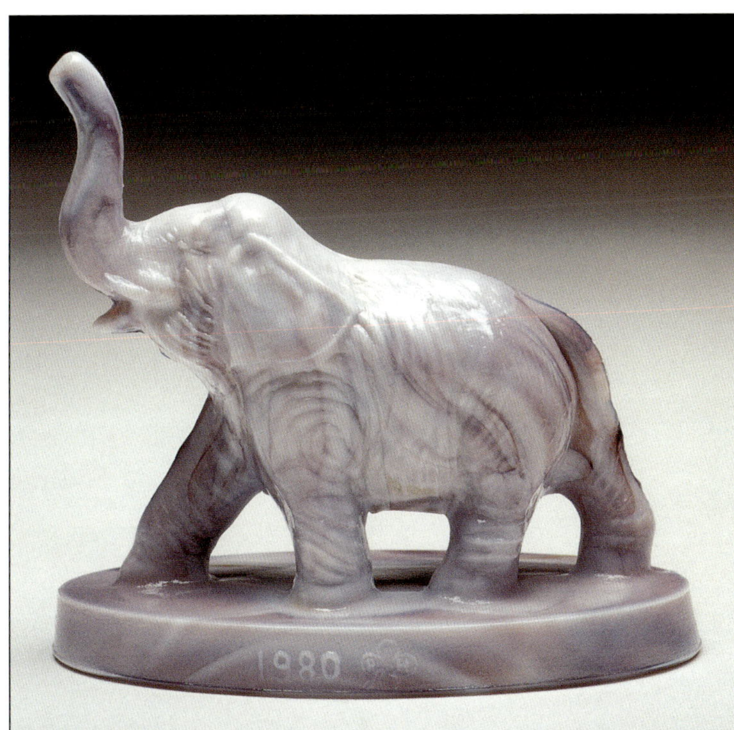

Contract work: Bimbah Elephant, "Taffy" a purple slag color, made for Robert T. Henry, 4.5" tall 5" long, only 994 made, November 1980, **$29.50**

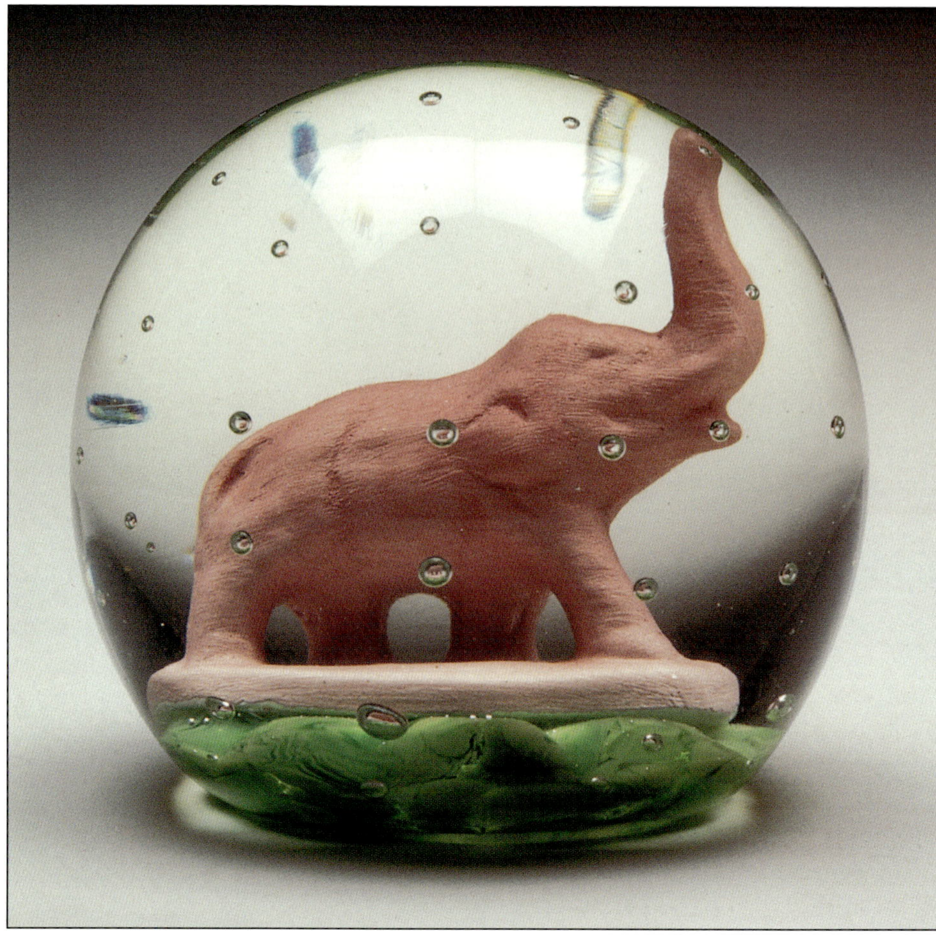

Contract work: Bimbah Elephant Paperweight, Crystal with controlled bubbles, pink with green base, marked on base Bimbah RH in clover, 3.5" tall, 3.75" diameter, Circa 1982, **$35.00**

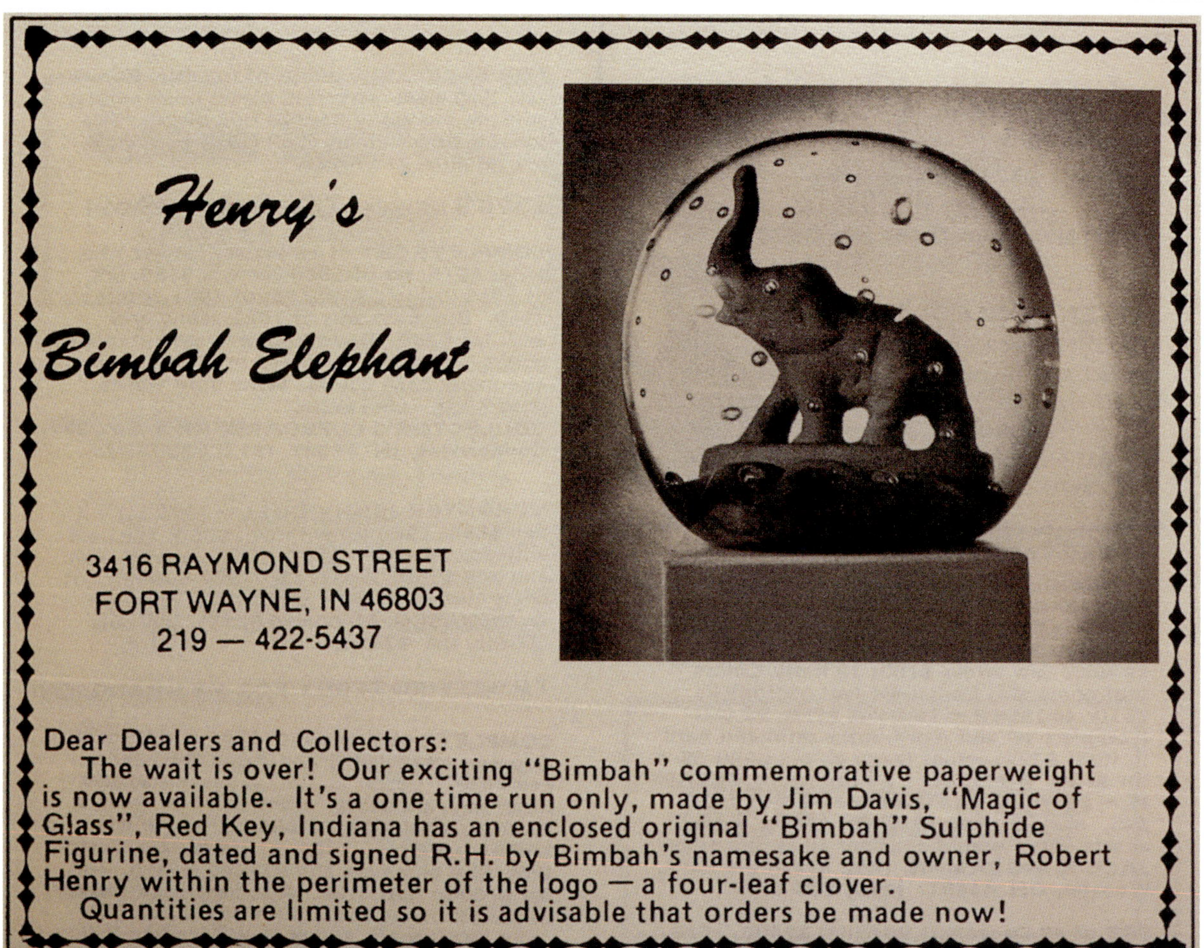

Original ad for Bimbah paperweight

New Martinsville Glass Company 1901-1944

Mark Douglas and George Matting, who had been with Specialty and West Virginia Glass Company at one time, arrived at New Martinsville, Ohio, in November, 1900, with the goal of creating a new glassmaking company. They founded New Martinsville Glass Company in 1901 and the company began by producing lamps, novelties, and tableware. David Fisher was the manager of the company from 1908 to 1916, when he founded Paden City Glass Company. He was followed to Paden City by some of the more skilled New Martinsville employees.

In 1926, New Martinsville brought glass animals into their line, hoping to attract new customers. As part of further promotions in 1932, a local theater gave New Martinsville glass novelties to each of their customers attending matinees. One of these included an elephant, and it was also an incense burner.

New Martinsville had made glass for other companies to sell, as well, but when they noticed the success these companies had selling their products, they decided to direct their attention back to themselves and make their own success.

A tragic event occurred in 1943, when a flood badly damaged the plant. Unable to adequately make repairs and allocate funding, the directors were forced to close the factory in 1944.

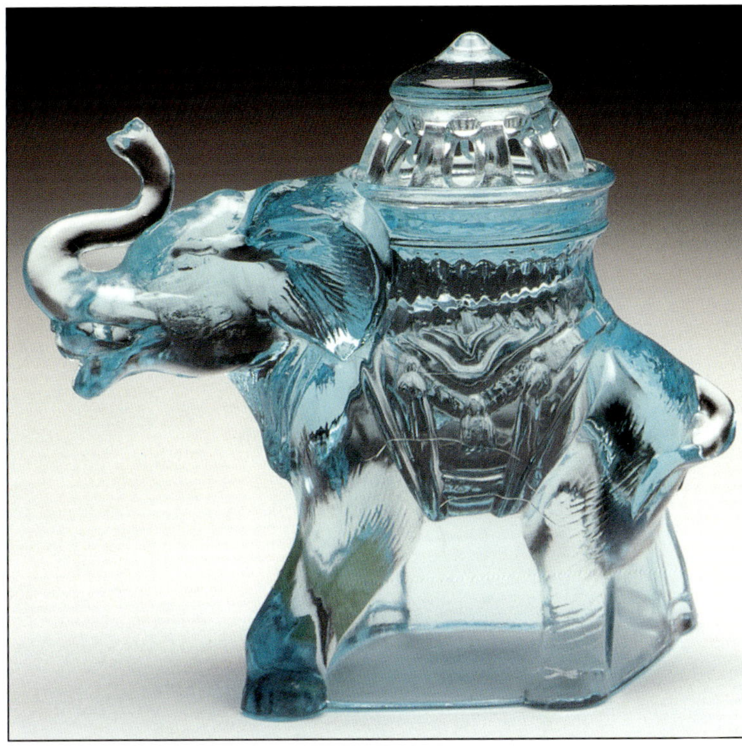

Elephant incense burner #201, Blue, Note, has original label (one with this label would add an additional $50.00 to the value), 5.8" tall, 6.25" long, Circa 1930 to early 1940's, **$350.00**

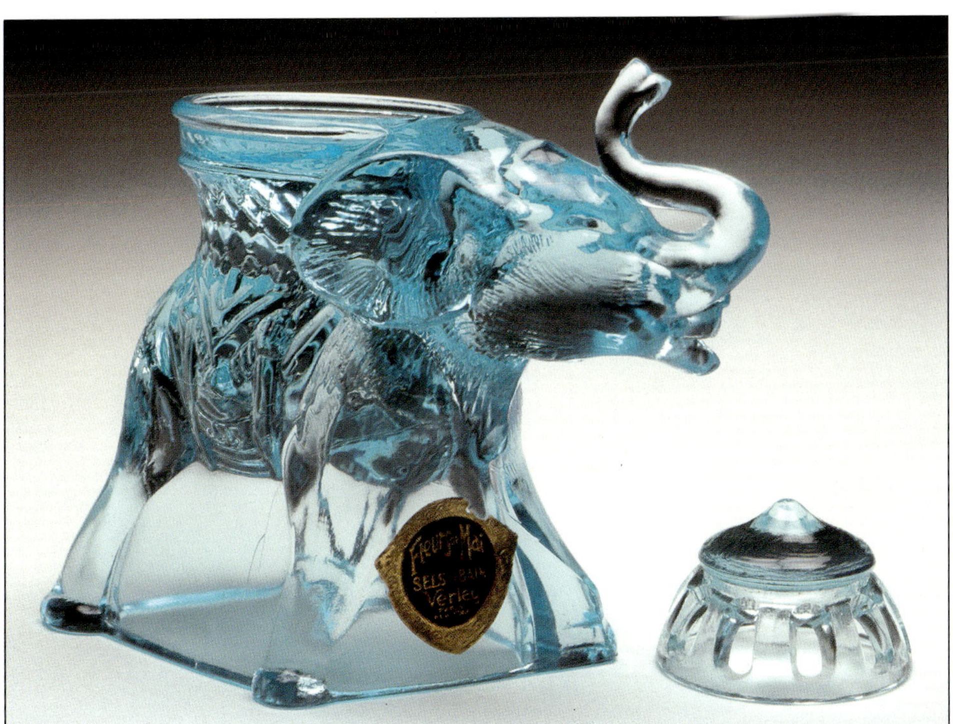

Shown with label found on the blue elephant incense burner #201. The label says the following: "Fleurs de Mai - SELS de BAIN - Verlys - Paris - New York". Cover shown off showing detail

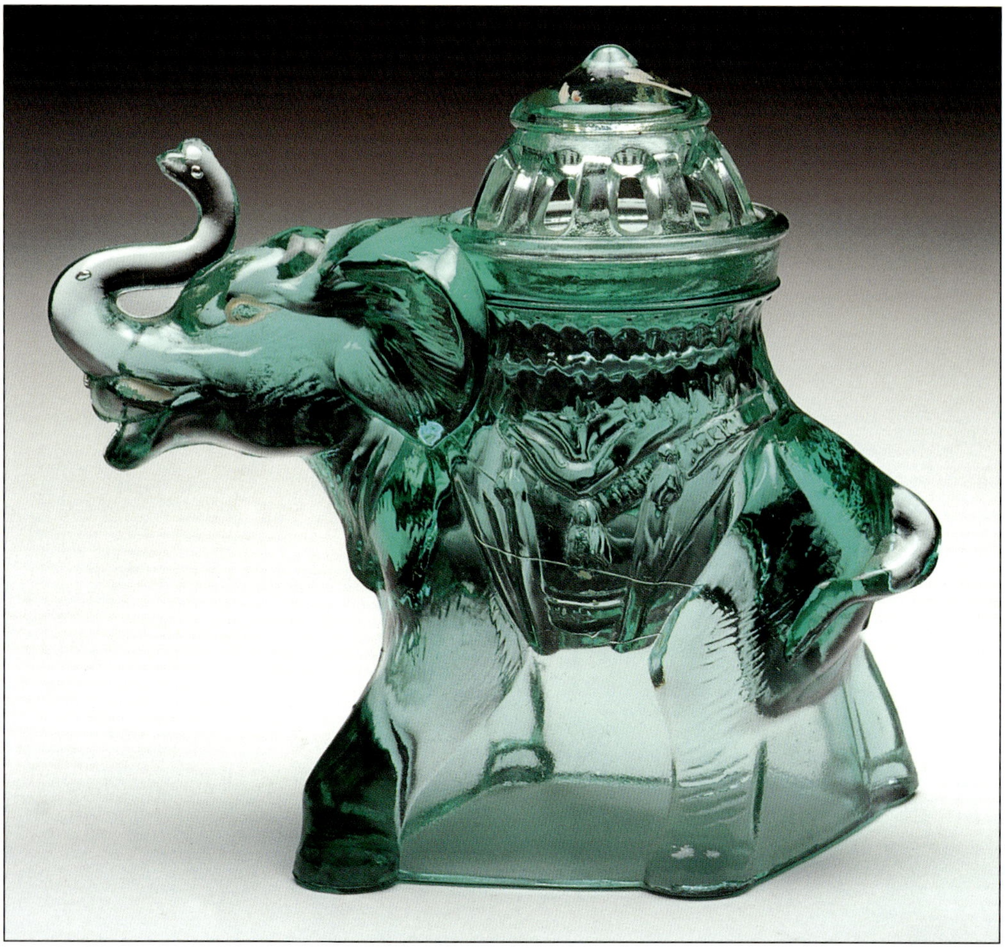

Elephant incense burner #201, Green, 5.8" tall, 6.25" long, Circa 1930 to early 1940's, **$350.00**

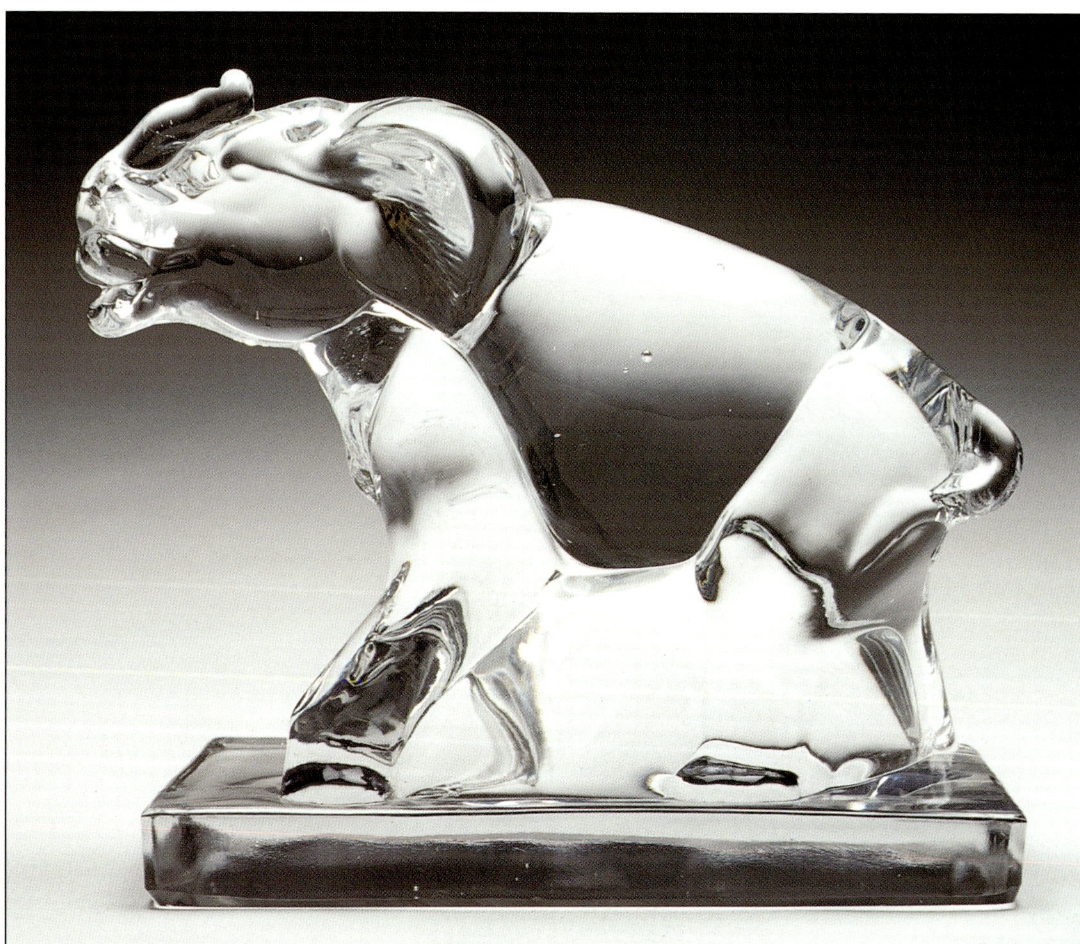

Elephant bookend #237, Crystal, 5.25" tall, 6" long, Circa 1942-44, **$95.00**

Oneida
1880-Present

In 1880, Oneida Community Limited was founded in Oneida, New York, as a small work society. Their roots were in a communal-like environment in which they were closely bonded with family, religion and culture. They deemed their background as utopian and strived for perfection while combining their community and work together, which ultimately led to success and high production. When their leader died, the community was changed to a joint stock company.

Oneida is a leading supplier of crystal, glassware, and silverware. Today, they pride themselves with continuing success because of their past beliefs and foundation.

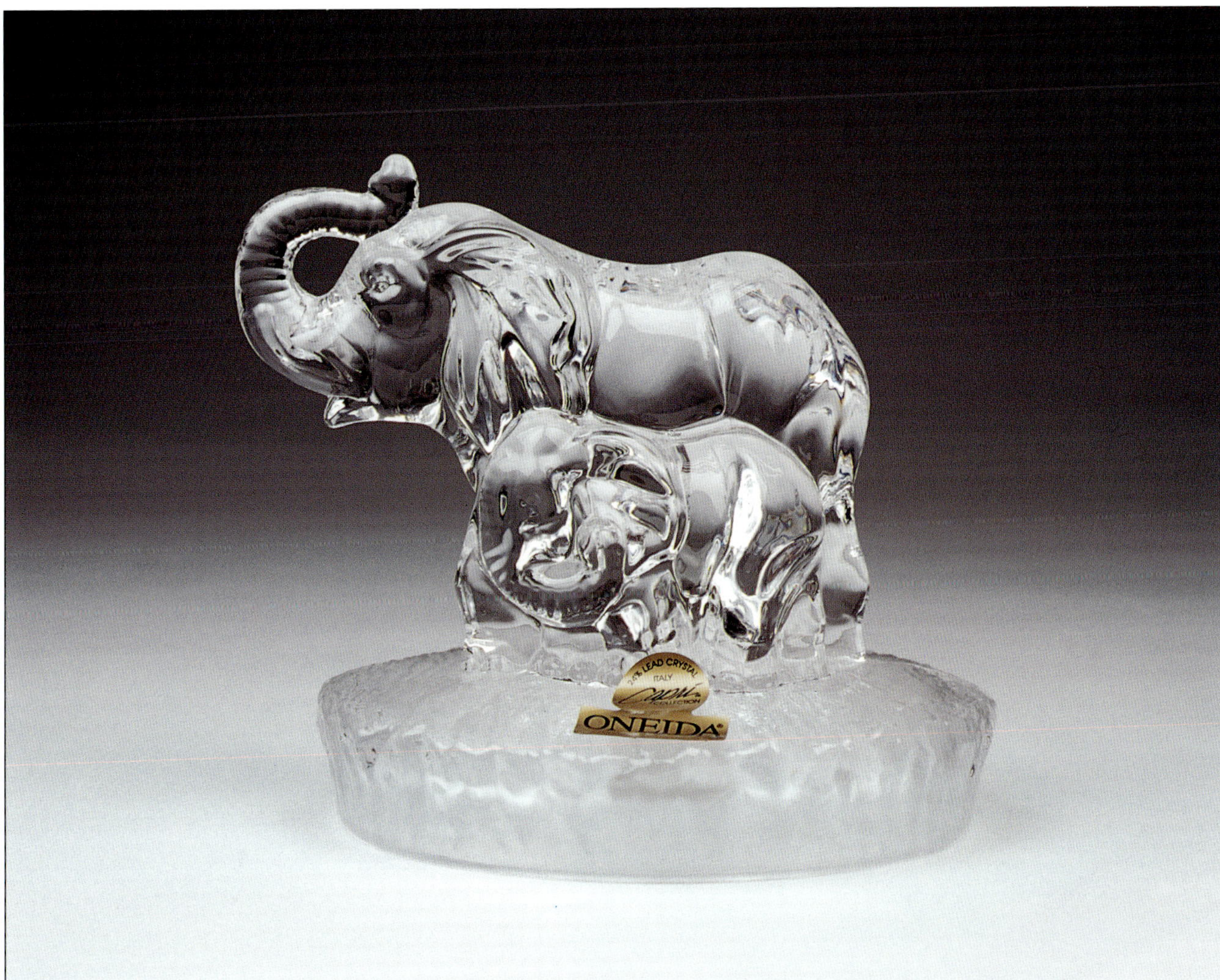

Elephant mother with trunk up and baby, Capri Collection, Crystal with round base, 4.5" tall, Circa 1990's, **$24.00**

Orient & Flume 1972-Present

In 1972, Douglas Boyd founded the company Orient & Flume in Chico, California. He bought a carriage house at the corner of Orient and Flume Streets and transformed it into a glass studio. Their promotions claim their products are "nationally acclaimed for excellence in design, the glass of Orient & Flume utilizes both traditional and contemporary motifs and can be found in the permanent collections of the Metropolitan Museum, the Chrysler Museum, the Chicago Art Institute, and the Corning Glass Museum."

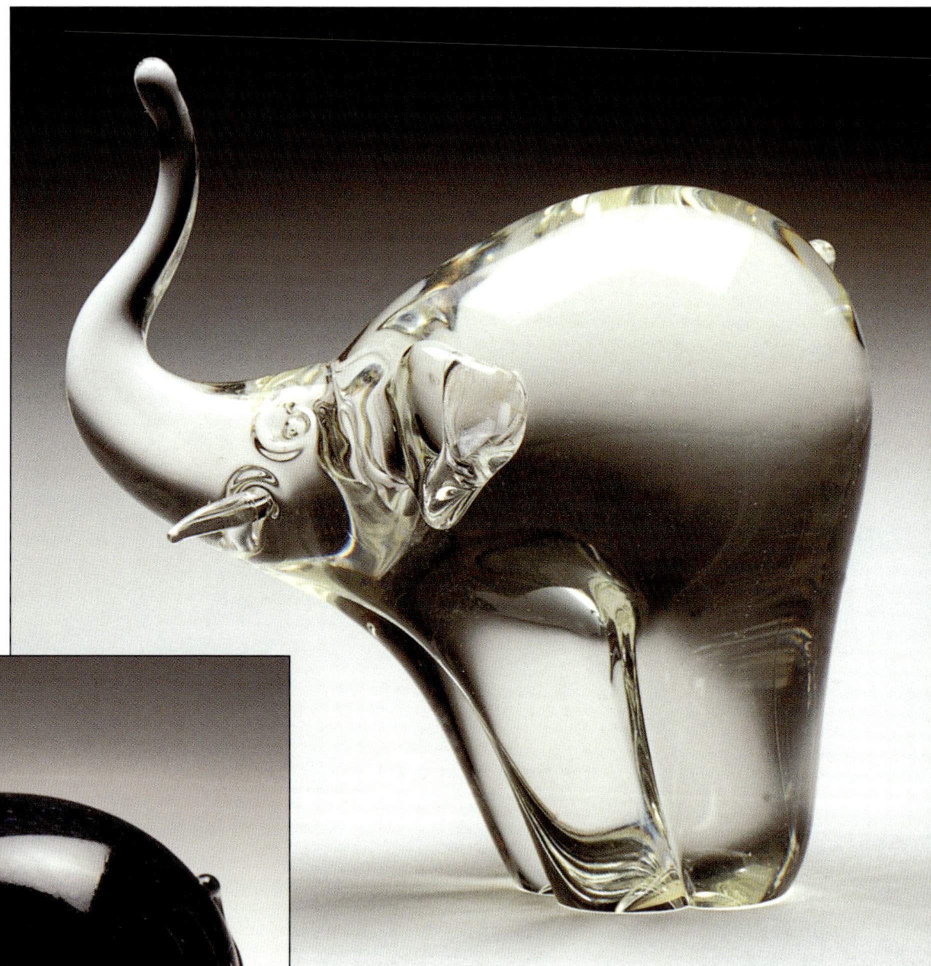

Elephant with raised trunk, Crystal, marked on bottom Orient and Flume GG74, 5.3" tall, 5" long, Circa 1980-90's, **$150.00**

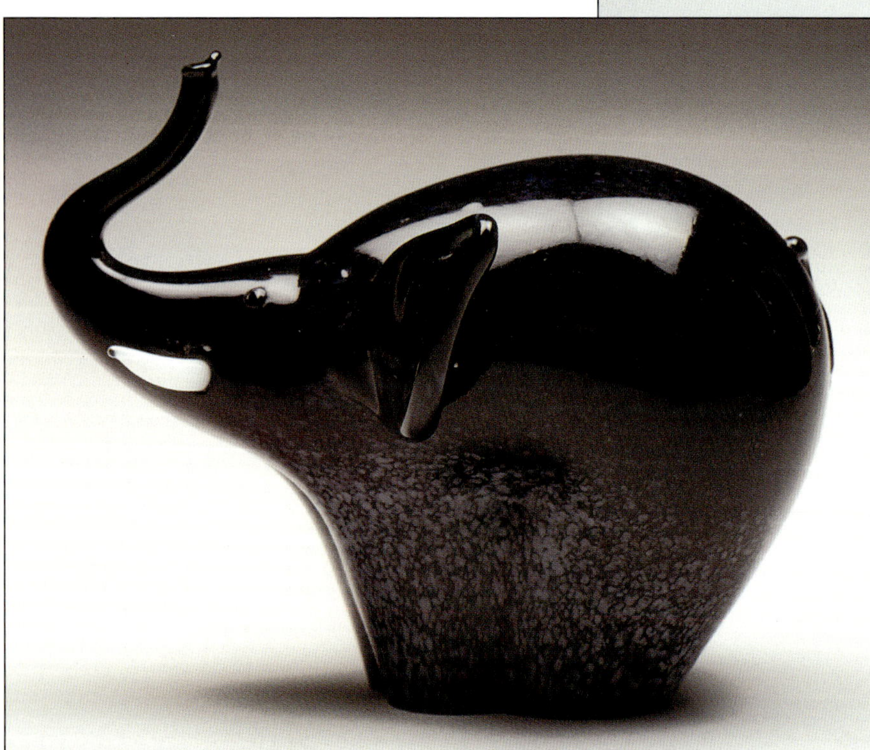

Elephant with raised trunk, Dark Green-looks black, white splatter at base, marked on bottom Orient and Flume W268477, 4.5" tall, 5.25" long, Circa 1980-90's, **$175.00**

Pairpoint Crystal Company
1918-Present

The Pairpoint Crystal Company can be found today in Bedford, Massachusetts. There were high demands for fine glass at the time of the opening of their predecessor company, the Pairpoint Corporation, in 1918, and that company flourished for nearly twenty years. The Pairpoint Corporation ended in 1938, when Gunderson Glass Works took over. In 1952, Robert Gunderson died and there was a lapse in the company's operation. Robert Bryden reinstated the Pairpoint Corporation again in 1957, and the name changed once more in 1970, to become the Pairpoint Crystal Company.

Distinguished colors can be found in Pairpoint crystal, including:

Amethyst
Auroria, which is a reddish-amber
Black
Canaria, which is green-yellow
Chrysophrase, which is a brown
Cobalt
Flambeau, which is red-orange
Green
Gold
Marina Blue
Rosaria, which is a cranberr
Selenium Rubies

Pairpoint markings can be found on the glass itself, or on paper labels. The symbol is a capital P in a diamond.

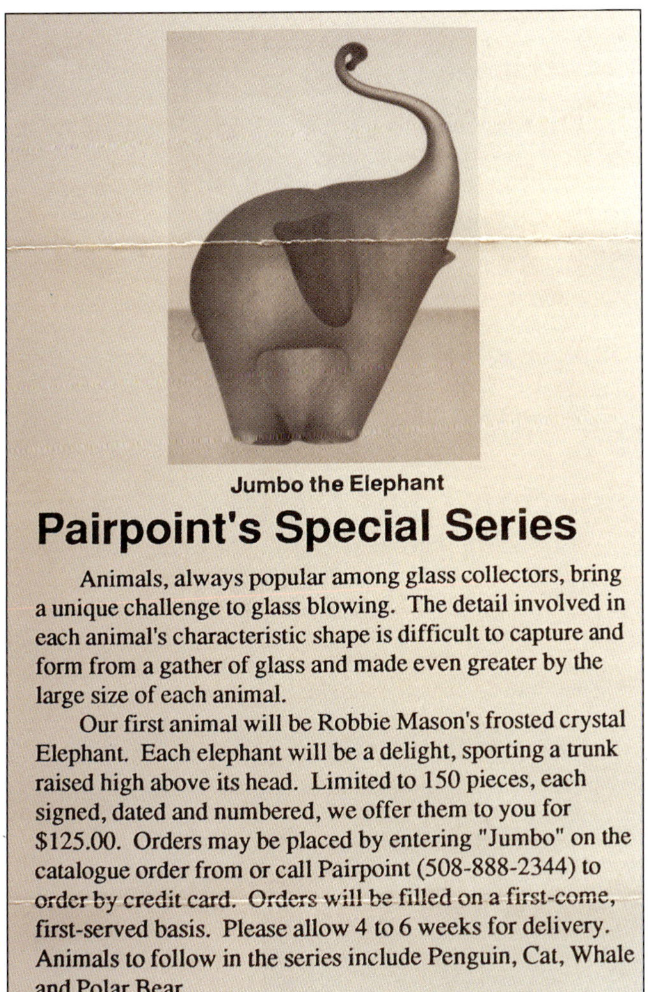

Original brochure showing "Jumbo The Elephant", limited to 150, November 1999. Reprinted with permission from OPairpoint Crystal Company

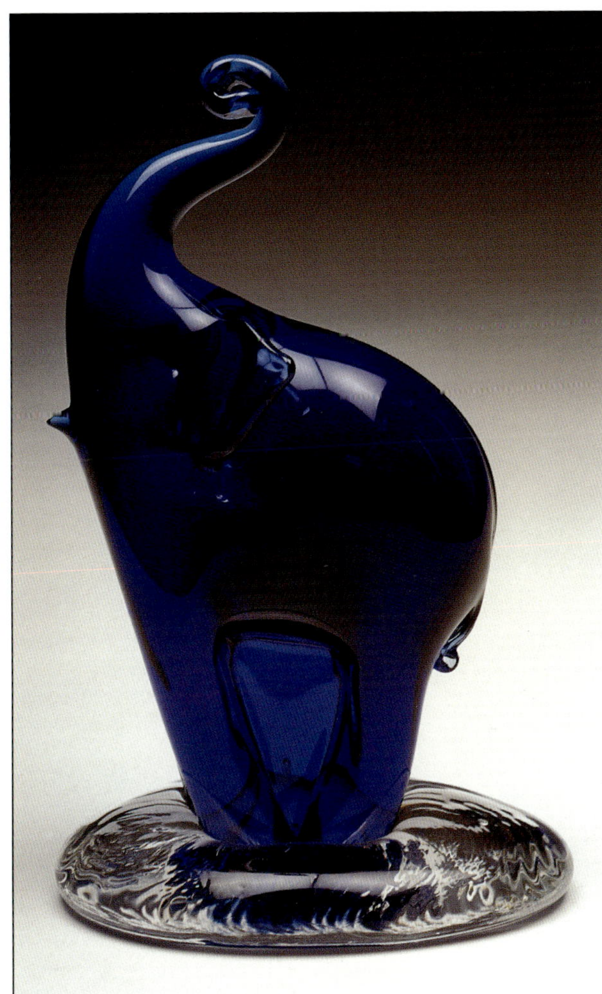

Standing Elephant, #4032, cobalt with crystal base, 6.5" tall, 4" long, Circa 1990's, **$95.00**

Quality Glass Incorporated
1970s

Quality Glass Incorporated, in Cambridge, Ohio, was part of a conglomerate of contemporary companies located in relatively the same area. Quality had a specialty in hand-blown lamp parts, unique novelties, and private mould work.

Glass Review issues had ads which pictured Quality's milk glass animals in 1979, and they have helped to give some insight to this elusive company. The very limited knowledge about them has made it unknown how long their glass elephants were made, how many were made, or even specific company details.

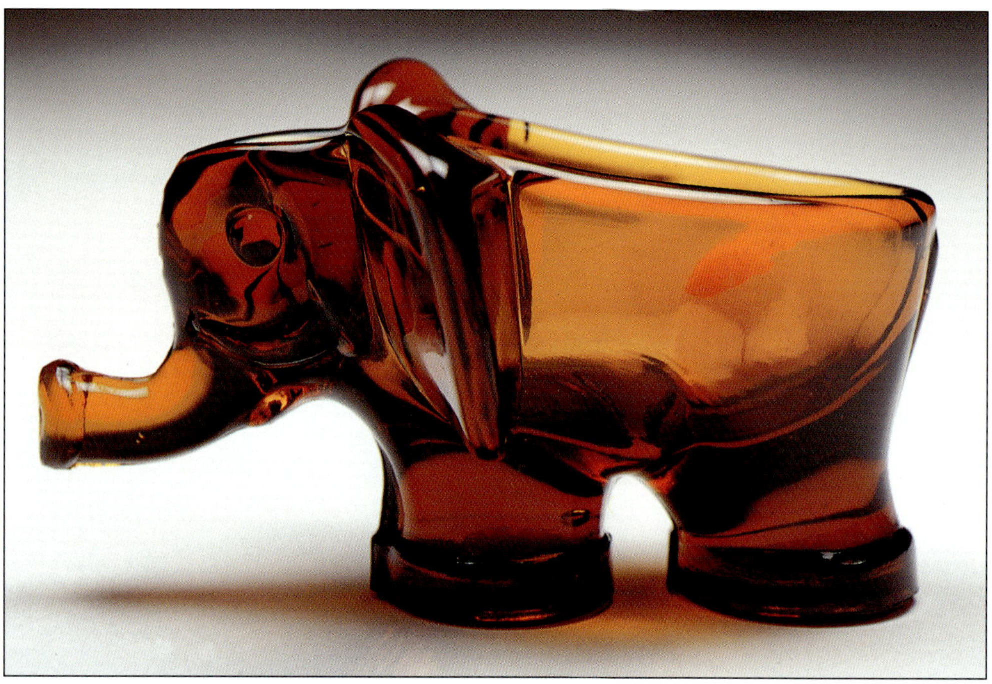

Elephant ashtray, Amber, open back, 2.25" tall, 3.75" long, Circa 1970's, **$8.50**

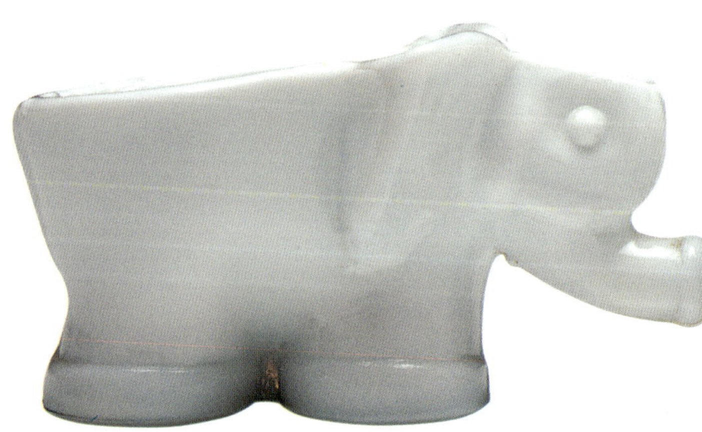

Elephant ashtray, Milk Glass, open back, 2.25" tall, 3.75" long, Circa 1970's, **$6.50**

Rainbow Glass Company 1939-1972

Rainbow Glass Company, of Huntington, West Virginia, was begun in 1939 to decorate glass. They would buy glass items from other companies, decorate them, and sell them to their customers. After a few years, they began making their own glass. In 1954, Rainbow was purchased by Viking Glass Company. For almost two decades, Viking let them remain as Rainbow, doing their own work, under their own name. In 1972, Viking overtook them all together, and the Rainbow name ceased to exist.

The marking for Rainbow consisted of an oval paper label with "Rainbow," a star above the name, and "Huntington, West Virginia, USA" below the name. These labels helped to distinguish Rainbow from other companies of the time.

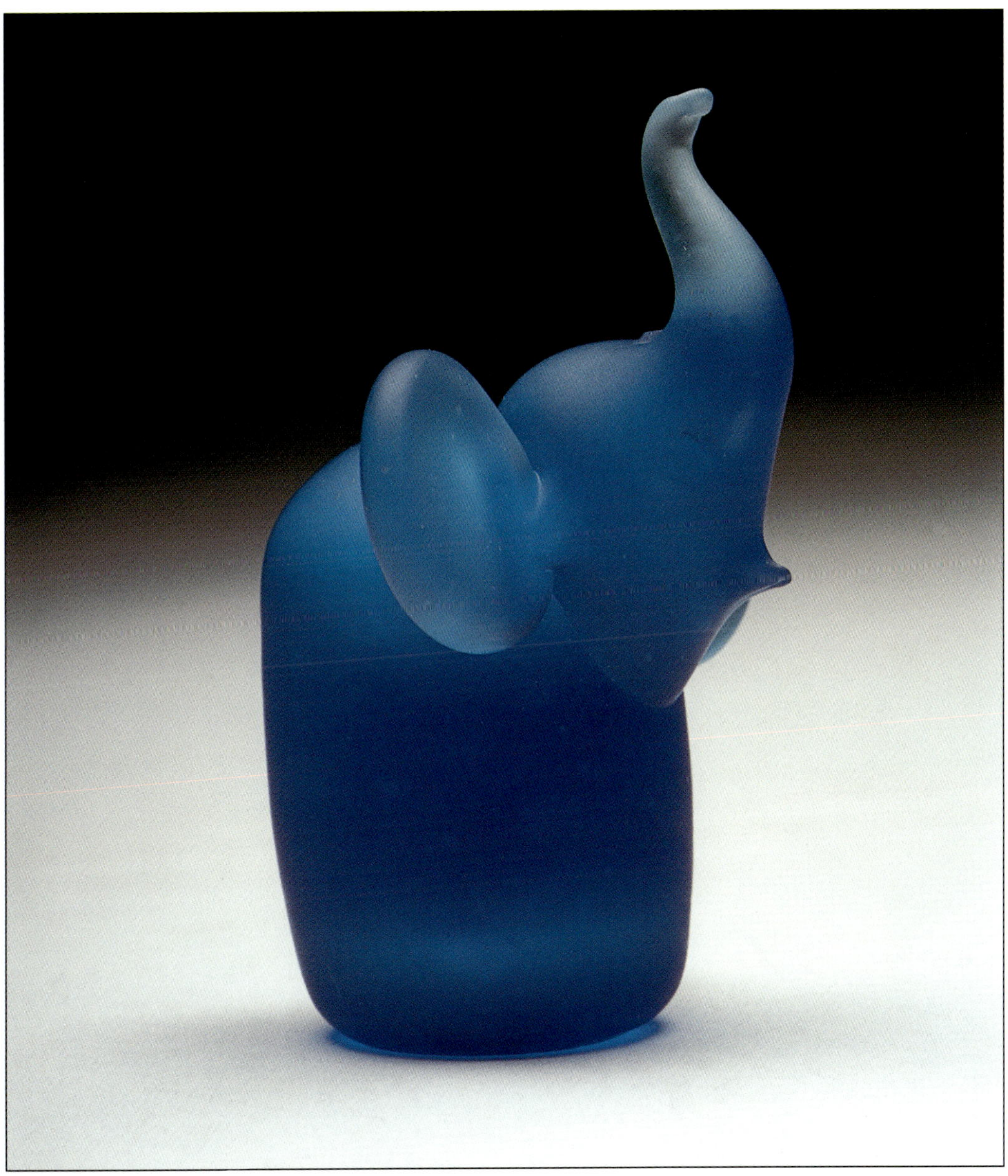

Elephant with trunk up, hand blown, Blue with satin finish, 4.1" tall, 3" wide, Circa 1950's, **$24.50**

L.E. Smith Glass Company 1907-Present

Every glass company has a special story of how they began, and this company is no different. Lewis E. Smith was a gourmet cook who came up with his own mustard recipe in 1907. He wanted to produce and market his mustard, so he bought a closed glass factory in Mt. Pleasant, Pennsylvania. To ensure that things would run smoothly, and to free-up his own time to focus on marketing his mustard, Smith hired highly experienced glass workers. His sales kept growing through 1911, when Smith had an urge to create a new venture and went in a new direction, leaving the glass workers to manage the company.

Luckily, the employees were highly dedicated and the company continued to prosper and a variety of tableware designs were created. During the 1930s, they bought Greensburg Glass Company as a means for expansion. Since then, L. E. Smith Glass Company has had several different owners, though they continue to be successful.

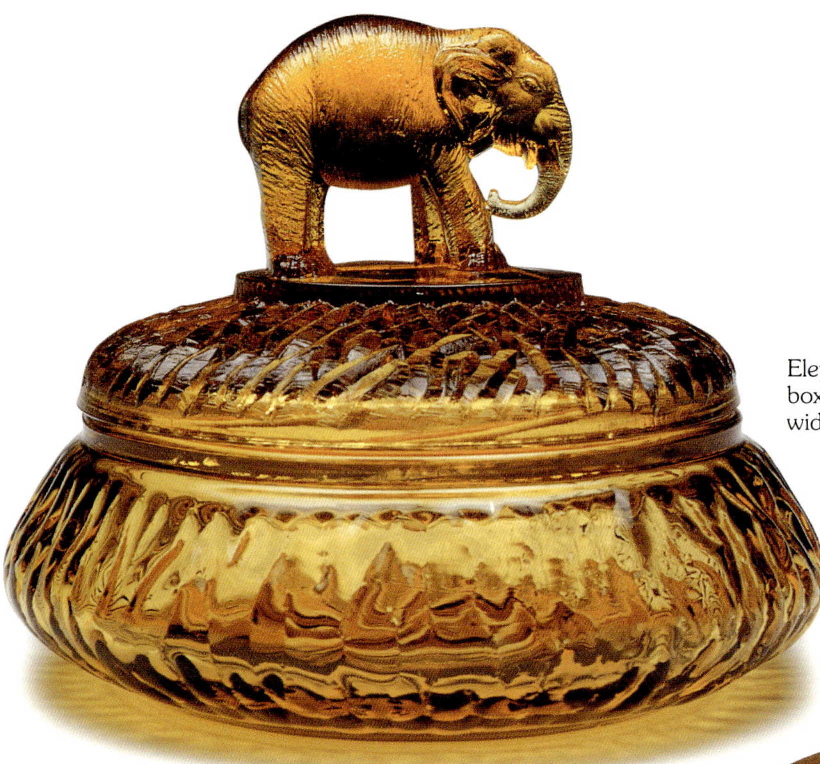

Elephant trunk up covered powder box (candy), Amber, 5" tall, 6" wide, Circa 1930's, **$95.00**

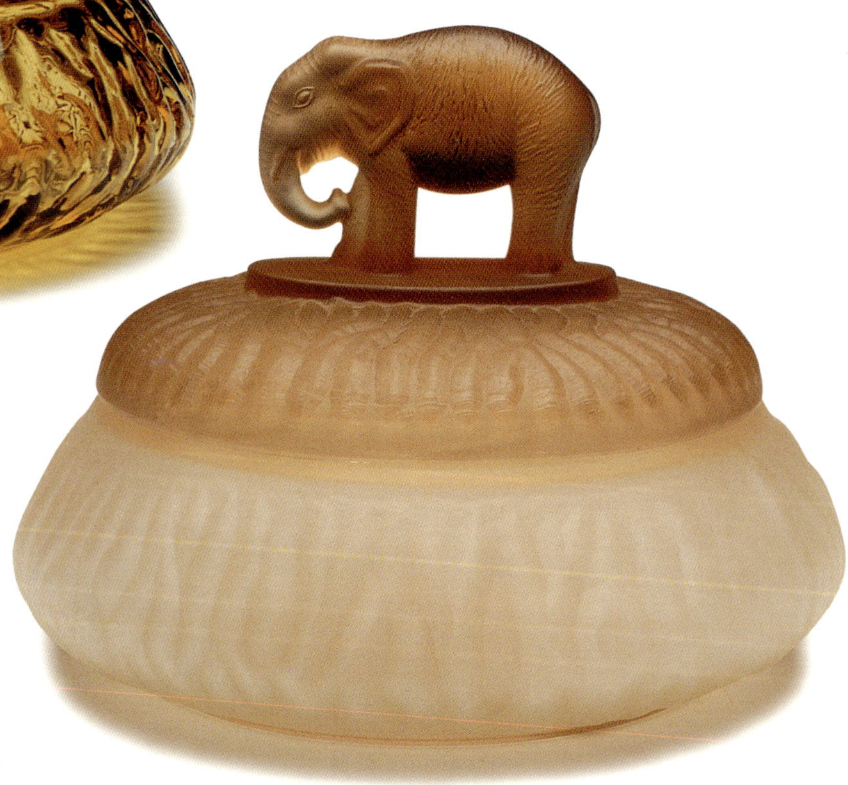

Elephant trunk up covered powder box (candy), Pink with satin finish, 5" tall, 6" wide, Circa 1930's, **$125.00**

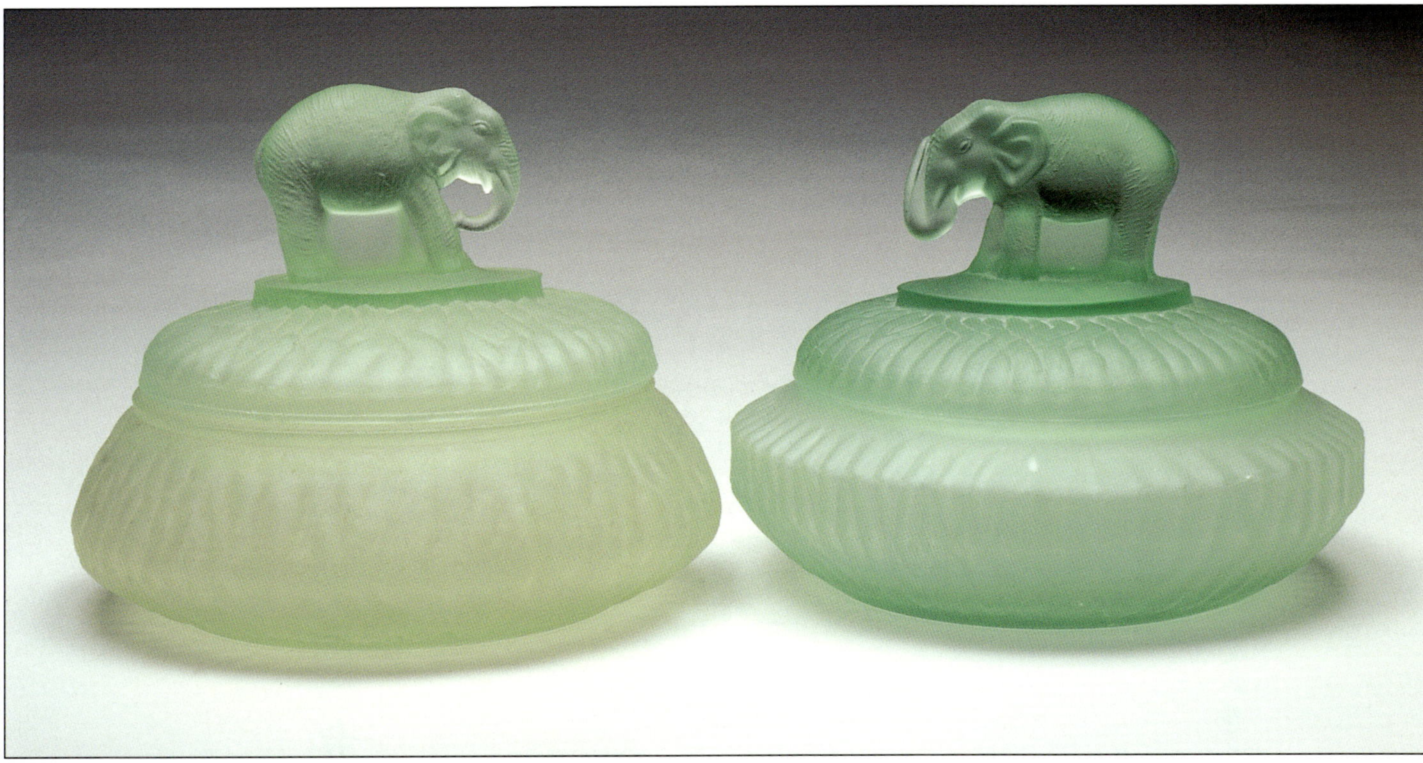

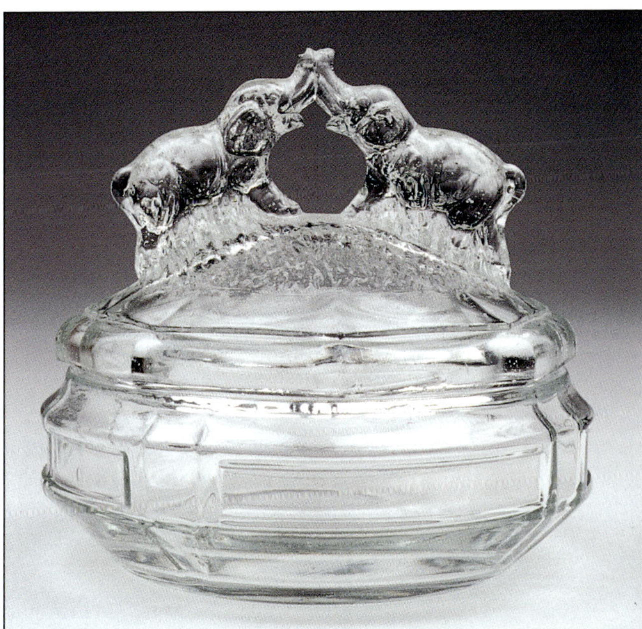

Left: Elephant trunk up covered powder box (candy), Green with satin finish, 5" tall, 6" wide, Circa 1930's, **$125.00**
Right: Elephant trunk down covered powder box (candy), Green with satin finish, 5" tall, 6" wide, Circa 1930's, **$145.00**

Elephants with trunks up and intertwined, covered powder box (candy), Crystal, 6" tall, 6" wide, Circa 1930's, **$95.00**

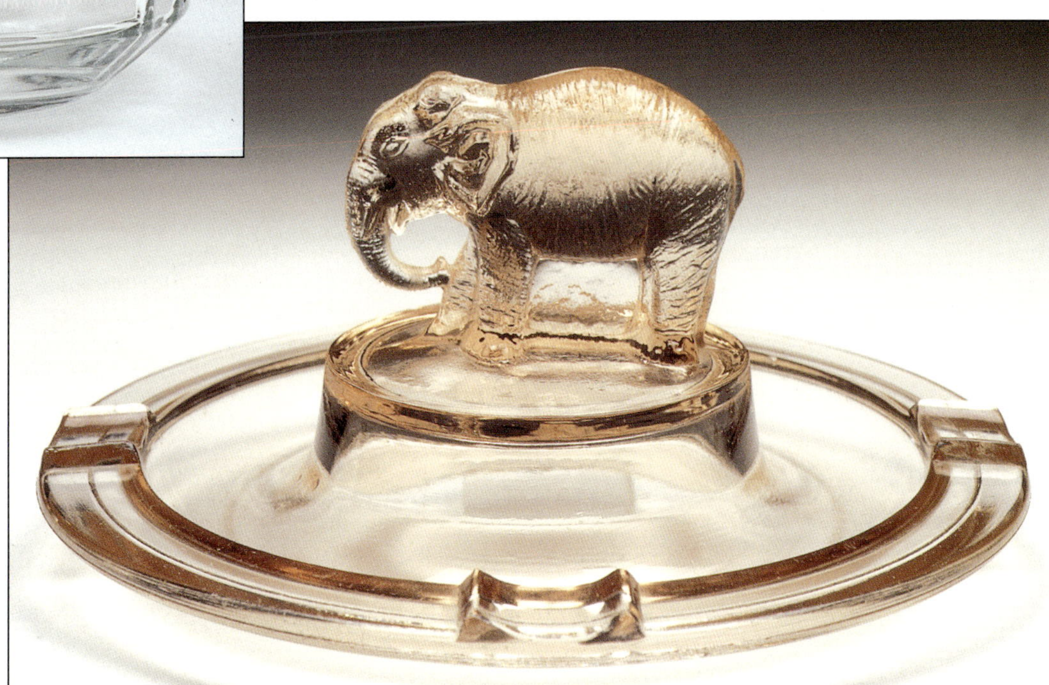

Elephant center handled ashtray, Pink, 2.75" tall, 6.25" diameter, Circa 1930's, **$60.00**

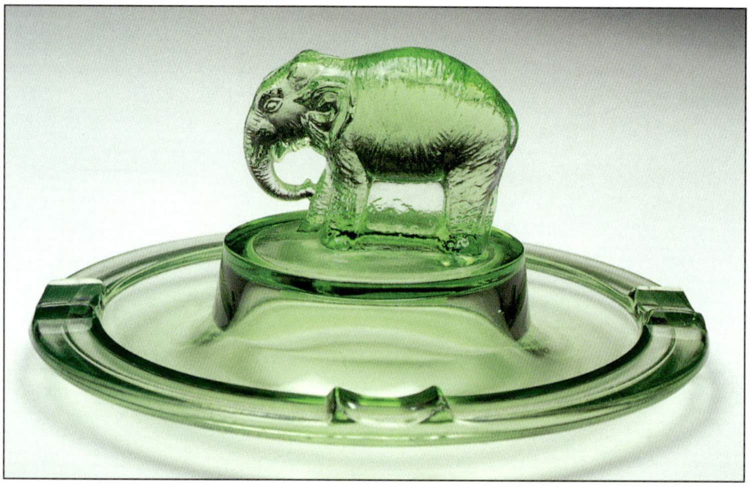

Elephant center handled ashtray, Green, 2.75" tall, 6.25" diameter, Circa 1930's, **$60.00**

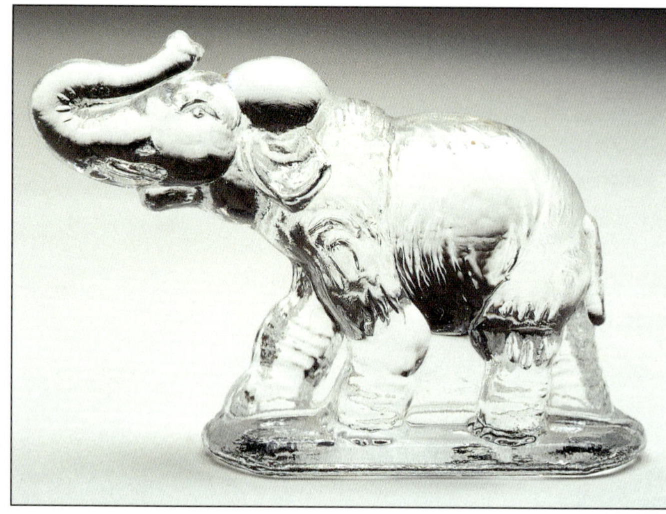

Elephant with trunk up, Crystal, 1.75" tall, 2.4" long, Circa 1950's, **$16.00**

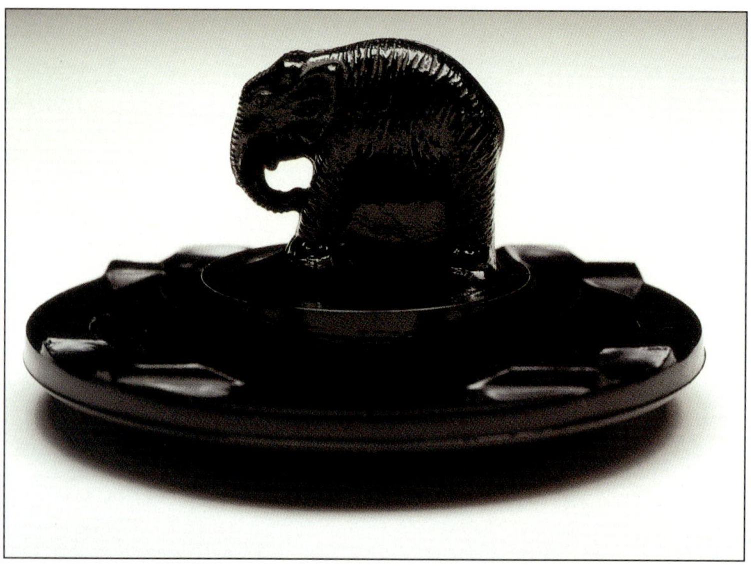

Elephant center handled ashtray, Black, 2.25" tall, 4" wide, Circa 1930's, **$48.00**

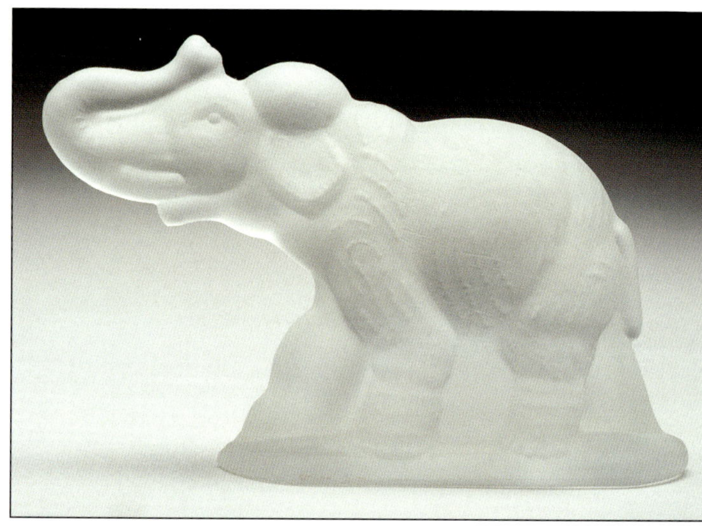

Elephant with trunk up, Crystal with satin finish, 1.75" tall, 2.4" long, Circa 1950's, **$14.00**

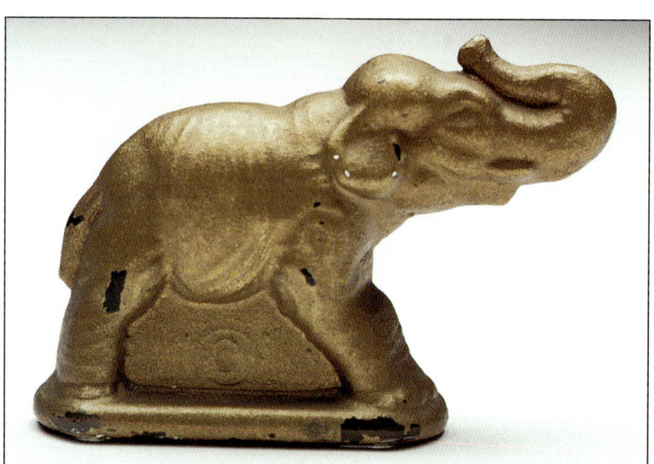

Elephant with trunk up, Crystal with gold painted, 1.75" tall, 2.4" long, Circa 1930 - 1940's, **$18.00**

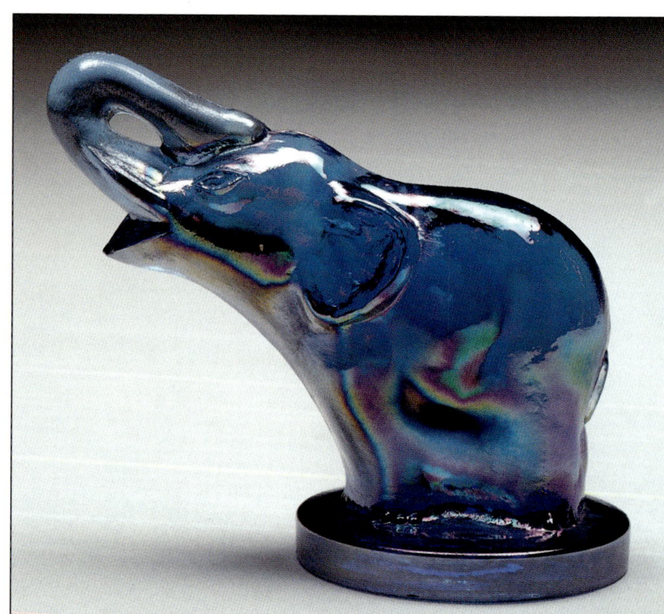

Elephant with raised trunk, Blue Carnival, 2.75" tall, 3.25" long, Circa 1950's **$28.00**

Summit Art Glass Company 1972-Present

Russel and Joann Vogelsong started Summit Art Glass Company, in Ravenna, Ohio, in 1972. The company is still running strong today.

Summit has bought a variety of moulds from such companies as Cambridge, Imperial, Westmoreland, and St. Clair. Island Mould also made moulds for Summit. They pride themselves on making quality novelty glass.

Summit pieces have been advertised as authentic reproductions in *Glass Review* during the 1970s and 1980s.

Summit created a new elephant in 1982 that was advertised as a "new and amazing limited edition Clown Elephant." This is a standing elephant, 5" tall, and is dressed in a suit, complete with a derby hat. It was marketed as a circus memory. Issued in 12 different colors, it was given the following boy names for each color: Jimmy, Tommy, Billy, Joey, Timmy, Bobby, Davy, Frank, Ernie, Jerry, Danny, and Ron. Every mould would be made in just a few colors, and once the edition was complete, the mould would be destroyed so that the market would not become saturated.

Within their current catalog you can find a variety of pieces, however none of them is offered as a limited edition, although a certain color may be offered on a limited basis. Very few Summit elephants bear their trademarked capital V in a circle.

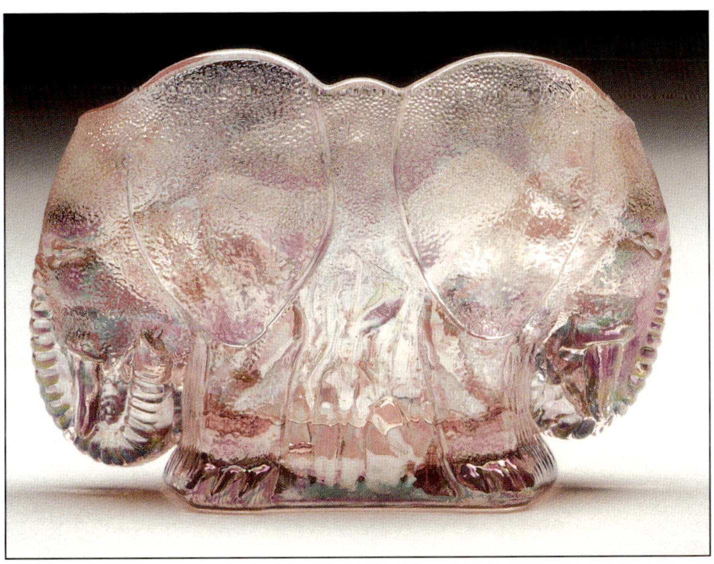

Double Elephant head toothpick #544, Pink Iridescent (carnival), V in circle mark, 2.4" tall, 3.5" long, Circa 1979, **$15.00**

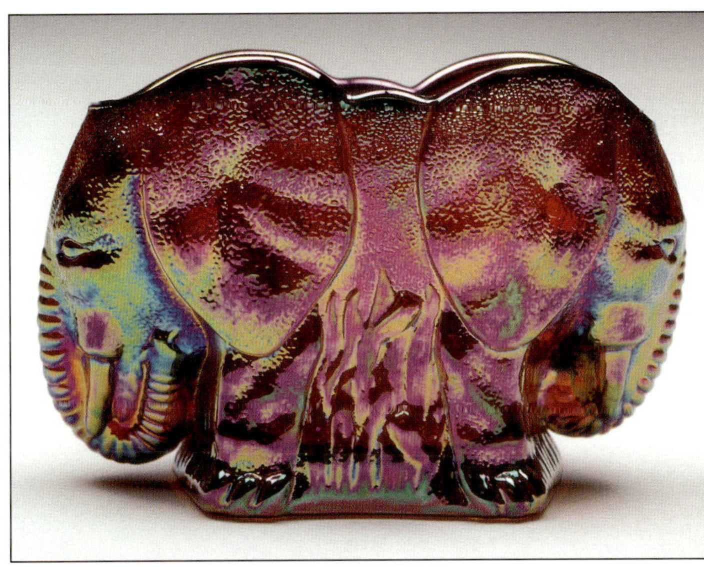

Double Elephant Head toothpick #544, Red Carnival, V in circle mark, 2.4" tall, 3.5" long, Circa 1979, **$18.00**

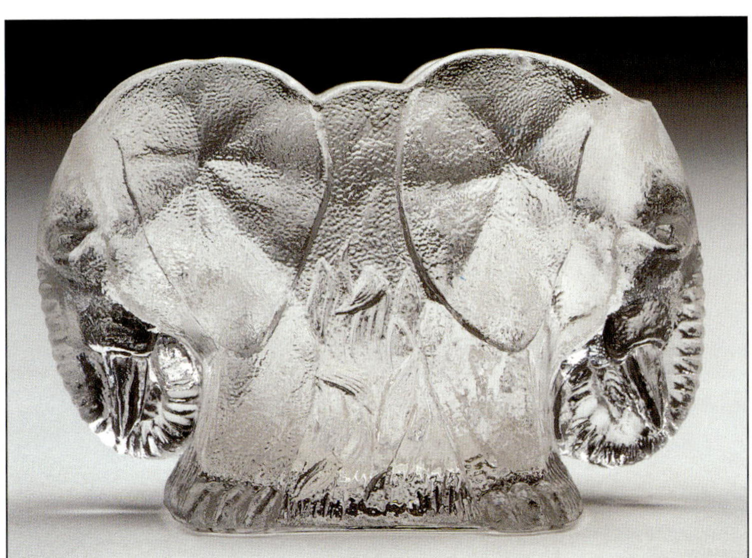

Double Elephant head toothpick #544, Crystal, 2.4" tall, 3.5" long, Circa 1980's, **$10.00**

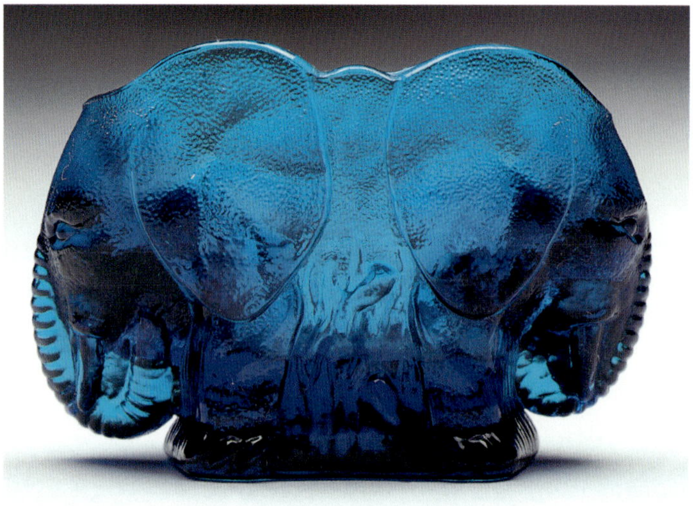

Double Elephant head toothpick #544, Teal, V in circle mark, 2.4" tall, 3.5" long, Circa 1995, **$12.00**

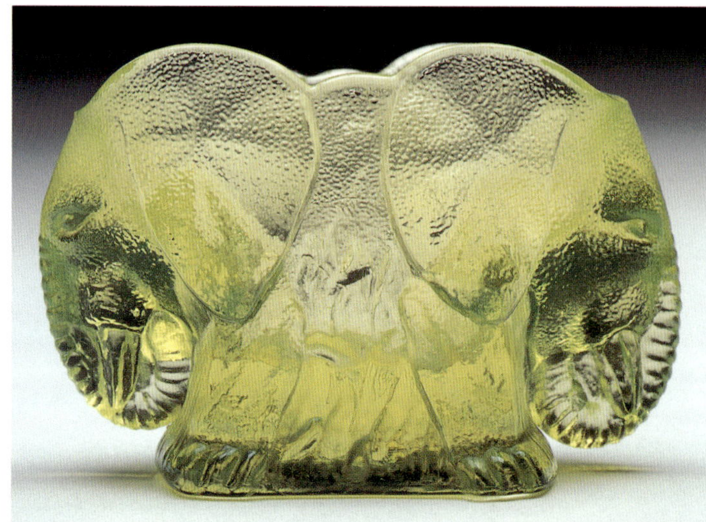

Double Elephant Head toothpick #544, Vaseline, V in circle mark, 2.4" tall, 3.5" long, Circa 1998, **$10.00**

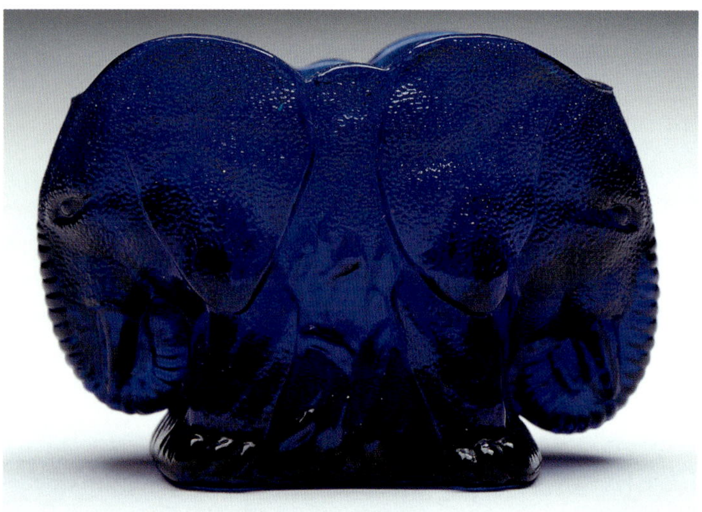

Double Elephant Head toothpick #544, Cobalt, V in circle mark, 2.4" tall, 3.5" long, Circa 1998, **$10.00**

Below:
Double Elephant Head toothpick #544, shown for color comparison
Top row: Vaseline and Pink Iridized
Bottom row: Cobalt, Red Carnival and Teal

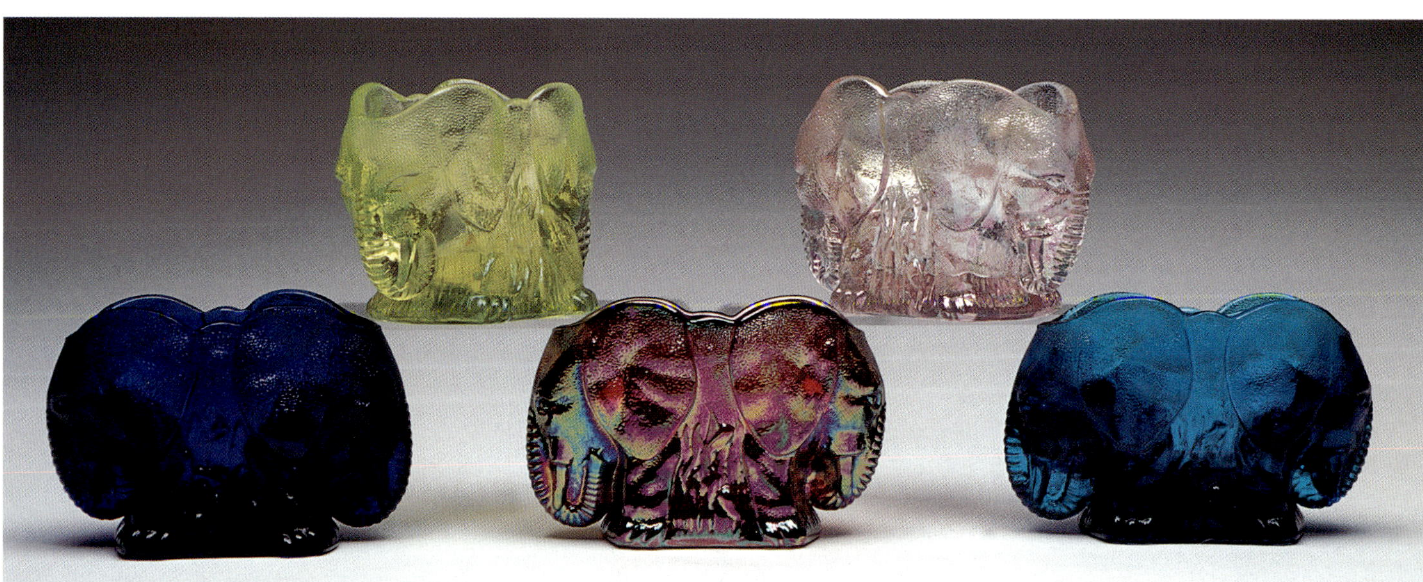

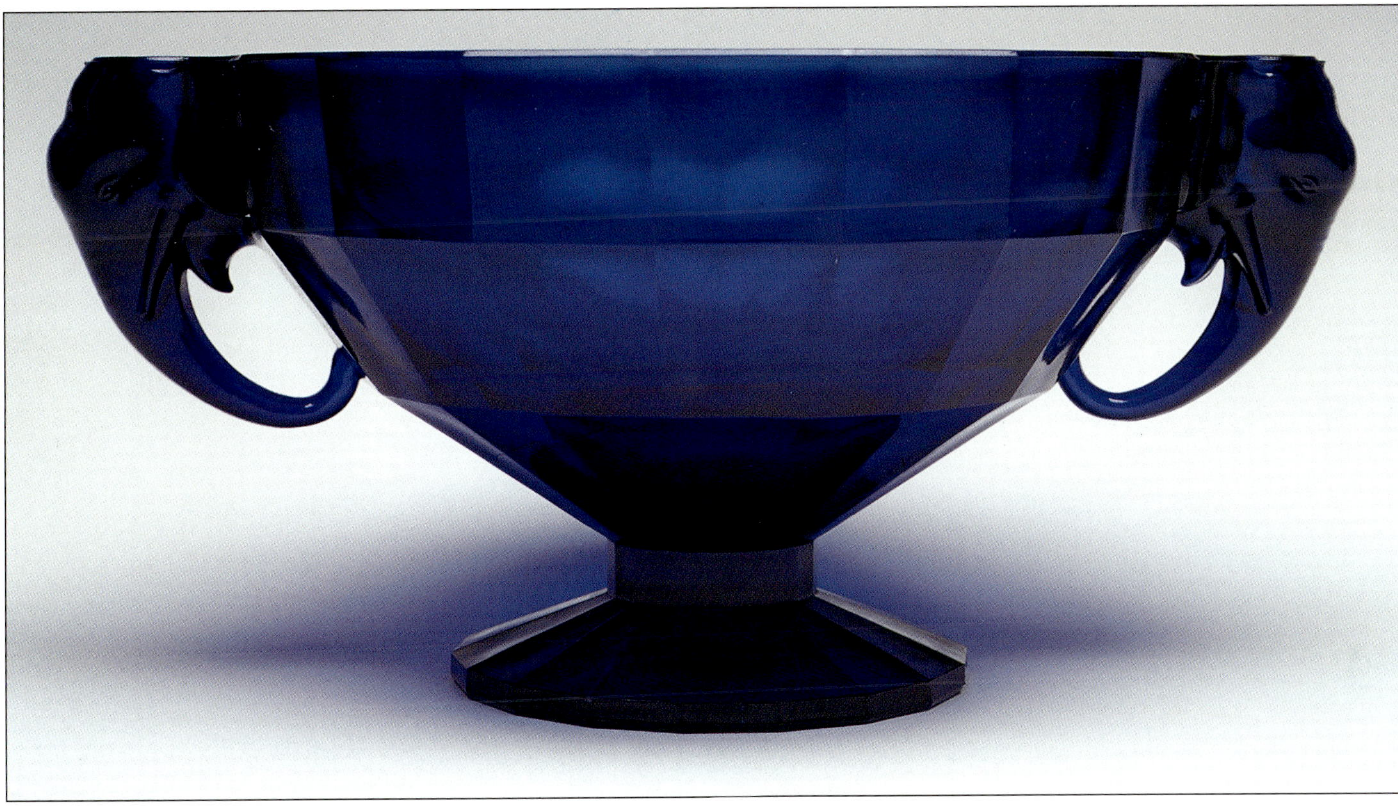

Double Elephant Head Candle holder Bowl, Cobalt, Note, this mould was obtained from Westmoreland Glass Company, 5.6" tall, 11.75" wide, Circa 1990's, **$65.00**

Double Elephant Head Candle holder Bowl shown with candles as it would be used, Teal, Note, this mould was obtained from Westmoreland Glass Company, 5.6" tall, 11.75" wide, Circa 1990's, **$75.00**

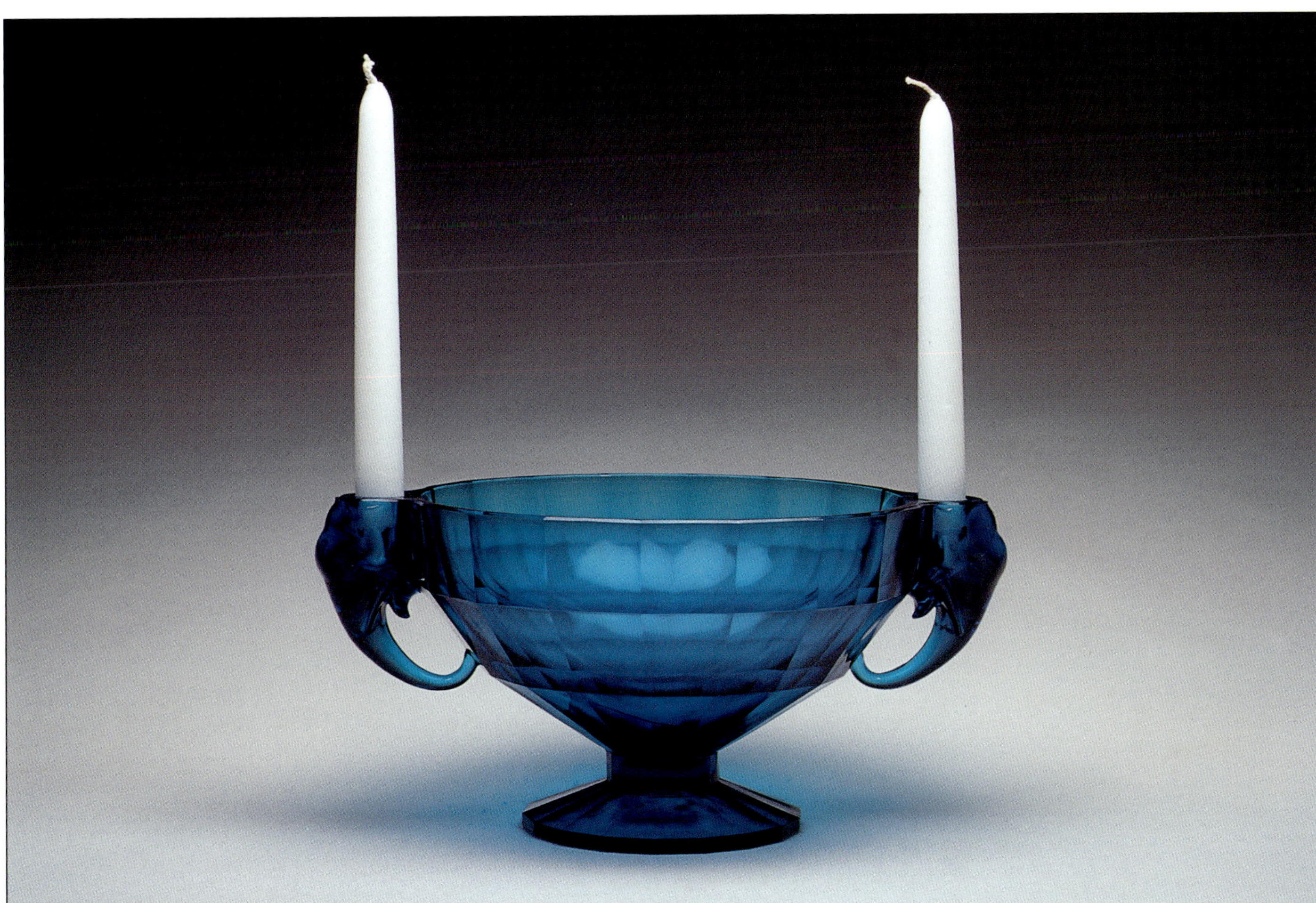

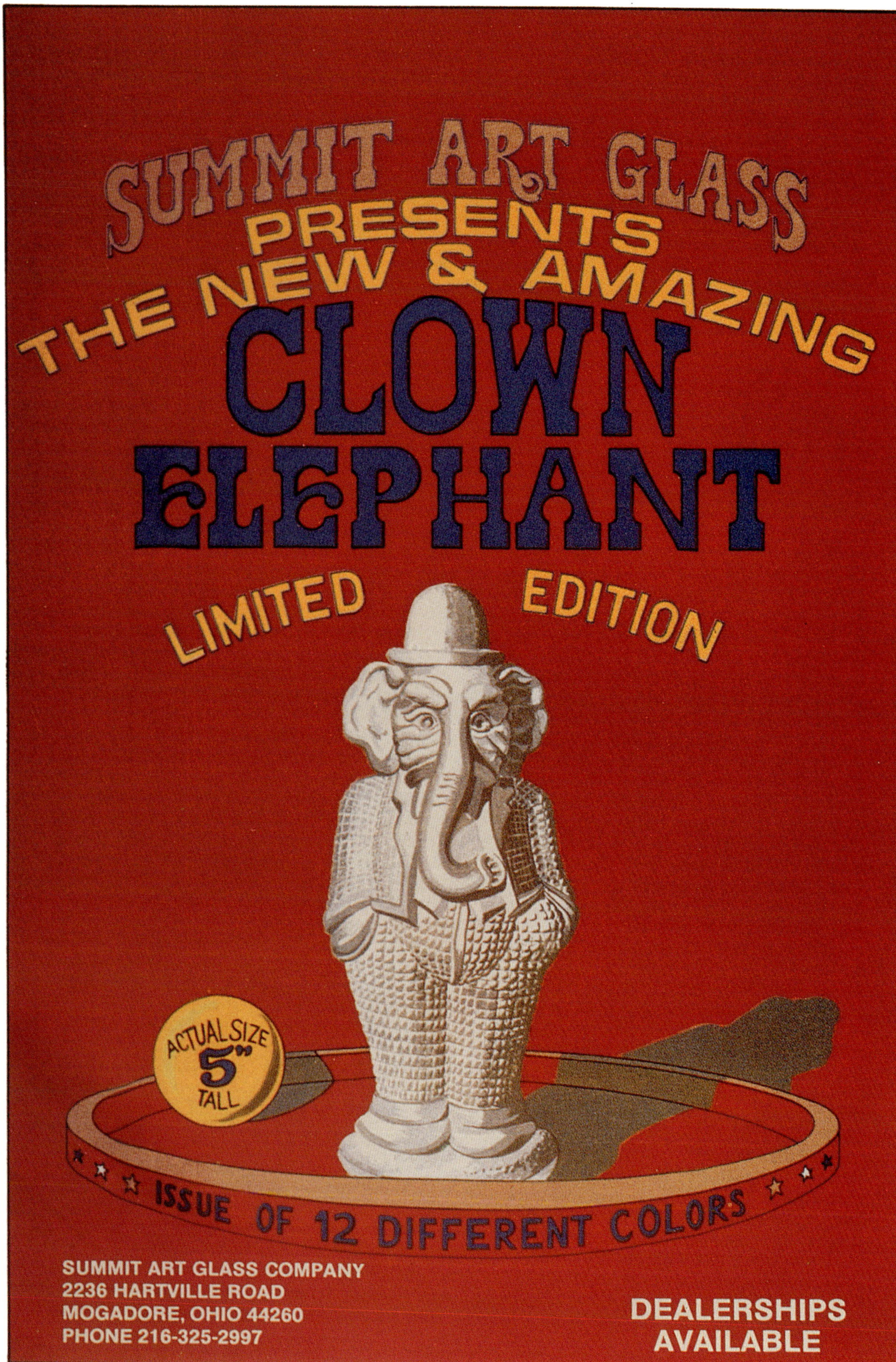

Original ad of Clown Elephant, Circa 1982. Reprinted with permission of Summit Art Glass Company

Tiara Company 1970-1998

In 1970, the Tiara Company was formed as a specific division of the Indiana Glass Company. The goal was to have a line that could be distributed at popular home parties.

At the start, Tiara was a glass dinnerware. Once the dinnerware was established and successful, novelty pieces and giftware were added. To bring further interest to the line, old moulds from Lancaster Colony, the parent company of Indiana Glass, were obtained to make glassware in new colors. These moulds came from the now-closed glass companies including Duncan & Miller, Federal, Fostoria, and Imperial. Many Fenton Art Glass moulds were also obtained for use in the Tiara line. While the Indiana Glass company had made a large number of Tiara's items, Fenton Art Glass Company also had made various items for Tiara.

At Tiara, women became essential parts of the marketing work force by running home parties. Insufficient sales caused the Tiara line to be eliminated in 1998.c

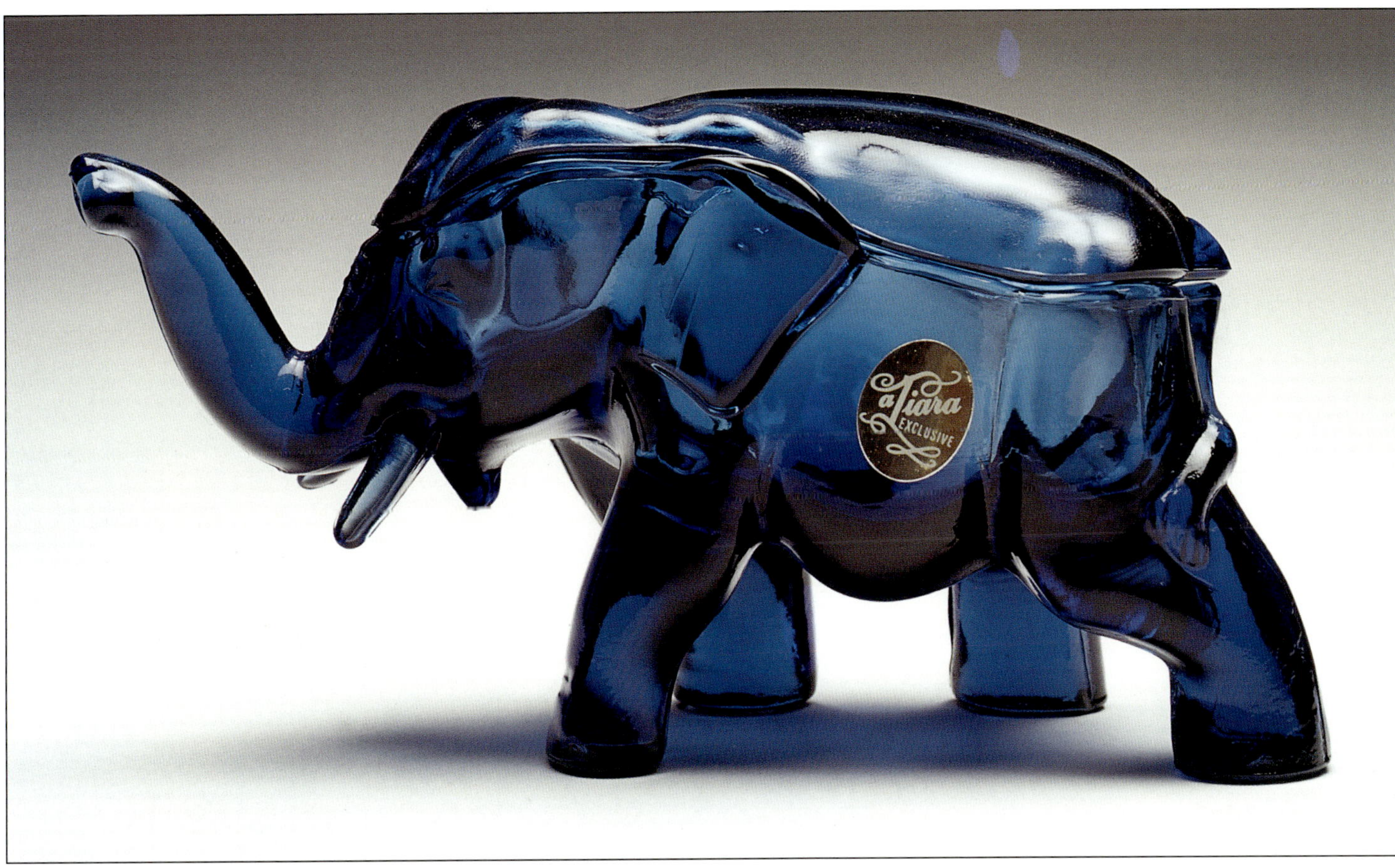

Elephant covered dish, Dark Blue, Note original black and silver label, 4.25" tall, 7.5" long, Circa 1980's, **$24.00**

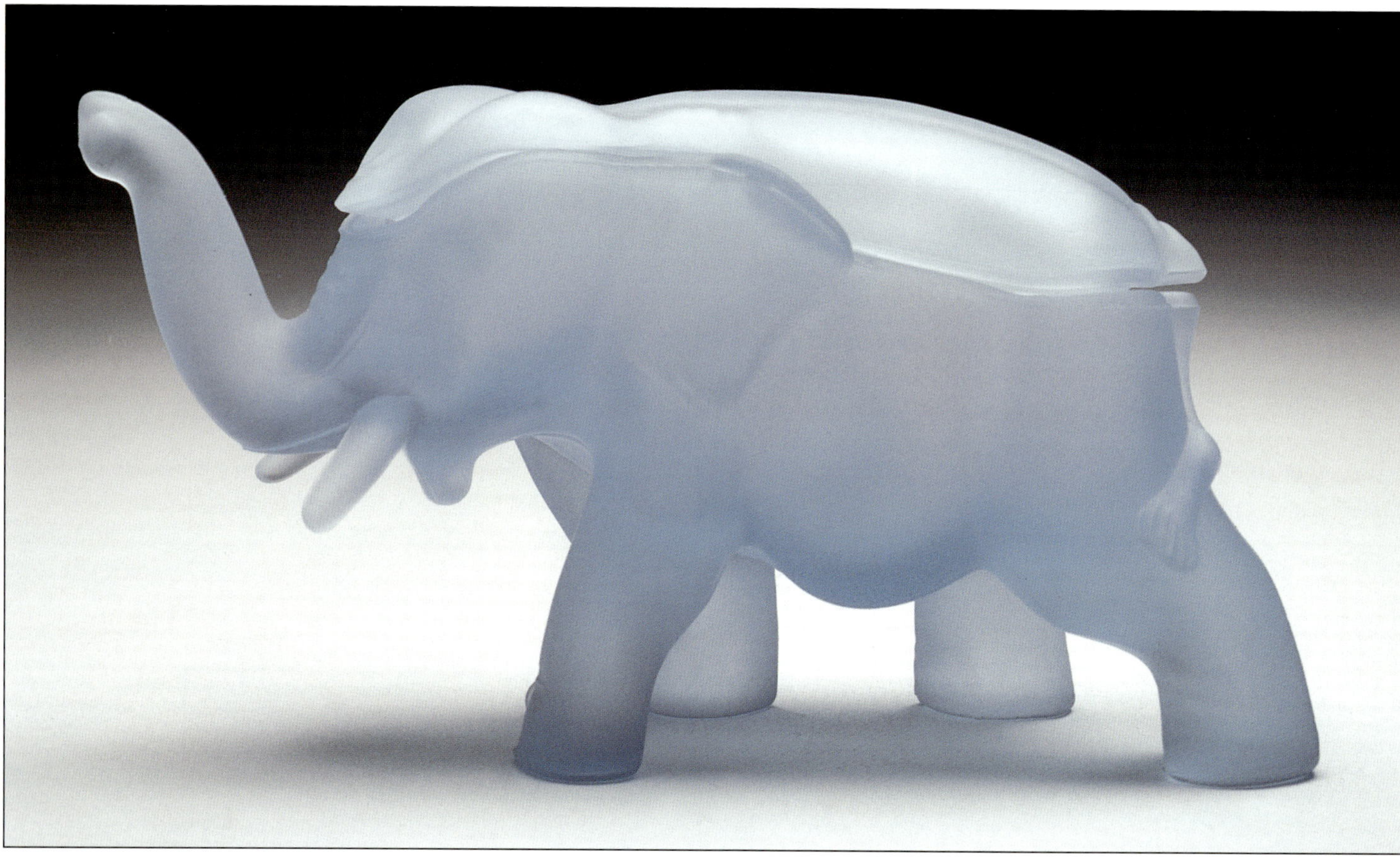

Elephant covered dish, Blue with satin finish, 4.25" tall, 7.5" long, Circa 1980's, **$18.00**

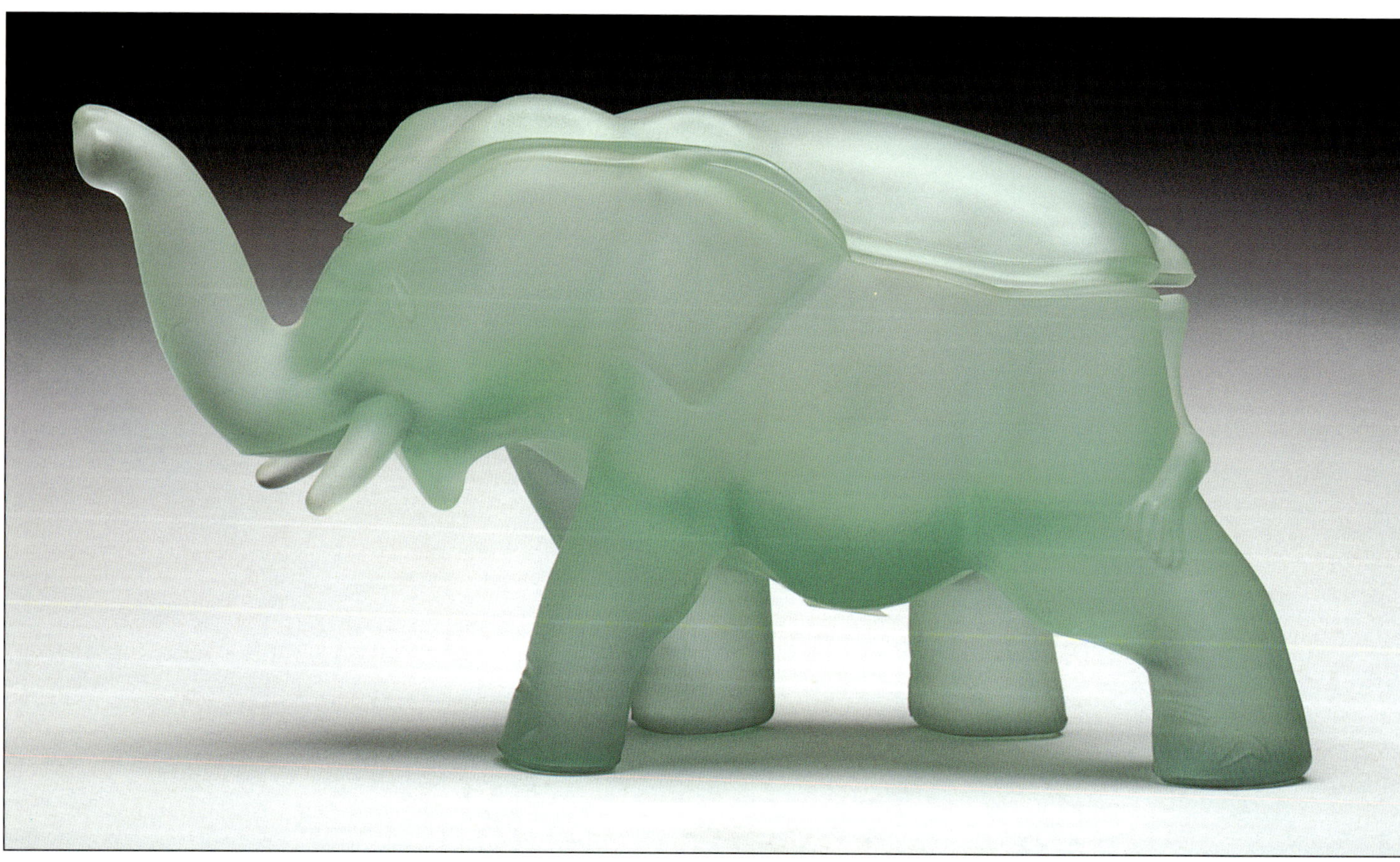

Elephant covered dish, Green with satin finish, 4.25" tall, 7.5" long, Circa 1988-90, **$18.00**

Viking Glass Company (Dalzell-Viking) 1944-1998

When the New Martinsville Glass Company closed in 1944, a stockholder by the name of G.R. Cummings purchased the company. He instituted many changes and it reopened with the new name of Viking. The hope was that this new company would attract new investors.

Through Swedish influences, new styles, colors, and designs were begun to transform the company. In addition, Harry Barth sold his business to Viking in 1952 and the Rainbow Glass Company was purchased in 1954. Sales of Viking glass were good in the 1970s.

During the 1980s, sales slumped and money issues arose. Viking closed in 1986.

Kenneth Dalzell, who formerly worked at Fostoria Glass, purchased Viking Glass Company in 1988 and renamed it Dalzell-Viking. Carl Hoffman, who was a former Fostoria employee, came over to Dalzell-Viking and created a new glass formula for the animal line. The animals were revamped to a higher quality. However, in 1998, Dalzell experienced several problems and finally had to close the company.

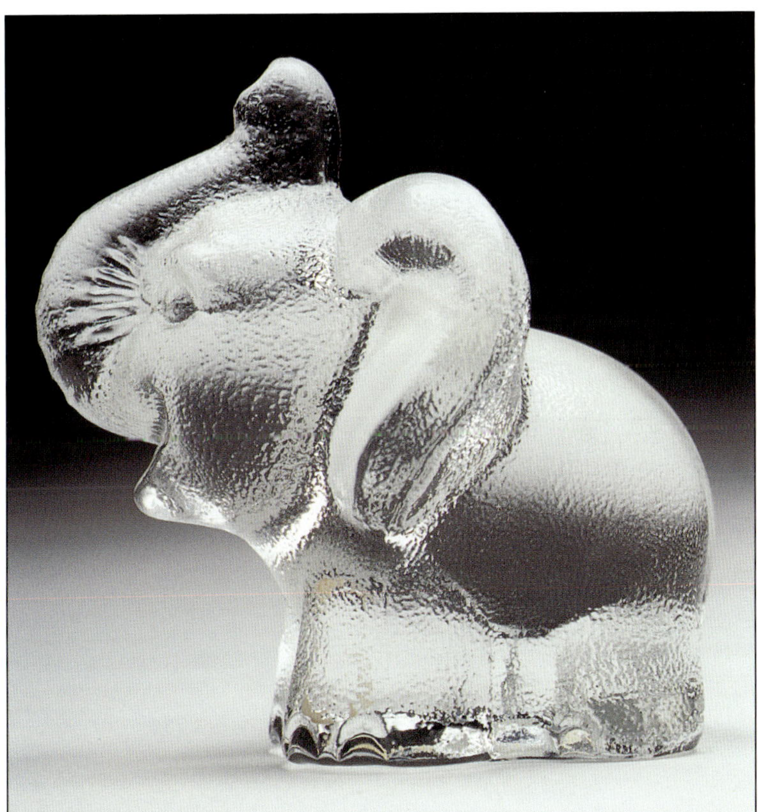

Elephant, Crystal with satin finish highlighting, 3.75" tall, 3.5" long, Circa late 1970's, **$35.00**

Wheaton Glass Company 1888-Present

Wheaton Glass Company was created in 1888 in Millville, New Jersey. They began their productions with bottles and later made commemorative decanters. To expand their lines to include products for home-party sales, Wheaton Glass created Wheatonware in 1965 as a separate division. In the early 1970s, several Kemple moulds were added to this line. However, within just a few years, the new line was not successful enough to survive, so the Wheatonware line was closed.

Avon Products had approached Wheaton Glass in the 1960s to make decorative decanters for them, and this contract work continues today. Wheaton was sold in 1996 to Alusuisse Lonza, a Swiss company. Alcan Packaging bought the company in 2000 and changed its name to Wheaton USA.

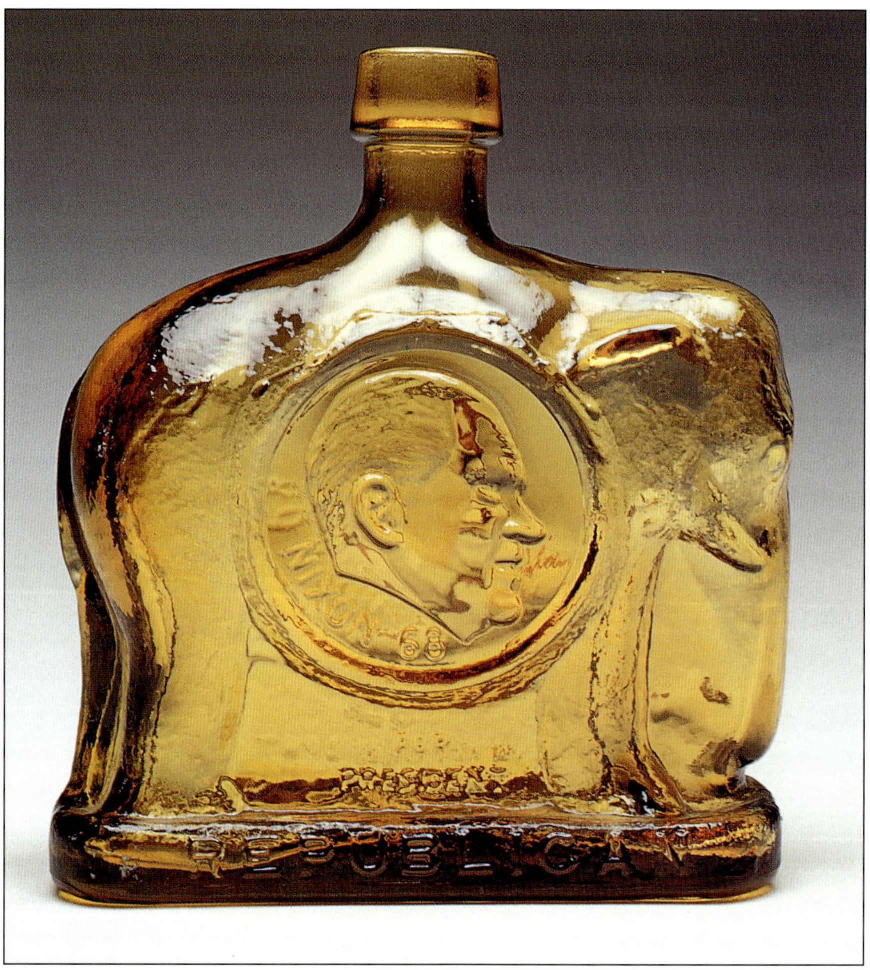

Elephant bottle, Amber, marked on right side: "Nixon 68 for President, Republican". marked on left side: Agnew for Vice President" campaign. marked on bottom: Wheaton NJ First Edition, 5" tall 6.5" long, Circa 1968, **$18.00**

Wilkerson Glass Company 1984-Present

Fred Wilkerson, Sr. strived for a glass company of his own. He had gained experience in the glassmaking field with Fostoria since 1958. Around 1971, he started making his own glass, but kept it a part-time interest. However, when Fostoria Glass Company closed in 1983, he saw an opportunity to have his own company. He started Wilkerson Glass Company, in Moundsville, West Virginia, and taught his son the art of glassmaking that enabled him to run a small family business. Fred Jr. has done a wonderful job and he teaches glassmaking at Oglebay Institute, in Wheeling, West Virginia.

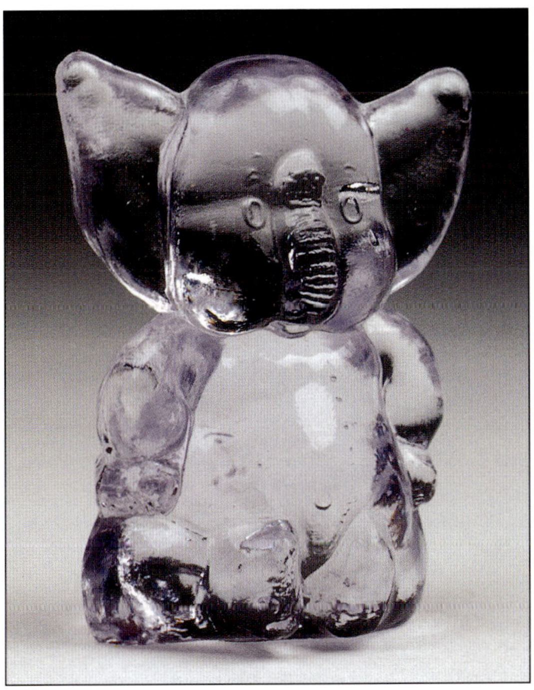

Elephant sitting up and trunk up, Crystal, 2.25" tall, 1.5" wide, Circa 1990's, **$12.00**

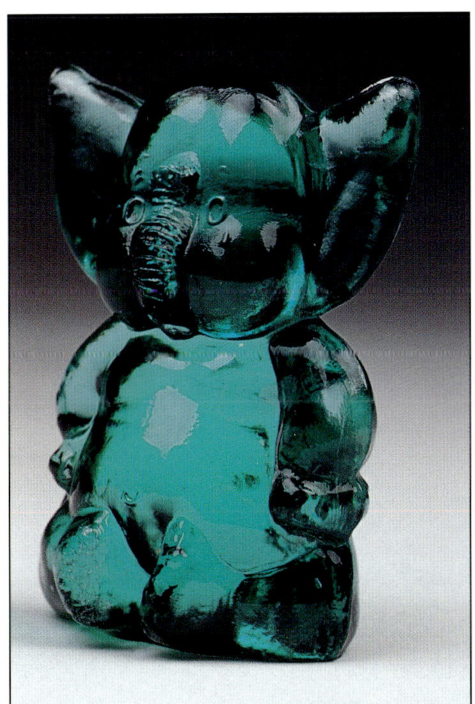

Elephant sitting up and trunk up, Teal, 2.25" tall, 1.5" wide, Circa 1990's, **$12.00**

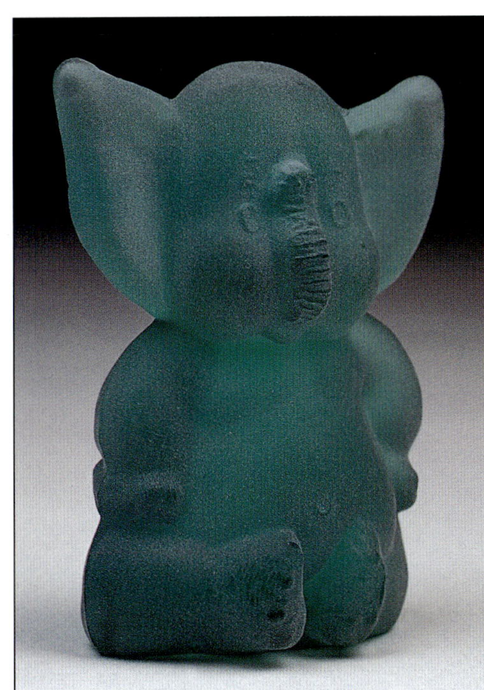

Elephant sitting up and trunk up, Teal with satin finish, 2.25" tall, 1.5" wide, Circa 1990's, **$12.00**

Unknowns

There are several elephants for which specific information could not be obtained. Here I turn to my fellow collectors for their assistance. These elephants have showed up in many places before, and it would be most useful if I could identify them. However, they are believed to be American, so they are included in this reference. Let me know your thoughts about them.

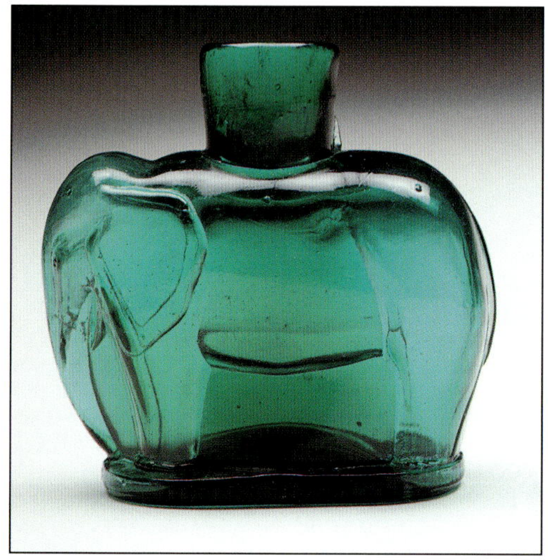

Elephant Perfume Bottle, Teal, 3" tall, 2.75" long, Circa 1930's, **$24.00**

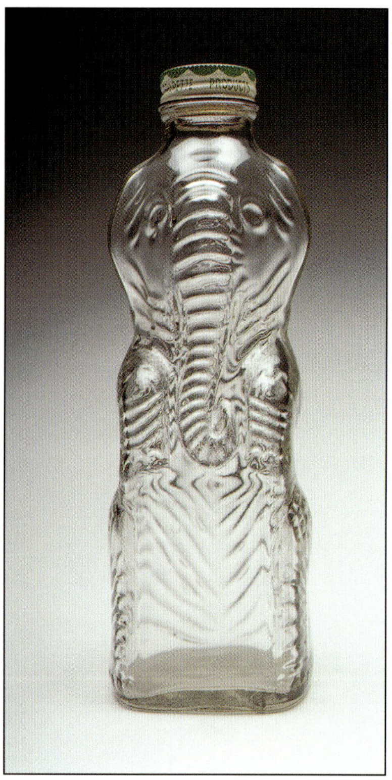

Elephant bottle, Crystal, metal lid that screws off, says Grapette Family Beverage Syrup on top, around side Grapette Products, Company Camden, Ark, marked on bottom of glass Grapette Products Co. 15 o in an oval 3, larger 3 Camden, Ark (Arkansas), 7.25" tall, 2.75" wide, Circa 1930's, **$35.00**

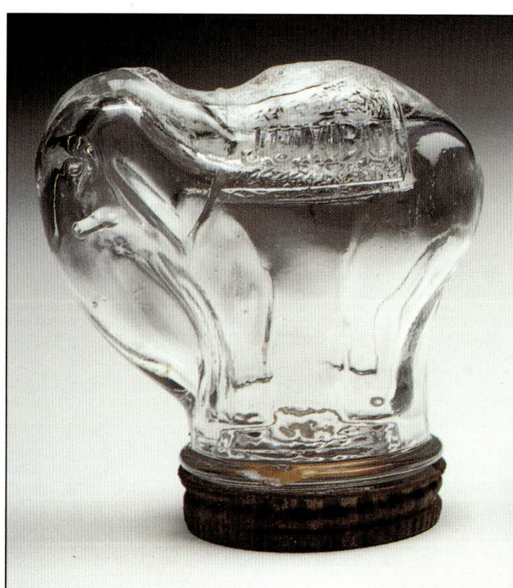

Elephant container, Crystal, Embossed on blanket: Peanut Butter on one side, Jumbo on other, on metal lid it says Jumbo Peanut Butter 3.5 oz., 3.5" tall, 3" long, Circa 1920's, **$48.00**

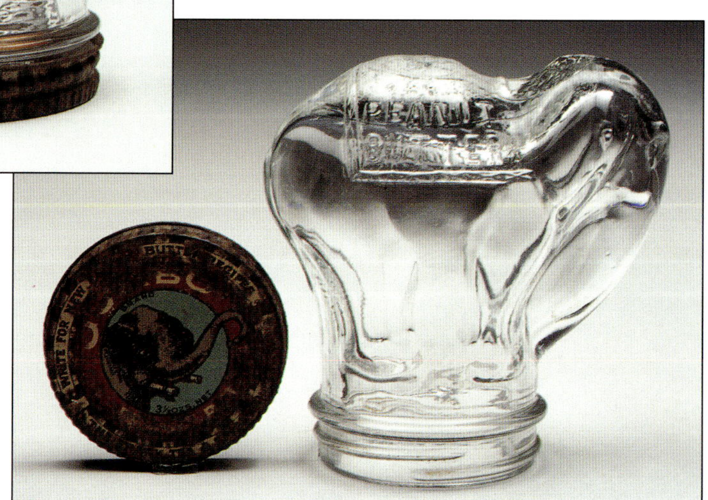

Elephant container, Crystal, shown with screw on lid off for look at detail

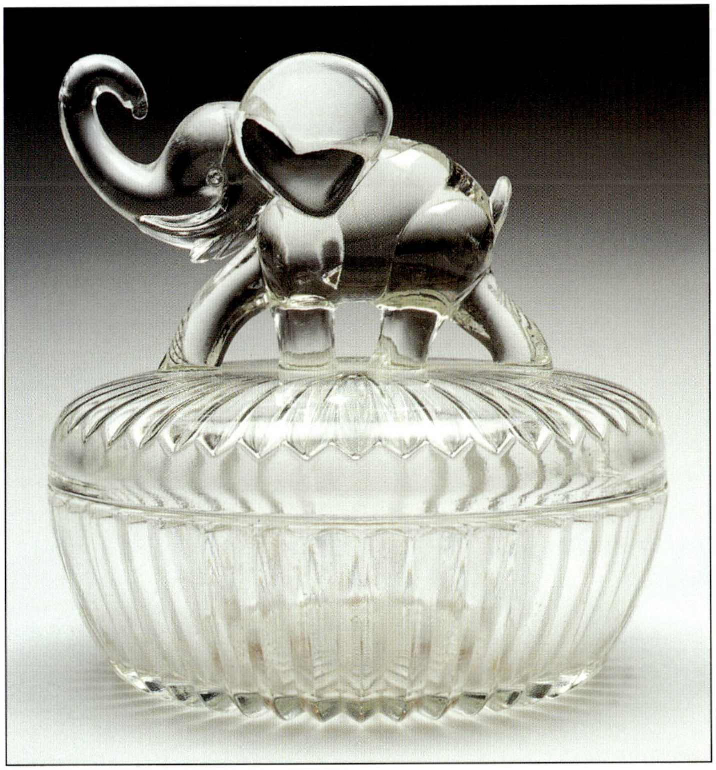

Elephant trunk up covered powder dish, Crystal, 5.75" tall, 5.5" wide, Circa 1930's, **$45.00**

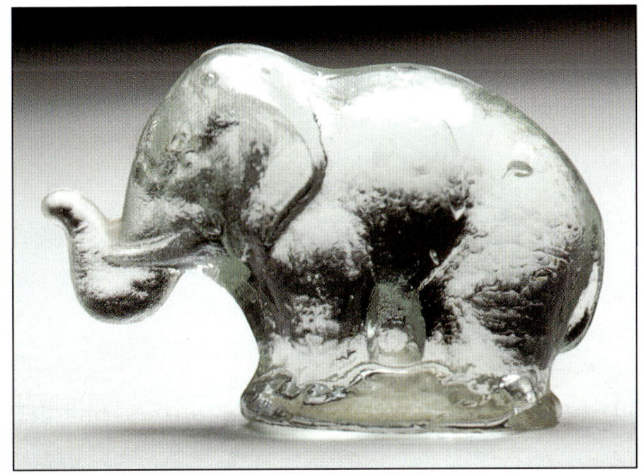

Standing, Trunk up, Crystal, 1.5" tall, 2.5" long, Circa 1930's, **$6.00**

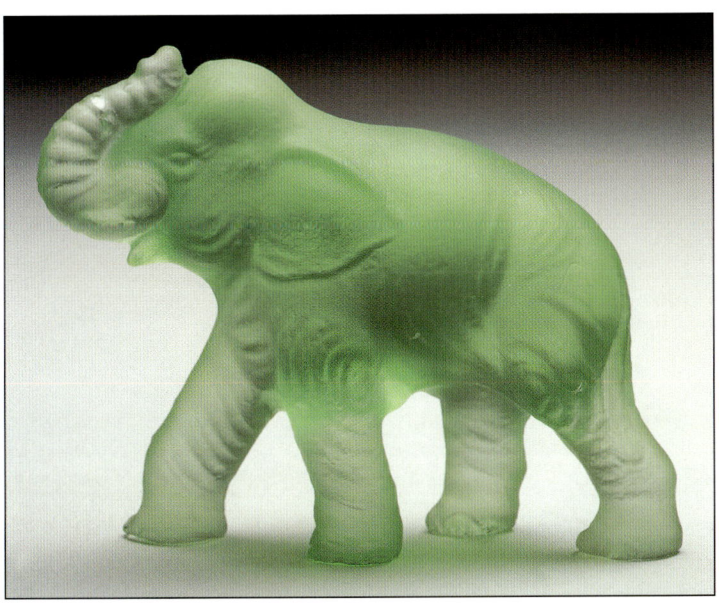

Elephant walking with trunk up, Green with satin finish, 2.75" tall, 3.25" long, Circa 1930's, **$60.00**

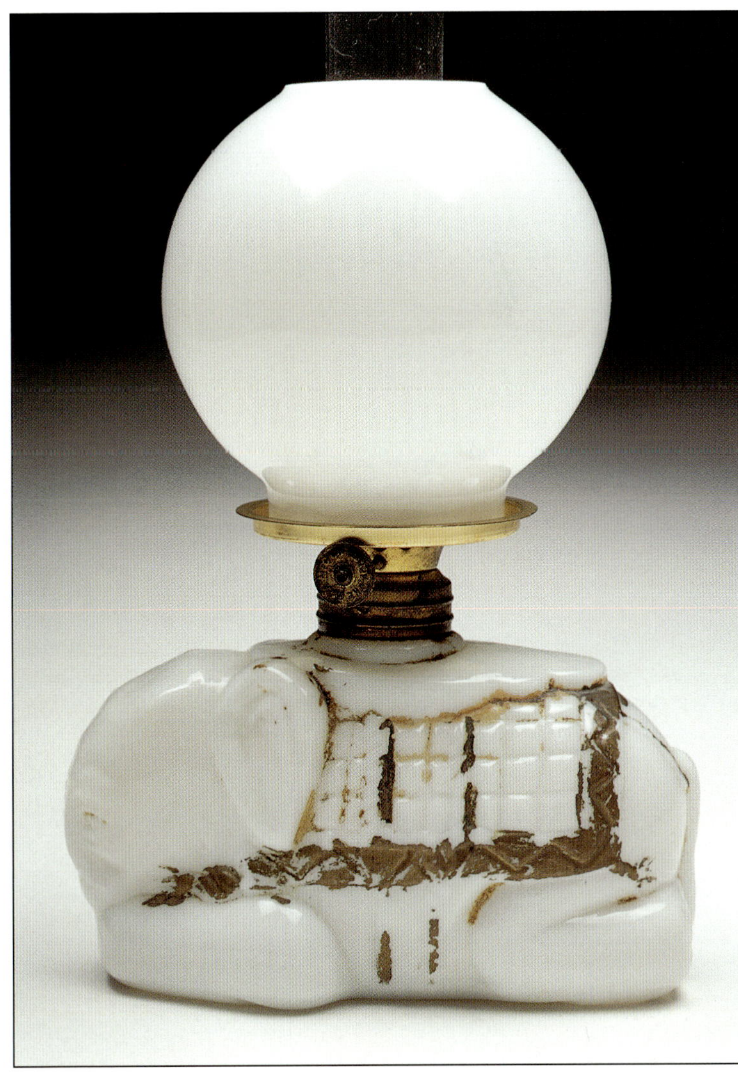

Elephant, Milk glass, kerosene lamp (Note, also came with basket weave shade and add $50.00 for it) listed in Butler Brothers catalog, 8.25" tall, 5" long, Circa 1900, **$195.00**

Collector Organizations

Collecting glass is more interesting if you belong to an organization that promotes education about specific items. By gathering with other enthusiasts, it becomes possible to form a beneficial network. I recommend joining such a non-profit organization that strives for the preservation of information about glass companies, general related education, and overall support of collecting interests. The national organizations that are listed here provide information through educational newsletters, study guides, reprinting of company catalogs, seminars, sanctioning conventions, having a museum, and other educational activities. These are a few suggestions, and there are many other organizations as well.

Boyd Art Glass Collectors Guild
P. O. Box 52, Hatboro, PA 19040

Fostoria Glass Society
P. O. Box 826, Moundsville, WV 26041
304-845-9188
$16/year 8 newsletters a year
www.fostoriaglass.org

Heisey Collectors of America
169 West Church Street, Newark, OH 43055
740-345-2932
$22/year 12 newsletters a year
www.heiseymuseum.org

Jody and Darrell's Glass Collectibles (Boyd glass)
P. O. Box 180833
Arlington, TX 76096-0833
$27/yr

National American Glass Club
Box 8489, Silver Springs, MD 20907
607-974-8357
$25/yr 4 newsletters
www.glassclub.org

National Imperial Glass Collectors Society
P. O. Box 534, Bellaire, OH 43906
410-995-1254
$15/year 4 newsletters a year
www.imperialglass.org

Pacific NW Fenton Association
P. O. Box 881, Tillamook, OR 97141
503-842-4815
$23/year 4 newsletters and exclusive piece of Fenton glass
www.glasscastle.com/pnwfa.htm

West Virginia Museum of American Glass
304-269-5006
P. O. Box 574, Weston, WV 26452
$25/year 4 newsletters
http://members.aol.com/wvmuseumofglass

Bibliography

Belknap, E.M. *Milk Glass.* New York City, New York: Crown Publishers, 1949.

Blenko Glass Company. *Company Catalogs.* Milton, West Virginia: Blenko Glass Company, 1990s -2003.

Bredehoft, Neila & Tom. *Heisey Glass 1896-1957.* Paducah, Kentucky: Collector Books, 2001.

Boyd, Bernard, John & Sue. *Boyd's Crystal Art Glass.* Cambridge, Ohio: Boyd Family, 1990.

Boyd, Bernard, John & Sue. *Boyd's Newsletters.* Cambridge, Ohio: Boyd Family, 1985-2003.

Boyd, Bernard F. & Sue. *Personal correspondence*, Cambridge, Ohio: Boyd Family, 2003.

Coe, Debbie & Randy. *Glass Animals & Figurines.* Atglen, Pennsylvania: Schiffer Publishing, 2003.

Coe, Myra. *Fenton's Elephants PNWFA convention seminar,* Springfield, Oregon: Myra Coe, 1998.

Corning Glass Museum. *Archival material and microfiche.* Corning, New York: Corning Glass Museum, 2000.

Coyle, Robert; Lynne Bloch & Art Hartman. *The Heisey Animals, Etc Book II.* Lahaska, Pennsylvania: Lynne-Art's Glass House Inc., 1978.

Craig, Betty. *New Glass Collectibles.* Fort Wayne, Indiana: Betty Craig, 1980 & 1981.

Cudd, Viola. *Heisey Glassware.* Brenham, Texas: Herrmann Print Shop, 1969.

Degenhart Glass Museum. *Company Catalog.* Cambridge, Ohio: Degenhart Glass Museum, 2002.

Dereume Glass. *Company Catalogs.* Punxsutawney, Pennsylvania: Dereume Glass, 1990s.

Dezso, Douglas & J. Leon & Rose Poirier. *Collectors Guide to Candy Containers.* Paducah, Kentucky: Collector Books, 1998.

Fenton Art Glass Co. *Company Catalogs.* Williamstown, West Virginia: Fenton Art Glass Co., 1958-2003.

Fenton, Frank M. *Personal correspondence.* Williamstown, West Virginia: Fenton Art Glass Company, 2003.

Ferson, Mary & Regis. *Yesterday's Milk Glass Today.* Greensburg, Pennsylvania: Chas M. Henry Printing, 1981.

Font, Walter. *Personal correspondence*, Fort Wayne, Indiana: Fort Wayne Museum, 2003.

Florence, Gene. *Degenhart Glass & Paperweights.* Cambridge, Ohio: Degenhart & Paperweight and Glass Museum, Inc., 1982.

Fostoria Glass Company. *Company Catalogs.* Moundsville, West Virginia: Fostoria Glass Co., 1930-1980s.

Fostoria Glass Society. *Facets of Fostoria newsletters.* Moundsville, West Virginia: Fostoria Glass Society, 1980s-1990s.

Franklin Mint, www.franklinmint.com, 2003.

Furr's Gifts Co. *Company Catalogs.* Deep Gap, North Carolina: Furr's Gifts Company, 1970.

Garmon, Lee & Dick Spencer. *Glass Animals of the Depression Era.* Paducah, Kentucky: Collector Books, 1993.

Gibson Glass. *Company Catalogs.* Milton, West Virginia: Gibson Glass, 1990s-2002.

Hahn, Frank & Paul Kikeli. *Collectors Guide to Heisey & Heisey by Imperial Glass Animals.* Lima, Ohio: Golden Era Publications, 1991.

Hastin, Bud. *Avon Products & California Perfume Co. Collectors Encyclopedia.* Fort Lauderdale, Florida: Bud Hastin, 1998.

Heacock, Bill. *Collecting Glass Volume 1.* Marietta, Ohio: Richardson Printing Corp., 1984.

Heacock, Bill. *Collecting Glass Volume II.* Marietta, Ohio: Richardson Printing Corp., 1985.

Heacock, Bill. *Collecting Glass Volume III.* Marietta, Ohio: Richardson Printing Corp., 1986.

Heacock, Bill. *Fenton Glass The First Twenty Five Years.* Marietta, Ohio: O-Val Advertising Corporation, 1978.

Heacock, Bill. *Fenton Glass The Second Twenty Five Years.* Marietta, Ohio. O-Val Advertising Corporation, 1980.

Heacock, Bill. *Fenton Glass The Third Twenty Five Years.* Marietta, Ohio: O-Val Advertising Corporation, 1989.

Heacock, Bill. *The Glass Collector #2 to #6.* Columbus, Ohio: Peacock Publications, 1982.

Heisey Collectors of America. *Heisey Catalog & Price List #32.* Newberg, Oregon: Headrick Buchdruckerei, 1994.

Heisey Collectors of America. *Heisey News newsletters.* Newark, Ohio: Heisey Collectors of America,1980-2001.

Holmes, Todd & Ann. *Boyd's Art Glass Production 1978-1992.* Kansas City, Missouri: Todd & Ann Holmes, 1992.

Holmes, Todd & Ann. *Boyd Glass Coloring Book.* Kansas City, Missouri: Todd & Ann Holmes, 1993.

Imperial Glass Corporation. *Company Brochure.* Bellaire, Ohio: Imperial Glass Corporation, 1947.

Imperial Glass Corporation. *Company Brochures.* Bellaire, Ohio: Imperial Glass Corporation, 1950s.

Kerr, Ann. *Fostoria.* Paducah, Kentucky: Collector Books, 1994.

Long, Milbra & Emily Seate. *Fostoria Useful & Ornamental.* Paducah, Kentucky: Collector Books, 2000.

Measell, James. *Fenton Glass The 1980s Decade.* Marietta, Ohio: The Glass Press, 1996.

Measell, James. *Fenton Glass The 1990s Decade.* Marietta, Ohio: The Glass Press, 2000.

Measell, James. *Imperial Glass Encyclopedia Volume II.* Marietta, Ohio: The Glass Press, 1997.

Measell, James. *Imperial Glass Encyclopedia Volume III.* Marietta, Ohio: The Glass Press, 1999.

Measell, James. *New Martinsville Glass 1900-44.* Marietta, Ohio: Antique Publications, 1994.

McDermott, James. *Heisey Animals Book I.* Lima, Ohio: Golden Era Publications, 1973.

Miller, Everett & Addie, *The New Martinsville Glass Story.* Marietta, Ohio: Richardson Publishing Co.,1972.

Mosser Glass Company. *Company Catalogs.* Cambridge, Ohio: Mosser Glass Company, 1990-2003.

National Imperial Glass Collectors Society. *Imperial Glass Catalog #66A.* Marietta, Ohio: Richardson Printing Corporation,1991.

National Imperial Glass Collectors Society. *Imperial Collectors Gazettes.* Bellaire, Ohio: National Imperial Glass Collectors,1990-2001.

Newbound, Betty & Bill, *Collector's Encyclopedia of Milk Glass.* Paducah, Kentucky: Collector Books, 1995.

Newbound, Betty. *Figurine Facts and Figures.* Union Lake, Michigan: Bill Newbound, 1982.

Newark Heisey Collectors Club. *Heisey by Imperial.* Newark, Ohio: Heisey Collectors of America, 1982.

Oneida, www.oneida.com. 2003.

Orient & Flume, www.orientflume.com. 2003.

Pacific NW Fenton Association. *Nor'Wester newsletters.* Tillamook, Oregon: Pacific NW Fenton Association, 1994-2002.

Padgett, Leonard. Pairpoint Glass. Des Moines, Iowa: Wallace Homestead, 1979.

Pairpoint Glass Works. *Company Catalogs 1990-2003.* Sagamore, Massachusetts: Pairpoint Glass Works, 1990-2003.

Piña, Leslie. *Blenko Glass 1962-1971 Catalogs.* Atglen, Pennsylvania: Schiffer Publications, 2000.

Piña, Leslie. *Popular "50s and '60s Glass.* Atglen, Pennsylvania: Schiffer Publications, 1995.

Rainbow Art Co. *Company Catalog.* Huntington, West Virginia: Rainbow Art Co.,1944.

Revi, Albert Christian. *Spinning Wheel. magazines,* Hanover, Pennsylvania: Everybody's Press, 1970s.

Rice, Ferill J.. *Caught in the Butterfly Net.* Williamstown, West Virginia: Fenton Art Glass Collectors of America, 1991.

Richardson, David. *Glass Collectors Digest.* Marietta, Ohio: Richardson Printing Corp., 1980-1990s.

Robinson, Dorothy & Bill Feeny. *Official Price Guide to American Pottery & Porcelain.* Orlando, Florida: House of Collectibles, 1980.

Saffell, Jon. *Personal correspondence.* Williamstown, West Virginia: Fenton Art Glass Company, 2003.

Shaeffer, Barbara, *Glass Review.* Marietta, Ohio: Barbara Shaeffer, 1980-1986.

Smith, L.E. *Company Catalogs.* Mt. Pleasant, Pennsylvania: L E Smith Glass Company, 1990-2002.

Summit Art Glass Co. *Company Brochures 1990-2002.* Ravenna, Ohio: Summit Art Glass Co., 1990-2003.

Taylor, Dorothy, *Encore by Dorothy Book I.* Kansas City, Missouri: Dorothy Taylor, 1985.

Taylor, Dorothy, *Encore by Dorothy Book II.* Kansas City, Missouri: Dorothy Taylor, 1986.

Taylor, Dorothy, *Encore by Dorothy Book III.* Kansas City, Missouri: Dorothy Taylor, 1990.

Teal, Ron Sr., *Tiara Exclusives.* Marietta, Ohio: The Glass Press, 2000.

Tiara Exclusives, *Company Catalogs 1970s-1990s.* Dunkirk, Indiana: Tiara Exclusives, 1970s-1990s.

Tumbusch, Tom, *Tomart's Illustrated Disneyana Catalog & Price Guide.* Dayton, Ohio: Tomart Publications, 1985.

Van Pelt, Mary. *Fantastic Figurines.* Westminster, California: Mary Van Pelt, 1973.

Van Pelt, Mary. *Figurines in Crystal.* Westminster, California: Mary Van Pelt, 1975.

Viking Glass Co. *Company Catalogs.* New Martinsville, West Virginia: Viking Glass Co., 1960-1980s.

Vogel, Clarence. *Heisey's Early & Late Years.* Galion, Ohio: Fisher Printing, 1971.

Vogel, Clarence. *Heisey's Art & Colored Glass.* Galion, Ohio: Fisher Printing, 1970.

Walk, John, *Fenton Glass Compendium 1970-1985.* Atglen, Pennsylvania: Schiffer Publishing, 2001.

Walk, John, *Fenton Rarities 1940-1985.* Atglen, Pennsylvania: Schiffer Publishing, 2002.

Weatherman, Hazel Marie. *Fostoria the First 50 Years.* Springfield, Missouri: The Weatherman's, 1972.

Weatherman, Hazel Marie. *Colored Glassware of the Depression Era.* Springfield, Missouri: Weatherman Glass Books, 1974.

West Virginia Museum of American Glass. *Archival Material.* Weston, West Virginia: West Virginia Museum of American Glass, 2001.

Wheaton Glass Co. *Company Catalogs 1970s.* Millville, New Jersey: Wheaton Glass Co., 1970s.

Whitmyer, Kenn & Margaret. *Fenton Art Glass Patterns 1939-1980.* Paducah, Kentucky: Collector Books, 1999.

Whitmyer, Kenn & Margaret. *Fenton Art Glass 1907-1939.* Paducah, Kentucky: Collector Books, 1999.

Williams, Juanita. *Figurals by Fostoria Glass Study Guide.* California: Juanita Williams, 1990.

Yeakley, Virginia & Loren. *Heisey Glass in Color.* Marietta, Ohio: Richardson Printing Corporation, 1978.

Zemel, Evelyn. *American Glass Animals A to Z.* North Miami, Florida: A to Z Productions, 1978.